LONGMAN CRITICAL READERS

General Editor:

STAN SMITH, Professor of English, University of Dundee

Published titles:

K.M. NEWTON, *George Eliot*

MARY EAGLETON, *Feminist Literary Criticism*

GARY WALLER, *Shakespeare's Comedies*

JOHN DRAKAKIS, *Shakespearean Tragedy*

RICHARD WILSON AND RICHARD DUTTON, *New Historicism and Renaissance Drama*

PETER BROOKER, *Modernism/Postmodernism*

PETER WIDDOWSON, *D. H. Lawrence*

RACHEL BOWLBY, *Virginia Woolf*

FRANCIS MULHERN, *Contemporary Marxist Literary Criticism*

ANNABEL PATTERSON, *John Milton*

CYNTHIA CHASE, *Romanticism*

MICHAEL O'NEILL, *Shelley*

STEPHANIE TRIGG, *Medieval English Poetry*

ANTONY EASTHOPE, *Contemporary Film Theory*

TERRY EAGLETON, *Ideology*

IDEOLOGY

Edited and Introduced by

TERRY EAGLETON

LONGMAN
LONDON AND NEW YORK

Longman Group UK Limited,
Longman House, Burnt Mill,
Harlow, Essex CM20 2JE, England
and Associated Companies throughout the world.

Published in the United States of America
by Longman Publishing, New York

First published 1994

ISBN 0 582 23715 7 CSD
ISBN 0 582 23716 5 PPR

British Library Cataloguing in Publication Data

A catalogue record for this book is
available from the British Library

Library of Congress Cataloging-in-Publication Data

Set by 14 in 8\10 Palatino
Produced by Longman Sinapore Publishers (Pte) Ltd.
Printed in Singapore

Ideology / edited and introduced by Terry Eagleton.
        p.   cm. — (Longman critical readers)
    Includes bibliographical references and index.
    ISBN 0-582-23715-7. — ISBN 0-582-23716-5 (pbk.)
      1. Ideology. I. Eagleton, Terry, 1943– . II. Series.
    B823.3.I346 1994
    140—dc20   93-48939
                                                    CIP

Contents

General Editors' Preface

The outlines of contemporary critical theory are now often taught as a standard feature of a degree in literary studies. The development of particular theories has seen a thorough transformation of literary criticism. For example, Marxist and Foucauldian theories have revolutionised Shakespeare studies, and 'deconstruction' has led to a complete reassessment of Romantic poetry. Feminist criticism has left scarcely any period of literature unaffected by its searching critiques. Teachers of literary studies can no longer fall back on a standardised, received, methodology.

Lecturers and teachers are now urgently looking for guidance in a rapidly changing critical environment. They need help in understanding the latest revisions in literary theory, and especially in grasping the practical effects of the new theories in the form of theoretically sensitised new readings. A number of volumes in the series anthologise important essays on particular theories. However, in order to grasp the full implications and possible uses of particular theories it is essential to see them put to work. This series provides substantial volumes of new readings, presented in an accessible form and with a significant amount of editorial guidance.

Each volume includes a substantial introduction which explores the theoretical issues and conflicts embodied in the essays selected and locates areas of disagreement between positions. The pluralism of theories has to be put on the agenda of literary studies. We can no longer pretend that we all tacitly accept the same practices in literary studies. Neither is a *laissez-faire* attitude any longer tenable. Literature departments need to go beyond the mere toleration of theoretical differences: it is not enough merely to agree to differ; they need actually to 'stage' the differences openly. The volumes in this series all attempt to dramatise the differences, not necessarily with a view to resolving them but in order to foreground the choices presented by different theories or to argue for a particular route through the impasses the differences present.

The theory 'revolution' has had real effects. It has loosened the grip of traditional empiricist and romantic assumptions about language and literature. It is not always clear what is being proposed as the new agenda for literary studies, and indeed the very notion of 'literature' is questioned by the post-structuralist strain in theory. However, the uncertainties and obscurities of contemporary theories appear much less worrying when we see what the best critics have been able to do with them in practice. This series aims to disseminate the best of recent criticism and to show that it is possible to re-read the canonical texts of literature in new and challenging ways.

RAMAN SELDEN AND STAN SMITH

The Publishers and fellow Series Editor regret to record that Raman Selden died after a short illness in May 1991 at the age of fifty-three. Ray Selden was a fine scholar and a lovely man. All those he has worked with will remember him with much affection and respect.

Acknowledgements

We are grateful to the following for permission to reproduce copyright material:

Basil Blackwell Ltd for 'Ideology' by Jurgen Habermas from *Interpretations of Marx* edited by Tom Bottomore (Oxford: Basil Blackwell, 1988) pp. 299–309, 'Marxism & Literary History' by Professor John Frow from *Marxism and Literary History* (Oxford: Basil Blackwell, 1986) pp. 62–7, 'Belief, Bias and Ideology' by Jon Elster from *Rationality and Relativism* edited by Martin Hollis and Steven Lukes (Oxford: Bail Blackwell, 1982) pp. 123–148; Cambridge University Press and the author for 'Ideology' by Raymond Cuess from *The Idea of a Critical Theory* pp. 4–22; Janet Walker Gouldner for 'Ideological Discourse as Rationality and False Consciousness' from *The Dialectic of Ideology and Technology* by the late Alvin Gouldner (London: Macmillan, 1976); Harper Collins Ltd for Fontana and the editor, Professor David E. Apter for 'Ideology as a Cultural System' by Clifford Geertz from both *The Interpretation of Cultures* (Fontana) pp. 208–233 and *Ideology and Discontent* edited by D. Apter (Copyright 1964 by The Free Press of Glencoe – a division of Macmillan & Co) pp. 47–56; The Macmillan Press Ltd for 'Problems and Advances in the Theory of Ideology' from *On Law and Ideology* by Paul Hirst (London: Macmillan, 1979) pp. 29–39; the author, John Mepham and the editor of *Radical Philosophy* for 'The Theory of Ideology in *Capital*' from *Radical Philosophy* 2, Summer 1972, pp. 12–19; MIT Press for 'Class Consciousness' by George Lukacs from *History and Class Consciousness* (Cambridge, Mass: MIT Press 1971) pp. 46–70; Oxford University Press for 'Ideology' by Raymond Williams from *Marxism and Literature.* © Oxford University Press 1977; the editor of *Radical Philosophy* for 'On the theory of Ideology – Althusser's Politics' by Jacques Ranciere from *Radical Philosophy* 7, Spring 1974, pp. 2–15; Random House UK Ltd/Hill & Wang, a division of Farrar, Straus & Giroux Inc. for extracts from 'Myth Today' by Roland Barthes from *Mythologies*, translated by Annette Lavers. Translation copyright © 1972 by Jonathan Cape Ltd; Routledge for extracts from *Ideology and Utopia* by Karl Mannheim (London: Routledge & Kegan Paul, 1936) pp. 49–74; Verso Ltd for extracts by Louis Althusser from *For Marx* (London: New Left Books, 1969) pp. 232–4, 'On Ideology and Ideological State Apparatus' by Louis Althusser from *Lenin and Philosophy* (London: New Left Books, 1971) pp. 136–65, 'The Capitalist State and Ideologies' by Nicos Poulantzas from *Political Power and Social Classes* (London: New Left Books, 1973) pp. 195–210; Washington State University Press for 'The Epistemology of

Sociology' by Lucien Goldman from *Method in the Sociology of Literature* (Oxford: Basil Blackwell, 1981) originally printed under WSUP 'TELOS' imprint.

Introduction

1 Ideology and Enlightenment

Like much else in the modern world, the concept of ideology is a child of the Enlightenment. For most of us nowadays 'ideology' has something of a pejorative ring to it, evoking as it does a whole array of negative notions from false consciousness to fanaticism, mental blockage to mystification. In ordinary conversation, to claim that someone is thinking or speaking 'ideologically' is usually to suggest that their view of things is skewed by a set of rigid preconceptions. If only they were to shuck off this conceptual straitjacket, they might begin to see the world as it truly is. But this is not at all how the term 'ideology' started life. 'Ideology' means, literally, the study or knowledge of ideas; and as such it belongs to the great dream of the eighteenth-century Enlightenment that it might somehow be possible to chart the human mind with the sort of delicate precision with which we can map the motions of the body. What if that most obscure and elusive of realities, consciousness itself, could be *scientifically* known? What if it were possible to demonstrate a certain lawful regularity in its operations – in the way we generate ideas from sensations, in the manner in which those ideas are permutated, and so on all the way up to our loftiest spiritual conceptions? Can there be a materialism of the mind – of that which seems the very opposite of matter?

In this sense, the nearest modern equivalent to the classical notion of ideology would be the science of psychology. But there is an important difference between the two. Ideology, in its Enlightenment sense, is concerned with ideas as *social* phenomena, as modern-day psychology is usually not. Its aim is not just to map some abstraction known as 'consciousness', but (at least for some Enlightenment theorists) to uncover the laws of a system of social thought. And to this extent it hovers ambiguously between what we know as psychology, and what nowadays would be termed the 'sociology of knowledge'. Ideologists believed that particular social ideas could be traced back to certain universal operations of the mind; but the point of doing this was to give them the capacity to alter men's and women's ways of thinking. If, for example, we could show that the mind worked by certain principles of association, then it might be possible to alter our social environment so that we associated *x* with *y* rather than *a* with *b*, and so developed ideas which were conducive to human dignity, freedom and justice rather than to superstition and oppression. All this, to be sure, has something of a quaint ring for us today; but it reflects the naive utopianism of a revolutionary age, which was busy sweeping away idols and fetishes of various kinds, and which did not hesitate to carry this campaign into the very inner sanctum of humanity. Ideology, then, begins life as nothing less than an ambitious project of mental engineering, which will sweep clean the Augean stables of mind and society together, and in doing so free men and women from the taboos and mystifications under which they have languished. The hardest form of emancipation is always self-emancipation; and the science of ideology, flushed with all the euphoria of an age of Reason, believes that the revolution against false gods must be carried into the inmost recesses of consciousness itself.

What this amounts to is that ideology is the equivalent in the mental realm of the overthrow of priest and king in the political one. And to this extent, ironically enough, the science of ideology is itself ideological – a reflex in the sphere of consciousness of real material conditions. The man who actually coined the term, the French revolutionary aristocrat Destutt de Tracy, did so in a prison cell during the Reign of Terror, firm in his belief that reason, not violence, was the key to social reconstruction. Reason must replace religion: which is to say that custodianship of the mind and soul must be wrested from the priests and invested instead in an élite of scientific specialists who would be, so to speak, technicians of social consciousness. As Antonio Gramsci recognised in his celebrated concept of 'hegemony', no successful transformation in the sphere of politics can neglect the business of influencing hearts and minds; and the science of ideology, born in the blood and turmoil of the French revolution, was the first attempt to systematise this project in the modern age. Ideology, then, belongs to modernity – to the brave new epoch of secular, scientific rationality which aims to liberate men and women from their mystifications and irrationalisms, their false reverence for God, aristocrat and absolute monarch, and restore to them instead their dignity as fully rational, self-determining beings. It is the bourgeois revolution at the level of the mind itself; and its ambition is nothing less than to reconstruct that mind from the ground up, dissecting the ways we receive and combine our sense-data so as to intervene in this process and deflect it to desirable political ends.

If this bold enterprise scandalised the reactionaries, it was because it represented an impious meddling with sacred mysteries. For surely the mind is the one place where we are free – free of the drearily determining laws which govern our physiological life, and perhaps our social existence as well. Ideology for its opponents is a form of vulgar reductionism, seeking to model the very pith of our dignity and autonomy – consciousness itself – on all that threatens to enslave it. Intoxicated with a mythology of pure reason, it sets out to purge humanity of its essential mystery, converting the mind itself into a sort of material object as mechanically predictable as the circulation of the blood. It is, in short, a kind of madness of Reason – a hubristic campaign to blueprint our elusive spiritual being, and to do so, moreover, for the purposes of controlling and manipulating it. Those traditional guardians of the human psyche – the priests – knew at least that it was inviolable and irreducible, as the inscription of God himself in humanity; now this last bastion of our freedom is to be rudely invaded by the same grubby hands which broke open the Bastille. In its own day, then, the new science of ideology attracted all the virulent opposition which has been reserved in our own time for psychoanalysis. For the scandal of Freud is not finally his embarrassing revelations about infantile sexuality or the precariousness of gender; it is the fact that the human psyche itself can now, apparently, be scientifically dissected like a muscle, and this not just in its topmost, more socially obvious layer ('consciousness') but in its murkiest unconscious depths.

The conflict in our own time between 'theorists' and 'humanists' is a legacy of these eighteenth-century quarrels. 'System', Roland Barthes once commented, 'is the enemy of Man' – meaning that the 'Man' of the humanist is all that cannot be analysed and tabulated, all that slips through the net of theoretical enquiry. In late eighteenth-century England, the names for this running battle were Paine and Burke: Thomas Paine, with his revolutionary fervour and serene confidence in reason; Edmund Burke, for whom the whole notion that the social order can be submitted to rational critique is a kind of blasphemy. For Burke, human affairs are too intricate, intuitive and opaque, too much the product of immemorial custom and spontaneous habit, to be charted with any certainty; and this belief is inevitably coupled with a conservative politics. For if the skein of social life is so elusively tangled, then only those delicate refurbishings and readjustments we know as reform can avoid shearing brutally through it. For this standpoint, we cannot put our social life into radical question precisely because we are the products of it, because we bear in our bones and fibres the very traditions we are foolishly seeking to objectify. Radical critique would thus involve some impossible hauling of ourselves up by our own bootstraps, some doomed attempt to examine ourselves as though we were not present on the scene of enquiry. And where exactly would we have to be standing to perform such an operation? A rejection of ideology is thus an endorsement of the political status quo, just as the opponents of 'theory' today tend to be conservative. In modern English history, 'ideologists' have generally been known as 'intellectuals', and the term carries a significantly disparaging resonance. Intellectuals are bloodless, clinical creatures bereft of the ordinary human affections, crushing spontaneity and intuition with their cerebral convolutions. They are *alien* animals because they strive to 'estrange' our familiar forms of life, casting upon them the coldly critical eye of a Martian or a visiting anthropologist. Like the early French ideologues, they try to uncover the laws or 'deep structures' by which our most taken-for-granted institutions work; and this might only succeed in disabling those institutions, exposing them to a rigorous scepticism under whose baleful glare they might wilt and wither. The traditional quarrel between ideologue and conservative is being rehearsed today in the battle between those radical theorists who believe that a fundamental critique of a particular social order is both possible and necessary, and those pragmatist descendants of Nietzsche or Heidegger or Wittgenstein or John Dewey for whom this is mere intellectualist fantasy.[1] For if human beings are actually constituted to their roots by their social practices, how could they ever hope to leap out of them in imagination and subject them to thoroughgoing critical analysis? Would this not be like the eye trying to catch itself seeing something, or trying to shin up a rope you are yourself holding?

The pragmatist case against the 'ideologist' is that to do what she aims to do, she would have to be standing at some Archimedean point outside the culture she hopes to criticise. Not only does no such point exist, but even if it did it would be far too remote from our form of life to gain any effective hold upon it. This, in my view, is a misguided notion: it is perfectly possible, as with the Marxist concept of an 'immanent' critique, to launch a radical critique of a culture from somewhere inside it, not least from those internal fissures or fault-lines which betray its underlying contradictions. But if the pragmatist charge is not generally valid, it would certainly seem to apply to the early French ideologues. These men sought to submit their societies to the gaze of Reason; but whose reason, and reason of what kind? For them reason really was a 'transcendental' faculty, sublimely untainted by social factors. Yet this, ironically, contradicts the whole spirit of their project, which sets out precisely to examine how the human mind is conditioned by its social and material environment. How come that *their* minds – their notions of reason – are so immune from their own doctrine? What if the grand science of ideology was no more than a socially conditioned reflex in the head of its founder? If everything is to be exposed to the clear light of reason, must this not include reason itself? And would we not then discover that this supposedly timeless, transcendental faculty was no more than the style of rationality of a particular, newly dominant social class at a specific historical time? What we might find, in short, is that ideology in the classical sense of the word is ideology in one contemporary sense: the partisan perspective of a social group or class, which then mistakes itself as universal and eternal.

For some theorists of our time, notably the Marxist philosopher Louis Althusser and his progeny, ideology is the opposite of science; so it is ironic that the concept was born precisely as an exciting new science. For some other thinkers, notably the early Marx and Engels of *The German Ideology*, ideology means ideas which have floated free of their material foundation and deny its existence; so it is a further irony that ideology in its infancy was part of a more general materialist enquiry into society as a whole. Indeed for the founder of the discipline, Destutt de Tracy, it was part of 'zoology': of a science of humanity in general. How then did it come about that, not long after its inception, 'ideology' came to mean idle abstractions, illusions and chimeras with no root in the real world? The answer, in a word, may be Napoleon. As Napoleon tightened his authoritarian political control, the French ideologues rapidly became his *bêtes noires*; and the concept of ideology itself entered the field of ideological struggle. Tracy and his kind, so he complained, were 'dreamers' and 'windbags', intent on destroying the consoling illusions by which men and women lived. Before long he was seeing ideologues under every bed, and even blamed them for his defeat in Russia. The ideologues, he charged, had substituted a 'diffuse metaphysics' for a 'knowledge of the human heart and of the lessons of history' – an ironic enough accusation, since it was precisely 'metaphysics' that the materialistically-minded ideologues were out to combat. The confrontation between Napoleon and Tracy, then, is an early instance of the conflict between the pragmatist who appeals to custom, piety, intuition and concrete experience, and the sinister 'intellectual' who puts all of this in brackets in his remorseless rationalism. The French exponents of ideology were not in fact metaphysicians; as we have seen, they believed in a close interrelation between ideas and material circumstances. But they did believe that ideas were at the very foundation of social life, and so were an odd mixture of materialist and idealist. It is this belief in the primacy of ideas which Napoleon, who claimed to have invented the term 'ideologue' himself as a derogatory label for his opponents, seized on in his campaign to discredit them. The kernal of his accusation is that there is something irrational about excessive rationalism. In his eyes, these thinkers have pursued their enquiry into the laws of reason to the point where they have become locked within their own abstract space, as divorced from material reality as a psychotic. So it is that the term ideology veers on its axis, as a word originally synonymous with scientific rationalism ends up denoting an idle and speculative idealism.

2 The Marxist heritage

The belief that ideas are socially conditioned is now so obvious to us that it requires a leap of imagination to envisage how anyone might think differently. But the belief is not of course obvious at all, not least for those brands of philosophical dualism or idealism for which consciousness is one thing and the material world quite another. Before the French ideologues, a good many thinkers had speculated in a rather crudely materialist vein on the influence on our minds of climate, or physiology, or national character; and for English empiricism it is sense-perception which lies at the source of all our concepts. But none of this is quite what the modern sense of the term 'ideology' is trying to capture. The study of ideology is more than just some sociology of ideas; more particularly, it claims to show how ideas are related to real material conditions by masking or dissembling them, displacing them into other terms, speciously resolving their conflicts and contradictions, converting these situations into apparently natural, immutable, universal ones. Ideas, in short, are here granted an active political force, rather than being grasped as mere reflections of their world; and in its day the Marxist tradition has sought to describe ideology in terms of any or all of these various strategies. The source text for this tradition is Marx and Engels's *The German Ideology*, in which the authors see ideology as essentially an inversion of the relation between consciousness and reality as they themselves conceive it. For a materialist like Marx, consciousness is inseparably bound up with social practice, and is secondary to it; for the Hegelian philosophers whom they oppose, ideas are thought to be both autonomous of such practice, and to be the root cause of social existence. By granting such primacy to ideas, Marx's antagonists would seem to suggest that if you change people's minds, you change their conditions of life. Marx himself wants to insist that you could only transform human consciousness by transforming the material conditions which create it. A materialist analysis, in short, goes hand in hand with a revolutionary politics. The rationalist creed that one should combat false ideas with true ones is decisively rejected; and so is the related idealist doctrine that consciousness is the key to social reality. In a pathbreaking move, then, *The German Ideology* rejects rationalism, idealism and any mere 'sociology of knowledge'; instead, in an audacious reformulation, it insists that consciousness is essentially *practical*, and that one of its practical uses is to distract men and women from their oppression and exploitation by generating illusions and mystifications. Paradoxically, then, ideas *are* practically related to real life; but that relation takes the mystifying form of a non-relation, in the shape of the idealist fantasy that consciousness is grandly independent of all material determinants. To put the point another way: there is an apparent non-correspondence between ideas and reality in class society, but this non-correspondence is structural to that form of life, and fulfils an important function within it.

It would appear, then, that to dub an idea 'ideological' is not just to call it false or deceptive, but to claim that it fulfils a particular kind of deceptive or mystifying function within social life as a whole. And as far as that goes, it might be thought that true ideas might do just as well as false ones. In the end, for this style of thought, an ideological notion is one which is somehow convenient for our rulers – one which conceals or naturalises or otherwise legitimates an unjust form of power. And in *The German Ideology*, given the thinkers the authors are out to assail, these ideas are most often metaphysical fantasies and chimeras of various sorts which downgrade the importance of material struggle. But this means that there is, from the outset, a tension in Marx's thought between two rather different senses of the term ideology. On the one hand, ideology has a point, a function, a practical political force; on the other hand it would seem a mere set of illusions, a set of ideas which have come unstuck from reality and now conduct an apparently autonomous life in isolation from it. This tension is not exactly a contradiction: one can see well enough how encouraging certain religious or metaphysical illusions may serve to mystify men and women as to their real material interests, and so have some practical force. But to see ideology just as 'illusion' has seemed to many later thinkers to deny its materiality, as well as to overlook the fact that many of the notions which we call ideological may succeed as well as they do precisely because they are true. People who enjoy dwelling upon Winston Churchill's dogged resilience and powers of leadership are probably speaking ideologically, but they are not thereby lying. *The German Ideology* makes it sound as though all ideology is idealist; but this is plainly not the case. The thought of the French ideologues or English empiricists is certainly in some sense materialist, but it is not hard to point out its ideological functions. So, at the very origin of the tradition we are examining, there is a revealing ambiguity: is ideology primarily an *epistemological* affair, concerned with what Theodor Adorno once termed 'socially necessary illusion', or is it a *sociological* matter, insisting on the way certain ideas intersect with power? Can thought have a firm anchorage in material life and still be ideological? And if ideology, as with the early Marx and Engels, means ideas independent of that life, how can this be so if all consciousness is in truth practical consciousness?

Whatever these difficulties, the early Marxian claim that 'the ideas of the ruling class are in every epoch the ruling ideas' is a remarkably bold and original formulation. For this is to assert a startlingly direct hook-up between consciousness and power, which goes far beyond any mere insistence that ideas are socially conditioned. We are moving instead towards the proposition, more fully elaborated by later Marxists, that ideas are weapons in a field of struggle – that an 'ideological' discourse, properly understood, means one which, deciphered and decoded in certain ways, will betray in its limits and emphases, its silences, gaps and internal contradictions, the imprint of real material conflicts. On this view, ideology is a form of thought generated or skewed out of shape by the exigencies of power; but if it is therefore traced through with significant tensions and inconsistencies, it also represents an attempt to mask the very conflicts from which it springs, either by denying that they exist, or by asserting their unimportance or inevitability. Ideologies are sets of discursive strategies for displacing, recasting or spuriously accounting for realities which prove embarrassing to a ruling power; and in doing so, they contribute to that power's self-legitimation.

Such, at least, is one strong contemporary understanding of ideology. It is not one without its problems, as we shall see in this book. For some thinkers, like the later Karl Marx, ideology is less a matter of thought or discourse than of the very objective structure of class society itself. For others like Althusser, it is less consciousness than unconsciousness; for others again, ideology is less a 'tool' of a ruling power than an effect of a social and political situation as a whole, a complex field in which different groups and classes ceaselessly negotiate their relations rather than a well-bounded form of consciousness which can be neatly assigned to this group or the other. There are difficulties, too, about the fact that 'ideology' is sometimes used to cover radical or oppositional ideas: if ideology means the ideas of the ruling class, why does Lenin speak approvingly of 'socialist ideology', and why would many people want to claim that feminism or anarchism or republicanism were 'ideological'? For the moment, however, we can stay with the conception of ideology as a set of discursive strategies for legitimating a dominant power, and enquire more precisely into what these strategies consist in. We should note before we do, however, that the concept of a 'dominant ideology', as a coherent bloc of ideas which effectively secures the power of a governing group, has been greeted with scepticism in certain quarters, a view made plain by the work of Nicholas Abercrombie and his colleagues.[2]

Ideologies are often seen as *rationalisations* of a set of (normally unjust) social interests. I say 'normally unjust', because one would think that a set of just social interests would hardly need rationalising. But some plainly unjust views do not need rationalising either: ancient society saw nothing reprehensible in slave-owning, and felt no need to dress it up in some plausible apologia as we would have to do today. For one extreme sort of contemporary free marketeer, there is no reason to justify the suffering that *laissez-faire* generates: for him, the weak can simply go to the wall. But much ideological rationalisation does of course go on; and rationalisation, which is essentially a psychoanalytic category, can be defined as 'a procedure whereby the subject attempts to present an explanation that is either logically consistent or ethically acceptable for attitudes, ideas, feelings, etc., whose true motives are not perceived'.[3] Whether all ruling powers fail to perceive how discreditable their true motives really are is in fact questionable. Someone who behaves disreputably but conceals the fact from himself is known as self-deceived – a concept which is of vital importance in the study of ideology. And it is true that ruling powers are often enough engaged in what the linguisticians would call a 'performative contradiction' between what they say they are doing and what they are actually doing – a contradiction which it may be part of the function of their discourse to mask even from themselves. But we should beware of excessive charity here: dominant groups and classes are quite frequently well aware of how shabby their conduct is, and simply seek to hide this from their subordinates rather than from themselves. Some such groups feel no urge to rationalise their motives, either because they do not regard them as shameful or because they are not in fact so; but others will engage in more or less systematic attempts to provide plausible justifications for conduct that might otherwise be the object of criticism. For some sociologists of a Nietzschean bent, notably Vilfedo Pareto in his *Treatise of General Sociology* (1916), all social interests are in fact irrational, so that the whole of our social discourse is in effect ideological, substituting apparently rational belief for affective or instinctual motives. Rationalisation may involve trying to square a discrepancy between conscious belief and unconscious motivation; or it may involve trying to square the circle between two sets of contradictory beliefs. (Whether it is in fact possible for us to hold contradictory beliefs simultaneously, and how this might come about, is a fascinating aspect of the theory of ideology.) Rationalising our beliefs in this way may help to promote and legitimate them; but there is the occasional case of interests which get promoted precisely because they do not rationalise themselves, as in the case of a self-confessed hedonist who wins our sympathy by his or her disarming candour. A stoical or fatalistic world-view may rationalise the wretchedness of some oppressed group's conditions of life; but it will not necessarily serve to advance their interests, other than in the sense of supplying them with an opiate. In this situation, it is not simply a question of the group's beliefs being at odds with its interests, but of its having conflicting kinds of interests. Indeed we should note here that oppressed groups may engage in rationalisation just as full-bloodedly as their masters, persuading themselves that their misery is inevitable, or that they deserve to suffer, or that everyone else does too, or that the alternative might be a good deal worse. Such rationalisations on the part of the oppressed may not promote their interests; but they may certainly advance those of their rulers.

Ideologies are commonly felt to be both *naturalising* and *universalising*. By a set of complex discursive devices, they project what are in fact partisan, controversial, historically specific values as true of all times and all places, and so as natural, inevitable and unchangeable. That much of the language we dub ideological engages in such manoeuvres is undoubted; but we should hesitate before viewing this as characteristic of all ideology without exception. Ideology very often presents itself as obvious – as an 'Of

course!' or 'That goes without saying.' But not all ideological doctrines
appear obvious, even to their most ardent adherents: think of the Roman
Catholic dogma of the Assumption of the Blessed Virgin, which is hardly a
matter of plain common sense even for a devout Catholic. Many people
revere the monarchy, or are enthusiasts for multinational capitalism; but
they are not always obtuse enough to believe that the world would simply
grind to a halt without these institutions, or that they have existed from
time immemorial. The case that ideology always and everywhere
dehistoricises the world, making it appear natural and ineluctable, is based
on the dubious assumption that ideology is never able to reflect upon itself
– that, as Louis Althusser observes, it is never able to announce 'I am
ideological.' But 'never' is surely too strong. 'I know I'm a terrible
reactionary, but I just can't see that women are equal to men'; 'I'm a racist
and proud of it'; 'Sorry to be so disgustingly bourgeois, but would you
mind removing that pig from the drawing room?': all of these statements
may serve as coy or defiant self-rationalisations, but they reveal in ideology
a limited degree of self-awareness which any full-blooded 'naturalisation'
thesis perilously overlooks. For the 'naturalising' thesis, ideologies are
sealed universes which curve back on themselves rather like the cosmos,
and admit of no outside or alternative. They can also acknowledge no
origin, since that which was born can always die. Ideologies, on this view,
are thus parentless and without siblings. But many apologists for
capitalism or patriarchy are well aware that alternatives to them exist; it is
just that they do not agree with them. And hardly any devotees of
parliamentary democracy are dim-witted enough to believe that it
flourished among the ancient Druids. Besides, not everything which is
natural is ideological. It is natural to human beings – proper to their
material constitution – to be born, eat, engage in sexual activity,
associate with one another, suffer from time to time, laugh, labour and
die. The fact that all of these activities assume different cultural forms is
no argument against their naturalness, however nervous of the term a
certain fashionable culturalism may be. Any society which legislated
against our laughing would be unnatural, and could be opposed on those
grounds. When the rulers of the *ancien régimes* of eighteenth-century
Europe heard the word 'Nature', they reached for their traditional
privileges.

Just as some human practices are natural, so some are genuinely
universal. Ideologies do often enough deceptively generalise their own
highly particular beliefs to global or transhistorical status; but sometimes –
as, for instance, with the liberal doctrine that all human beings should be
equally accorded justice and dignity – they are quite right to do so. Marx
and Engels believed that new social movements or classes, on their first
revolutionary emergence, quite often present themselves as representing
the interests of all; but while this is sometimes mystifying, it is also

sometimes true. It would indeed be ultimately in the interests of everybody, even of men, if patriarchy were to be brought low.

Many theories of ideology regard it as a kind of screen or blockage which intervenes between us and the real world. If only we could nip around this screen, we would see reality aright. But there is, of course, no way of viewing reality except from a particular perspective, within the frame of specific interests or assumptions, which is one reason why some people have considered that all of our thought and perception is in fact ideological. But this is surely to widen the term to the point of uselessness. Any term which tries to cover too much threatens to cancel all the way through and end up signifying nothing. 'Ideological' is not synonymous with 'cultural': it denotes, more precisely, the points at which our cultural practices are interwoven with political power. Whether this is always a *dominant* power, or whether it always and everywhere involves naturalising, falsity, mystification, the masking or rationalising of injustice or the spurious resolution of social contradictions, are controversial issues in the theory of ideology; but if ideology just means something like 'a specific way of seeing', or even 'a set of doctrinal beliefs' then it rapidly dwindles in interest. We would not usually call a set of beliefs about whether lamb is tastier than haddock ideological, even though it is true that there is no belief which *could* not be ideological, given the appropriate circumstances. It all depends on who is saying what to whom, with what intentions and with what effects. Ideology, in short, is a matter of *discourse* – of practical communication between historically situated subjects – rather than just of *language* (of the kinds of propositions we utter). And it is not just a matter of discourse which is slanted or prejudiced or partisan, since there is no human discourse which is not.

Let us return, however, to the notion of ideology as a kind of screen or blockage between us and the world – one thrown up, perhaps, by social interests or 'false consciousness'. The model depends on a distinction between appearance and reality: there is a real state of affairs out there, but we represent it to ourselves or others in distorting or obscuring ways. A psychological analogy might be appropriate here: over there is reality, and over here the fantasies we entertain about it. But it is part of Freud's enterprise to deconstruct this duality: for him, what we term 'reality' is itself shot through with psychical fantasy, as much a construct of our unconscious desires as of our conscious perception There is some sense in which the appearances are here actually part of the reality, not a mere screen which we could slide aside to see things as they really are. Much the same is true of Marx's later theory of ideology, as it can be pieced together from his economic studies in *Capital*. What Marx argues here is that our ideological misperceptions are not just the upshot of distorted ideas or 'false consciousness', but somehow inherent in the material structure of· capitalist society itself. It is just in the nature of that society that it presents itself to our consciousness other than how it is; and this dislocation between appearance and reality is structural to it, an unavoidable effect of its routine operations. Thus, the wage contract for Marx involves exploitation, but it presents itself spontaneously as an equal exchange. Competition operates to obscure the ways in which value under capitalism is determined by labour-time. And the real social relations between men and women are concealed by the celebrated 'fetishism of commodities', in which what are actually social interchanges take the form of interactions between commodities. Ideology, which for the younger Marx was a matter of illusions and chimeras, is now folded into the material world itself, anchored no longer in consciousness but in the day-to-day workings of the capitalist system. There is a kind of dissembling or duplicity built into the very economic structures of capitalism, such that it simply cannot help appearing to us in ways at odds with what it is.

This is a deeply suggestive theory; but it hardly covers all of what we mean by ideology, and (along with certain dubious epistemological assumptions) it runs the risk of reducing ideology to the economic. The great tradition of Western Marxism, from Georg Lukács to Louis Althusser, has in general reacted sharply against economic reductionism, seeking to restore to Marxist theory the centrality of culture, practice and consciousness. Perhaps the key text in this lineage is Lukács's *History and Class Consciousness* (1923), a bold and brilliant attempt to reintroduce the importance of social consciousness to a Marxism previously afflicted by economic determinism. For Lukács, social consciousness – in particular the class consciousness of the proletariat – is not just a reflection of social conditions, but a transformative force within them. Thought and reality are part of the same dialectical process; and if a particular social class is able to dominate others, it is because it has managed to impose its own peculiar consciousness or world-view upon them. Capitalist society in general is ridden with reification, experienced as a set of discrete, isolated entities whose connections have been hidden from view; but it is in the interests of a subject class – in this case, the proletariat – to grasp that social order in its dynamic totality, and in doing so it becomes conscious of its own commodified status within it. The self-consciousness of the working class, then, is the transformative moment in which it grasps itself as a subject rather than an object, recognising that it is itself through its labour the author of this society which appears to it as alien and opaque, and reclaiming that alienated product through revolutionary action.

In a breathtakingly original move, Lukács has here rewritten Marxist theory in terms of Hegel's philosophy of the subject; and no subsequent Marxist thinking about ideology was to be immune from its effects. There is, nevertheless, much in Lukács's doctrine which is open to criticism. For one thing, in the typically 'historicist' style of Western Marxism, he assumes that social classes can best be seen as 'subjects', each equipped with a distinctive and cohesive form of consciousness. It is doubtful, though, that any 'class consciousness' is that pure and unified: ideology is perhaps best seen as a field of struggle and negotiation between various social groups and classes, not as some world-view intrinsic to each of them. For another thing, Lukács assigns too high an importance to 'consciousness' within social life as a whole. Ideology may be an indispensable part of political rule; but it is surely not what *centrally* secures such government, which is normally a question of much more material techniques. What is especially interesting in Lukács, however, is his supposed theory of 'false consciousness', which raises some difficult epistemological issues. In reaction to the scientistic conceptions of truth and falsehood typical of so much of the Marxism he inherited, Lukács locates truth instead in the fullest possible consciousness of an historically 'progressive' class. Truth is no longer an abstract, contemplative affair, but a function of the practical coming to consciousness of a class which must in its own interests grasp more of the dynamic totality of society than those which have come before it. Among other problems, there is a real danger here of relativism: what is true or false is tied to the historical situation of a specific social class, rather than being (as we might think of many propositions) true or false regardless of who is uttering them. But this does not mean that Lukács holds that the consciousness of non-progressive classes is therefore false, in the sense of giving a distorting image of reality as it is. On the contrary, he believes that the consciousness of the bourgeoisie truthfully reflects the reified, atomised social conditions in which they find themselves – so that, intriguingly, 'false consciousness' means less a view of things which is false to the true situation, than a view of things which is true to a false situation. Quite what is meant by a 'false situation' is a thorny issue; but Lukács is working here with the interesting notion of a social consciousness which is, so to speak, true as far as it goes, but structurally bound and limited by the historical situation which produced it. On this view, an ideological discourse is not just false or mystificatory; it is rather that in delivering some undoubted truths, it continually finds itself pressing up against certain limits or frontiers inherent in its style of thought, which are the inscription within it of certain 'limits' in historical reality itself. This, in effect, is what Marx thought was ideological about the discourse of the bourgeois political economist with whom he did battle; and it descends to modern 'structuralist' Marxists as the concept of a 'problematic'.

Another of the great Western Marxists – Antonio Gramsci – had rather little of originality to say of the concept of ideology, since it is subsumed for him under the more encompassing notion of 'hegemony'. Hegemony for Gramsci suggests the varied techniques by which ruling classes secure the consent of their subordinates to be ruled; and though ideology is certainly part of this process, it includes a great many other measures too.

Indeed Gramsci develops his idea of hegemony partly because the theories of ideology of the 'orthodox' Marxism of his day had grown dismally impoverished, reducing social consciousness for the most part to a mere reflex of economic conditions. It was left to the French Marxist philosopher Louis Althusser to incorporate some aspects of Gramsci's concept of hegemony into a strikingly novel theoretical synthesis, which along with Gramsci drew heavily on structuralism and psychoanalysis. For Althusser, ideology works primarily at the level of the unconscious; its function is to constitute us as historical subjects equipped for certain tasks in society; and it does this by drawing us into an 'imaginary' relation with the social order which persuades us that we and it are centred on and indispensable to one another. Ideology is not thereby false, since, first of all, this relation is more a matter of unconscious feelings and images than of falsifiable propositions, and secondly because all of this goes on within certain material practices and institutions – 'ideological state apparatuses', as Althusser calls them – which are indubitably real. An 'ideological' problematic for Althusser is in effect a closed universe which continually returns us to the same starting-point; and science, or Marxist theory, is to be sharply counterposed to it. Ideology 'subjects' us in a double sense, constructing our subjectivity by persuading us into into internalising an oppressive Law; but since it is thus at the very root of what it is to be a subject, inseparable from our lived experience itself, it is an essential dimension of any society whatsoever, even a communist one. With several of his challenging theses – that ideology has nothing to with falsehood, that it is more unconscious than conscious, that it is the medium of our very subjectivity, that it is more a question of ritual practice than conscious doctrine, that it is 'eternal' in its duration and immutable in its structure – Althusser at once returned the whole topic of ideology to a central place in radical thinking, and sought to overturn many of that thinking's presuppositions.

3 Ideology and irrationalism

No single conception of ideology – least of all Althusser's, with its many questionable assumptions – has commanded universal assent from those at work in this field. Indeed it is hardly an exaggeration to claim that there are almost as many theories of ideology as there are theorists of it. For Theodor Adorno, ideology is essentially a kind of 'identity thinking', erasing difference and otherness at the level of the mind as remorselessly as commodity exchange does at the level of the material. For the American sociologist Martin Seliger, ideology is best seen as a set of action-oriented beliefs, whose truth or falsehood, conservatism or radicalism, is quite irrelevant.[4] A whole span of thinkers – Jürgen Habermas, Nicos Poulantzas and Alvin Gouldner among them – take ideology to be a wholly modern, secular, quasi-scientific phenomenon, in contrast to earlier brands of mythical, religious or metaphysical thought. Karl Mannheim, by contrast, sees ideology as essentially antiquated forms of thought out of sync with what the age demands. Definitions of ideology range from 'systematically distorted communication' (Habermas) to 'semiotic closure' (post-structuralism), from 'the confusion of linguistic and phenomenal reality' (Paul de Man) to a discourse marked by certain significant absences and elisions (Pierre Macherey). For those like Lukács and his discipline Lucien Goldmann, ideology is a 'genetic' affair, its truth to be located in the historical class or situation from which it springs; for others, ideology is a functional matter, a question of the effects of certain utterances whatever their source. Many theorists now consider the truth-value of ideological statements to be irrelevant to the business of classifying them as ideological in the first place; others hold that ideology may indeed contain important truths, but ones deformed by the impact of social interests or the exigencies of action. A history of the concept ideology could be written in terms of what is taken as its opposite, all the way from 'seeing reality as it is' (the early Marx and Engels) and 'a consciousness of totality' (Lukács) to 'science' (Althusser) and 'a recognition of difference' (Adorno). Ideology can be theoretically elaborate (Thomism, Social Darwinism) or a set of spontaneous, automated habits (what the French sociologist Pierre Bourdieu calls *habitus*). It can mean, too vaguely, 'socially conditioned or socially interested thought' or, too narrowly, 'false ideas which help to legitimate an unjust political power'. The term may be pejorative, as with Marx or Mannheim; positive, as (sometimes) with Lenin; or neutral, as with Althusser. There are those like Lucien Goldmann for whom ideologies are highly structured, internally coherent formations, and others like Pierre Macherey for whom they are amorphous and diffuse.[5] Whereas Adorno sees ideology as falsely homogenising, Fredric Jameson views its essential gesture as an absolute binary opposition.[6] And there is the odd right-wing academic like Kenneth Minoghue for whom left-wingers have ideology while conservatives see things as they really are.[7]

Theories of ideology are, among other things, attempts to explain why it is that men and women come to hold certain views; and to this extent they examine the relation between thought and social reality. However that relation is conceived – as reflection or contradiction, correspondence or dislocation, inversion or imaginary construction – these theories assume that there are specific historical reasons why people come to feel, reason, desire and imagine as they do. It may be because they are in the grip of embattled sectional interests, or because they are hoodwinked by the false forms in which the social world presents itself, or because a screen of fantasy interposes itself between that world and themselves.

With Louis Althusser, however, we touch on the rather more alarming claim that some kind of imaginary misperception of both self and world is actually latent in the very structure of human subjectivity. Without this misperception, human beings for Althusser would simply not be able to function as their societies require them to; so that this flaw or misconception is absolutely necessary to what we are, structurally indispensable to the human animal. Sectional interests might be abolished, screens of fantasy removed and social structures transformed; but if ideology lies at the very root of our being, then a much gloomier picture begins to emerge. Behind Althusser's claim, whether consciously or not, lies the thought of Friedrich Nietzsche, for whom all purposive action depends on the consoling fiction that we are unified selves, and on a necessary oblivion of the random, ineffably complex and shameful determinants of our actual human existence. For Althusser, the 'imaginary' self of ideology is a coherent one, which is why it is able to undertake socially essential action; but 'theory' is grimly aware that such unity is in fact a myth, that the human subject – like the social order itself – is no more than a decentred assemblage of elements. The paradox emerges, then, that we become subjects only by a repression of the determinants which go into our making; and this is precisely the major insight of Sigmund Freud. We become subjects for Freud by passing more or less successfully through the Oedipal trauma; but to operate effectively we must repress that hideous drama, and we do so by opening up within us the place known as the unconscious, driving our insatiable desire underground. Forgetting is then for Freud our 'normal' condition, and remembering is simply forgetting to forget. For these thinkers, then, there is something chronically askew about human beings, a kind of original sin by which all perception includes misperception, all action involves incapacity, all cognition is inseparable from error. One name for this line of thought in our own time has been post-structuralism; but that particular discourse is just the latest phase of a long post-Romantic tradition, which stretches from the German philosopher Arthur Schopenhauer to his disciple Nietzsche and on to Freud and a whole host of twentieth-century thinkers. For this lineage, one cannot really speak of false consciousness because now *all* consciousness is inherently false; whoever says 'consciousness' says delusion, distortion, estrangement. Reason is just a blundering instrument in the service of Will (Schopenhauer), power (Nietzsche) or desire (Freud); and it is in the nature of this accidental spin-off of evolution to miss the mark, to be self-deceived, to be tragically blinded to its own deeper determinations. Freud, to be sure, inherits much of the Enlightenment tradition too, with his courageous belief in the 'talking cure', in the power of analysis to set right some of our discontents; but for this 'irrationalist' heritage in general, ideology is a useless notion since it covers more or less all we know as the conscious mind. Consciousness is now itself a monstrous aberration, and is divided by some unspannable abyss from the reality it vainly seeks to embrace.

There seems little doubt that this powerful philosophical tradition captures some of the way the human mind is. But if the Enlightenment errs on the side of a hubristic rationalism, this current of thought is too ready to sweep aside as so much trivia those *particular* social mechanisms which cause men and women to languish in the grip of oppressive ideas, and so to collude in their own wretchedness. To this extent, one could view the 'irrationalist' tradition as at once an essential corrective to some vulgar notion that we could emancipate our minds simply by rationally reorganising our society, and as an ideology in exactly the Marxist sense, naturalising and universalising specific forms of irrationality to the structure of human consciousness as such. If all consciousness is false consciousness, then the term covers too much and drops out of sight; and this is one major reason why there has been so little talk of ideology in a postmodern age. For the relativist climate of postmodernism is in general wary of concepts of truth, suspecting them to be absolutist and authoritarian; and if one cannot speak of truth, then one cannot logically speak of falsehood either. To identify an ideological view, so the argument goes, you would need to be in secure possession of the truth, to see things precisely as they are; but since any such claim is epistemologically overweening, there is no point in speaking of ideology. To which the first response is that ideology, as we have seen, is at least as much concerned with the functions, effects and motivations of discourses as with their truth-value; and the second response is that it is plainly false to imagine that, in order to spot a falsehood, distortion or deception, you must have some access to absolute truth. Those postmodernists who assert that this last statement is untrue have just undermined their own case. The notion of absolute truth is simply a bugbear here; we do not need intuitive access to the Platonic Forms to be aware that apartheid is a social system which leaves something to be desired. What most theories of ideology assert is that for oppressed and exploited peoples to emancipate themselves, a knowledge of how the social system works, and how they stand within it, is essential to their project; so that the opposite of ideology here would be less 'science' or 'totality' than 'emancipatory knowledge'. The theory of ideology claims further that it is in the interests of the system in question to forestall such accurate knowledge of its workings, and that fetishism, mystification, naturalisation and the rest are among the devices by which it achieves these ends. There are those for whom accurate knowledge is vital, just because they need urgently to change their situations; and there are others (postmodernist academics among them) who can afford their cognitive indeterminacy. Because seeking a true self-understanding, in conditions of illusion and obscurantism, involves certain virtues (of honesty, realism, tenacity and so forth), emancipatory knowledge is at once cognitive and ethical, bridging a gap which Immanuel Kant declared unspannable.

Postmodernism is an 'end of ideology' world, just as it has been declared to be the end of history. But this, of course, is true only for postmodern theorists. It is hardly true for American Evangelicals, Egyptian fundamentalists, Ulster Unionists or British fascists. Some ideologies (those of neo-Stalinism, for instance) may have crumbled, while others (patriarchy, racism, neo-colonialism, free-marketeering) remain as virulent as ever. We must ponder, then, the extraordinary irony that, in a world gripped by powerful, sometimes death-dealing ideologies, the intellectuals have decided that the ideological party is over. In part, of course, this merely reflects their customary distance from the world in which most people have to live; in part, it reflects their mistaking the media and the shopping mall for the rest of social reality. It is also the consequence of a fashionable cult of neo-Nietzscheanism: if power, desire and sectional interests are the very stuff of reality, why bother to speak of ideologies as though there was anything beyond them, or as though they could ever be changed? But it springs also from certain alterations in the nature of capitalism, which in its more classical period sought to justify itself by rhetorical appeals to moral value, but is nowadays often enough content to appeal to self-interest and consumerist hedonism. An 'end to ideology' is in this sense an ideology all in itself: what it recommends is that we forget about moral justifications altogether and simply concentrate on enjoying ourselves. In this sense, our present end-of-ideology climate differs from the 'end of ideology' current during the Cold War. What this came down to, in effect, was that while the Soviet Union was in the grip of ideology, the United States saw things as they really were. Sending one's tanks into Hungary is an instance of ideological fanaticism; subverting the democratically elected government of Chile is a matter of adapting realistically to the facts.

There is a common dystopian fantasy of a world so thoroughly ideologised that all dissent has been contained, all conflicts papered over, all rebellion rendered unthinkable. For some, this fantasy is not so distant: we live, so the argument goes, in a world of doped telly-viewers who have long since been cowed into apathetic conformity. In this dark vision, the powers which rule our lives have now become thoroughly internalised; and it is true that any dominant ideology which wishes to succeed must aim precisely at this. For it is not enough to win the mere outward obedience of men and women; ideally, they should come to identify that power with their own inward being, so that to rebel against it would be a form of self-transgression. Power must become at one with the very form of our subjectivity; indeed for a political pessimist like Michel Foucault, it is power which actually produces that subjectivity in the first place. The

Law must be inscribed on our hearts and bodies, since it demands of us not simply a passive tolerance but an ardent embrace. Its ultimate aim is not simply to induce us to accept oppression, but cheerfully to collude in it; women under patriarchy are kept in place not primarily by coercion, but by guilt, low self-esteem, a misplaced sense of duty, feelings of powerlessness, fear of alienating the love and approval of others, anxieties about appearing unfeminine, a feeling of solidarity with similarly placed women, and so on. The Law is not satisfied with a mere ritual obedience; it wants us instead to look it in the eyes and whisper that we have understood. And if this were indeed our situation, then the dystopian cynics would be right. But there are excellent psychoanalytic reasons for believing that this all-powerful authority is itself a psychological fantasy. First, not all power or authority is of course oppressive: deployed by the right hands in the right ways, it can be a source of human benefit. Secondly, the ego's relationship to the superego (or internalised source of authority) will never cease to be ambivalent, torn as it is between fear and affection, duty and dissent, guilty acquiescence and smouldering resentment. Every oppressive form of rule harbours the secret knowledge that it lives only in the active consent of those it subjugates, and that were this consent to be withdrawn on any major scale, it would be struck powerless. If an unjust authority cannot secure such widespread consent, then it will be often enough forced to resort to coercion; but in doing so it will tend to suffer a massive loss of credibility, alienating its subjects even more thoroughly. Every such authority knows also that men and women will only grant it their consent if there is something in it for them – if that authority is capable of yielding them, however meagrely, some gratification to be going on with. If it is able to do this, then individuals will quite often put up heroically with various kinds of misery; but the moment it ceases to grant them any such fulfilments, they will rebel against it as surely as night follows day. The dystopian vision is wrong on this account; but it is wrong also to imagine that what keeps us in our allotted places is mainly some omnipotent ideology. For there is no reason to suppose that people who meekly acquiesce in some unjust social order do so because they have obediently internalised its values. Many of the British people accepted the government of Margaret Thatcher; but it appears that only a minority of them actually endorsed her values. There are much more humdrum reasons why people will fall into line: because they can see no workable alternative to what they have, because they are too busy caring for their children and worrying about their jobs, because they are frightened of the consequences of opposing a particular regime. Ideology plays a part in persuading people to tolerate unjust situations; but it is probably not the major part, and it almost never does so without a struggle.

Finally, a brief note on the material in this book. All of the pieces it contains are theoretical, dealing with the concept of ideology itself rather than discussing or exemplifying this or that ideological position. The aim of the book is two-fold: to make available some of the classical texts on the subject, and to illustrate something of the variety of modern debate about it. No single view of ideology emerges from these pages; instead, there is a constant clash of standpoints, as one essay implicitly challenges or qualifies another. This interplay of perspectives is inevitable, given the complexity of the field and the degree of disagreement within it; nobody has yet come up with a single comprehensive definition of ideology acceptable to all concerned, since the term has been made in its day to serve a whole variety of purposes, many of them useful but not all of them mutually compatible. If the majority of texts in the volume bear some sort of relation to the Marxist tradition, this is not chiefly because of the predilections of the editor, but because of the simple historical fact that most writing on the subject of ideology has in fact sprung from this area. But several of the modern extracts are critical of the Marxist heritage from a variety of viewpoints; and the book thus tries to do justice to the range of accounts and analyses which are now available.

Notes

1. For an excellent analysis of some of these arguments, see CHRISTOPHER NORRIS, *Deconstruction and the Interests of Theory* (London: Routledge, 1989).
2. See N. ABERCROMBIE et al., *The Dominant Ideology Thesis* (London: George Allen and Unwin, 1980).
3. J. LAPLANCHE and J. B. PONTALIS, *The Language of Psycho-Analysis* (London: The Hogarth Press, 1980), p. 375.
4. See MARTIN SELIGER, *The Marxist Conception of Ideology* (Cambridge: Cambridge University Press, 1977).
5. See PIERRE MACHEREY, *A Theory of Literary Production* (London: Routledge, 1978), Part 1.
6. See THEODOR ADORNO, *Negative Dialectics* (London: Routledge, 1973), Introduction, and FREDRIC JAMESON, *The Political Unconscious* (London, Methuen, 1981), pp. 115ff.
7. See KENNETH MINOGHUE, *Alien Powers* (London: Weidenfeld and Nicolson, 1985), p. 5.

Part One
The Classical Tradition

1 Selected Texts*

KARL MARX and FRIEDRICH ENGELS

Karl Marx (1818–83) and Friedrich Engels (1820–95) were the founders of historical materialism, the key doctrine of which is that the conflict between exploiting and exploited classes throughout history is closely linked to the rise, development and demise of modes of material production. Marx and Engels never produced a fully-fledged theory of ideology; but their writings on other matters contain suggestive ideas in this direction, and their early work *The German Ideology* (1845–46) engages the topic directly. The book was written in opposition to the so-called Young Hegelians, who in Marx and Engels's view gave undue prominence to the power of ideas in society. Against the idealism of Hegel, Marx and Engels want to assert that all human consciousness is rooted in material conditions, and can be changed only by transforming these conditions.

The passage from the Preface to *A Contribution to the Critique of Political Economy* (1859) contains the fullest formulation of the so-called 'base and superstructure' doctrine: the claim that the various legal, political and cultural forms of thought of a society are determined by its social relations of production. As these social relations change, so our forms of social thought change with them. It is the 'social being' of humanity which determines its consciousness, not – as the philosophical idealists hold – the other way round. The extract from 'On the Fetishism of Commodities' is taken from volume one of Marx's *Capital* (1867), and proposes a rather different model of ideology: the notion that the capitalist system spontaneously breeds deceptive appearances. Commodities are human products; but under capitalism they detach themselves from social control and come to have a fetishistic life of their own, so that it is the transactions between them which govern human relations, rather than vice versa. This, note, is not

---

*Reprinted from KARL MARX and FRIEDRICH ENGELS, *The German Ideology*, ed. C. J. Arthur (New York: International Publishers, 1986), pp. 47, 64; MARX and ENGELS, *Selected Works* (London: Lawrence and Wishart, 1968), p. 180; KARL MARX, *Capital*, Vol. 1 (London: George Allen and Unwin, 1971), pp. 41–7.

just a question of appearance: under capitalism, so Marx argues, commodity exchange actually *does* determine human lives, and does so in ways which blind individuals to their true social relations.

The ideas of the ruling class are in every epoch the ruling ideas, i.e. the class which is the ruling *material* force of society, is at the same time its ruling *intellectual* force. The class which has the means of material production at its disposal has control at the same time over the means of mental production, so that thereby, generally speaking, the ideas of those who lack the means of mental production are subject to it. The ruling ideas are nothing more than the ideal expression of the dominant material relationships, the dominant material relationships grasped as ideas; hence of the relationships which make the one class the ruling one, therefore, the ideas of its dominance. The individuals composing the ruling class possess among other things consciousness, and therefore think. Insofar, therefore, as they rule as a class and determine the extent and compass of an epoch, it is self-evident that they do this in its whole range, hence among other things rule also as thinkers, as producers of ideas, and regulate the production and distribution of the ideas of their age: thus their ideas are the ruling ideas of the epoch. . . .

The production of ideas, of conceptions, of consciousness, is at first directly interwoven with the material activity and the material intercourse of men, the language of real life. Conceiving, thinking, the mental intercourse of men, appear at this stage as the direct efflux of their material behaviour. The same applies to mental production as expressed in the language of politics, laws, morality, religion, metaphysics, etc. of a people. Men are the producers of their conceptions, ideas, etc. – real, active men, as they are conditioned by a definite development of their productive forces and of the intercourse corresponding to these, up to its furthest forms. Consciousness can never be anything else than conscious existence, and the existence of men is their actual life-process. If in all ideology men and their circumstances appear upside-down as in a *camera obscura*, this phenomenon arises just as much from their historical life-process as the inversion of objects on the retina does from their physical life-process.

In direct contrast to German philosophy which descends from heaven to earth, here we ascend from earth to heaven. That is to say, we do not set out from what men say, imagine, conceive, nor from men as narrated, thought of, imagined, conceived, in order to arrive at men in the flesh. We set out from real, active men, and on the basis of their real life-process we demonstrate the development of the ideological reflexes and echoes of this life-process. The phantoms formed in the human brain are also, necessarily, sublimates of their material life-process, which is empirically verifiable and bound to material premises. Morality, religion, metaphysics, all the rest of ideology and their corresponding forms of consciousness, thus no longer retain the semblance of independence. They have no history, no development; but men, developing their material production and their material intercourse, alter, along with this their real existence, their thinking and the products of their thinking. Life is not determined by consciousness, but consciousness by life. In the first method of approach the starting-point is consciousness taken as the living individual; in the second method, which conforms to real life, it is the real living individuals themselves, and consciousness is considered solely as *their* consciousness.

(From *The German Ideology*, 1845–46)

In the social production of their life, men enter into definite relations that are indispensable and independent of their will, relations of production which correspond to a definite stage of development of their material productive forces. The sum total of these relations of production constitutes the economic structure of society, the real foundation, on which rises a legal and political superstructure and to which correspond definite forms of social consciousness. The mode of production of material life conditions the social, political and intellectual life process in general. It is not the consciousness of men that determines their being, but, on the contrary, their social being that determines their consciousness.

(From the Preface to *A Contribution to the Critique of Political Economy*, 1859)

The fetishism of commodities and the secret thereof

A commodity appears, at first sight, a very trivial thing, and easily understood. Its analysis shows that it is, in reality, a very queer thing, abounding in metaphysical subtleties and theological niceties. So far as it is a value in use, there is nothing mysterious about it, whether we consider it from the point of view that by its properties it is capable of satisfying human wants, or from the point that those properties are the product of human labour. It is as clear as noon-day, that man, by his industry, changes the forms of the materials furnished by nature, in such a way as to make them useful to him. The form of wood, for instance, is altered, by making a table out of it. Yet, for all that, the table continues to be that common, everyday thing, wood. But, so soon as it steps forth as a commodity, it is changed into something transcendent. It not only stands with its feet on the ground, but, in relation to all other commodities, it stands on its head, and evolves out of its wooden brain grotesque ideas, far more wonderful than 'table-turning' ever was.

The mystical character of commodities does not originate, therefore, in their use-value. Just as little does it proceed from the nature of the determining factors of value. For, in the first place, however varied the useful kinds of labour, or productive activities, may be, it is a physiological fact, that they are functions of the human organism, and that each such function, whatever may be its nature or form, is essentially the expenditure of human brain, nerves, muscles, &c. Secondly, with regard to that which forms the ground-work for the quantitative determination of value, namely, the duration of that expenditure, or the quantity of labour, it is quite clear that there is a palpable difference between its quantity and quality. In all states of society, the labour-time that it costs to produce the means of subsistence, must necessarily be an object of interest to mankind, though not of equal interest in different stages of development.[1] And lastly, from the moment that men in any way work for one another, their labour assumes a social form.

Whence, then, arises the enigmatical character of the product of labour, so soon as it assumes the form of commodities? Clearly from this form itself. The equality of all sorts of human labour is expressed objectively by their products all being equally values; the measure of the expenditure of labour-power by the duration of that expenditure, takes the form of the quantity of value of the products of labour; and finally, the mutual relations of the producers, within which the social character of their labour affirms itself, take the form of a social relation between the products.

A commodity is therefore a mysterious thing, simply because in it the social character of men's labour appears to them as an objective character stamped upon the product of that labour, because the relation of the producers to the sum total of their own labour is presented to them as a social relation, existing not between themselves, but between the products of their labour. This is the reason why the products of labour become commodities, social things whose qualities are at the same time perceptible and imperceptible by the senses. In the same way the light from an object is perceived by us not as the subjective excitation of our optic nerve, but as the objective form of something outside the eye itself. But, in the act of seeing, there is at all events, an actual passage of light from one thing to another, from the external object to the eye. There is a physical relation between physical things. But it is different with commodities. There, the existence of the things *qua* commodities, and the value relation between the products of labour which stamps them as commodities, have absolutely no connection with their physical properties and with the material relations arising therefrom. There is a definite social relation between men, that assumes, in their eyes, the fantastic form of a relation between things. In order, therefore, to find an analogy, we must have recourse to the mist-enveloped regions of the religious world. In that world the productions of the human brain appear as independent beings endowed with life, and entering into relation both with one another and the human race. So it is in the world of commodities with the products of men's hands. This I call the Fetishism which attaches itself to the products of labour, so soon as they are produced as commodities, and which is therefore inseparable from the production of commodities.

This Fetishism of commodities has its origin, as the foregoing analysis has already shown, in the peculiar social character of the labour that produces them.

As a general rule, articles of utility become commodities, only because they are products of the labour of private individuals or groups of individuals who carry on their work independently of each other. The sum total of the labour of all these private individuals forms the aggregate labour of society. Since the producers do not come into social contact with each other until they exchange their products, the specific social character of each producer's labour does not show itself except in the act of exchange. In other words, the labour of the individual asserts itself as a part of the labour of society, only by means of the relations which the act of exchange establishes directly between the products, and indirectly, through them, between the producers. To the latter, therefore, the relations connecting the labour of one individual with that of the rest appear, not as direct social relations between individuals at work, but as what they really are, material relations between persons and social relations between things. It is only by being exchanged that the products of labour acquire, as values, one uniform social status, distinct from their varied forms of existence as objects of utility. This division of a product into a useful thing and a value becomes practically important, only when exchange has acquired such an extension that useful articles are produced for the purpose of being exchanged, and their character as values has therefore to be taken into account, beforehand, during production. From this moment the labour of the individual producer acquires socially a two-fold character. On the one hand, it must, as a definite useful kind of labour, satisfy a definite social want, and thus hold its place as part and parcel of the collective labour of all, as a branch of a social division of labour that has sprung up spontaneously. On the other hand, it can satisfy the manifold wants of the individual producer himself, only in so far as the mutual exchangeability of all kinds of useful private labour is an established social fact, and therefore the private useful labour of each producer ranks on an equality with that of all others. The equalisation of the most different kinds of labour can be the result only of an abstraction from their inequalities, or of reducing them to their common denominator, viz., expenditure of human labour power or human labour in the abstract. The two-fold social character of the labour of the individual appears to him, when reflected in his brain, only under

those forms which are impressed upon that labour in everyday practice by
the exchange of products. In this way, the character that his own labour
possesses of being socially useful takes the form of the condition, that the
product must be not only useful, but useful for others, and the social
character that his particular labour has of being the equal of all other
particular kinds of labour, takes the form that all the physically different
articles that are the products of labour, have one common quality, viz., that
of having value.

Hence, when we bring the products of our labour into relation with
each other as values, it is not because we see in these articles the material
receptacles of homogeneous human labour. Quite the contrary: whenever,
by an exchange, we equate as values our different products, by that very
act, we also equate, as human labour, the different kinds of labour
expended upon them. We are not aware of this, nevertheless we do it.[2]
Value, therefore, does not stalk about with a label describing what it is. It is
value, rather, that converts every product into a social hieroglyphic. Later
on, we try to decipher the hieroglyphic, to get behind the secret of our own
social products; for to stamp an object of utility as a value, is just as much a
social product as language. The recent scientific discovery, that the
products of labour, so far as they are values, are but material expressions of
the human labour spent in their production, marks, indeed, an epoch in the
history of the development of the human race, but, by no means, dissipates
the mist through which the social character of labour appears to us to be an
objective character of the products themselves. The fact, that in the
particular form of production with which we are dealing, viz., the
production of commodities, the specific social character of private labour
carried on independently, consists in the equality of every kind of that
labour, by virtue of its being human labour, which character, therefore,
assumes in the product the form of value – this fact appears to the
producers, notwithstanding the discovery above referred to, to be just as
real and final, as the fact, that, after the discovery by science of the
component gases of air the atmosphere itself remained unaltered.

What, first of all, practically concerns producers when they make an
exchange, is the question, how much of some other product they get for
their own? in what proportions the products are exchangeable? When
these proportions have, by custom, attained a certain stability, they appear
to result from the nature of the products, so that, for instance, one ton of
iron and two ounces of gold appear as naturally to be of equal value as a
pound of gold and a pound of iron in spite of their different physical and
chemical qualities appear to be of equal weight. The character of having
value, when once impressed upon products, obtains fixity only by reason
of their acting and re-acting upon each other as quantities of value. These
quantities vary continually, independently of the will, foresight and action
of the producers. To them, their own social action takes the form of the

action of objects, which rule the producers instead of being ruled by them. It requires a fully developed production of commodities before, from accumulated experience alone, the scientific conviction springs up, that all the different kinds of private labour, which are carried on independently of each other, and yet as spontaneously developed branches of the social division of labour, are continually being reduced to the quantitative proportions in which society requires them. And why? Because, in the midst of all the accidental and ever fluctuating exchange-relations between the products, the labour-time socially necessary for their production forcibly asserts itself like an overriding law of nature. The law of gravity thus asserts itself when a house falls about our ears.[3] The determination of the magnitude of value by labour-time is therefore a secret, hidden under the apparent fluctuations in the relative values of commodities. Its discovery, while removing all appearance of mere accidentality from the determination of the magnitude of the values of products, yet in no way alters the mode in which that determination takes place.

Man's reflections on the forms of social life, and consequently, also, his scientific analysis of those forms, take a course directly opposite to that of their actual historical development. He begins, *post festum*, with the results of the process of development ready to hand before him. The characters that stamp products as commodities, and whose establishment is a necessary preliminary to the circulation of commodities, have already acquired the stability of natural, self-understood forms of social life, before man seeks to decipher, not their historical character, for in his eyes they are immutable, but their meaning. Consequently it was the analysis of the prices of commodities that alone led to the determination of the magnitude of value, and it was the common expression of all commodities in money that alone led to the establishment of their characters as values. It is, however, just this ultimate money form of the world of commodities that actually conceals, instead of disclosing, the social character of private labour, and the social relations between the individual producers. When I state that coats or boots stand in a relation to linen, because it is the universal incarnation of abstract human labour, the absurdity of the statement is self-evident. Nevertheless, when the producers of coats and boots compare those articles with linen, or, what is the same thing, with gold or silver, as the universal equivalent, they express the relation between their own private labour and the collective labour of society in the same absurd form.

The categories of bourgeois economy consist of such like forms. They are forms of thought expressing with social validity the conditions and relations of a definite, historically determined mode of production, viz., the production of commodities. The whole mystery of commodities, all the magic and necromancy that surrounds the products of labour as long as they take the form of commodities, vanishes therefore, so soon as we come to other forms of production.   (From *Capital*, Vol. I, 1867)

Notes

1. Among the ancient Germans the unit for measuring land was what could be harvested in a day, and was called *Tagwerk, Tagwanne* (*jurnale,* or *terra jurnalis,* or *diornalis*), Mannsmaad, &c. (See G.L. VON MAURER, *Einleitung zur Geschichte der Mark –, &c.* (München: Verfassung, 1859, pp. 129–59.)
2. When, therefore, Galiani says: Value is a relation between persons – 'La Ricchezza è una ragione tra due persone' – he ought to have added: a relation between persons expressed as a relation between things. (GALIANI: *Della Moneta,* p. 221, V, III, of Custodi's collection of 'Scrittori Classici Italiani di Economia Politica', Parte Moderna, Milano, 1803.)
3. 'What are we to think of a law that asserts itself only by periodical revolutions? It is just nothing but a law of Nature, founded on the want of knowledge of those whose action is the subject of it' (FRIEDRICH ENGELS: 'Umrisse zu einer Kritik der Nationalökonomie', in the *Deutsch-französische Jahrbücher,* ed. Arnold Ruge and Karl Marx, Paris, 1844.)

2 Class Consciousness*

GEORG LUKÁCS

Georg Lukács (1885–1971) is considered by many to be the greatest
Marxist literary critic of our epoch. Born in Hungary, he was a
Communist activist for much of his life, falling out of favour with the
Comintern on several occasions and dedicated to an Hegelian or
humanist revision of orthodox Marxism which sometimes reinforced,
sometimes resisted the power of Stalinism. Among his major works of
literary criticism are *Theory of the Novel* (1920; London: Merlin Press,
1971), *Studies in European Realism* (1939; London: Merlin Press, 1972)
and *The Historical Novel* (1947; London: Merlin Press, 1962).

Lukács's undoubtedly greatest work, however, is *History and Class
Consciousness* (1923), written in the wake of the wave of proletarian
insurgency which broke across Europe in the years around the First
World War. Inspired by these turbulent events, Lukács turns severely
upon the mechanically deterministic Marxism then in favour,
reinstating the centrality of consciousness as practical activity and
political force. With astonishing boldness, the book rewrites mainstream
European philosophy in terms of the commodity form, and develops a
theory of alienation and reification which strikingly parallels the
writings of the young Marx, at that point undiscovered. Lukács is the
chief representative of an Hegelian or 'historicist' brand of Marxism,
which substitutes the self-consciousness of the oppressed class for
Hegel's 'Subject', and views socialist revolution as the drama in which
this self-alienated subject reclaims its estranged social existence. It is
against Lukács's pioneering work that many of the theses of the
'anti-humanist' Marxist Louis Althusser are silently directed.

> The question is not what goal is *envisaged* for
> the time being by this or that member of
> the proletariat, or even by the proletariat

*Reprinted from GEORG LUKÁCS, *History and Class Consciousness* (1923; Cambridge,
Mass.: MIT Press, 1971), pp. 46–55, 59–70.

> as a whole. The question is *what is the proletariat*
> and what course of action will it be forced
> historically to take in conformity with its own
> *nature.*

(Marx, *The Holy Family*)

Marx's chief work breaks off just as he is about to embark on the definition of class. This omission was to have serious consequences both for the theory and the practice of the proletariat. For on this vital point the later movement was forced to base itself on interpretations, on the collation of occasional utterances by Marx and Engels and on the independent extrapolation and application of their method. In Marxism the division of society into classes is determined by position within the process of production. But what, then, is the meaning of class consciousness? The question at once branches out into a series of closely interrelated problems. First of all, how are we to understand class consciousness (in theory)? Second, what is the (practical) function of class consciousness, so understood, in the context of the class struggle? This leads to the further question: is the problem of class consciousness a 'general' sociological problem or does it mean one thing for the proletariat and another for every other class to have emerged hitherto? And lastly, is class consciousness homogeneous in nature and function, or can we discern different gradations and levels in it? And if so, what are their practical implications for the class struggle of the proletariat?

In his celebrated account of historical materialism[1] Engels proceeds from the assumption that although the essence of history consists in the fact that 'nothing happens without a conscious purpose or an intended aim', to understand history it is necessary to go further than this. For on the one hand,

> the many individual wills active in history for the most part produce results quite other than those intended – often quite the opposite; *their motives, therefore, in relation to the total result are likewise of only secondary importance.* On the other hand, the further question arises: *what driving forces in turn stand behind these motives?* What are the historical causes which transform themselves into these motives in the brain of the actors?

He goes on to argue that these driving forces ought themselves to be determined, in particular those which 'set in motion great masses, whole peoples and again whole classes of the people; and which create *a lasting action resulting in a great transformation*'. The essence of scientific Marxism consists, then, in the realisation that the real motor forces of history are independent of man's (psychological) consciousness of them.

At a more primitive stage of knowledge this independence takes the form of the belief that these forces belong, as it were, to nature and that in them and in their causal interactions it is possible to discern the 'eternal' laws of nature. As Marx says of bourgeois thought:

> Man's reflections on the forms of social life and consequently also his scientific analysis of those forms, take a course directly opposite to that of their actual historical development. He begins *post festum*, with the results of the process of development ready to hand before him. The characters . . . have already acquired the stability of natural self-understood forms of social life, before man seeks to decipher not their historical character (for in his eyes they are immutable) but their meaning.[2]

This is a dogma whose most important spokesmen can be found in the political theory of classical German philosophy and in the economic theory of Adam Smith and Ricardo. Marx opposes to them a critical philosophy, a theory of theory and a consciousness of consciousness. This critical philosophy implies above all historical criticism. It dissolves the rigid, unhistorical, natural appearance of social institutions; it reveals their historical origins and shows therefore that they are subject to history in every respect including historical decline. Consequently history does not merely unfold *within* the terrain mapped out by these institutions. It does not resolve itself into the evolution of *contents*, of men and situations, etc., while the *principles* of society remain eternally valid. Nor are these institutions the *goal* to which all history aspires, such that when they are realised history will have fulfilled her mission and will then be at an end. On the contrary, history is precisely *the history of these institutions*, of the changes they undergo *as* institutions which bring men together in societies. Such institutions start by controlling economic relations between men and go on to permeate all human relations (and hence also man's relations with himself and with nature, etc.).

At this point bourgeois thought must come up against an insuperable obstacle, for its starting-point and its goal are always, if not always consciously, an apologia for the existing order of things or at least the proof of their immutability.[3] 'Thus there has been history, but there is no longer any',[4] Marx observes with reference to bourgeois economics, a dictum which applies with equal force to all attempts by bourgeois thinkers to understand the process of history. (It has often been pointed out that this is also one of the defects of Hegel's philosophy of history.) As a result, while bourgeois thought is indeed able to conceive of history as a problem, it remains an *intractable* problem. Either it is forced to abolish the process of history and regard the institutions of the present as eternal laws of nature which for 'mysterious' reasons and in a manner wholly at odds with the principles of a rational science were held to have failed to establish themselves firmly, or indeed at all, in the past. (This is characteristic of bourgeois sociology.) Or else, everything meaningful or purposive is banished from history. It then becomes impossible to advance beyond the mere 'individuality' of the various epochs and their social and human representatives. History must then insist with Ranke that every age is 'equally close to God', i.e. has attained an equal degree of perfection and that – for quite different reasons – there is no such thing as historical development.

In the first case it ceases to be possible to understand the *origin* of social institutions.[5] The objects of history appear as the objects of immutable, eternal laws of nature. History becomes fossilised in a *formalism* incapable of comprehending that the real nature of socio-historical institutions is that they consist of *relations between men*. On the contrary, men become estranged from this, the true source of historical understanding and cut off from it by an unbridgeable gulf. As Marx points out,[6] people fail to realise 'that these definite social relations are just as much the products of men as linen, flax, etc.'.

In the second case, history is transformed into the irrational rule of blind forces which is embodied at best in the 'spirit of the people' or in 'great men'. It can therefore only be described pragmatically but it cannot be rationally understood. Its only possible organisation would be aesthetic, as if it were a work of art. Or else, as in the philosophy of history of the Kantians, it must be seen as the instrument, senseless in itself, by means of which timeless, suprahistorical, ethical principles are realised.

Marx resolves this dilemma by exposing it as an illusion. The dilemma means only that the contradictions of the capitalist system of production are reflected in these mutually incompatible accounts of the same object. For in this historiography with its search for 'sociological' laws or its formalistic rationale, we find the reflection of man's plight in bourgeois society and of his helpless enslavement by the forces of production. 'To them, *their own social action*', Marx remarks,[7] 'takes the form of the action of objects which rule the producers instead of being ruled by them.' This law was expressed most clearly and coherently in the purely natural and rational laws of classical economics. Marx retorted with the demand for a historical critique of economics which resolves the totality of the reified objectivities of social and economic life into *relations between men*. Capital and with it every form in which the national economy objectifies itself is, according to Marx, 'not a thing but a social relation between persons mediated through things'.[8]

However, by reducing the objectivity of the social institutions so hostile to man to relations between men, Marx also does away with the false implications of the irrationalist and individualist principle, i.e. the other side of the dilemma. For to eliminate the objectivity attributed both to social institutions inimical to man and to their historical evolution means the restoration of this objectivity to their underlying basis, to the relations between men; it does not involve the elimination of laws and objectivity independent of the will of man and in particular the wills and thoughts of individual men. It simply means that this objectivity is the self-objectification of human society at a particular stage in its development; its laws hold good only within the framework of the historical context which produced them and which is in turn determined by them.

It might look as though by dissolving the dilemma in this manner we were denying consciousness any decisive role in the process of history. It is true that the conscious reflexes of the different stages of economic growth remain historical facts of great importance; it is true that while dialectical materialism is itself the product of this process, it does not deny that men perform their historical deeds themselves and that they do so consciously. But as Engels emphasises in a letter to Mehring,[9] this consciousness is false. However, the dialectical method does not permit us simply to proclaim the 'falseness' of this consciousness and to persist in an inflexible confrontation of true and false. On the contrary, it requires us to investigate this 'false consciousness' concretely as an aspect of the historical totality and as a stage in the historical process.

Of course bourgeois historians also attempt such concrete analyses; indeed they reproach historical materialists with violating the concrete uniqueness of historical events. Where they go wrong is in their belief that the concrete can be located in the empirical individual of history ('individual' here can refer to an individual man, class or people) and in his empirically given (and hence psychological or mass-psychological) consciousness. And just when they imagine that they have discovered the most concrete thing of all: *society as a concrete totality*, the system of production at a given point in history and the resulting division of society into classes – they are in fact at the furthest remove from it. In missing the mark they mistake something wholly abstract for the concrete. 'These relations', Marx states, 'are not those between one individual and another, but between worker and capitalist, tenant and landlord, etc. Eliminate these relations and you abolish the whole of society; your Prometheus will then be nothing more than a spectre without arms or legs. . . .'[10]

Concrete analysis means then: the relation to society *as a whole*. For only when this relation is established does the consciousness of their existence that men have at any given time emerge in all its essential characteristics. It appears, on the one hand, as something which is *subjectively* justified in the social and historical situation, as something which can and should be understood, i.e. as 'right'. At the same time, *objectively*, it bypasses the essence of the evolution of society and fails to pinpoint it and express it adequately. That is to say, objectively, it appears as a 'false consciousness'.

On the other hand, we may see the same consciousness as something which fails *subjectively* to reach its self-appointed goals, while furthering and realising the *objective* aims of society of which it is ignorant and which it did not choose.

This twofold dialectical determination of 'false consciousness' constitutes an analysis far removed from the naive description of what men *in fact* thought, felt and wanted at any moment in history and from any given point in the class structure. I do not wish to deny the great importance of this, but it remains after all merely the *material* of genuine historical analysis. The relation with concrete totality and the dialectical determinants arising from it transcend pure description and yield the category of objective possibility. By relating consciousness to the whole of society it becomes possible to infer the thoughts and feelings which men would have in a particular situation if they were *able* to assess both it and the interests arising from it in their impact on immediate action and on the whole structure of society. That is to say, it would be possible to infer the thoughts and feelings appropriate to their objective situation. The number of such situations is not unlimited in any society. However much detailed researches are able to refine social typologies there will always be a number of clearly distinguished basic types whose characteristics are determined by the types of position available in the process of production. Now class consciousness consists in fact of the appropriate and rational reactions 'imputed' (*zugerechnet*) to a particular typical position in the process of production.[11] This consciousness is, therefore, neither the sum nor the average of what is thought or felt by the single individuals who make up the class. And yet the historically significant actions of the class as a whole are determined in the last resort by this consciousness and not by the thought of the individual – and these actions can be understood only by reference to this consciousness.

This analysis establishes right from the start the distance that separates class consciousness from the empirically given, and from the psychologically describable and explicable ideas which men form about their situation in life. But it is not enough just to state that this distance exists or even to define its implications in a formal and general way. We must discover, firstly, whether it is a phenomenon that differs according to the manner in which the various classes are related to society as a whole and whether the differences are so great as to produce *qualitative distinctions*. And we must discover, secondly, the *practical* significance of these different possible relations between the objective economic totality, the imputed class consciousness and the real, psychological thoughts of men about their lives. We must discover, in short, the *practical, historical function* of class consciousness.

Only after such preparatory formulations can we begin to exploit the category of objective possibility systematically. The first question we must ask is how far is it *in fact* possible to discern the whole economy of a society from inside it? It is essential to transcend the limitations of particular individuals caught up in their own narrow prejudices. But it is no less vital not to overstep the frontier fixed for them by the economic structure of society and establishing their position in it.[12] Regarded abstractly and formally, then, class consciousness implies a class-conditioned *unconsciousness* of one's own socio-historical and economic condition.[13] This condition is given as a definite structural relation, a definite formal nexus which appears to govern the whole of life. The 'falseness', the illusion implicit in this situation is in no sense arbitrary; it is simply the intellectual reflex of the objective economic structure. Thus, for example, 'the value or price of labour-power takes on the appearance of the price or value of labour itself . . . ' and 'the illusion is created that the totality is paid labour. . . . ' In contrast to that, under slavery even that portion of labour which is paid for appears unpaid for.[14] Now it requires the most painstaking historical analysis to use the category of objective possibility so as to isolate the conditions in which this illusion can be exposed and a real connection with the totality established. For if from the vantage point of a particular class the totality of existing society is not visible; if a class thinks the thoughts imputable to it and which bear upon its interests right through to their logical conclusion and yet fails to strike at the heart of that totality, then such a class is doomed to play only a subordinate role. It can never influence the course of history in either a conservative or progressive direction. Such classes are normally condemned to passivity, to an unstable oscillation between the ruling and the revolutionary classes, and if perchance they do erupt then such explosions are purely elemental and aimless. They may win a few battles but they are doomed to ultimate defeat.

For a class to be ripe for hegemony means that its interests and consciousness enable it to organise the whole of society in accordance with those interests. The crucial question in every class struggle is this: which class possesses this capacity and this consciousness at the decisive moment? This does not preclude the use of force. It does not mean that the class-interests destined to prevail and thus to uphold the interests of society as a whole can be guaranteed an automatic victory. On the contrary, such a transfer of power can often only be brought about by the most ruthless use of force (as e.g. the primitive accumulation of capital). But it often turns out that questions of class consciousness prove to be decisive in just those situations where force is unavoidable and where classes are locked in a life-and-death struggle. Thus the noted Hungarian Marxist Erwin Szabó is mistaken in criticising Engels for maintaining that the Great Peasant War (of 1525) was essentially a reactionary movement. Szabó argues that the peasants' revolt was suppressed *only* by the ruthless use of force and that its defeat was not grounded in socio-economic factors and in the class consciousness of the peasants. He overlooks the fact that the deepest reason for the weakness of the peasantry and the superior strength of the princes is to be sought in class consciousness. Even the most cursory student of the military aspects of the Peasants' War can easily convince himself of this.

It must not be thought, however, that all classes ripe for hegemony have a class consciousness with the same inner structure. Everything hinges on the extent to which they can become conscious of the actions they need to perform in order to obtain and organise power. The question then becomes: how far does the class concerned perform the actions history has imposed on it 'consciously' or 'unconsciously'? And is that consciousness 'true' or 'false'? These distinctions are by no means academic. Quite apart from problems of culture where such fissures and dissonances are crucial, in all practical matters too the fate of a class depends on its ability to elucidate and solve the problems with which history confronts it. And here it becomes transparently obvious that class consciousness is concerned neither with the thoughts of individuals, however advanced, nor with the state of scientific knowledge. For example, it is quite clear that ancient society was broken economically by the limitations of a system built on slavery. But it is equally clear that neither the ruling classes nor the classes that rebelled against them in the name of revolution or reform could perceive this. In consequence the practical emergence of these problems meant that the society was necessarily and irremediably doomed.

The situation is even clearer in the case of the modern bourgeoisie, which, armed with its knowledge of the workings of economics, clashed with feudal and absolutist society. For the bourgeoisie was quite unable to perfect its fundamental science, its own science of classes: the reef on which it foundered was its failure to discover even a theoretical solution to the problem of crises. The fact that a scientifically acceptable solution does exist is of no avail. For to accept that solution, even in theory, would be tantamount to observing society *from a class standpoint other than that of the bourgeoisie*. And no class can do that – unless it is willing to abdicate its power freely. Thus the barrier which converts the class consciousness of the bourgeoisie into 'false' consciousness is objective; it is the class situation itself. It is the objective result of the economic set-up, and is neither arbitrary, subjective nor psychological. The class consciousness of the bourgeoisie may well be able to reflect all the problems of organisation entailed by its hegemony and by the capitalist transformation and penetration of total production. But it becomes obscured as soon as it is called upon to face problems that remain within its jurisdiction but which point beyond the limits of capitalism. The discovery of the 'natural laws' of economics is pure light in comparison with mediaeval feudalism or even the mercantilism of the transitional period, but by an internal dialectical twist they became 'natural laws based on the unconsciousness of those who are involved in them'.[15]

It would be beyond the scope of these pages to advance further and attempt to construct a historical and systematic typology of the possible degrees of class consciousness. That would require – in the first instance – an exact study of the point in the total process of production at which the interests of the various classes are most immediately and vitally involved. Secondly, we would have to show how far it would be in the interest of any given class to go beyond this immediacy, to annul and transcend its immediate interest by seeing it as a factor within a totality. And lastly, what is the nature of the totality that is then achieved? How far does it really embrace the true totality of production? It is quite evident that the quality and structure of class consciousness must be very different if, e.g. it remains stationary at the separation of consumption from production (as with the Roman *Lumpenproletariat*) or if it represents the formation of the interests of circulation (as with merchant capital). Although we cannot embark on a systematic typology of the various points of view it can be seen from the foregoing that these specimens of 'false' consciousness differ from each other both qualitatively, structurally and in a manner that is crucial for the activity of the classes in society. . . .

Bourgeoisie and proletariat are the only pure classes in bourgeois society. They are the only classes whose existence and development are entirely dependent on the course taken by the modern evolution of production and only from the vantage point of these classes can a plan for the total organisation of society *even be imagined*. The outlook of the other classes (petty bourgeois or peasants) is ambiguous or sterile because their existence is not based exclusively on their role in the capitalist system of production but is indissolubly linked with the vestiges of feudal society. Their aim, therefore, is not to advance capitalism or to transcend it, but to reverse its action or at least to prevent it from developing fully. Their class interest concentrates on *symptoms of development* and not on development itself, and on elements of society rather than on the construction of society as a whole.

The question of consciousness may make its appearance in terms of the objectives chosen or in terms of action, as for instance in the case of the petty bourgeoisie. This class lives at least in part in the capitalist big city and every aspect of its existence is directly exposed to the influence of capitalism. Hence it cannot possibly remain wholly unaffected by the *fact* of class conflict between bourgeoisie and proletariat. But as a 'transitional class in which the interests of two other classes become simultaneously blunted . . . ' it will imagine itself 'to be above all class antagonisms'.[16] Accordingly it will search for ways whereby it will 'not indeed eliminate the two extremes of capital and wage labour, but will weaken their antagonism and transform it into harmony'.[17] In all decisions crucial for society its actions will be irrelevant and it will be forced to fight for both sides in turn but always without consciousness. In so doing its own objectives – which exist exclusively in its own consciousness – must become progressively weakened and increasingly divorced from social action. Ultimately they will assume purely 'ideological' forms. The petty bourgeoisie will only be able to play an active role in history as long as these objectives happen to coincide with the real economic interests of capitalism. This was the case with the abolition of the feudal estates during the French Revolution. With the fulfilment of this mission its utterances, which for the most part remain unchanged in form, become more and more remote from real events and turn finally into mere caricatures (this was true, e.g., of the Jacobinism of the Montagne, 1848–51).

This isolation from society as a whole has its repercussions on the internal structure of the class and its organisational potential. This can be seen most clearly in the development of the peasantry. Marx says on this point:[18]

> The small-holding peasants form a vast mass whose members live in similar conditions but without entering into manifold relations with each other. Their mode of production isolates them from one another instead of bringing them into mutual intercourse. . . . Every single peasant family . . . thus acquires its means of life more through exchange with nature than in intercourse with society. . . . In so far as millions of families live under economic conditions of existence that separate their mode of life, their interests and their culture from those of other classes and place them in opposition to them, they constitute a class. In so far as there is only a local connection between the small-holding peasants, and the identity of their interests begets no community, no national unity and no political organisation, they do not constitute a class.

Hence *external* upheavals, such as war, revolution in the towns, etc. are needed before these masses can coalesce in a unified movement, and even then they are incapable of organising it and supplying it with slogans and a positive direction corresponding to their own interests.

Whether these movements will be progressive (as in the French Revolution of 1789 or the Russian Revolution of 1917), or reactionary (as with Napoleon's *coup d'état*) will depend on the position of the other classes involved in the conflict, and on the level of consciousness of the parties that lead them. For this reason, too, the *ideological* form taken by the class consciousness of the peasants changes its content more frequently than that of other classes: this is because it is always borrowed from elsewhere. Hence parties that base themselves wholly or in part on this class consciousness always lack really firm and secure support in critical situations (as was true of the Socialist Revolutionaries in 1917 and 1918).

This explains why it is possible for peasant conflicts to be fought out under opposing flags. Thus it is highly characteristic of both Anarchism and the 'class consciousness' of the peasantry that a number of counter-revolutionary rebellions and uprisings of the middle and upper strata of the peasantry in Russia should have found the anarchist view of society to be a satisfying ideology. We cannot really speak of class consciousness in the case of these classes (if, indeed, we can even speak of them as classes in the strict Marxist sense of the term): for a full consciousness of their situation would reveal to them the hopelessness of their particularist strivings in the face of the inevitable course of events. Consciousness and self-interest then are *mutually incompatible* in this instance. And as class consciousness was defined in terms of the problems of imputing class interests the failure of their class consciousness to develop in the immediately given historical reality becomes comprehensible philosophically.

With the bourgeoisie, also, class consciousness stands in opposition to class interest. But here the antagonism is *not contradictory but dialectical*.

The distinction between the two modes of contradiction may be briefly described in this way: in the case of the other classes, a class consciousness is prevented from emerging by their position within the process of production and the interests this generates. In the case of the bourgeoisie, however, these factors combine to produce a class consciousness but one which is cursed by its very nature with the tragic fate of developing an insoluble contradiction at the very zenith of its powers. As a result of this contradiction it must annihilate itself.

The tragedy of the bourgeoisie is reflected historically in the fact that even before it had defeated its predecessor, feudalism, its new enemy, the proletariat, had appeared on the scene. Politically, it became evident when at the moment of victory, the 'freedom' in whose name the bourgeoisie had joined battle with feudalism, was transformed into a new repressiveness. Sociologically, the bourgeoisie did everything in its power to eradicate the fact of class conflict from the consciousness of society, even though class conflict had only emerged in its purity and became established as an historical fact with the advent of capitalism. Ideologically, we see the same contradiction in the fact that the bourgeoisie endowed the individual with an unprecedented importance, but at the same time that same individuality was annihilated by the economic conditions to which it was subjected, by the reification created by commodity production.

All these contradictions, and the list might be extended indefinitely, are only the reflection of the deepest contradictions in capitalism itself as they appear in the consciousness of the bourgeoisie in accordance with their position in the total system of production. For this reason they appear as dialectical contradictions in the class consciousness of the bourgeoisie. They do not merely reflect the inability of the bourgeoisie to grasp the contradictions inherent in its own social order. For, on the one hand, capitalism is the first system of production able to achieve a total economic penetration of society,[19] and this implies that in theory the bourgeoisie should be able to progress from this central point to the possession of an (imputed) class consciousness of the whole system of production. On the other hand, the position held by the capitalist class and the interests which determine its actions ensure that it will be unable to control its own system of production even in theory.

There are many reasons for this. In the first place, it only seems to be true that for capitalism production occupies the centre of class consciousness and hence provides the theoretical starting-point for analysis. With reference to Ricardo 'who had been reproached with an exclusive concern with production', Marx emphasised[20] that he 'defined distribution as the sole subject of economics'. And the detailed analysis of the process by which capital is concretely realised shows in every single instance that the interest of the capitalist (who produces not goods but commodities) is necessarily confined to matters that must be peripheral in terms of production. Moreover, the capitalist, enmeshed in what is for him the decisive process of the expansion of capital, must have a standpoint from which the most important problems become quite invisible.[21]

The discrepancies that result are further exacerbated by the fact that there is an insoluble contradiction running through the internal structure of capitalism between the social and the individual principle, i.e. between the function of capital as private property and its objective economic function. As the *Communist Manifesto* states: 'Capital is a social force and not a personal one.' But it is a social force whose movements are determined by the individual interests of the owners of capital – who cannot see and who are necessarily indifferent to all the social implications of their activities. Hence the social principle and the social function implicit in capital can only prevail unbeknown to them and, as it were, against their will and behind their backs. Because of this conflict between the individual and the social, Marx rightly characterised the stock companies as the 'negation of the capitalist mode of production itself'.[22] Of course, it is true that stock companies differ only in inessentials from individual capitalists and even the so-called abolition of the anarchy in production through cartels and trusts only shifts the contradiction elsewhere, without, however, eliminating it. This situation forms one of the decisive factors governing the class consciousness of the bourgeoisie. It is true that the bourgeoisie acts as a class in the objective evolution of society. But it understands the process (which it is itself instigating) as something external which is subject to objective laws which it can only experience passively.

Bourgeois thought observes economic life consistently and necessarily from the standpoint of the individual capitalist and this naturally produces a sharp confrontation between the individual and the overpowering supra-personal 'law of nature' which propels all social phenomena.[23] This leads both to the antagonism between individual and class interests in the event of conflict (which, it is true, rarely becomes as acute among the ruling classes as in the bourgeoisie), and also to the logical impossibility of discovering theoretical and practical solutions to the problems created by the capitalist system of production.

'This sudden reversion from a system of credit to a system of hard cash heaps theoretical fright on top of practical panic; and the dealers by whose agency circulation is effected shudder before the impenetrable mystery in which their own economic relations are shrouded.'[24] This terror is not unfounded, that is to say, it is much more than the bafflement felt by the individual capitalist when confronted by his own individual fate. The facts and the situations which induce this panic force something into the consciousness of the bourgeoisie which is too much of a brute fact for its existence to be wholly denied or repressed. But equally it is something that the bourgeoisie can never fully understand. For the recognisable background to this situation is the fact that 'the *real barrier* of capitalist production is *capital itself*'.[25] And if this insight were to become conscious it would indeed entail the self-negation of the capitalist class.

In this way the objective limits of capitalist production become the limits of the class consciousness of the bourgeoisie. The older 'natural' and 'conservative' forms of domination had left unmolested[26] the forms of production of whole sections of the people they ruled and therefore exerted by and large a traditional and unrevolutionary influence. Capitalism, by contrast, is a revolutionary form *par excellence. The fact that it must necessarily remain in ignorance of the objective economic limitations of its own system expresses itself as an internal, dialectical contradiction in its class consciousness.*

This means that *formally* the class consciousness of the bourgeoisie is geared to economic consciousness. And indeed the highest degree of unconsciousness, the crassest form of 'false consciousness' always manifests itself when the conscious mastery of economic phenomena appears to be at its greatest. From the point of view of the relation of consciousness to society this contradiction is expressed as the *irreconcilable antagonism between ideology and economic base*. Its dialectics are grounded in the irreconcilable antagonism between the (capitalist) individual, i.e. the stereotyped individual of capitalism, and the 'natural' and inevitable process of development, i.e. the process not subject to consciousness. In consequence theory and practice are brought into irreconcilable opposition to each other. But the resulting dualism is anything but stable; in fact it constantly strives to harmonise principles that have been wrenched apart and thenceforth oscillate between a new 'false' synthesis and its subsequent cataclysmic disruption.

This internal dialectical contradiction in the class consciousness of the bourgeoisie is further aggravated by the fact that the objective limits of capitalism do not remain purely negative. That is to say that capitalism does not merely set 'natural' laws in motion that provoke crises which it cannot comprehend. On the contrary, those limits acquire a historical embodiment with its own consciousness and its own actions: the proletariat.

Most 'normal' shifts of perspective produced by the capitalist point of view in the image of the economic structure of society tend to 'obscure and mystify the true origin of surplus value'.[27] In the 'normal', purely theoretical view this mystification only attaches to the organic composition of capital, viz. to the place of the employer in the productive system and the economic function of interest, etc., i.e. it does no more than highlight the failure of observers to perceive the true driving forces that lie beneath the surface. But when it comes to practice this mystification touches upon the central fact of capitalist society: the class struggle.

In the class struggle we witness the emergence of all the hidden forces that usually lie concealed behind the façade of economic life, at which the capitalists and their apologists gaze as though transfixed. These forces appear in such a way that they cannot possibly be ignored. So much so that even when capitalism was in the ascendant and the proletariat could only give vent to its protests in the form of vehement spontaneous explosions, even the ideological exponents of the rising bourgeoisie acknowledged the class struggle as a basic fact of history. (For example, Marat and later historians such as Mignet.) But in proportion as the theory and practice of the proletariat made society conscious of this unconscious, revolutionary principle inherent in capitalism, the bourgeoisie was thrown back increasingly on to a conscious defensive. The dialectical contradiction in the 'false' consciousness of the bourgeoisie became more and more acute: the 'false' consciousness was converted into a mendacious consciousness. What had been at first an objective contradiction now became subjective also: the theoretical problem turned into a moral posture which decisively influenced every practical class attitude in every situation and on every issue.

Thus the situation in which the bourgeoisie finds itself determines the function of its class consciousness in its struggle to achieve control of society. The hegemony of the bourgeoisie really does embrace the whole of society; it really does attempt to organise the whole of society in its own interests (and in this it has had some success). To achieve this it was forced both to develop a coherent theory of economics, politics and society (which in itself presupposes and amounts to a *Weltanschauung*), and also to make conscious and sustain its faith in its own *mission* to control and organise society. The tragic dialectics of the bourgeoisie can be seen in the fact that it is not only desirable but essential for it to clarify its own class interests on *every particular issue*, while at the same time such a clear awareness becomes fatal when it is extended to *the question of the totality*. The chief reason for this is that the rule of the bourgeoisie can only be the rule of a minority. Its hegemony is exercised not merely *by* a minority but *in the interest* of that minority, so the need to deceive the other classes and to ensure that their class consciousness remains amorphous is inescapable for a bourgeois regime. (Consider here the theory of the state that stands 'above' class antagonisms, or the notion of an 'impartial' system of justice.)

But the veil drawn over the nature of bourgeois society is indispensable to the bourgeoisie itself. For the insoluble internal contradictions of the system become revealed with increasing starkness and so confront its supporters with a choice. Either they must consciously ignore insights which become increasingly urgent or else they must suppress their own moral instincts in order to be able to support with a good conscience an economic system that serves only their own interests.

Without overestimating the efficacy of such ideological factors it must be agreed that the fighting power of a class grows with its ability to carry out its own mission with a good conscience and to adapt all phenomena to its own interests with unbroken confidence in itself. If we consider Sismondi's criticism of classical economics, German criticisms of natural law and the youthful critiques of Carlyle it becomes evident that from a very early stage the ideological history of the bourgeoisie was *nothing but a desperate resistance to every insight into the true nature of the society it had created and thus to a real understanding of its class situation*. When the *Communist Manifesto* makes the point that the bourgeoisie produces its own gravediggers this is valid ideologically as well as economically. The whole of bourgeois thought in the nineteenth century made the most strenuous efforts to mask the real foundations of bourgeois society; everything was tried: from the greatest falsifications of fact to the 'sublime' theories about the 'essence' of history and the state. But in vain: with the end of the century the issue was resolved by the advances of science and their corresponding effects on the consciousness of the capitalist élite.

This can be seen very clearly in the bourgeoisie's greater readiness to accept the idea of conscious organisation. A greater measure of concentration was achieved first in the stock companies and in the cartels and trusts. This process revealed the social character of capital more and more clearly without affecting the general anarchy in production. What it did was to confer near-monopoly status on a number of giant individual capitalists. Objectively, then, the social character of capital was brought into play with great energy but in such a manner as to keep its nature concealed from the capitalist class. Indeed this illusory elimination of economic anarchy successfully diverted their attention from the true situation. With the crises of the War and the post-war period this tendency has advanced still further: the idea of a 'planned' economy has gained ground at least among the more progressive elements of the bourgeoisie. Admittedly this applies only within quite narrow strata of the bourgeoisie and even there it is thought of more as a theoretical experiment than as a practical way out of the impasse brought about by the crises.

When capitalism was still expanding it rejected every sort of social organisation on the grounds that it was 'an inroad upon such sacred things as the rights of property, freedom and unrestricted play for the initiative of the individual capitalist'.[28] If we compare that with current attempts to harmonise a 'planned' economy with the class interests of the bourgeoisie, we are forced to admit that what we are witnessing is *the capitulation of the class consciousness of the bourgeoisie before that of the proletariat*. Of course, the section of the bourgeoisie that accepts the notion of a 'planned' economy does not mean by it the same as does the proletariat: it regards it as a last attempt to save capitalism by driving its internal contradictions to breaking-point. Nevertheless this means jettisoning the last theoretical line of defence. (As a strange counterpart to this we may note that *at just this point in time* certain sectors of the proletariat *capitulate before the bourgeoisie* and adopt this, the most problematic form of bourgeois organisation.)

With this the whole existence of the bourgeoisie and its culture is plunged into the most terrible crisis. On the one hand, we find the utter sterility of an ideology divorced from life, of a more or less conscious attempt at forgery. On the other hand, a cynicism no less terribly jejune lives on in the world-historical irrelevances and nullities of its own existence and concerns itself only with the defence of that existence and with its own naked self-interest. This ideological crisis is an unfailing sign of decay. The bourgeoisie has already been thrown on the defensive; however aggressive its *weapons* may be, it is fighting for self-preservation. *Its power to dominate has vanished beyond recall*.

In this struggle for consciousness historical materialism plays a crucial role. Ideologically no less than economically, the bourgeoisie and the proletariat are mutually interdependent. The same process that the bourgeoisie experiences as a permanent crisis and gradual dissolution appears to the proletariat, likewise in crisis-form, as the gathering of strength and the springboard to victory. Ideologically this means that the same growth of insight into the nature of society, which reflects the protracted death struggle of the bourgeoisie, entails a steady growth in the strength of the proletariat. For the proletariat the truth is a weapon that brings victory; and the more ruthless, the greater the victory. This makes more comprehensible the desperate fury with which bourgeois science assails historical materialism: for as soon as the bourgeoisie is forced to take up its stand on this terrain, it is lost. And, at the same time, this explains why the proletariat and *only* the proletariat can discern in the correct understanding of *the nature of society* a power-factor of the first, and perhaps decisive importance.

The unique function of consciousness in the class struggle of the proletariat has consistently been overlooked by the vulgar Marxists who have substituted a petty 'Realpolitik' for the great battle of principle which reaches back to the ultimate problems of the objective economic process. Naturally we do not wish to deny that the proletariat must proceed from the facts of a given situation. But it is to be distinguished from other classes by the fact that it goes beyond the contingencies of history; far from being driven forward by them, it is itself their driving force and impinges centrally upon the process of social change. When the vulgar Marxists detach themselves from this central point of view, i.e. from the point where a proletarian class consciousness arises, *they thereby place themselves on the level of consciousness of the bourgeoisie*. And that the bourgeoisie fighting on its own ground will prove superior to the proletariat both economically and ideologically can come as a surprise only to a vulgar Marxist. Moreover only a vulgar Marxist would infer from this fact, which after all derives exclusively from his own attitude, that the bourgeoisie *generally* occupies the stronger position. For quite apart from the very real force at its disposal, it is self-evident that the bourgeoisie *fighting on its own ground* will be both more experienced and more expert. Nor will it come as a surprise if the bourgeoisie automatically obtains the upper hand when its opponents abandon their own position for that of the bourgeoisie.

As the bourgeoisie has the intellectual, organisational and every other advantage, the superiority of the proletariat must lie exclusively in its ability to see society from the centre, as a coherent whole. This means that it is able to act in such a way as to change reality; in the class consciousness of the proletariat theory and practice coincide and so it can consciously throw the weight of its actions onto the scales of history – and this is the deciding factor. When the vulgar Marxists destroy this unity they cut the nerve that binds proletarian theory to proletarian action. They reduce theory to the 'scientific' treatment of the symptoms of social change and as for practice they are themselves reduced to being buffeted about aimlessly and uncontrollably by the various elements of the process they had hoped to master.

The class consciousness that springs from this position must exhibit the same internal structure as that of the bourgeoisie. But when the logic of events drives the same dialectical contradictions to the surface of consciousness the consequences for the proletariat are even more disastrous than for the bourgeoisie. For despite all the dialectical contradictions, despite all its objective falseness, the self-deceiving 'false' consciousness that we find in the bourgeoisie is at least in accord with its class situation. It cannot save the bourgeoisie from the constant exacerbation of these contradictions and so from destruction, but it can enable it to continue the struggle and even engineer victories, albeit of short duration.

But in the case of the proletariat such a consciousness not only has to overcome these internal (bourgeois) contradictions, but it also conflicts with the course of action to which the economic situation necessarily commits the proletariat (regardless of its own thoughts on the subject). The proletariat must act in a proletarian manner, but its own vulgar Marxist theory blocks its vision of the right course to adopt. The dialectical contradiction between necessary proletarian action and vulgar Marxist (bourgeois) theory becomes more and more acute. As the decisive battle in the class struggle approaches, the power of a true or false theory to accelerate or retard progress grows in proportion. The 'realm of freedom', the end of the 'pre-history of mankind' means precisely that the power of the objectified, reified relations between men begins to revert to *man*. The closer this process comes to its goal the more urgent it becomes for the proletariat to understand its own historical mission and the more vigorously and directly proletarian class consciousness will determine each of its actions. For the blind power of the forces at work will only advance 'automatically' to their goal of self-annihilation as long as that goal is not within reach. When the moment of transition to the 'realm of freedom' arrives this will become apparent just because the blind forces really will hurtle blindly towards the abyss, and only the conscious will of the proletariat will be able to save mankind from the impending catastrophe. In other words, when the final economic crisis of capitalism develops, *the fate of the revolution (and with it the fate of mankind) will depend on the ideological maturity of the proletariat, i.e. on its class consciousness.*

We have now determined the unique function of the class consciousness of the proletariat in contrast to that of other classes. The proletariat cannot liberate itself as a class without simultaneously abolishing class society as such. For that reason its consciousness, the last class consciousness in the history of mankind, must both lay bare the nature of society and achieve an increasingly inward fusion of theory and practice. 'Ideology' for the proletariat is no banner to follow into battle, nor is it a cover for its true objectives: it is the objective and the weapon itself. Every non-principled or unprincipled use of tactics on the part of the proletariat debases historical materialism to the level of mere 'ideology' and forces the proletariat to use bourgeois (or petty bourgeois) tactics. It thereby robs it of its greatest strength by forcing class consciousness into the secondary or inhibiting role of a bourgeois consciousness, instead of the active role of a proletarian consciousness.

Notes

1. *Feuerbach and the End of Classical German Philosophy* (SW II), pp. 354ff.
2. *Capital* I, p. 75.

3. And also of the 'pessimism' which *perpetuates* the present state of affairs and represents it as the uttermost limit of human development just as much as does 'optimism'. In this respect (and in this respect alone) Hegel and Schopenhauer are on a par with each other.

4. *The Poverty of Philosophy*, p. 135.

5. Ibid., p. 117.

6. Ibid., p. 122.

7. *Capital* I, p. 75 (my italics). Cf. also ENGELS, *The Origin of the Family, Private Property and the State*, (SW II), pp. 292–3.

8. *Capital* I, p. 766. Cf. also *Wage Labour and Capital* (SW II), p. 83; on machines see *The Poverty of Philosophy*, p. 149; on money, ibid., p. 89, etc.

9. *Dokumente des Sozialismus* II, p. 76.

10. *The Poverty of Philosophy*, p. 112.

11. In this context it is unfortunately not possible to discuss in greater detail some of the ramifications of these ideas in Marxism, e.g. the very important category of the 'economic persona'. Even less can we pause to glance at the relation of historical materialism to comparable trends in bourgeois thought (such as Max Weber's ideal types).

12. This is the point from which to gain an historical understanding of the great utopians such as Plato or Sir Thomas More. Cf. also Marx on Aristotle, *Capital* I, pp. 59–60.

13. 'But although ignorant of this, yet he says it', Marx says of Franklin (*Capital* I, p. 51). And similarly: 'They know not what they do, but they do it' (ibid., p. 74).

14. *Wages, Price and Profit* (SW I), pp. 388–9.

15. ENGELS, *Umriss zu einer Kritik der Nationalökonomie* (Nachlass I), p. 449.

16. *The Eighteenth Brumaire of Louis Bonaparte* (SW I), p. 252.

17. Ibid., p. 249.

18. Ibid., pp. 302–3.

19. But no more than the tendency. It is Rosa Luxemburg's great achievement to have shown that this is not just a passing phase but that capitalism can only survive – economically – while it moves society in the direction of capitalism but has not yet fully penetrated it. This economic self-contradiction of any purely capitalist society is undoubtedly one of the reasons for the contradictions in the class consciousness of the bourgeoisie.

20. *A Contribution to the Critique of Political Economy*, p. 285.

21. *Capital* III, pp. 136, 307–8, 318, etc. It is self-evident that the different groups of capitalists, such as industrialists and merchants, etc., are differently placed; but the distinctions are not relevant in this context.

22. Ibid., p. 428.

23. On this point cf. the essay 'The Marxism of Rosa Luxemburg'.

24. *A Contribution to the Critique of Political Economy*, p. 198.

25. *Capital* III, pp. 245 and also p. 252.

26. This applies also to e.g. primitive forms of hoarding (see *Capital* I, p. 131) and even to certain expressions of (what is relatively) 'pre-capitalist' merchants' capital. Cf. *Capital* III, p. 329.

27. *Capital* III, pp. 165 and also pp. 151, 373–6, 383, etc.

28. *Capital* I, p. 356.

3 Ideology and Utopia*

KARL MANNHEIM

Karl Mannheim (1893–1947), a refugee from Nazism who held an appointment at the London School of Economics, collaborated with Georg Lukács in his youth, and though not himself a Marxist was strongly influenced by Marxist and historicist thought. His major work, *Ideology and Utopia* (1936, first published in 1929), is a classic of the 'sociology of knowledge' tradition, and was to be supplemented by his posthumously published *Essays in the Sociology of Knowledge* (London: Routledge and Kegan Paul, 1968). Ideology for Mannheim means ideas which deceptively rationalise a particular partisan standpoint, or, more generally, a body of beliefs which is inadequate to a specific stage of historical development. Against this he posits the disinterested analysis of 'world-views' as a whole, seeking to reveal their historical base in a style of thought which will pass into the 'genetic structuralism' of Lucien Goldmann. Mannheim thus belongs to a German hermeneutical tradition which seeks to decipher the meanings of collective mental structures; and this for him is the true aim of a 'scientific' sociology of knowledge which – unlike a more partisan 'ideology critique' – aims to understand systems of ideas rather than to unmask and discredit them.

Definition of concepts

In order to understand the present situation of thought, it is necessary to start with the problems of 'ideology'. For most people, the term 'ideology' is closely bound up with Marxism, and their reactions to the term are largely determined by the association. It is therefore first necessary to state that although Marxism contributed a great deal to the original statement of the problem, both the word and its meaning go farther back in history than

*Reprinted from KARL MANNHEIM, *Ideology and Utopia* (London: Routledge and Kegan Paul, 1936), pp. 49–62, 67–74.

Marxism, and ever since its time new meanings of the word have emerged, which have taken shape independently of it.

There is no better introduction to the problem than the analysis of the meaning of the term 'ideology': firstly we have to disentangle all the different shades of meaning which are blended here into a pseudo-unity, and a more precise statement of the variations in the meanings of the concept, as it is used to-day, will prepare the way for its sociological and historical analysis. Such an analysis will show that in general there are two distinct and separable meanings of the term 'ideology' – the particular and the total.

The particular conception of ideology is implied when the term denotes that we are sceptical of the ideas and representations advanced by our opponent. They are regarded as more or less conscious disguises of the real nature of a situation, the true recognition of which would not be in accord with his interests. These distortions range all the way from conscious lies to half-conscious and unwitting disguises; from calculated attempts to dupe others to self-deception. This conception of ideology, which has only gradually become differentiated from the common-sense notion of the lie, is particular in several senses. Its particularity becomes evident when it is contrasted with the more inclusive total conception of ideology. Here we refer to the ideology of an age or of a concrete historico-social group, e.g. of a class, when we are concerned with the characteristics and composition of the total structure of the mind of this epoch or of this group.

The common as well as the distinctive elements of the two concepts are readily evident. The common element in these two conceptions seems to consist in the fact that neither relies solely on what is actually said by the opponent in order to reach an understanding of his real meaning and intention.[1] Both fall back on the subject, whether individual or group, proceeding to an understanding of what is said by the indirect method of analysing the social conditions of the individual or his group. The ideas expressed by the subject are thus regarded as functions of his existence. This means that opinions, statements, propositions, and systems of ideas are not taken at their face value but are interpreted in the light of the life-situation of the one who expresses them. It signifies further that the specific character and life-situation of the subject influence his opinions, perceptions, and interpretations.

Both these conceptions of ideology, accordingly, make these so-called 'ideas' a function of him who holds them, and of his position in his social milieu. Although they have something in common, there are also significant differences between them. Of the latter we mention merely the most important:

(a) Whereas the particular conception of ideology designates only a part of the opponent's assertions as ideologies – and this only with reference to their content, the total conception calls into question the opponent's total

Weltanschauung (including his conceptual apparatus), and attempts to understand these concepts as an outgrowth of the collective life of which he partakes.

(b) The particular conception of 'ideology' makes its analysis of ideas on a purely psychological level. If it is claimed for instance that an adversary is lying, or that he is concealing or distorting a given factual situation, it is still nevertheless assumed that both parties share common criteria of validity – it is still assumed that it is possible to refute lies and eradicate sources of error by referring to accepted criteria of objective validity common to both parties. The suspicion that one's opponent is the victim of an ideology does not go so far as to exclude him from discussion on the basis of a common theoretical frame of reference. The case is different with the total conception of ideology. When we attribute to one historical epoch one intellectual world and to ourselves another one, or if a certain historically determined social stratum thinks in categories other than our own, we refer not to the isolated cases of thought-content, but to fundamentally divergent thought-systems and to widely differing modes of experience and interpretation. We touch upon the theoretical or noological level whenever we consider not merely the content but also the form, and even the conceptual framework of a mode of thought as a function of the life-situation of a thinker. 'The economic categories are only the theoretical expressions, the abstractions, of the social relations of production. . . . The same men who establish social relations conformably with their material productivity, produce also the principles, the ideas, the categories, conformably with their social relations' (Karl Marx, *The Poverty of Philosophy*, being a translation of *Misère de la Philosophie*, with a preface by Frederick Engels, translated by H. Quelch, Chicago, 1910, p. 119). These are the two ways of analysing statements as functions of their social background; the first operates only on the psychological, the second on the noological level.

(c) Corresponding to this difference, the particular conception of ideology operates primarily with a psychology of interests, while the total conception uses a more formal functional analysis, without any reference to motivations, confining itself to an objective description of the structural differences in minds operating in different social settings. The former assumes that this or that interest is the cause of a given lie or deception. The latter presupposes simply that there is a correspondence between a given social situation and a given perspective, point of view, or apperception mass. In this case, while an analysis of constellations of interests may often be necessary it is not to establish causal connections but to characterize the total situation. Thus interest psychology tends to be displaced by an analysis of the correspondence between the situation to be known and the forms of knowledge.

Since the particular conception never actually departs from the psychological level, the point of reference in such analyses is always the individual. This is the case even when we are dealing with groups, since all psychic phenomena must finally be reduced to the minds of individuals. The term 'group ideology' occurs frequently, to be sure, in popular speech. Group existence in this sense can only mean that a group of persons, either in their immediate reactions to the same situation or as a result of direct psychic interaction, react similarly. Accordingly, conditioned by the same social situation, they are subject to the same illusions. If we confine our observations to the mental processes which take place in the individual and regard him as the only possible bearer of ideologies, we shall never grasp in its totality the structure of the intellectual world belonging to a social group in a given historical situation. Although this mental world as a whole could never come into existence without the experiences and productive responses of the different individuals, its inner structure is not to be found in a mere integration of these individual experiences. The individual members of the working class, for instance, do not experience *all* the elements of an outlook which could be called the proletarian *Weltanschauung*. Every individual participates only in certain fragments of this thought-system, the totality of which is not in the least a mere sum of these fragmentary individual experiences. As a totality the thought-system is integrated systematically, and is no mere casual jumble of fragmentary experiences of discrete members of the group. Thus it follows that the individual can only be considered as the bearer of an ideology as long as we deal with that conception of ideology which, by definition, is directed more to detached contents than to the whole structure of thought, uncovering false ways of thought and exposing lies. As soon as the total conception of ideology is used, we attempt to reconstruct the whole outlook of a social group, and neither the concrete individuals nor the abstract sum of them can legitimately be considered as bearers of this ideological thought-system as a whole. The aim of the analysis on this level is the reconstruction of the systematic theoretical basis underlying the single judgments of the individual. Analyses of ideologies in the particular sense, making the content of individual thought largely dependent on the interests of the subject, can never achieve this basic reconstruction of the whole outlook of a social group. They can at best reveal the collective psychological aspects of ideology, or lead to some development of mass psychology, dealing either with the different behaviour of the individual in the crowd, or with the results of the mass integration of the psychic experiences of many individuals. And although the collective-psychological aspect may very often approach the problems of the total ideological analysis, it does not answer its questions exactly. It is one thing to know how far my attitudes and judgments are influenced and altered by the co-existence of other human beings, but it is another thing to know what are the theoretical implications of my mode of thought which are identical with those of my fellow members of the group or social stratum.

We content ourselves here merely with stating the issue without attempting a thorough-going analysis of the difficult methodological problems which it raises.

The concept ideology in historical perspective

Just as the particular and total conceptions of ideology can be distinguished from one another on the basis of their differences in meaning, so the historical origins of these two concepts may also be differentiated even though in reality they are always intertwined. We do not as yet possess an adequate historical treatment of the development of the concept of ideology, to say nothing of a sociological history of the many variations[2] in its meaning. Even if we were in a position to do so, it would not be our task, for the purposes we have in mind, to write a history of the changing meanings in the concept of ideology. Our aim is simply to present such facts from the scattered evidence as will most clearly exhibit the distinction between the two terms made in the previous chapter, and to trace the process which gradually led to the refined and specialized meaning which the terms have come to possess. Corresponding to the dual meaning of the term ideology which we have designated here as the particular and total conceptions, respectively, are two distinct currents of historical development.

The distrust and suspicion which men everywhere evidence towards their adversaries, at all stages of historical development, may be regarded as the immediate precursor of the notion of ideology. But it is only when the distrust of man toward man, which is more or less evident at every stage of human history, becomes explicit and is methodically recognized, that we may properly speak of an ideological taint in the utterances of others. We arrive at this level when we no longer make individuals personally responsible for the deceptions which we detect in their utterances, and when we no longer attribute the evil that they do to their malicious cunning. It is only when we more or less consciously seek to discover the source of their untruthfulness in a social factor, that we are properly making an ideological interpretation. We begin to treat our adversary's views as ideologies only when we no longer consider them as calculated lies and when we sense in his total behaviour an unreliability which we regard as a function of the social situation in which he finds himself. The particular conception of ideology therefore signifies a phenomenon intermediate between a simple lie at one pole, and an error, which is the result of a distorted and faulty conceptual apparatus, at the other. It refers to a sphere of errors, psychological in nature, which, unlike deliberate deception, are not intentional, but follow inevitably and unwittingly from certain causal determinants.

According to this interpretation, Bacon's theory of the *idola* may be regarded to a certain extent as a forerunner of the modern conception of ideology. The 'idols' were 'phantoms' or 'preconceptions', and there were, as we know, the idols of the tribe, of the cave, of the market, and of the theatre. All of these are sources of error derived sometimes from human nature itself, sometimes from particular individuals. They may also be attributed to society or to tradition. In any case, they are obstacles in the path to true knowledge.[3] There is certainly some connection between the modern term 'ideology' and the term as used by Bacon, signifying a source of error. Furthermore, the realization that society and tradition may become sources of error is a direct anticipation of the sociological point of view.[4] Nevertheless, it cannot be claimed that there is an actual relationship, directly traceable through the history of thought, between this and the modern conception of ideology.

It is extremely probable that everyday experience with political affairs first made man aware of and critical toward the ideological element in his thinking. During the Renaissance, among the fellow citizens of Machiavelli, there arose a new adage calling attention to a common observation of the time – namely that the thought of the palace is one thing, and that of the public square is another.[5] This was an expression of the increasing degree to which the public was gaining access to the secrets of politics. Here we may observe the beginning of the process in the course of which what had formerly been merely an occasional outburst of suspicion and scepticism toward public utterances developed into a methodical search for the ideological element in all of them. The diversity of the ways of thought among men is even at this stage attributed to a factor which might, without unduly stretching the term, be denominated as sociological. Machiavelli, with his relentless rationality, made it his special task to relate the variations in the opinions of men to the corresponding variations in their interests. Accordingly when he prescribes a *medicina forte* for every bias of the interested parties in a controversy,[6] he seems to be making explicit and setting up as a general rule of thought what was implicit in the common-sense adage of his time.

There seems to be a straight line leading from this point in the intellectual orientation of the Western world to the rational and calculating mode of thought characteristic of the period of the Enlightenment. The psychology of interests seems to flow from the same source. One of the chief characteristics of the method of rational analysis of human behaviour, exemplified by Hume's *History of England*, was the presupposition that men were given to 'feigning'[7] and to deceiving their fellows. The same characteristic is found in contemporary historians who operate with the particular conception of ideology. This mode of thought

will always strive in accordance with the psychology of interests to cast
doubt upon the integrity of the adversary and to deprecate his motives.
This procedure, nevertheless, has positive value as long as in a given case
we are interested in discovering the genuine meaning of a statement that
lies concealed behind a camouflage of words. This 'debunking' tendency
in the thought of our time has become very marked.[8] And even though in
wide circles this trait is considered undignified and disrespectful (and
indeed in so far as 'debunking' is an end in itself, the criticism is justified),
this intellectual position is forced upon us in an era of transition like our
own, which finds it necessary to break with many antiquated traditions
and forms.

From the particular to the total conception of ideology

It must be remembered that the unmasking which takes place on the
psychological level is not to be confused with the more radical scepticism
and the more thoroughgoing and devastating critical analysis which
proceeds on the ontological and noological levels. But the two cannot be
completely separated. The same historical forces that bring about
continuous transformations in one are also operative in the other. In the
former, psychological illusions are constantly being undermined, in the
latter, ontological and logical formulations arising out of given
world-views and modes of thought are dissolved in a conflict between the
interested parties. Only in a world in upheaval, in which fundamental new
values are being created and old ones destroyed, can intellectual conflict go
so far that antagonists will seek to annihilate not merely the specific beliefs
and attitudes of one another, but also the intellectual foundations upon
which these beliefs and attitudes rest.

As long as the conflicting parties lived in and tried to represent the
same world, even though they were at opposite poles in that world, or as
long as one feudal clique fought against its equal, such a thoroughgoing
mutual destruction was inconceivable. This profound disintegration of
intellectual unity is possible only when the basic values of the contending
groups are worlds apart. At first, in the course of this ever-deepening
disintegration, naive distrust becomes transformed into a systematic
particular notion of ideology, which, however, remains on the
psychological plane. But, as the process continues, it extends to the
noological–epistemological sphere. The rising bourgeoisie which brought
with it a new set of values was not content with merely being assigned a
circumscribed place within the old feudal order. It represented a new
'economic system' (in Sombart's sense), accompanied by a new style of
thought which ultimately displaced the existing modes of interpreting and

explaining the world. The same seems to be true of the proletariat today as well. Here too we note a conflict between two divergent economic views, between two social systems, and, correspondingly, between two styles of thought.

What were the steps in the history of ideas that prepared the way for the total conception of ideology? Certainly it did not merely arise out of the attitude of mistrust which gradually gave rise to the particular conception of ideology. More fundamental steps had to be taken before the numerous tendencies of thought moving in the same general direction could be synthesized into the total conception of ideology. Philosophy played a part in the process, but not philosophy in the narrow sense (as it is usually conceived) as a discipline divorced from the actual context of living. Its role was rather that of the ultimate and fundamental interpreter of the flux in the contemporary world. This cosmos in flux is in its turn to be viewed as a series of conflicts arising out of the nature of the mind and its responses to the continually changing structure of the world. We shall indicate here only the principal stages in the emergence of the total conception of ideology on the noological and ontological levels.

The first significant step in this direction consisted in the development of a philosophy of consciousness. The thesis that consciousness is a unity consisting of coherent elements sets a problem of investigation which, especially in Germany, has been the basis of monumental attempts at analysis. The philosophy of consciousness has put in place of an infinitely variegated and confused world an organization of experience the unity of which is guaranteed by the unity of the perceiving subject. This does not imply that the subject merely reflects the structural pattern of the external world, but rather that, in the course of his experience with the world, he spontaneously evolves the principles of organization that enable him to understand it. After the objective ontological unity of the world had been demolished, the attempt was made to substitute for it a unity imposed by the perceiving subject. In the place of the medieval-Christian objective and ontological unity of the world, there emerged the subjective unity of the absolute subject of the Enlightenment – 'consciousness in itself'.

Henceforth the world as 'world' exists only with reference to the knowing mind, and the mental activity of the subject determines the form in which the world appears. This constitutes in fact the embryonic total conception of ideology, though it is, as yet, devoid of its historical and sociological implications.

At this stage, the world is conceived as a structural unity, and no longer as a plurality of disparate events as it seemed to be in the intermediate period when the breakdown of the objective order seemed to bring chaos. It is related in its entirety to a subject, but in this case the subject is not a concrete individual. It is rather a fictitious 'consciousness in itself'. In this view, which is particularly pronounced in Kant, the noological level is sharply differentiated from the psychological one. This is the first stage in the dissolution of an ontological dogmatism which regarded the 'world' as existing independently of us, in a fixed and definitive form.

The second stage in the development of the total conception of ideology is attained when the total but super-temporal notion of ideology is seen in historical perspective. This is mainly the accomplishment of Hegel and the Historical school. The latter, and Hegel to an even greater degree, start from the assumption that the world is a unity and is conceivable only with reference to a knowing subject. And now at this point, what is for us a decisive new element is added to the conception – namely, that this unity is in a process of continual historical transformation and tends to a constant restoration of its equilibrium on still higher levels. During the Enlightenment the subject, as carrier of the unity of consciousness, was viewed as a wholly abstract, super-temporal, and super-social entity: 'consciousness in itself'. During this period the *Volksgeist*, 'folk spirit', comes to represent the historically differentiated elements of consciousness, which are integrated by Hegel into the 'world spirit'. It is evident that the increasing concreteness of this type of Philosophy results from the more immediate concern with the ideas arising from social interaction and the incorporation of historical-political currents of thought into the domain of philosophy. Thenceforth, however, the experiences of everyday life are no longer accepted at face value, but are thought through in all their implications and are traced back to their presuppositions. It should be noted, however, that the historically changing nature of mind was discovered not so much by philosophy as by the penetration of political insight into the everyday life of the time.

The reaction following upon the unhistorical thought of the period of the French Revolution revitalized and gave new impetus to the historical perspective. In the last analysis, the transition from the general, abstract, world-unifying subject ('consciousness in itself') to the more concrete subject (the nationally differentiated 'folk spirit') was not so much a philosophical achievement as it was the expression of a transformation in the manner of reacting to the world in all realms of experience. This change may be traced to the revolution in popular sentiment during and after the Napoleonic Wars when the feeling of nationality was actually born. The fact that more remote antecedents may be found for both the historical perspective and the *Volksgeist* does not detract from the validity of this observation.[9]

The final and most important step in the creation of the total conception of ideology likewise arose out of the historical – social process. When 'class' took the place of 'folk' or nation as the bearer of the historically evolving consciousness, the same theoretical tradition, to which we have already referred, absorbed the realization which meanwhile had grown up through the social process, namely, that the structure of society and its corresponding intellectual forms vary with the relations between social classes.

Just as at an earlier time, the historically differentiated 'folk spirit' took the place of 'consciousness as such', so now the concept of *Volksgeist*, which is still too inclusive, is replaced by the concept of class consciousness, or more correctly class ideology. Thus the development of these ideas follows a two-fold trend – on the one hand, there is a synthesizing and integrating process through which the concept of consciousness comes to furnish a unitary centre in an infinitely variable world; and on the other, there is a constant attempt to make more pliable and flexible the unitary conception which has been too rigidly and too schematically formulated in the course of the synthesizing process.

The result of this dual tendency is that instead of a fictional unity of a timeless, unchanging 'consciousness as such' (which was never actually demonstrable) we get a conception which varies in accordance with historic periods, nations, and social classes. In the course of this transition, we continue to cling to the unity of consciousness, but this unity is now dynamic and in constant process of becoming. This accounts for the fact that despite the surrender of the static conception of consciousness, the growing body of material discovered by historical research does not remain an incoherent and discontinuous mass of discrete events. This latest conception of consciousness provides a more adequate perspective for the comprehension of historical reality.

Two consequences flow from this conception of consciousness: first we clearly perceive that human affairs cannot be understood by an isolation of their elements. Every fact and event in an historical period is only explicable in terms of meaning, and meaning in its turn always refers to another meaning. Thus the conception of the unity and interdependence of meaning in a period always underlies the interpretation of that period. Secondly, this interdependent system of meanings varies both in all its parts and in its totality from one historical period to another. Thus the reinterpretation of that continuous and coherent change in meaning becomes the main concern of our modern historical sciences. Although Hegel has probably done more than anyone else in emphasizing the need for integrating the various elements of meaning in a given historical experience, he proceeded in a speculative manner, while we have arrived at a stage of development where we are able to translate this constructive notion, given us by the philosophers, into empirical research.

What is significant for us is that although we separated them in our analysis, the two currents which led to the particular and total conceptions of ideology, respectively, and which have approximately the same historical origin, now begin to approach one another more closely. The particular conception of ideology merges with the total. This becomes apparent to the observer in the following manner: previously, one's adversary, as the representative of a certain political – social position, was accused of conscious or unconscious falsification. Now, however, the critique is more thoroughgoing in that, having discredited the total structure of his consciousness, we consider him no longer capable of thinking correctly. This simple observation means, in the light of a structural analysis of thought, that in earlier attempts to discover the sources of error, distortion was uncovered only on the psychological plane by pointing out the personal roots of intellectual bias. The annihilation is now more thoroughgoing since the attack is made on the noological level and the validity of the adversary's theories is undermined by showing that they are merely a function of the generally prevailing social situation. Herewith a new and perhaps the most decisive stage in the history of modes of thought has been reached. It is difficult, however, to deal with this development without first analysing some of its fundamental implications. The total conception of ideology raises a problem which has frequently been adumbrated before, but which now for the first time acquires broader significance, namely the problem of how such a thing as the 'false consciousness' (*falsches Bewusstsein*) – the problem of the totally distorted mind which falsifies everything which comes within its range – could ever have arisen. It is the awareness that our total outlook as distinguished from its details may be distorted, which lends to the total conception of ideology a special significance and relevance for the understanding of our social life. Out of this recognition grows the profound disquietude which we feel in our present intellectual situation, but out of it grows also whatever in it is fruitful and stimulating. . . .

The transition from the theory of ideology to the sociology of knowledge

The previous chapter traced a process of which numerous examples can be found in social and intellectual history. In the development of a new point of view one party plays the pioneering role, while other parties, in order to cope with the advantage of their adversary in the competitive struggle, must of necessity themselves make use of this point of view. This is the case with the notion of ideology. Marxism merely discovered a clue to understanding and a mode of thought, in the gradual rounding out of which the whole nineteenth century participated. The complete formulation of this idea is not the sole achievement of any single group and is not linked exclusively with any single intellectual and social position. The role that Marxism played in this process was one that deserves a high rank in intellectual history and should not be minimized. The process, however, by which the ideological approach is coming into general use, is

going on before our very eyes, and hence is subject to empirical
observation.

It is interesting to observe that, as a result of the expansion of the
ideological concept, a new mode of understanding has gradually come into
existence. This new intellectual standpoint constitutes not merely a change
of degree in a phenomenon already operating. We have here an example of
the real dialectical process which is too often misinterpreted for scholastic
purposes – for here we see indeed a matter of difference in degree
becoming a matter of difference in kind. For as soon as all parties are able
to analyse the ideas of their opponents in ideological terms, all elements of
meaning are qualitatively changed and the word ideology acquires a totally
new meaning. In the course of this all the factors with which we dealt in
our historical analysis of the meaning of the term are also transformed
accordingly. The problems of 'false consciousness' and of the nature of
reality henceforth take on a different significance. This point of view
ultimately forces us to recognize that our axioms, our ontology, and our
epistemology have been profoundly transformed. We will limit ourselves
in what follows to pointing out through what variations in meaning the
conception of ideology has passed in the course of this transformation.

We have already traced the development from the particular to the total
conception. This tendency is constantly being intensified. Instead of being
content with showing that the adversary suffers from illusions or
distortions on a psychological or experiential plane, the tendency now is to
subject his total structure of consciousness and thought to a thoroughgoing
sociological analysis.[10]

As long as one does not call his own position into question but regards
it as absolute, while interpreting his opponents' ideas as a mere function of
the social positions they occupy, the decisive step forward has not yet been
taken. It is true, of course, that in such a case the total conception of
ideology is being used, since one is interested in analysing the structure of
the mind of one's opponent in its totality, and is not merely singling out a
few isolated propositions. But since, in such an instance, one is interested
merely in a sociological analysis of the opponent's ideas, one never gets
beyond a highly restricted, or what I should like to call a special,
formulation of the theory. In contrast to this special formulation, the
general[11] form of the total conception of ideology is being used by the
analyst when he has the courage to subject not just the adversary's point of
view but all points of view, including his own, to the ideological analysis.

At the present stage of our understanding it is hardly possible to avoid
this general formulation of the total conception of ideology, according to
which the thought of all parties in all epochs is of an ideological character.
There is scarcely a single intellectual position, and Marxism furnishes no
exception to this rule, which has not changed through history and which
even in the present does not appear in many forms. Marxism, too, has

taken on many diverse appearances. It should not be too difficult for a Marxist to recognize their social basis.

With the emergence of the general formulation of the total conception of ideology, the simple theory of ideology develops into the sociology of knowledge. What was once the intellectual armament[12] of a party is transformed into a method of research in social and intellectual history generally. To begin with, a given social group discovers the 'situational determination' (*Seinsgebundenheit*) of its opponents' ideas. Subsequently the recognition of this fact is elaborated into an all-inclusive principle according to which the thought of every group is seen as arising out of its life conditions.[13] Thus, it becomes the task of the sociological history of thought to analyse without regard for party biases all the factors in the actually existing social situation which may influence thought. This sociologically-oriented history of ideas is destined to provide modern men with a revised view of the whole historical process.

It is clear, then, that in this connection the conception of ideology takes on a new meaning. Out of this meaning two alternative approaches to ideological investigation arise. The first is to confine oneself to showing everywhere the interrelationships between the intellectual point of view held and the social position occupied. This involves the renunciation of every intention to expose or unmask those views with which one is in disagreement.

In attempting to expose the views of another, one is forced to make one's own view appear infallible and absolute, which is a procedure altogether to be avoided if one is making a specifically non-evaluative investigation. The second possible approach is nevertheless to combine such a non-evaluative analysis with a definite epistemology. Viewed from the angle of this second approach there are two separate and distinct solutions to the problem of what constitutes reliable knowledge – the one solution may be termed *relationism*, and the other *relativism*.

Relativism is a product of the modern historical–sociological procedure which is based on the recognition that all historical thinking is bound up with the concrete position in life of the thinker (*Standortsgebundenheit des Denkers*). But relativism combines this historical–sociological insight with an older theory of knowledge which was as yet unaware of the interplay between conditions of existence and modes of thought, and which modelled its knowledge after static prototypes such as might be exemplified by the proposition $2 \times 2 = 4$. This older type of thought, which regarded such examples as the model of all thought, was necessarily led to the rejection of all those forms of knowledge which were dependent upon the subjective standpoint and the social situation of the knower, and which were, hence, merely 'relative'. Relativism, then, owes its existence to the discrepancy between this newly-won insight into the actual processes of thought and a theory of knowledge which had not yet taken account of this new insight.

If we wish to emancipate ourselves from this relativism we must seek to understand with the aid of the sociology of knowledge that it is not epistemology in any absolute sense but rather a certain historically transitory type of epistemology which is in conflict with the type of thought oriented to the social situation. Actually, epistemology is as intimately enmeshed in the social process as is the totality of our thinking, and it will make progress to the extent that it can master the complications arising out of the changing structure of thought.

A modern theory of knowledge which takes account of the relational as distinct from the merely relative character of all historical knowledge must start with the assumption that there are spheres of thought in which it is impossible to conceive of absolute truth existing independently of the values and position of the subject and unrelated to the social context. Even a god could not formulate a proposition on historical subjects like $2 \times 2 = 4$, for what is intelligible in history can be formulated only with reference to problems and conceptual constructions which themselves arise in the flux of historical experience.

Once we recognize that all historical knowledge is relational knowledge, and can only be formulated with reference to the position of the observer, we are faced, once more, with the task of discriminating between what is true and what is false in such knowledge. The question then arises: which social standpoint *vis-à-vis* of history offers the best chance for reaching an optimum of truth? In any case, at this stage the vain hope of discovering truth in a form which is independent of an historically and socially determined set of meanings will have to be given up. The problem is by no means solved when we have arrived at this conclusion, but we are, at least, in a better position to state the actual problems which arise in a more unrestricted manner. In the following we have to distinguish two types of approach to ideological inquiry arising upon the level of the general-total conception of ideology: first, the approach characterized by freedom from value-judgments and, second, the epistemological and metaphysically oriented normative approach. For the time being we shall not raise the question of whether in the latter approach we are dealing with relativism or relationism.

The non-evaluative general-total conception of ideology is to be found primarily in those historical investigations, where, provisionally and for the sake of the simplification of the problem, no judgments are pronounced as to the correctness of the ideas to be treated. This approach confines itself to discovering the relations between certain mental structures and the life-situations in which they exist. We must constantly ask ourselves how it comes about that a given type of social situation gives rise to a given interpretation. Thus the ideological element in human thought, viewed at this level, is always bound up with the existing life-situation of the thinker.

According to this view human thought arises, and operates, not in a social vacuum but in a definite social milieu.

We need not regard it as a source of error that all thought is so rooted. Just as the individual who participates in a complex of vital social relations with other men thereby enjoys a chance of obtaining a more precise and penetrating insight into his fellows, so a given point of view and a given set of concepts, because they are bound up with and grow out of a certain social reality, offer, through intimate contact with this reality, a greater chance of revealing its meaning. (The example cited earlier showed that the proletarian-socialistic point of view was in a particularly favourable position to discover the ideological elements in its adversaries' thought.) The circumstance, however, that thought is bound by the social- and life-situation in which it arises creates handicaps as well as opportunities. It is clearly impossible to obtain an inclusive insight into problems if the observer or thinker is confined to a given place in society. For instance, as has already been pointed out, it was not possible for the socialist idea of ideology to have developed of itself into the sociology of knowledge. It seems inherent in the historical process itself that the narrowness and the limitations which restrict one point of view tend to be corrected by clashing with the opposite points of view. The task of a study of ideology, which tries to be free from value-judgments, is to understand the narrowness of each individual point of view and the interplay between these distinctive attitudes in the total social process. We are here confronted with an inexhaustible theme. The problem is to show how, in the whole history of thought, certain intellectual standpoints are connected with certain forms of experience, and to trace the intimate interaction between the two in the course of social and intellectual change. In the domain of morals, for instance, it is necessary to show not only the continuous changes in human conduct but the constantly altering norms by which this conduct is judged. Deeper insight into the problem is reached if we are able to show that morality and ethics themselves are conditioned by certain definite situations, and that such fundamental concepts as duty, transgression, and sin have not always existed but have made their appearance as correlatives of distinct social situations.[14] The prevailing philosophic view which cautiously admits that the content of conduct has been historically determined, but which at the same time insists upon the retention of eternal forms of value and of a formal set of categories, is no longer tenable. The fact that the distinction between the content and the forms of conduct was made and recognized is an important concession to the historical–sociological approach which makes it increasingly difficult to set up contemporary values as absolutes.

Having arrived at this recognition it becomes necessary also to remember that the fact that we speak about social and cultural life in terms of values is itself an attitude peculiar to our time. The notion of 'value' arose and was diffused from economics, where the conscious choice between values was the starting-point of theory. This idea of value was later transferred to the ethical, æsthetic, and religious spheres, which brought about a distortion in the description of the real behaviour of the human being in these spheres. Nothing could be more wrong than to describe the real attitude of the individual when enjoying a work of art quite unreflectively, or when acting according to ethical patterns inculcated in him since childhood, in terms of conscious choice between values.

The view which holds that all cultural life is an orientation toward objective values is just one more illustration of a typically modern rationalistic disregard for the basic irrational mechanisms which govern man's relation to his world. Far from being permanently valid the interpretation of culture in terms of objective values is really a peculiar characteristic of the thought of our own time. But even granting for the moment that this conception had some merit, the existence of certain formal realms of values and their specific structure would be intelligible only with reference to the concrete situations to which they have relevance and in which they are valid.[15] There is, then, no norm which can lay claim to formal validity and which can be abstracted as a constant universal formal element from its historically changing content.

Today we have arrived at the point where we can see clearly that there are differences in modes of thought, not only in different historical periods but also in different cultures. Slowly it dawns upon us that not only does the content of thought change but also its categorical structure. Only very recently has it become possible to investigate the hypothesis that, in the past as well as in the present, the dominant modes of thought are supplanted by new categories when the social basis of the group, of which these thought-forms are characteristic, disintegrates or is transformed under the impact of social change.

Research in the sociology of knowledge promises to reach a stage of exactness if only because nowhere else in the realm of culture is the interdependence in the shifts of meaning and emphasis so clearly evident and precisely determinable as in thought itself. For thought is a particularly sensitive index of social and cultural change. The variation in the meaning of words and the multiple connotations of every concept reflect polarities of mutually antagonistic schemes of life implicit in these nuances of meaning.[16]

Nowhere in the realm of social life, however, do we encounter such a clearly traceable interdependence and sensitivity to change and varying emphasis as in the meaning of words. The word and the meaning that attaches to it is truly a collective reality. The slightest nuance in the total system of thought reverberates in the individual word and the shades of meaning it carries. The word binds us to the whole of past history and, at the same time, mirrors the totality of the present. When, in communicating with others, we seek a common level of understanding the word can be used to iron out individual differences of meaning. But, when necessary, the word may become an instrument in emphasizing the differences in meaning and the unique experiences of each individual. It may then serve as a means for detecting the original and novel increments that arise in the course of the history of culture, thereby adding previously imperceptible values to the scale of human experience. In all of these investigations use will be made of the total and general conception of ideology in its non-evaluative sense.

Notes

1. If the interpretation relies solely upon that which is actually said we shall speak of an 'immanent interpretation': if it transcends these data, implying thereby an analysis of the subject's life-situation, we shall speak of a 'transcendental interpretation'. A typology of these various forms of interpretation is to be found in the author's 'Ideologische und soziologische Interpretation der geistigen Gebilde', *Jahrbuch für Soziologie*, vol. ii (Karlsruhe, 1926), pp. 424ff.
2. As a partial bibliography of the problem, the author indicates the following of his own works: K. MANNHEIM, 'Das Problem einer Soziologie des Wissens', *Archiv für Sozialwissenschaft und Sozialpolitik*, 1925, vol. 54; K. MANNHEIM, 'Ideologische und soziologische Interpretation der geistigen Gebilde', *Jahrbuch für Soziologie*, ed. Gottfried Salomon, ii (Karlsruhe, 1926), pp. 424ff.

   Other relevant materials are to be found in: W.T. KRUG, *Allgemeines Handwörterbuch der philosophischen Wissenschaften nebst ihrer Literatur und Geschichte*, 2nd edn (Leipzig, 1833); EISLER's *Philosophisches Wörterbuch;* LALANDE, *Vocabulaire de la philosophie* (Paris, 1926); SALOMON, G., 'Historischer Materialismus und Ideologienlehre', *Jahrbuch für Soziologie*, ii, pp. 386ff.; H.O. ZIEGLER, 'Ideologienlehre', *Archiv für Sozialwissenschaft und Sozialpolitik*, vol. 57, pp. 657ff.

   The majority of the studies of ideology never reach the level of attempting a systematic analysis, confining themselves usually to historical references or to the most general considerations. As examples, we cite the well-known works of Max Weber, Georg Lukács, Carl Schmitt, and more recently, HANS KELSEN, 'Die philosophischen Grundlagen der Naturrechtslehre und der Rechtspositivismus', No. 31 of the *Vorträge der Kant Gesellschaft*, 1928.

   The standard works of W. Sombart, Max Scheler, and Franz Oppenheimer are too widely known to require detailed reference.

   In a wider connection the following studies are of especial interest: K. RIEZLER, 'Idee und Interesse in der politischen Geschichte', *Die Dioskuren*, vol. iii (Munich, 1924); PAUL SZENDE, *Verhüllung und Enthüllung* (Leipzig, 1922); GEORG ADLER, *Die Bedeutung der Illusionen für Politik und soziales Leben* (Jena, 1904); JANKELEVITCH, 'Du rôle des idées dans l'évolution des sociétés', *Revue philosophique*, vol. 66, 1908, pp. 256ff.; M. MILLIOUD, 'La formation de l'idéal', ibid., pp. 138ff.; A. DIETRICH, 'Kritik der politischen Ideologien', *Archiv für Geschichte und Politik* (1923).

3. A characteristic passage from Bacon's *Novum Organum*, § 38. 'The idols and false notions which have already preoccupied the human understanding and are deeply rooted in it, not only so beset men's minds that they become difficult of access, but even when access is obtained will again meet, and trouble us in the instauration of the sciences, unless mankind when forewarned guard themselves with all possible care against them'. *The Physical and Metaphysical Works of Lord Bacon* (including the *Advancement of Learning* and *Novum Organum*) ed. Joseph Devey, p. 389 (London: G. Bell and Sons, 1891).

4. 'There are also idols formed by the reciprocal intercourse and society of man with man, which we call idols of the market from the commerce and association of men with each other; for men converse by means of language, but words are formed at the will of the generality, and there arises from a bad and unapt formation of words a wonderful obstruction to the mind.' BACON, op. cit., p. 390, § 43. Cf. also § 59.

On 'the idol of tradition' Bacon says:

The human understanding, when any proposition has once been laid down (either from general admission and belief, or from the pleasure it affords), forces everything else to add fresh support and confirmation: and although most cogent and abundant instances exist to the contrary, yet either does not observe or despises them or gets rid of and rejects them by some distinction, with violent and injurious prejudice, rather than sacrifice the authority of its first conclusion.

(Op. cit., § 46, p. 392)

That we are confronted here with a source of error is evinced by the following passage: 'The human understanding resembles not a dry light, but admits a tincture of the will and passions, which generate their own system accordingly, for man always believes more readily that which he prefers' (op. cit., § 49, pp. 393–4). Cf. also § 52.

5. MACHIAVELLI, *Discorsi*, vol. ii, p. 47. Cited by MEINECKE, *Die Idee der Staats* (Munich and Berlin, 1925), p. 40.

6. Cf. MEINECKE, ibid.

7. FR. MEUSEL, *Edmund Burke und die französische Revolution* (Berlin, 1913), p. 102, note 3.

8. Carl Schmitt analysed this characteristic contemporary manner of thought very well when he said that we are in continual fear of being misled. Consequently we are perpetually on guard against disguises, sublimations, and refractions. He points out that the word *simulacra*, which appeared in the political literature of the seventeenth century, may be regarded as a forerunner of the present attitude (*Politische Romantik*, 2nd edn (Munich and Leipzig, 1925), p. 19).

9. For future reference, we state here that the sociology of knowledge, unlike the orthodox history of ideas, does not aim at tracing ideas back to all their remote historical prototypes. For if one is bent on tracing similar motifs in thought to their ultimate origins, it is always possible to find 'precursors' for every idea. There is nothing which has been said, which has not been said before (*Nullum est iam dictum, quod non sit dictum prius*). The proper theme of our study is to observe how and in what form intellectual life at a given historical moment is related to the existing social and political forces. Cf. my study, 'Das konservative Denken', loc. cit., p. 103, note 57.

10. This is not meant to imply that for certain aspects of the struggles of everyday life the particular conception of ideology is inapplicable.

11. We add here another distinction to our earlier one of 'particular and total', namely that of 'special and general'. While the first distinction concerns the question as to whether single isolated ideas or the entire mind is to be seen as ideological, and whether the social situation conditions merely the psychological manifestations of concepts, or whether it even penetrates to the noological meanings, in the distinction of special *versus* general, the decisive question is whether the thought of all groups (including our own) or only that of our adversaries is recognized as socially determined.

12. Cf. the Marxist expression 'To forge the intellectual weapons of the proletariat'.

13. By the term 'situational determination of knowledge' I am seeking to differentiate the propagandistic from the scientific sociological content of the ideological concept.

14. Cf. MAX WEBER, *Wirtschaft und Gesellschaft*. Grundriss der Sozialökonomik, Part iii, p. 794, dealing with the social conditions which are requisite to the genesis of the moral.

15. Cf. E. LASK, *Die Logik der Philosophie und die Kategorienlehre* (Tübingen, 1911), uses the term *hingelten* in order to explain that categorical forms are not valid in themselves but only with reference to their always changing content which inevitably reacts upon their nature.

16. For this reason the sociological analysis of meanings will play a significant role in the following studies. We may suggest here that such an analysis might be developed into a symptomatology based upon the principle that in the social realm, if we can learn to observe carefully, we can see that each element of the situation which we are analysing contains and throws light upon the whole.

4 The Epistemology of Sociology*

LUCIEN GOLDMANN

Lucien Goldmann (1913–70) was born in Bucharest but spent most of his working life in Paris, where he became Director of Studies at the Ecole Pratique des Hautes Etudes. As a sociologist of culture, he synthesised the insights of Max and Piaget to produce what he termed 'genetic structuralism', a form of analysis which dissects the structures of a cultural artefact or of a 'world vision' but which also relates them to their historical conditions. In his major work, *The Hidden God* (1956; London: Routledge, 1964), Goldmann locates a common structure in the work of Racine and Pascal, one homologous to the 'world vision' of a particular religious group (the Jansenists) of seventeenth-century France. Great works of art, in his view, embody in their fullest form a 'collective consciousness' or 'transindividual mental structure', an idea somewhat akin to Georg Lukács's notion of 'possible consciousness'. Indeed Goldmann's work is broadly Lukácsian in tone, much indebted to the brand of Hegelian or 'historicist' Marxism which regards social classes as 'subjects' equipped with a distinctive outlook or vision. Goldmann seeks to differentiate such coherent, comprehensive 'world visions', typical of a social class at its zenith, from 'ideologies', which for him signify a more partial, sectoral perspective on the world; but much of what he has to say of a 'world vision' can in fact be read as a Hegelian-Marxist contribution to the theory of ideology.

In the human sciences, the moment one approaches any problem at a sufficiently general level, one finds oneself in a circle where the researcher himself is part of the society that he intends to study and that plays a pre-eminent role in the elaboration of his mental categories. (Jean Piaget has shown the existence of this circle on many levels, notably in the classification of the sciences and their interdependence.)

We encounter this same circle in broaching the study of sociological

---

*Reprinted from LUCIEN GOLDMANN, *Method in the Sociology of Literature* (1967; Oxford: Basil Blackwell, 1981), pp. 55–72.

knowledge and that of the sociology of knowledge. If, like all other scientific disciplines, sociology is a science based on an aggregation of categories forming an intellectual structure, then these categories and this structure are themselves social facts that sociology brings into relief. Inversely, mental categories, which are also social facts, justify sociological thought in their turn.

Yet, if we are in the presence neither of a vicious circle nor an insurmountable obstacle here, we still have a particular situation in the human sciences from which no researcher can escape. This situation implies certain epistemological and methodological consequences concerning the relation between thought and action in the socio-historical realm and, thus, it involves the very structure of sociological objectivity.

Furthermore, when we approach the study of society in general, and the facts of individual and collective consciousness in particular, we must never lose sight of the following points:

(1) If the concept of 'collective consciousness' is an operation notion indicating an aggregation of individual consciousnesses and their relationships, it does not correspond to any reality that could be situated outside these consciousnesses. As Marx said,

> Above all, one must avoid making 'society' an abstraction in relation to individuals. The individual is a social essence. His exteriorization – even if it does not appear in the immediate form of an exteriorization accomplished in common with others – is, then, an exteriorization and confirmation of social life. The life of the individual man and the life of the species are not different.[1]

And Piaget reiterates this: 'Sociology must consider society as a whole, although this whole, as distinct from the sum of individuals, may only be the aggregation of the relations or interactions among these individuals.'[2]

(2) Socio-historical reality is a structured aggregation of the conscious behavior of individuals – whether this consciousness be true or false, adequate or inadequate – within a determinate natural and social environment.

(3) The structuring process results from the fact that individuals – and the social groups that they constitute (groups formed by individuals finding themselves related to one another and, in certain more or less important aspects, in similar situations) – seek to give unitary and coherent responses to the aggregation of problems posed by their relations with the surrounding environment. Or to put it another way, they tend by their action (praxis) to establish a balance between themselves and this environment.

The results of the thesis are:

(a) Every fact of consciousness is strictly bound in an immediate or relatively mediated way to praxis, just as all praxis is mediately or immediately, explicitly or implicitly, bound to a specific structure of consciousness.

(b) Just as the psychologist must conceive of an individual's psychological life as a complex effort tending toward an integral but difficult balance between the subject and his environment, so the sociologist must study every social group in an effort to find an integral and coherent response to the problems common to all members of the group in relation to their social and natural environment.

Obviously, for each individual, these problems are only one part of his consciousness, the whole of which is connected to all the groups to which he belongs. Thus, each individual is a mixture and a source of a different structuring process in relation to other members of the group.

All the same, the sociologist can make an abstraction of these differences in order to disengage the reality of a common process, of a relatively thwarted attempt by each individual consciousness to provide a coherent solution to an aggregation of problems common to all members of the group.

(c) Within these observations, which are valid for all social groups, certain groups present a privileged character both by their conscious life and by their social and historical praxis. For these groups praxis is oriented toward a global structuring of society, that is, toward a certain balance among the constitutive groups of the entire society, and between the society and the physical world.

The conscious aspect of the life of these groups appears to be the essential factor in the genesis of their cultural life and praxis, a decisive element of historical life.

It appears equally true that, at least with regard to much of modern history, it is social classes that have constituted these privileged groups.

(4) The existence of social groups constitutes a process of equilibration between a collective subject and a social and natural environment. Thus, the group is a structure within the wider relative totality that encompasses it, while its own constitutive elements are relative totalities in themselves, albeit more structures.

Subjectivity and objectivity: the establishing of facts and values

On the basis of the fact that every sociologist himself belongs to a social group, will himself be one of the constitutive elements of a structure that will be another element of study, traditional dialectical thinkers – notably Hegel and Lukács – speak about the identity of the subject and object in action and historical thought. In this perspective, the study of society would be a positive body of knowledge in which the collective subject could itself be known through an individual mind: it would, therefore, be a type of consciousness.

For reasons to be indicated later, this apparently extreme thesis is opposed to the inverse position – in our view, a completely wrong one – of the possibility of attaining a degree of objectivity in the social sciences similar to that in the natural sciences.

Indeed, all social reality is simultaneously constituted by material and intellectual facts which, in turn, structure the consciousness of the researcher and naturally imply value judgments. That is why a rigorously objective study of society appears impossible. The formula 'the identity of the subject and the object' is too general, given that the value judgments that make up a part of the object studied can be mediately or immediately related with the values that structure the consciousness of the researcher. Thus, for example, even if total objectivity is beyond the reach of contemporary French sociologists, the maximum attainable degree of objectivity varies, depending upon whether one studies the Eskimos, the thought of Marsile Ficin, the Florence of the Medicis, or contemporary transformations of the French proletariat.

That is why it is necessary to isolate as much as possible the specific degree of identity between the subject and object in each instance and thereby isolate the degree of accessible objectivity. Furthermore, this relationship between values and social reality implies a complementary result. If values structure the researcher's consciousness and introduce an element of distortion, the latter's thought in its turn also constitutes an element of reality. By the simple fact of its elaboration and expression, the researcher's thought modifies reality, mostly in an insignificant way, but at times appreciably.

Beginning with the relationship between thought and praxis, then, how can we pose the problem of objectivity with regard to knowledge in general, and the human sciences in particular?

From Marx up to the contemporary works of Jean Piaget, many epistemological and historical investigations have established the strict bond between the categorical structure of human thought and praxis, a relation as valid for daily thought and the natural sciences as for the human sciences. In the case of the natural sciences, nevertheless, we can today speak of objective thought to the extent that its goal, man's mastery over nature and the resulting categorical structure, is the same for all actually existing groups. That is why physics is practised the same way in Moscow and Washington, Paris and Warsaw. The differences, which are in the final instance secondary, depend upon the scientific and professional education of the researchers, upon their talent, their intelligence and, to a certain extent, upon the social network of university relations, their traditions, and so on. These differences do not, at any rate, depend upon the fundamental structure of global societies and the categories that such a structure engenders.

Without any serious danger of distortion, the physicist concerned with the problems of method can place himself exclusively on the level of theoretical research without concerning himself with the problems of his relationship to praxis, since this relation is implicit in the discussion.

But the situation is very different in the human sciences. Today, man's growing mastery over nature is unanimously accepted by nearly everyone. When one analyses social life, however, the values determining the categorical structure of consciousness nearly always have a specific and, thus, deforming character. In other words, by making this consciousness abstract, one implicitly forms an ideology rather than a positive science.

Thus, one of the most important tasks of the serious researcher is to know and to make known to others his value judgments by making them explicit. This will help him attain the maximum degree of objectivity that is subjectively accessible to him the moment he writes. This will also help future researchers working in the same perspective and will afford them a better comprehension of reality. They will more easily be able to use his works and go beyond them.

Specific value judgments are inevitably part of all historical and sociological research, either in an explicit or implicit way, and this participation has an immediate and technical character in the development and elaboration of ideas in social life. Thus, even the most honest, scrupulous and critical sociological study can be characterized as an explicit or implicit wager, both theoretically and practically: theoretically with regard to the maximum possible conformity to the object studied; practically, with regard to the possibility of transforming society or stabilizing it.

Structures and world views

Most concrete sociological or psychological studies from Marx and Freud to Piaget are inspired by genetic structuralism. In other words, they are based on the hypotheses stated above: first, to be aware that one's subjective life is closely bound to praxis; second, that this life is presented on both the individual and collective levels under the form of dynamic realities oriented toward a coherent equilibrium between the subject and its surrounding environment, that is, toward structuring processes; third, that within these global processes one's subjective life, and within this the realm of thought, constitutes a relative totality in its turn, a structuring process directed toward a significant and coherent state of equilibrium.

In the privileged case of groups oriented toward a global organization of society, we have called these psychic structurations world views.

By limiting ourselves to the structuring processes of world views and to their conceptual expression – theory and value scales (there are also imaginary expressions such as literature and art) – it seems evident that the latter are not sums of independent elements, isolated atoms coupled to each other. On the contrary, they are aggregations, the constitutive parts of which are interdependent and bound together by specific rules and have limited possibilities of transformation.

World views could not be purely individual facts. No matter how great the creative imagination of an individual may be, given the limits of his life and his experiences, he could at best only partially elaborate such an aggregation of categories. This process of elaboration is a slow and complex one, usually spread out over several generations. It presupposes the joint praxis of a considerable number of individuals who constitute a social group and, when we are dealing with the elaboration of a world view, a privileged social group.

Such a world view constitutes the 'collective consciousness' of a group and this general formula must, in each particular case, be replaced by the 'consciousness of a specific group'. Still, it is obvious that a world view exists only in the individual consciousness of those making up the group. In each individual this world vision is presented under the form of a relatively global apprehension of the group, as the process of the aggregate's structuration. It follows that a sociology of knowledge must, above all, study the socio-historical processes of the structuring process of large systems at the general level characteristic of the systems of formal logic and at the level of more specific and particular totalities, world views. It follows also that this could only be done by reconnecting these processes of intellectual genesis to the universal praxis of individuals as such (for formal logic) and to the specific social praxis of certain privileged groups, notably, social class (for world views).

Self-regulation and progress – accommodation and assimilation

Furthermore, one must always remember that when dealing with social facts in general and with the processes of intellectual structuration, which, within the tendencies of global balance, constitutes the genesis of world views, in particular, one is dealing with processes of an average duration governed by a rather complex dynamism. This has been identified in history by Marx and in psychology by Piaget.

As a world vision is being elaborated, and this process is part of a larger one in which a collective subject attempts to achieve a balance with its social and natural environment, opposite but complementary processes will sooner or later be manifested. Marx has called this tension the conflict between the relations of production and the development of productive forces. On the psychological level, Piaget has called it the antagonism between assimilation into the existing mental structures and accommodation to the structures of the external world.

In fact, every process of structuration implies the tendency to incorporate into the state of equilibrium a greater and greater area of the surrounding social and physical world. This tendency, however, can conflict with three kinds of obstacles, two of which are originally exogenous and one endogenous:

(1) The fact that certain sectors of the external world do not lend themselves to integration into the structure being elaborated.

(2) The fact that certain structures of the external world are transformed in such a way that, although they may have been able to be integrated before, this integration becomes increasingly difficult and finally impossible.

(3) The fact that individuals in the group, who are responsible for generating the processes of equilibrium, transform the surrounding social and physical environment, thereby creating situations that hinder the continuation of the structuring processes generating them.

For these three reasons, every process of equilibrium sooner or later ceases to constitute the optimal response to the need to find a significant balance between the collective subject and its environment. Phenomena will then appear with the process that Piaget calls accommodation to reality. This is a structuring process oriented toward a new equilibrium, one better adapted than the previous one to the present praxis of the group.

In this sense, particularly with regard to the sociology of knowledge and the life of the spirit, the sociologist nearly always finds himself faced with extremely complex processes. More precisely, he is faced with the deviation of old structuring processes and the old equilibrium, as well as with the gradual birth of the structuring process of a new equilibrium.

From the perspective of concrete research, this situation poses the problem of knowing to what extent empirical facts can be described on the basis of the old and deviated structuring process (which Piaget would call accommodation) and to what extent they can be described on the basis of the new structuring process still charged with the surviving elements of the old process, which it has replaced.

In philosophical language, this is the problem designated by Hegel and Marx as the passage from quantity to quality.

Isolating the object of study

In his practical research, the sociologist is immediately confronted by a very difficult problem: that of isolating synchronically and diachronically the object of his study.

As we have already said, all human reality tends toward an equilibrium that transforms the surrounding world, and the very processes of equilibrium are also transformed by a self-regulatory process making up the new equilibrium. In a less abstract way, one could say that history is made by the effort of human groups to find a coherent and significant aggregate of responses to the problems posed by their relations with the surrounding world. These responses, however, are each time exceeded by the transformations of this surrounding world, which the very praxis of the group carries out and which, by an extension of the range of this praxis, generates new processes of equilibrium. The individuals of the group and their environment, the two elements making up such an orientation toward a meaningful equilibrium, however, are far from being immediate givens for the researcher.

We have here the well-known dialectical distinction between appearance and essence, between the empirical given presented in an abstract way and its concretization through the mediation of the concept.

The data of immediate experience is most often presented to the researcher torn from its global context and, as such, separated from its meaning, that is, its essence. Data can only be made concrete by inserting it into the destructuring process of an old structure and into the structuring process of a new equilibrium. In this way one may judge the objective meaning of data as well as its relative importance in the aggregate.

The first step of such an analysis, then, is to isolate the object to be studied. In other words, one must bring to light a totality in which the objective meaning of a major part of the empirical data under study can be attained. Such a totality will also permit one to study the transformations of this data. We assume, however, that the aggregate of these empirical facts is taken as the starting point of research and that the possibility of accounting for them is the sole objective criterion for judging its validity. It should also be stressed that this initial isolation of the object determines the rest of the analysis and that, frequently, the ideological factor intervenes precisely at this point by influencing the later results of research in advance.

Here is an example: it was impossible to isolate the tragic vision of Pascal's *Pensées* in so far as one was seeking, as most scholars of Pascal were, a valid internal coherence both for *Les Provinciales* and the *Pensées*. It is impossible to understand the specific traits of the First Empire, Stalinism or Nazism on the basis of the idea that there exists a social fact having fixed qualities which, as such, can be studied sociologically under the concept of 'dictatorship'.

Although the process of isolating the object is unique for each study, there are some general rules. Notably, the objects studied must be significant structures. It is on the basis of their position in the aggregate that specific elements and their transformations may be understood. Then, one must eliminate such typical concepts as 'dictatorship', 'hierarchy', and 'scandal' as well as purely individual facts. The former must be eliminated because they derive from an abstraction based on some common characteristics that have different and even opposite meanings in each particular case; the latter because they remain insufficiently defined so long as they have not been inserted into a wider dynamic totality in which they can be made concrete. Such a totality can eventually be reconciled with other related structures. As a result, between the poles of positivist and abstract sociology and anecdotal history, there is a place for a concrete science of social facts that could only be a historical sociology or a sociological history.

Real consciousness and possible consciousness

Having isolated the object of his research, the scholar finds himself faced with another important problem. In fact, social reality is far too rich and complex to be analysed in its totality, even in the framework of a validly isolated object. Furthermore, no definitions of the object under study are ever valid in the absolute sense. One always begins with an approximation and, as research continues, one is obliged to modify it. As the structure under study is drawn with more detail, certain facts prove irrelevant while others, which at first seemed out of place, now fit. Thus, the researcher must base himself on two conceptual instruments that only rarely correspond to empirical reality in a sufficiently close way: the balanced and coherent structure toward which the old structuring process was tending, but which is now being superseded, and the structure toward which the principal structuring process is now tending.

In sociology, schematizations such as 'feudal society', 'capitalist society', 'totemism', 'Protestantism', and 'Jansenism' are at the root of all important research. Obviously, it is clear that there are good and bad schematizations determining the value of practical research. For example, a number of contemporary ethnologists have questioned the validity of the concept 'totemism'. To prove their position, they will have to replace it with another concept better suited to empirical reality, but this one will also be a schematization.

When studying mental categories and consciousness in general, the most functional schematizations appear to be those corresponding to the concept first elaborated by Marx and Lukács as *zugerechnetes Bewusstsein* (consciousness as 'calculated' or 'constructed' by the researcher), a term that we have translated as possible consciousness.

We may, then, conceive of social life as a totality of the processes through which groups of individuals try to achieve a satisfying and coherent equilibrium with their social and natural environment. The facts of consciousness constitute an essential and interdependent part of this effort. These processes, along with their conscious element, come into conflict with innumerable incidental or structural obstacles that make up the empirical environment. Furthermore, these obstacles do not remain purely external but have a distorting effect on the consciousness of the subject.

In the resulting relationship between the subject and his environment, the subject (both on the individual and transindividual levels) never reacts univocally but projects a relatively large gamut of possible responses. Within this gamut different responses can be alternated at will.

Depending on the level of research, the important thing is not to know the effective consciousness of the group at a given moment, but rather the field within which this knowledge and these responses can vary without there being an essential modification of existing structures and processes. If sociological research is not yet able to make an inventory of these possible responses, it can, on the other hand, establish at least two privileged modalities within this field. They are effective consciousness and the maximum possible consciousness (i.e., the maximum degree of knowledge able to admit the processes and structures being studied and still conform to reality, this 'maximum' being a crucial conceptual instrument for the understanding of reality).

To carry out this sort of analysis, it is particularly important to study groups oriented toward a global structuration of society. If the secondary processes and structures (i.e., those not absolutely indispensable to the existence of such a group) are neglected at the outset, the maximum possible consciousness compatible with the existence of these basic groups, known historically as social classes, can be determined. It is, moreover, at the level of the possible consciousness of the great classes of modern European society (the proletariat, the bourgeoisie, and even the court aristocracy and the nobility) that this concept has been elaborated and defined, a conceptual instrument that appears to be of primary importance in the understanding of human reality. It is also crucial with respect to the structured grouping of the facts of consciousness, a fact which is particularly obvious when one is dealing with the sociology of cultural creations (literary, artistic and philosophical) and the sociology of political action.

Indeed, if the real consciousness of groups rarely matches their possible consciousness, the great cultural works seem precisely to express this maximum to an advanced and nearly coherent degree (and this on such levels as the concept, the verbal imagination, the visual, etc.). It is this aspect that makes them characteristic of human societies. Thus, cultural works are both collective and individual to the extent that the world view they correspond to has been elaborated over several years and several generations by the collectivity. The author, however, is the first, or at least one of the first, to express this world view at a level of advanced coherence, whether on the theoretical level or on the artistic, by creating an imaginary universe of characters, objects and relations.

This manner of considering the facts of consciousness represents a considerable upheaval in the sociology of culture. Until Lukács and those inspired by him, in fact, this discipline was oriented toward the research of analogies between the content of the collective consciousness and that of cultural creations. The results were easily foreseeable: similarities were often discovered, but these did not concern the totality of the work and its unity, i.e., its specifically cultural character. Instead, they concerned a relatively large number of partial elements all the more numerous as the work was less original and merely reproduced the author's personal experience without distilling it. But genetic structuralism seeks instead a homology, an intelligible relationship, between the structures of the collective consciousness and the structures of cultural works that express an integral and coherent universe, it being understood that the two rigorously homologous structures can have entirely different contents.

In this perspective it is precisely those works in which the author has completely distilled the experience of the group that prove to approach most closely the structure of a collective consciousness. For this reason also, they are the most accessible to sociological research. But works that reflect only an individual experience usually represent a mixture best studied by a biographical methodology, since they lack a coherent structure. (Far from reflecting the consciousness of his group, the true creator reveals what those in the group were thinking and feeling unbeknownst to themselves, i.e., where they were implicitly and confusedly headed. For example, in order to know whether or not the works of Pascal or Racine are Jansenist, it is not necessary to compare them to the thought of Arnauld or Nicole, but to the possible consciousness of the group to which they belong. This would permit one to show that their works go beyond the thought of other Jansenists, and it is in relation to them that one measures the degree of Jansenism in the other characters studied by anecdotal history.)

Similarly, the concept of possible consciousness is of primary importance for sociology and, particularly, for political action. The latter, in fact, is a conscious attempt to intervene in social life in order to transform it. It is true that in a stable period a politician wishing to be elected or to stay in office can limit himself to an intuitive or scientific knowledge of the real consciousness of groups. Every attempt to transform the structure of this consciousness, however, poses the problem of its solidarity and the

limits in which it can be modified without radically transforming the
present structure of these groups. A well-known example illustrates this
problem. Up to 1917, international socialist thought was rather strictly
oriented toward the maintenance and development of a state-controlled or
cooperative agricultural system. But in 1917 the success of the Russian
Revolution depended essentially on the possibility of the Bolsheviks
obtaining the peasants' support. That is why Lenin radically modified
these traditional positions by explaining to his comrades that the idea of
the great exploitation of the land went so far beyond the possible
consciousness of the Russian peasant that the revolution proved
impossible. Nor could they accept it in the future. In other respects,
however, such as their loyalty to the czar, their spirit of obedience, etc.,
their consciousness could be changed rather easily. Analyses of the same
kind could undoubtedly be elaborated for a number of contemporary
political events. They show that positivist sociology, oriented only toward
the exploitation of real consciousness, is insufficient and misses the most
important aspects of reality.

Comprehension and explanation

With regard to social facts, the genetic structuralist perspective also
clarifies one of the most controversial points concerning methodology in
the human sciences. The description of the states of equilibrium toward
which particular social processes tend and the attempt to explain why
these specific structures have an optimal functional value within a
structure of the whole constitutes a positive and rigorous definition of
what has often been designated in a vague way by the concept of
comprehension.

Frequently, in fact, the latter has been defined only by an affective label,
such as sympathy or empathy. Indeed, without denying the variable
importance that these factors can have on the researcher and the progress
of his work, there are still external and intellectual conditions rigorously
defined as the description of the essential relationships between the
elements of a structure and the discovery of its optimal functioning.

In this perspective, explanation is no longer a process apart from
comprehension. In fact, a structure's optimal function, indispensable to
comprehension, is an element of explanation. This function is especially
evident when we place ourselves in a genetic perspective rather than a
static one. In effect, changes within a structure naturally involve
modifications of this optimal function and, implicitly, the major or minor
characteristics of the collective subject and its structural characteristics.
These changes in the object, i.e., in the environment, can be either of an

exogenous or an endogenous origin, as we have already said. In either case, though, these changes entail a new orientation of the structuring process, which in turn requires a new comprehensive description. This means that the comprehensive description of the genesis of a global structure has an explanatory function with regard to the evolution and transformations of the particular structures that make up the global one. According to this perspective, then, comprehension and explanation are one and the same intellectual process, though related to two different points of reference: one an englobing structure and the other an englobed one.

To give an example: the description of the tragic vision and its expression in Pascal's *Pensées* and Racine's tragedies constitutes a comprehensive study of these writings. But the structural and comprehensive description of the Jansenist movement has an explanatory value for the genesis of Pascal's and Racine's writings. Of course, in cases where the dynamism of the transformations is predominantly endogenous, the simple fact of a genetic study at the level of the given structure already has, as such, an explanatory character. More often, however, the origins of the transformation are both exogenous and endogenous. Thus, all serious investigation must explore both the great transformations of the englobing structure and, at as precise a level as possible, the genesis and transformation of the structure constituting the object proper to the work. This is the middle level of research, then, that at which one wishes to disengage only those transformations that have an explanatory value for the englobed structure and not the totality of the englobing structure.

The starting points of research: progress from the abstract to the concrete

Our perspective, then, supports the idea that individual empirical facts must be inserted into a structuring process in order to obtain their meaning and have knowledge of their nature. This process, in turn, can only be known by studying the elements and relationships composing it. By proceeding from the immediate and abstract empirical given – or from the abstract global hypothesis – to concrete and mediated reality, one cannot hope to follow a linear progress which begins from a necessary starting point, whether empirical or rational.

Similarly, to the extent that the facts one proposes to study constitute a structure and not a class, one cannot see rigorously valid definitions for all these facts and for them only.

Class is defined by the closest genus and the characteristics of the species; structure, on the other hand, is defined by the internal description of its states of equilibrium and the genetic analysis of its functionality. In his attempt to define intelligence, Piaget comes up against the same difficulties and concludes: 'It remains possible to define intelligence by the direction which its development is oriented to without insisting on the question of limits, which become a matter of stages or of successive forms of equilibrium. Thus, one can simultaneously see it from the viewpoints of the functional situation and the structural mechanism.'[3]

In order to reach this point, research must start from several different points of the structuring process as well as from the wider structuring process that surrounds the object to be studied. Further, one must admit that certain starting points are relatively favorable to its progress. One can only advance by successive approximations obtained by a permanent *va-et-vient* between the whole and its parts. Progress in understanding a global structure most often involves the possibility of better understanding its elements. Inversely, progress in understanding the latter permits one to return to the whole in a functional manner.

Since the meaning of every group of facts depends upon their insertion into a structured whole, and since each global structure is, in turn, part of another structure that englobes it, it follows that no genetic structuralist analysis could end up with an exhaustive meaning and explanation. This is also a practical problem that must be resolved in each particular case, that of knowing into what processes of structuration one must insert the facts studied, in view of obtaining a sufficient number of meanings and pertinent explanations to attain the degree of precision proposed.

Determinism and equilibrium

Lastly, we should like to close this enumeration of the basic principles of a dialectical sociology (or, if you will, a structuralist and genetic sociology) by recalling another aspect of the circle with which we began this study.

The sociologist is part of the society he studies and which structures his consciousness. Because of this, it is impossible to separate radically judgments of fact from value judgments in the human sciences. It is equally important in doing concrete research to keep in mind the circle constituted by the action of the social conditions on thought and on the praxis of men and the action of praxis on these conditions.

One can always explain the thought or behavior of a group of men by the social conditions of the epoch (although only to a certain extent, not completely, because every aggregate of conditions limits the field of possible responses, but does not engender one univocally determined response). It is just as important, however, that the researcher keep in mind the fact that social life represents an aggregate of processes. To a large extent, social conditions themselves are the result of the praxis of individuals belonging to specific groups. Present praxis, then, modifies the environment. It creates the conditions in which the individuals of various groups will have to act and gives rise to the problems which they will have to resolve in the near future.

Here lies the most important difference between a dialectical sociology and an entirely positivist or mechanist one. Marx, who accounted for it perfectly, formulated it in the third Thesis on Feuerbach: 'The materialist doctrine which says that men are the products of circumstances and education, that consequently, transformed men may be the products of other circumstances and of a modified education, forgets that it is precisely men who transform circumstances and that the educator himself needs to be educated.'[4]

No determinist, mechanist or simply positivist conception of social life will effectively succeed in explaining why the relative equilibrium once established between the subject and the object does not remain definitive after a period of time elapses.

This type of sociology is obliged to introduce a group of exceptional beings into its scheme (gods, wise men, legislators, social technocrats), to admit the existence of irrational factors beyond the reach of science (accidents, happenings), or to ignore the problem altogether.

A genetic and dialectical perspective, on the other hand, sees here not only one of the essential aspects of the circle within which all reflection on social and historical life finds itself necessarily engaged, but also one of the elements that must be positively integrated into research if one wishes to keep in touch with reality. It is on this basis that one can understand why dialectical scholars refuse a narrow and mechanist determination. As Piaget writes, science based on the reflex theory too often tends to forget that from time to time it must really give meat to Pavlov's dog.

> Although too often forgotten on the theoretical level, one knows in practice that a conditioned reflex stabilizes itself only to the extent that it is confirmed or sanctioned: a signal associated with food does not give place to a lasting reaction if real food is not periodically given. Thus, the association must be inserted within a total behavior based on needs and their satisfaction (whether real, anticipated, or merely pertaining to a game).[5]

Dialectical scholars also refuse value judgments and categorical or hypothetical imperatives that are not based on reality. In order to understand social life and to have an effect on it, one must realize that in the social sciences the establishing of facts is bound closely to value judgments, and vice versa. Although we cannot deal with it here, another crucial problem concerns the important and even radical modifications that have brought about two particular structures in our general scheme: liberal capitalist society and advanced capitalist society, both having sectors that function in a nearly mechanical way. The problem involved here is that of reification, a process studied by Marx, Lukács and myself.

Notes

1. See KARL MARX, 'Economic and Philosophical Manuscripts', in MARX, *Early Writings* (New York, 1975), p. 350.
2. JEAN PIAGET, *Psychologie de l'intelligence* (Paris, 1952), p. 186.
3. *Psychologie de l'intelligence*, op. cit., p. 16.
4. Cf. KARL MARX, 'Theses on Feuerbach', in Lewis S. Feuer (ed.), *Marx and Engels: Basic Writings on Politics and Philosophy* (New York, 1959), p. 244.
5. *Psychologie de l'intelligence* op. cit., p. 110.

Part Two
Althusser and After

5   Selected Texts*

Louis Althusser

Louis Althusser (1918–90) was the leading Marxist philosopher of his day, a professor at the Ecole Normale Supérieure in Paris and a communist party activist. His chief works are *For Marx* (1965), *Reading Capital* (London: New Left Books, 1970), and *Lenin and Philosophy* (1971). Althusser's idiosyncratic brand of Marxism insisted on a sharp break between 'science' and 'ideology', dismissed humanism as ideological, and denigrated both history and subjectivity in favour of a rigorously structural Marxism influenced by Spinoza, Freud and French structuralism. He agitated within the French Communist party for a return to Leninist principles, harboured Maoist sympathies, and was throughout the 1970s something of a cult figure on the political Left. His theories, however, fell into some disfavour in the latter years of his life, marked as they were by personal tragedy: his murder of his wife while in the grip of psychosis, and his subsequent confinement to a psychiatric hospital.

In various passages in his collection of essays *For Marx*, Althusser develops his theory (derived in part from the psychoanalyst Jacques Lacan) of ideology as an 'imaginary' relation to one's real conditions of existence. Ideology is not a conceptual representation of the world, but the way we 'live' that world at the level of the unconscious. His celebrated essay on 'Ideology and Ideological State Apparatuses' in *Lenin and Philosophy*, perhaps the key text in the theory of ideology for our time, elaborates these Lacanian insights by showing how ideology constitutes us as human subjects, lending us the (fictional) sense of coherence and 'centredness' necessary for our agency within society. But the piece also offers some remarkable insights into the institutional nature of ideology, arguing as it does that it is always a question of material practices within material 'apparatuses'. Though published in

*Reprinted from Louis Althusser, *For Marx* (London: New Left Books, 1965), pp. 232–4, and Louis Althusser, *Lenin and Philosophy* (London: New Left Books, 1971), pp. 136–65.

the year of the momentous student uprising in Paris 1968, the essay takes a somewhat pessimistic political line, more concerned to examine how individuals are 'subjected' by a dominant ideology than how they might rebel against it. Its notably 'functionalist' approach to ideology has been heavily criticised, along with many of its epistemological theses; but it would hardly be an exaggeration to claim that, for all its limits, this single essay changed the course of thinking about ideology in our own day.

Ideology is as such an organic part of every social totality. It is as if human societies could not survive without these *specific formations*, these systems of representations (at various levels), their ideologies. Human societies secrete ideology as the very element and atmosphere indispensable to their historical respiration and life. Only an ideological world outlook could have imagined societies *without ideology* and accepted the utopian idea of a world in which ideology (not just one of its historical forms) would disappear without trace, to be replaced by *science*. For example, this utopia is the principle behind the idea that ethics, which is in its essence ideology, could be replaced by science or become scientific through and through; or that religion could be destroyed by science which would in some way take its place; that *art* could merge with knowledge or become 'everyday life', etc.

And I am not going to steer clear of the crucial question: *historical materialism cannot conceive that even a communist society could ever do without ideology*, be it ethics, art or 'world outlook'. Obviously it is possible to foresee important modifications in its ideological forms and their relations and even the disappearance of certain existing forms or a shift of their functions to neighbouring forms; it is also possible (on the premise of already acquired experience) to foresee the development of new ideological forms (e.g. the ideologies of 'the scientific world outlook' and 'communist humanism') but in the present state of Marxist theory strictly conceived, it is not conceivable that communism, a new mode of production implying determinate forces of production and relations of production, could do without a social organization of production, and corresponding ideological forms.

So ideology is not an aberration or a contingent excrescence of History: it is a structure essential to the historical life of societies. Further, only the existence and the recognition of its necessity enable us to act on ideology and transform ideology into an instrument of deliberate action on history.

It is customary to suggest that ideology belongs to the region of 'consciousness'. We must not be misled by this appellation which is still contaminated by the idealist problematic that preceded Marx. In truth, ideology has very little to do with 'consciousness', even supposing this term to have an unambiguous meaning. It is profoundly *unconscious*, even when it presents itself in a reflected form (as in pre-Marxist 'philosophy'). Ideology is indeed a system of representations, but in the majority of cases these representations have nothing to do with 'consciousness': they are usually images and occasionally concepts, but it is above all as *structures* that they impose on the vast majority of men, not via their 'consciousness'. They are perceived – accepted – suffered cultural objects and they act functionally on men via a process that escapes them. Men 'live' their ideologies as the Cartesian 'saw or did not see – if he was not looking at it – the moon two hundred paces away: *not at all as a form of consciousness, but as an object of their 'world'* – as their *'world'* itself. But what do we mean, then, when we say that ideology is a matter of men's 'consciousness'? First, that ideology is distinct from other social instances, but also that men *live* their actions, usually referred to freedom and 'consciousness' by the classical tradition, in ideology, *by and through ideology*; in short, that the 'lived' relation between men and the world, including History (in political action or inaction), passes through ideology, or better, *is ideology itself*. This is the sense in which Marx said that it is in ideology (as the locus of political struggle) that men *become conscious* of their place in the world and in history, it is within this ideological unconsciousness that men succeed in altering the 'lived' relation between them and the world and acquiring that new form of specific unconsciousness called 'consciousness'.

So ideology is a matter of the *lived* relation between men and their world. This relation, that only appears as *'conscious'* on condition that it is *unconscious*, in the same way only seems to be simple on condition that it is complex, that it is not a simple relation but a relation between relations, a second degree relation. In ideology men do indeed express, not the relation between them and their conditions of existence, but *the way* they live the relation between them and their conditions of existence: this presupposes both a real relation and an *'imaginary', 'lived'* relation. Ideology, then, is the expression of the relation between men and their 'world', that is, the (overdetermined) unity of the real relation and the imaginary relation between them and their real conditions of existence. In ideology the real relation is inevitably invested in the imaginary relation, a relation that *expresses a will* (conservative, conformist, reformist or revolutionary), a hope or a nostalgia, rather than describing a reality.

(From *For Marx*, 1965)

In order to advance the theory of the State it is indispensable to take into account not only the distinction between *State power* and *State apparatus*, but also another reality which is clearly on the side of the (repressive) State apparatus, but must not be confused with it. I shall call this reality by its concept: *the ideological State apparatuses*.

What are the ideological State apparatuses (ISAs)?

They must not be confused with the (repressive) State apparatus.

Remember that in Marxist theory, the State Apparatus (SA) contains: the Government, the Administration, the Army, the Police, the Courts, the Prisons, etc., which constitute what I shall in future call the Repressive State Apparatus. Repressive suggests that the State Apparatus in question 'functions by violence' – at least ultimately (since repression, e.g. administrative repression, may take non-physical forms).

I shall call Ideological State Apparatuses a certain number of realities which present themselves to the immediate observer in the form of distinct and specialized institutions. I propose an empirical list of these which will obviously have to be examined in detail, tested, corrected and reorganized. With all the reservations implied by this requirement, we can for the moment regard the following institutions as Ideological State Apparatuses (the order in which I have listed them has no particular significance):

- the religious ISA (the system of the different Churches),
- the educational ISA (the system of the different public and private 'Schools'),
- the family ISA,[1]
- the legal ISA,[2]
- the political ISA (the political system, including the different Parties),
- the trade-union ISA,
- the communications ISA (press, radio and television, etc.),
- the cultural ISA (Literature, the Arts, sports, etc.).

I have said that the ISAs must not be confused with the (Repressive) State Apparatus. What constitutes the difference?

As a first moment, it is clear that while there is *one* (Repressive) State Apparatus, there is a *plurality* of Ideological State Apparatuses. Even presupposing that it exists, the unity that constitutes this plurality of ISAs as a body is not immediately visible.

As a second moment, it is clear that whereas the – unified – (Repressive) State Apparatus belongs entirely to the *public* domain, much the larger part of the Ideological State Apparatuses (in their apparent dispersion) are part, on the contrary, of the *private* domain. Churches, Parties, Trade Unions, families, some schools, most newspapers, cultural ventures, etc., etc., are private.

We can ignore the first observation for the moment. But someone is bound to question the second, asking me by what right I regard as Ideological *State* Apparatuses, institutions which for the most part do not possess public status, but are quite simply *private* institutions. As a conscious Marxist, Gramsci already forestalled this objection in one sentence. The distinction between the public and the private is a distinction internal to bourgeois law, and valid in the (subordinate) domains in which bourgeois law exercises its 'authority'. The domain of the State escapes it because the latter is 'above the law': the State, which is the State *of* the ruling class, is neither public nor private; on the contrary, it is the precondition for any distinction between public and private. The same thing can be said from the starting-point of our State Ideological Apparatuses. It is unimportant whether the institutions in which they are realized are 'public' or 'private'. What matters is how they function. Private institutions can perfectly well 'function' as Ideological State Apparatuses. A reasonably thorough analysis of any one of the ISAs proves it.

But now for what is essential. What distinguishes the ISAs from the (Repressive) State Apparatus is the following basic difference: the Repressive State Apparatus functions 'by violence', whereas the Ideological State Apparatuses *function 'by ideology'.*

I can clarify matters by correcting this distinction. I shall say rather that every State Apparatus, whether Repressive or Ideological, 'functions' both by violence and by ideology, but with one very important distinction which makes it imperative not to confuse the Ideological State Apparatuses with the (Repressive) State Apparatus.

This is the fact that the (Repressive) State Apparatus functions massively and predominantly *by repression* (including physical repression), while functioning secondarily by ideology. (There is no such thing as a purely repressive apparatus.) For example, the Army and the Police also function by ideology both to ensure their own cohesion and reproduction, and in the 'values' they propound externally.

In the same way, but inversely, it is essential to say that for their part the Ideological State Apparatuses function massively and predominantly *by ideology*, but they also function secondarily by repression, even if ultimately, but only ultimately, this is very attenuated and concealed, even symbolic. (There is no such thing as a purely ideological apparatus.) Thus Schools and Churches use suitable methods of punishment, expulsion, selection, etc., to 'discipline' not only their shepherds, but also their flocks. The same is true of the Family. . . . The same is true of the cultural IS Apparatus (censorship, among other things), etc.

Is it necessary to add that this determination of the double 'functioning' (predominantly, secondarily) by repression and by ideology, according to whether it is a matter of the (Repressive) State Apparatus or the Ideological State Apparatuses, makes it clear that very subtle explicit or tacit combinations may be woven from the interplay of the (Repressive) State Apparatus and the Ideological State Apparatuses? Everyday life provides us with innumerable examples of this, but they must be studied in detail if we are to go further than this mere observation.

Nevertheless, this remark leads us towards an understanding of what constitutes the unity of the apparently disparate body of the ISAs. If the ISAs 'function' massively and predominantly by ideology, what unifies their diversity is precisely this functioning, in so far as the ideology by which they function is always in fact unified, despite its diversity and its contradictions, *beneath the ruling ideology*, which is the ideology of 'the ruling class'. Given the fact that the 'ruling class' in principle holds State power (openly or more often by means of alliances between classes or class fractions), and therefore has at its disposal the (Repressive) State Apparatus, we can accept the fact that this same ruling class is active in the Ideological State Apparatuses in so far as it is ultimately the ruling ideology which is realized in the Ideological State Apparatuses, precisely in its contradictions. Of course, it is a quite different thing to act by laws and decrees in the (Repressive) State Apparatus and to 'act' through the intermediary of the ruling ideology in the Ideological State Apparatuses. We must go into the details of this difference – but it cannot mask the reality of a profound identity. To my knowledge, *no class can hold State power over a long period without at the same time exercising its hegemony over and in the State Ideological Apparatuses.* I only need one example and proof of this: Lenin's anguished concern to revolutionize the educational Ideological State Apparatus (among others), simply to make it possible for the Soviet proletariat, who had seized State power, to secure the future of the dictatorship of the proletariat and the transition to socialism.[3]

This last comment puts us in a position to understand that the Ideological State Apparatuses may be not only the *stake*, but also the *site* of class struggle, and often of bitter forms of class struggle. The class (or class alliance) in power cannot lay down the law in the ISAs as easily as it can in the (repressive) State apparatus, not only because the former ruling classes are able to retain strong positions there for a long time, but also because the resistance of the exploited classes is able to find means and occasions to express itself there, either by the utilization of their contradictions, or by conquering combat positions in them in struggle.[4]

Let me run through my comments.

If the thesis I have proposed is well-founded, it leads me back to the classical Marxist theory of the State, while making it more precise in one point. I argue that it is necessary to distinguish between State power (and its possession by . . .) on the one hand, and the State Apparatus on the other. But I add that the State Apparatus contains two bodies: the body of institutions which represent the Repressive State Apparatus on the one hand, and the body of institutions which represent the body of Ideological State Apparatuses on the other.

But if this is the case, the following question is bound to be asked, even in the very summary state of my suggestions: what exactly is the extent of the role of the Ideological State Apparatuses? What is their importance based on? In other words: to what does the 'function' of these Ideological State Apparatuses, which do not function by repression but by ideology, correspond?

On the reproduction of the relations of production

I can now answer the central question which I have left in suspense for many long pages: *how is the reproduction of the relations of production secured?*

In the topographical language (Infrastructure, Superstructure), I can say: for the most part,[5] it is secured by the legal–political and ideological superstructure.

But as I have argued that it is essential to go beyond this still descriptive language, I shall say: for the most part,[6] it is secured by the exercise of State power in the State Apparatuses, on the one hand the (Repressive) State Apparatus, on the other the Ideological State Apparatuses.

What I have just said must also be taken into account, and it can be assembled in the form of the following three features:

(1) All the State Apparatuses function both by repression and by ideology, with the difference that the (Repressive) State Apparatus functions massively and predominantly by repression, whereas the Ideological State Apparatuses function massively and predominantly by ideology.

(2) Whereas the (Repressive) State Apparatus constitutes an organized whole whose different parts are centralized beneath a commanding unity, that of the politics of class struggle applied by the political representatives of the ruling classes in possession of State power, the Ideological State Apparatuses are multiple, distinct, 'relatively autonomous' and capable of providing an objective field to contradictions which express, in forms which may be limited or extreme, the effects of the clashes between the capitalist class struggle and the proletarian class struggle, as well as their subordinate forms.

(3) Whereas the unity of the (Repressive) State Apparatus is secured by its unified and centralized organization under the leadership of the representatives of the classes in power executing the politics of the class struggle of the classes in power, the unity of the different Ideological State Apparatuses is secured, usually in contradictory forms, by the ruling ideology, the ideology of the ruling class.

Taking these features into account, it is possible to represent the reproduction of the relations of production[7] in the following way, according to a kind of 'division of labour'.

The role of the repressive State apparatus, in so far as it is a repressive apparatus, consists essentially in securing by force (physical or otherwise) the political conditions of the reproduction of relations of production which are in the last resort *relations of exploitation*. Not only does the State apparatus contribute generously to its own reproduction (the capitalist State contains political dynasties, military dynasties, etc.), but also and above all, the State apparatus secures by repression (from the most brutal physical force, via mere administrative commands and interdictions, to

open and tacit censorship) the political conditions for the action of the
Ideological State Apparatuses.

In fact, it is the latter which largely secure the reproduction specifically
of the relations of production, behind a 'shield' provided by the repressive
State apparatus. It is here that the role of the ruling ideology is heavily
concentrated, the ideology of the ruling class, which holds State power. It is
the intermediation of the ruling ideology that ensures a (sometimes
teeth-gritting) 'harmony' between the repressive State apparatus and the
Ideological State Apparatuses, and between the different State Ideological
Apparatuses.

We are thus led to envisage the following hypothesis, as a function
precisely of the diversity of ideological State Apparatuses in their single,
because shared, role of the reproduction of the relations of production.

Indeed we have listed a relatively large number of ideological State
apparatuses in contemporary capitalist social formations: the educational
apparatus, the religious apparatus, the family apparatus, the political
apparatus, the trade union apparatus, the communications apparatus, the
'cultural' apparatus, etc.

But in the social formations of that mode of production characterized by
'serfdom' (usually called the feudal mode of production), we observe that
although there is a single repressive State apparatus which, since the
earliest known Ancient States, let alone the Absolute Monarchies, has been
formally very similar to the one we know today, the number of Ideological
State Apparatuses is smaller and their individual types are different. For
example, we observe that during the Middle Ages, the Church (the
religious ideological State apparatus) accumulated a number of functions
which have today devolved on to several distinct ideological State
apparatuses, new ones in relation to the past I am invoking, in particular
educational and cultural functions. Alongside the Church there was the
family Ideological State Apparatus, which played a considerable part,
incommensurable with its role in capitalist social formations. Despite
appearances, the Church and the Family were not the only Ideological
State Apparatuses. There was also a political Ideological State Apparatus
(the Estates General, the *Parlement*, the different political factions and
Leagues, the ancestors or the modern political parties, and the whole
political system of the free Communes and then of the *Villes*). There was
also a powerful 'proto-trade union' Ideological State Apparatus, if I may
venture such an anachronistic term (the powerful merchants' and bankers'
guilds and the journeymen's associations, etc.). Publishing and
Communications, even, saw an indisputable development, as did the
theatre; initially both were integral parts of the Church, then they became
more and more independent of it.

In the pre-capitalist historical period which I have examined extremely
broadly, it is absolutely clear that *there was one dominant Ideological State*

Apparatus, the Church, which concentrated within it not only religious functions, but also educational ones, and a large proportion of the functions of communications and 'culture'. It is no accident that all ideological struggle, from the sixteenth to the eighteenth century, starting with the first shocks of the Reformation, was *concentrated* in an anti-clerical and anti-religious struggle; rather this is a function precisely of the dominant position of the religious ideological State apparatus.

The foremost objective and achievement of the French Revolution was not just to transfer State power from the feudal aristocracy to the merchant-capitalist bourgeoisie, to break part of the former repressive State apparatus and replace it with a new one (e.g., the national popular Army) – but also to attack the number one Ideological State Apparatus: the Church. Hence the civil constitution of the clergy, the confiscation of ecclesiastical wealth, and the creation of new ideological State apparatuses to replace the religious ideological State apparatus in its dominant role.

Naturally, these things did not happen automatically: witness the Concordat, the Restoration and the long class struggle between the landed aristocracy and the industrial bourgeoisie throughout the nineteenth century for the establishment of bourgeois hegemony over the functions formerly fulfilled by the Church: above all by the Schools. It can be said that the bourgeoisie relied on the new political, parliamentary–democratic, ideological State apparatus, installed in the earliest years of the Revolution, then restored after long and violent struggles, for a few months in 1848 and for decades after the fall of the Second Empire, in order to conduct its struggle against the Church and wrest its ideological functions away from it, in other words, to ensure not only its own political hegemony, but also the ideological hegemony indispensable to the reproduction of capitalist relations of production.

That is why I believe that I am justified in advancing the following Thesis, however precarious it is. I believe that the ideological State apparatus which has been installed in the *dominant* position in mature capitalist social formations as a result of a violent political and ideological class struggle against the old dominant ideological State apparatus, is the *educational ideological apparatus.*

This thesis may seem paradoxical, given that for everyone, i.e. in the ideological representation that the bourgeoisie has tried to give itself and the classes it exploits, it really seems that the dominant ideological State apparatus in capitalist social formations is not the Schools, but the political ideological State apparatus, i.e. the regime of parliamentary democracy combining universal suffrage and party struggle.

However, history, even recent history, shows that the bourgeoisie has been and still is able to accommodate itself to political ideological State apparatuses other than parliamentary democracy: the First and Second Empires, Constitutional Monarchy (Louis XVIII and Charles X),

Parliamentary Monarchy (Louis-Philippe), Presidential Democracy (de Gaulle), to mention only France. In England this is even clearer. The Revolution was particularly 'successful' there from the bourgeois point of view, since unlike France, where the bourgeoisie, partly because of the stupidity of the petty aristocracy, had to agree to being carried to power by peasant and plebeian '*journées révolutionnaires*', something for which it had to pay a high price, the English bourgeoisie was able to 'compromise' with the aristocracy and 'share' State power and the use of the State apparatus with it for a long time (peace among all men of good will in the ruling classes!). In Germany it is even more striking, since it was behind a political ideological State apparatus in which the imperial Junkers (epitomized by Bismarck), their army and their police provided it with a shield and leading personnel, that the imperialist bourgeoisie made its shattering entry into history, before 'traversing' the Weimar Republic and entrusting itself to Nazism.

Hence I believe I have good reasons for thinking that behind the scenes of its political Ideological State Apparatus, which occupies the front of the stage, what the bourgeoisie has installed as its number one, i.e. as its dominant ideological State apparatus, is the educational apparatus, which has in fact replaced in its functions the previously dominant ideological State apparatus, the Church. One might even add: the School–Family couple has replaced the Church–Family couple.

Why is the educational apparatus in fact the dominant ideological State apparatus in capitalist social formations, and how does it function?

For the moment it must suffice to say:

(1) All ideological State apparatuses, whatever they are, contribute to the same result: the reproduction of the relations of production, i.e. of capitalist relations of exploitation.

(2) Each of them contributes towards this single result in the way proper to it. The political apparatus by subjecting individuals to the political State ideology, the 'indirect' (parliamentary) or 'direct' (plebiscitary or fascist) 'democratic' ideology. The communications apparatus by cramming every 'citizen' with daily doses of nationalism, chauvinism, liberalism, moralism, etc., by means of the press, the radio and television. The same goes for the cultural apparatus (the role of sport in chauvinism is of the first importance), etc. The religious apparatus by recalling in sermons and the other great ceremonies of Birth, Marriage and Death, that man is only ashes, unless he loves his neighbour to the extent of turning the other cheek to whoever strikes first. The family apparatus . . . but there is no need to go on.

(3) This concert is dominated by a single score, occasionally disturbed by contradictions (those of the remnants of former ruling classes, those of the proletarians and their organizations): the score of the Ideology of the current ruling class which integrates into its music the great themes of the

Humanism of the Great Forefathers, who produced the Greek Miracle even before Christianity, and afterwards the Glory of Rome, the Eternal City, and the themes of Interest, particular and general, etc. nationalism, moralism and economism.

(4) Nevertheless, in this concert, one ideological State apparatus certainly has the dominant role, although hardly anyone lends an ear to its music: it is so silent! This is the School.

It takes children from every class at infant-school age, and then for years, the years in which the child is most 'vulnerable', squeezed between the family State apparatus and the educational State apparatus, it drums into them, whether it uses new or old methods, a certain amount of 'know-how' wrapped in the ruling ideology (French, arithmetic, natural history, the sciences, literature) or simply the ruling ideology in its pure state (ethics, civic instruction, philosophy). Somewhere around the age of sixteen, a huge mass of children are ejected 'into production': these are the workers or small peasants. Another portion of scholastically adapted youth carries on: and, for better or worse, it goes somewhat further, until it falls by the wayside and fills the posts of small and middle technicians, white-collar workers, small and middle executives, petty bourgeois of all kinds. A last portion reaches the summit, either to fall into intellectual semi-employment, or to provide, as well as the 'intellectuals of the collective labourer', the agents of exploitation (capitalists, managers), the agents of repression (soldiers, policemen, politicians, administrators, etc.) and the professional ideologists (priests of all sorts, most of whom are convinced 'laymen').

Each mass ejected *en route* is practically provided with the ideology which suits the role it has to fulfil in class society: the role of the exploited (with a 'highly-developed' 'professional', 'ethical', 'civic', 'national' and apolitical consciousness); the role of the agent of exploitation (ability to give the workers orders and speak to them: 'human relations'), of the agent of repression (ability to give orders and enforce obedience 'without discussion', or ability to manipulate the demagogy of a political leader's rhetoric), or of the professional ideologist (ability to treat consciousnesses with the respect, i.e. with the contempt, blackmail, and demagogy they deserve, adapted to the accents of Morality, of Virtue, of 'Transcendence', of the Nation, of France's World Role, etc.).

Of course, many of these contrasting Virtues (modesty, resignation, submissiveness on the one hand, cynicism, contempt, arrogance, confidence, self-importance, even smooth talk and cunning on the other) are also taught in the Family, in the Church, in the Army, in Good Books, in films and even in the football stadium. But no other ideological State apparatus has the obligatory (and not least, free) audience of the totality of the children in the capitalist social formation, eight hours a day for five or six days out of seven.

But it is by an apprenticeship in a variety of know-how wrapped up in the massive inculcation of the ideology of the ruling class that the *relations of production* in a capitalist social formation, i.e. the relations of exploited to exploiters and exploiters to exploited, are largely reproduced. The mechanisms which produce this vital result for the capitalist regime are naturally covered up and concealed by a universally reigning ideology of the School, universally reigning because it is one of the essential forms of the ruling bourgeois ideology: an ideology which represents the School as a neutral environment purged of ideology (because it is . . . lay), where teachers respectful of the 'conscience' and 'freedom' of the children who are entrusted to them (in complete confidence) by their 'parents' (who are free, too, i.e. the owners of their children) open up for them the path to the freedom, morality and responsibility of adults by their own example, by knowledge, literature and their 'liberating' virtues.

I ask the pardon of those teachers who, in dreadful conditions, attempt to turn the few weapons they can find in the history and learning they 'teach' against the ideology, the system and the practices in which they are trapped. They are a kind of hero. But they are rare and how many (the majority) do not even begin to suspect the 'work' the system (which is bigger than they are and crushes them) forces them to do, or worse, put all their heart and ingenuity into performing it with the most advanced awareness (the famous new methods!). So little do they suspect it that their own devotion contributes to the maintenance and nourishment of this ideological representation of the School, which makes the School today as 'natural', indispensable, useful and even beneficial for our contemporaries as the Church was 'natural', indispensable and generous for our ancestors a few centuries ago.

In fact, the Church has been replaced today *in its role as the dominant Ideological State Apparatus* by the School. It is coupled with the Family just as the Church was once coupled with the Family. We can now claim that the unprecedentedly deep crisis which is now shaking the education system of so many States across the globe, often in conjunction with a crisis (already proclaimed in the *Communist Manifesto*) shaking the family system, takes on a political meaning, given that the School (and the School–Family couple) constitutes the dominant Ideological State Apparatus, the Apparatus playing a determinant part in the reproduction of the relations of production of a mode of production threatened in its existence by the world class struggle.

On ideology

When I put forward the concept of an Ideological State Apparatus, when I said that the ISAs 'function by ideology', I invoked a reality which needs a little discussion: ideology.

It is well known that the expression 'ideology' was invented by Cabanis, Destutt de Tracy and their friends, who assigned to it as an object the (genetic) theory of ideas. When Marx took up the term fifty years later, he gave it a quite different meaning, even in his Early Works. Here, ideology is the system of the ideas and representations which dominate the mind of a man or a social group. The ideologico-political struggle conducted by Marx as early as his articles in the *Rheinische Zeitung* inevitably and quickly brought him face to face with this reality and forced him to take his earliest intuitions further.

However, here we come upon a rather astonishing paradox. Everything seems to lead Marx to formulate a theory of ideology. In fact, *The German Ideology* does offer us, after the *1844 Manuscripts*, an explicit theory of ideology, but . . . it is not Marxist (we shall see why in a moment). As for *Capital*, although it does contain many hints towards a theory of ideologies (most visibly, the ideology of the vulgar economists), it does not contain that theory itself, which depends for the most part on a theory of ideology in general.

I should like to venture a first and very schematic outline of such a theory. The theses I am about to put forward are certainly not off the cuff, but they cannot be sustained and tested, i.e. confirmed or rejected, except by much thorough study and analysis.

Ideology has no history

One word first of all to expound the reason in principle which seems to me to found, or at least to justify, the project of a theory of ideology *in general*, and not a theory of particular ideolog*ies*, which, whatever their form (religious, ethical, legal, political), always express *class positions*.

It is quite obvious that it is necessary to proceed towards a theory of ideolog*ies* in the two respects I have just suggested. It will then be clear that a theory of ideolog*ies* depends in the last resort on the history of social formations, and thus of the modes of production combined in social formations, and of the class struggles which develop in them. In this sense it is clear that there can be no question of a theory of ideolog*ies in general*, since ideolog*ies* (defined in the double respect suggested above: regional and class) have a history, whose determination in the last instance is clearly situated outside ideologies alone, although it involves them.

On the contrary, if I am able to put forward the project of a theory of ideology *in general*, and if this theory really is one of the elements on which theories of ideolog*ies* depend, that entails an apparently paradoxical proposition which I shall express in the following terms: *ideology has no history*.

As we know, this formulation appears in so many words in a passage from *The German Ideology*. Marx utters it with respect to metaphysics, which, he says, has no more history than ethics (meaning also the other forms of ideology).

In *The German Ideology*, this formulation appears in a plainly positivist context. Ideology is conceived as a pure illusion, a pure dream, i.e. as nothingness. All its reality is external to it. Ideology is thus thought as an imaginary construction whose status is exactly like the theoretical status of the dream among writers before Freud. For these writers, the dream was the purely imaginary, i.e. null, result of 'day's residues', presented in an arbitrary arrangement and order, sometimes even 'inverted', in other words, in 'disorder'. For them, the dream was the imaginary, it was empty, null and arbitrarily 'stuck together' (*bricolê*), once the eyes had closed, from the residues of the only full and positive reality, the reality of the day. This is exactly the status of philosophy and ideology (since in this book philosophy is ideology *par excellence*) in *The German Ideology*.

Ideology, then, is for Marx an imaginary assemblage (*bricolage*), a pure dream, empty and vain, constituted by the 'day's residues' from the only full and positive reality, that of the concrete history of concrete material individuals materially producing their existence. It is on this basis that ideology has no history in *The German Ideology*, since its history is outside it, where the only existing history is, the history of concrete individuals, etc. In *The German Ideology*, the thesis that ideology has no history is therefore a purely negative thesis, since it means both:

(1) ideology is nothing in so far as it is a pure dream (manufactured by who knows what power: if not by the alienation of the division of labour, but that, too, is a *negative* determination);

(2) ideology has no history, which emphatically does not mean that there is no history in it (on the contrary, for it is merely the pale, empty and inverted reflection of real history) but that it has no history *of its own*.

Now, while the thesis I wish to defend formally speaking adopts the terms of *The German Ideology* ('ideology has no history'), it is radically different from the positivist and historicist thesis of *The German Ideology*.

For on the one hand, I think it is possible to hold that ideolog*ies have a history of their own* (although it is determined in the last instance by the class struggle); and on the other, I think it is possible to hold that ideology *in general has no history*, not in a negative sense (its history is external to it), but in an absolutely positive sense.

This sense is a positive one if it is true that the peculiarity of ideology is that it is endowed with a structure and a functioning such as to make it a non-historical reality, i.e. an *omni-historical* reality, in the sense in which that structure and functioning are immutable, present in the same form

INTRO

throughout what we can call history, in the sense in which the *Communist Manifesto* defines history as the history of class struggles, i.e. the history of class societies.

To give a theoretical reference-point here, I might say that, to return to our example of the dream, in its Freudian conception this time, our proposition: ideology has no history, can and must (and in a way which has absolutely nothing arbitrary about it, but, quite the reverse, is theoretically necessary, for there is an organic link between the two propositions) be related directly to Freud's proposition that the *unconscious is eternal*, i.e. that it has no history.

If eternal means, not transcendent to all (temporal) history, but omnipresent, trans-historical and therefore immutable in form throughout the extent of history, I shall adopt Freud's expression word for word, and write *ideology is eternal,* exactly like the unconscious. And I add that I find this comparison theoretically justified by the fact that the eternity of the unconscious is not unrelated to the eternity of ideology in general.

That is why I believe I am justified, hypothetically at least, in proposing a theory of ideology *in general*, in the sense that Freud presented a theory of the unconscious *in general*.

To simplify the phrase, it is convenient, taking into account what has been said about ideologies, to use the plain term ideology to designate ideology in general, which I have just said has no history, or, what comes to the same thing, is eternal, i.e. omnipresent in its immutable form throughout history (= the history of social formations containing social classes). For the moment I shall restrict myself to 'class societies' and their history.

Ideology is a 'representation' of the imaginary relationship of individuals to their real conditions of existence

In order to approach my central thesis on the structure and functioning of ideology, I shall first present two theses, one negative, the other positive. The first concerns the object which is 'represented' in the imaginary form of ideology, the second concerns the materiality of ideology.

THESIS I: Ideology represents the imaginary relationship of individuals to their real conditions of existence.

We commonly call religious ideology, ethical ideology, legal ideology, political ideology, etc., so many 'world outlooks'. Of course, assuming that we do not live one of these ideologies as the truth (e.g. 'believe' in God, Duty, Justice, etc. . . .), we admit that the ideology we are discussing from a critical point of view, examining it as the ethnologist examines the myths of a 'primitive society', that these 'world outlooks' are largely imaginary, i.e. do not 'correspond to reality'.

However, while admitting that they do not correspond to reality, i.e. that they constitute an illusion, we admit that they do make allusion to reality, and that they need only be 'interpreted' to discover the reality of the world behind their imaginary representation of that world (ideology = *illusion/allusion*).

There are different types of interpretation, the most famous of which are the *mechanistic* type, current in the eighteenth century (God is the imaginary representation of the real King), and the *'hermeneutic'* interpretation, inaugurated by the earliest Church Fathers, and revived by Feuerbach and the theologico-philosophical school which descends from him, e.g. the theologian Barth (to Feuerbach, for example, God is the essence of real Man). The essential point is that on condition that we interpret the imaginary transposition (and inversion) of ideology we arrive at the conclusion that in ideology 'men represent their real conditions of existence to themselves in an imaginary form'.

Unfortunately, this interpretation leaves one small problem unsettled: why do men 'need' this imaginary transposition of their real conditions of existence in order to 'represent to themselves' their real conditions of existence?

The first answer (that of the eighteenth century) proposes a simple solution: Priests or Despots are responsible. They 'forged' the Beautiful Lies so that, in the belief that they were obeying God, men would in fact obey the Priests and Despots, who are usually in alliance in their imposture, the Priests acting in the interests of the Despots or vice versa, according to the political positions of the 'theoreticians' concerned. There is therefore a cause for the imaginary transposition of the real conditions of existence: that cause is the existence of a small number of cynical men who base their domination and exploitation of the 'people' on a falsified representation of the world which they have imagined in order to enslave other minds by dominating their imaginations.

The second answer (that of Feuerbach, taken over word for word by Marx in his Early Works) is more 'profound', i.e. just as false. It, too, seeks and finds a cause for the imaginary transposition and distortion of men's real conditions of existence, in short, for the alienation in the imaginary of the representation of men's conditions of existence. This cause is no longer Priests or Despots, nor their active imagination and the passive imagination of their victims. This cause is the material alienation which reigns in the conditions of existence of men themselves. This is how, in *The Jewish Question* and elsewhere, Marx defends the Feuerbachian idea that men make themselves an alienated (= imaginary) representation of their conditions of existence because these conditions of existence are themselves alienating (in the *1844 Manuscripts*: because these conditions are dominated by the essence of alienated society – *'alienated labour'*).

All these interpretations thus take literally the thesis which they presuppose, and on which they depend, i.e. that what is reflected in the imaginary representation of the world found in an ideology is the conditions of existence of men, i.e. their real world.

Now I can return to a thesis which I have already advanced: it is not their real conditions of existence, their real world, that 'men' 'represent to themselves' in ideology, but above all it is their relation to those conditions of existence which is represented to them there. It is this relation which is at the centre of every ideological, i.e. imaginary, representation of the real world. It is this relation that contains the 'cause' which has to explain the imaginary distortion of the ideological representation of the real world. Or rather, to leave aside the language of causality it is necessary to advance the thesis that it is the *imaginary nature of this relation* which underlies all the imaginary distortion that we can observe (if we do not live in its truth) in all ideology.

To speak in a Marxist language, if it is true that the representation of the real conditions of existence of the individuals occupying the posts of agents of production, exploitation, repression, ideologization and scientific practice, does in the last analysis arise from the relations of production, and from relations deriving from the relations of production, we can say the following: all ideology represents in its necessarily imaginary distortion not the existing relations of production (and the other relations that derive from them), but above all the (imaginary) relationship of individuals to the relations of production and the relations that derive from them. What is represented in ideology is therefore not the system of the real relations which govern the existence of individuals, but the imaginary relation of those individuals to the real relations in which they live.

If this is the case, the question of the 'cause' of the imaginary distortion of the real relations in ideology disappears and must be replaced by a different question: why is the representation given to individuals of their (individual) relation to the social relations which govern their conditions of existence and their collective and individual life necessarily an imaginary relation? And what is the nature of this imaginariness? Posed in this way, the question explodes the solution by a 'clique',[8] by a group of individuals (Priests or Despots) who are the authors of the great ideological mystification, just as it explodes the solution by the alienated character of the real world. We shall see why later in my exposition. For the moment I shall go no further.

THESIS II: Ideology has a material existence.

I have already touched on this thesis by saying that the 'ideas' or 'representations', etc., which seem to make up ideology do not have an ideal (*idéale* or *idéelle*) or spiritual existence, but a material existence. I even suggested that the ideal (*idéale, idéelle*) and spiritual existence of 'ideas' arises exclusively in an ideology of the 'idea' and of ideology, and let me add, in an ideology of what seems to have 'founded' this conception since the emergence of the sciences, i.e. what the practicians of the sciences represent to themselves in their spontaneous ideology as 'ideas', true or false. Of course, presented in affirmative form, this thesis is unproven. I simply ask that the reader be favourably disposed towards it, say, in the name of materialism. A long series of arguments would be necessary to prove it.

This hypothetical thesis of the not spiritual but material existence of 'ideas' or other 'representations' is indeed necessary if we are to advance in our analysis ot the nature of ideology. Or rather, it is merely useful to us in order the better to reveal what every at all serious analysis of any ideology will immediately and empirically show to every observer, however critical.

While discussing the ideological State apparatuses and their practices, I said that each of them was the realization of an ideology (the unity of these different regional ideologies – religious, ethical, legal, political, aesthetic, etc. – being assured by their subjection to the ruling ideology). I now return to this thesis: an ideology always exists in an apparatus, and its practice, or practices. This existence is material.

Of course, the material existence of the ideology in an apparatus and its practices does not have the same modality as the material existence of a paving-stone or a rifle. But, at the risk of being taken for a Neo-Aristotelian (NB Marx had a very high regard for Aristotle), I shall say that 'matter is discussed in many senses', or rather that it exists in different modalities, all rooted in the last instance in 'physical' matter.

Having said this, let me move straight on and see what happens to the 'individuals' who live in ideology, i.e. in a determinate (religious, ethical, etc.) representation of the world whose imaginary distortion depends on their imaginary relation to their conditions of existence, in other words, in the last instance, to the relations of production and to class relations (ideology = an imaginary relation to real relations). I shall say that this imaginary relation is itself endowed with a material existence.

Now I observe the following.

An individual believes in God, or Duty, or Justice, etc. This belief derives (for everyone, i.e. for all those who live in an ideological representation of ideology, which reduces ideology to ideas endowed by definition with a spiritual existence) from the ideas of the individual concerned, i.e. from him as a subject with a consciousness which contains the ideas of his belief. In this way, i.e by means of the absolutely ideological 'conceptual' device (*dispositif*) thus set up (a subject endowed with a consciousness in which he freely forms or freely recognizes ideas in which he believes), the (material) attitude of the subject concerned naturally follows.

The individual in question behaves in such and such a way, adopts such and such a practical attitude, and, what is more, participates in certain regular practices which are those of the ideological apparatus on which 'depend' the ideas which he has in all consciousness freely chosen as a subject. If he believes in God, he goes to Church to attend Mass, kneels, prays, confesses, does penance (once it was material in the ordinary sense of the term) and naturally repents and so on. If he believes in Duty, he will have the corresponding attitudes, inscribed in ritual practices 'according to the correct principles'. If he believes in Justice, he will submit unconditionally to the rules of the Law, and may even protest when they are violated, sign petitions, take part in a demonstration, etc.

Throughout this schema we observe that the ideological representation of ideology is itself forced to recognize that every 'subject' endowed with a 'consciousness' and believing in the 'ideas' that his 'consciousness' inspires in him and freely accepts, must *act according to his ideas*, must therefore inscribe his own ideas as a free subject in the actions of his material practice. If he does not do so, 'that is wicked'.

Indeed, if he does not do what he ought to do as a function of what he believes, it is because he does something else, which, still as a function of the same idealist scheme, implies that he has other ideas in his head as well as those he proclaims, and that he acts according to these other ideas, as a man who is either 'inconsistent' ('no one is willingly evil') or cynical, or perverse.

In every case, the ideology of ideology thus recognizes, despite its imaginary distortion, that the 'ideas' of a human subject exist in his actions, or ought to exist in his actions, and if that is not the case, it lends him other ideas corresponding to the actions (however perverse) that he does perform. This ideology talks of actions: I shall talk of actions inserted into *practices*. *And* I shall point out that these practices are governed by the *rituals* in which these practices are inscribed, within the *material existence of an ideological apparatus*, be it only a small part of that apparatus: a small mass in a small church, a funeral, a minor match at a sports' club, a school day, a political party meeting, etc.

Besides, we are indebted to Pascal's defensive 'dialectic' for the wonderful formula which will enable us to invert the order of the notional schema of ideology. Pascal says more or less: 'Kneel down, move your lips in prayer, and you will believe.' He thus scandalously inverts the order of things, bringing, like Christ, not peace but strife, and in addition something hardly Christian (for woe to him who brings scandal into the world!) – scandal itself. A fortunate scandal which makes him stick with Jansenist defiance to a language that directly names the reality.

I will be allowed to leave Pascal to the arguments of his ideological struggle with the religious ideological State apparatus of his day. And I shall be expected to use a more directly Marxist vocabulary, if that is possible, for we are advancing in still poorly explored domains.

I shall therefore say that, where only a single subject (such and such an individual) is concerned, the existence of the ideas of his belief is material in that *his ideas are his material actions inserted into material practices governed by material rituals which are themselves defined by the material ideological apparatus from which derive the ideas of that subject*. Naturally, the four inscriptions of the adjective 'material' in my proposition must be affected by different modalities: the materialities of a displacement for going to mass, of kneeling down, of the gesture of the sign of the cross, or of the *mea culpa*, of a sentence, of a prayer, of an act of contrition, of a penitence, of a gaze, of a hand-shake, of an external verbal discourse or an 'internal' verbal discourse (consciousness), are not one and the same materiality. I shall leave on one side the problem of a theory of the differences between the modalities of materiality.

It remains that in this inverted presentation of things, we are not dealing with an 'inversion' at all, since it is clear that certain notions have purely and simply disappeared from our presentation, whereas others on the contrary survive, and new terms appear.

Disappeared: the term *ideas*.

Survive: the terms *subject, consciousness, belief, actions*.

Appear: the terms *practices, rituals, ideological apparatus*.

It is therefore not an inversion or overturning (except in the sense in which one might say a government or a glass is overturned), but a reshuffle (of a non-ministerial type), a rather strange reshuffle, since we obtain the following result.

Ideas have disappeared as such (in so far as they are endowed with an ideal or spiritual existence), to the precise extent that it has emerged that their existence is inscribed in the actions of practices governed by rituals defined in the last instance by an ideological apparatus. It therefore appears that the subject acts in so far as he is acted by the following system (set out in the order of its real determination): ideology existing in a material ideological apparatus, prescribing material practices governed by a material ritual, which practices exist in the material actions of a subject acting in all consciousness according to his belief.

But this very presentation reveals that we have retained the following notions: subject, consciousness, belief, actions. From this series I shall immediately extract the decisive central term on which everything else depends: the notion of the *subject*.

And I shall immediately set down two conjoint theses:

(1) there is no practice except by and in an ideology;

(2) there is no ideology except by the subject and for subjects.

I can now come to my central thesis.

Ideology interpellates individuals as subjects

This thesis is simply a matter of making my last proposition explicit: there is no ideology except by the subject and for subjects. Meaning, there is no ideology except for concrete subjects, and this destination for ideology is only made possible by the subject: meaning, *by the category of the subject* and its functioning.

By this I mean that, even if it only appears under this name (the subject) with the rise of bourgeois ideology, above all with the rise of legal ideology,[9] the category of the subject (which may function under other names: e.g., as the soul in Plato, as God, etc.) is the constitutive category of all ideology, whatever its determination (regional or class) and whatever its historical date – since ideology has no history.

I say: the category of the subject is constitutive of all ideology, but at the same time and immediately I add that *the category of the subject is only constitutive of all ideology in so far as all ideology has the function (which defines it) of 'constituting' concrete individuals as subjects*. In the interaction of this double constitution exists the functioning of all ideology, ideology being nothing but its functioning in the material forms of existence of that functioning.

In order to grasp what follows, it is essential to realize that both he who is writing these lines and the reader who reads them are themselves subjects, and therefore ideological subjects (a tautological proposition), i.e. that the author and the reader of these lines both live 'spontaneously' or 'naturally' in ideology in the sense in which I have said that 'man is an ideological animal by nature'.

That the author, in so far as he writes the lines of a discourse which claims to be scientific, is completely absent as a 'subject' from 'his' scientific discourse (for all scientific discourse is by definition a subjectless discourse, there is no 'Subject of science' except in an ideology of science) is a different question which I shall leave on one side for the moment.

As St Paul admirably put it, it is in the 'Logos', meaning in ideology, that we 'live, move and have our being'. It follows that, for you and for me, the category of the subject is a primary 'obviousness' (obviousnesses are always primary): it is clear that you and I are subjects (free, ethical, etc. . . .). Like all obviousnesses, including those that make a word 'name a thing' or 'have a meaning' (therefore including the obviousness of the 'transparency' of language), the 'obviousness' that you and I are subjects – and that that does not cause any problems – is an ideological effect, the elementary ideological effect.[10] It is indeed a peculiarity of ideology that it imposes (without appearing to do so, since these are 'obviousnesses') obviousnesses as obviousnesses, which we cannot *fail to recognize* and before which we have the inevitable and natural reaction of crying out (aloud or in the 'still, small voice of conscience'): 'That's obvious! That's right! That's true!'

At work in this reaction is the ideological *recognition* function which is one of the two functions of ideology as such (its inverse being the function of *misrecognition – méconnaissance*).

To take a highly 'concrete' example, we all have friends who, when they knock on our door and we ask, through the door, the question 'Who's there?', answer (since 'it's obvious') 'It's me.' And we recognize that 'it is him', or 'her'. We open the door, and 'it's true, it really was she who was there'. To take another example, when we recognize somebody of our (previous) acquaintance ((*re*)-*connaissance*) in the street, we show him that we have recognized him (and have recognized that he has recognized us) by saying to him 'Hello, my friend', and shaking his hand (a material ritual practice of ideological recognition in everyday life – in France, at least; elsewhere, there are other rituals).

In this preliminary remark and these concrete illustrations, I only wish to point out that you and I are *always already* subjects, and as such constantly practise the rituals of ideological recognition, which guarantees for us that we are indeed concrete, individual, distinguishable and (naturally) irreplaceable subjects. The writing I am currently executing and the reading you are currently[11] performing are also in this respect rituals of ideological recognition, including the 'obviousness' with which the 'truth' or 'error' of my reflections may impose itself on you.

But to recognize that we are subjects and that we function in the practical rituals of the most elementary everyday life (the hand-shake, the fact of calling you by your name, the fact of knowing, even if I do not know what it is, that you 'have' a name of your own, which means that you are recognized as a unique subject, etc.) – this recognition only gives us the 'consciousness' of our incessant (eternal) practice of ideological recognition – its consciousness, i.e. its *recognition* – but in no sense does it give us the (scientific) *knowledge* of the mechanism of this recognition. Now it is this knowledge that we have to reach, if you will, while speaking in ideology, and from within ideology we have to outline a discourse which tries to break with ideology, in order to dare to be the beginning of a scientific (i.e. subjectless) discourse on ideology.

Thus in order to represent why the category of the 'subject' is constitutive of ideology, which only exists by constituting concrete subjects as subjects, I shall employ a special mode of exposition: 'concrete' enough to be recognized, but abstract enough to be thinkable and thought, giving rise to a knowledge.

As a first formulation I shall say: *all ideology hails or interpellates concrete individuals as concrete subjects*, by the functioning of the category of the subject.

This is a proposition which entails that we distinguish for the moment between concrete individuals on the one hand and concrete subjects on the other, although at this level concrete subjects only exist in so far as they are supported by a concrete individual.

I shall then suggest that ideology 'acts' or 'functions' in such a way that it 'recruits' subjects among the individuals (it recruits them all), or 'transforms' the individuals into subjects (it transforms them all) by that very precise operation which I have called *interpellation* or hailing, and which can be imagined along the lines of the most commonplace everyday police (or other) hailing: 'Hey, you there!'[12]

Assuming that the theoretical scene I have imagined takes place in the street, the hailed individual will turn round. By this mere one-hundred-and-eighty-degree physical conversion, he becomes a *subject*. Why? Because he has recognized that the hail was 'really' addressed to him, and that 'it was *really him* who was hailed' (and not someone else). Experience shows that the practical telecommunication of hailings is such that they hardly ever miss their man: verbal call or whistle, the one hailed always recognizes that it is really him who is being hailed. And yet it is a strange phenomenon, and one which cannot be explained solely by 'guilt feelings', despite the large numbers who 'have something on their consciences'.

Naturally for the convenience and clarity of my little theoretical theatre I have had to present things in the form of a sequence, with a before and an after, and thus in the form of a temporal succession. There are individuals walking along. Somewhere (usually behind them) the hail rings out: 'Hey, you there!' One individual (nine times out of ten it is the right one) turns round, believing/suspecting/knowing that it is for him, i.e. recognizing that 'it really is he' who is meant by the hailing. But in reality these things happen without any succession. The existence of ideology and the hailing or interpellation of individuals as subjects are one and the same thing.

I might add: what thus seems to take place outside ideology (to be precise, in the street), in reality takes place in ideology. What really takes place in ideology seems therefore to take place outside it. That is why those who are in ideology believe themselves by definition outside ideology: one of the effects of ideology is the practical *denegation* of the ideological character of ideology by ideology: ideology never says, 'I am ideological.' It is necessary to be outside ideology, i.e. in scientific knowledge, to be able to say: I am in ideology (a quite exceptional case) or (the general case): I was in ideology. As is well known, the accusation of being in ideology only applies to others, never to oneself (unless one is really a Spinozist or a Marxist, which, in this matter, is to be exactly the same thing). Which amounts to saying that ideology *has no outside* (for itself), but at the same time *that it is nothing but outside* (for science and reality).

Spinoza explained this completely two centuries before Marx, who practised it but without explaining it in detail. But let us leave this point, although it is heavy with consequences, consequences which are not just theoretical, but also directly political, since, for example, the whole theory of criticism and self-criticism, the golden rule of the Marxist–Leninist practice of the class struggle, depends on it.

Thus ideology hails or interpellates individuals as subjects. As ideology is eternal, I must now suppress the temporal form in which I have presented the functioning of ideology, and say: ideology has always-already interpellated individuals as subjects, which amounts to making it clear that individuals are always-already interpellated by ideology as subjects, which necessarily leads us to one last proposition: *individuals are always-already subjects*. Hence the individuals are 'abstract' with respect to the subjects which they always-already are. This proposition might seem paradoxical.

That an individual is always-already a subject, even before he is born, is nevertheless the plain reality, accessible to everyone and not a paradox at all. Freud shows that individuals are always 'abstract' with respect to the subjects they always-already are, simply by noting the ideological ritual that surrounds the expectation of a 'birth', that 'happy event'. Everyone knows how much and in what way an unborn child is expected. Which amounts to saying, very prosaically, if we agree to drop the 'sentiments', i.e. the forms of family ideology (paternal/maternal/conjugal/fraternal) in which the unborn child is expected: it is certain in advance that it will bear its Father's Name, and will therefore have an identity and be irreplaceable. Before its birth, the child is therefore always-already a subject, appointed as a subject in and by the specific familial ideological configuration in which it is 'expected' once it has been conceived. I hardly need add that this familial ideological configuration is, in its uniqueness, highly structured, and that it is in this implacable and more or less 'pathological' (presupposing that any meaning can be assigned to that term) structure that the former subject-to-be will have to 'find' 'its' place, i.e. 'become' the sexual subject (boy or girl) which it already is in advance. It is clear that this ideological constraint and pre-appointment, and all the rituals of rearing and then education in the family, have some relationship with what Freud studied in the forms of the pre-genital and genital 'stages' of sexuality, i.e. in the 'grip' of what Freud registered by its effects as being the unconscious. But let us leave this point, too, on one side.

(From *Lenin and Philosophy*, 1971)

Notes

1. The family obviously has other 'functions' than that of an ISA. It intervenes in the reproduction of labour power. In different modes of production it is the unit of production and/or the unit of consumption.
2. The 'Law' belongs both to the (Repressive) State Apparatus and to the system of the ISAs.
3. In a pathetic text written in 1937, Krupskaya relates the history of Lenin's desperate efforts and what she regards as his failure.
4. What I have said in these few brief words about the class struggle in the ISAs is

obviously far from exhausting the question of the class struggle.

To approach this question, two principles must be borne in mind:

The first principle was formulated by Marx in the Preface to *A Contribution to the Critique of Political Economy*:

> In considering such transformations [a social revolution] a distinction should always be made between the material transformation of the economic conditions of production, which can be determined with the precision of natural science, and the legal, political, religious, aesthetic or philosophic – in short, ideological forms in which men become conscious of this conflict and fight it out.

The class struggle is thus expressed and exercised in ideological forms, thus also in the ideological forms of the ISAs. But the class struggle *extends far beyond* these forms, and it is because it extends beyond them that the struggle of the exploited classes may also be exercised in the forms of the ISAs, and thus turn the weapon of ideology against the classes in power.

This by virtue of the *second principle*: the class struggle extends beyond the ISAs because it is rooted elsewhere than in ideology, in the Infrastructure, in the relations of production, which are relations of exploitation and constitute the base for class relations.

5. For the most part. For the relations of production are first reproduced by the materiality of the processes of production and circulation. But it should not be forgotten that ideological relations are immediately present in these same processes.

6. As above.

7. *For that part* of reproduction to which the Repressive State Apparatus and the Ideological State Apparatus *contribute*.

8. I use this very modern term deliberately. For even in Communist circles, unfortunately, it is a commonplace to 'explain' some political deviation (left or right opportunism) by the action of a 'clique'.

9. Which borrowed the legal category of 'subject in law' to make an ideological notion: man is by nature a subject.

10. Linguists and those who appeal to linguistics for various purposes often run up against difficulties which arise because they ignore the action of the ideological effects in all discourses – including even scientific discourses.

11. NB: this double 'currently' is one more proof of the fact that ideology is 'eternal', since these two 'currentlys' are separated by an indefinite interval; I am writing these lines on 6 April 1969, you may read them at any subsequent time.

12. Hailing as an everyday practice subject to a precise ritual takes a quite 'special' form in the policeman's practice of 'hailing' which concerns the hailing of 'suspects'.

6 Problems and Advances in the Theory of Ideology*

PAUL HIRST

Paul Hirst is a sociologist and holds a Chair in the subject in the University of London. Throughout the 1970s, he and his fellow sociologist Barry Hindess were perhaps the leading exponents of Althusserian Marxism in Britain, adopting a trenchantly 'anti-humanist' posture and claiming Marxism as a rigorous science. With Hindess, Hirst produced a number of iconoclastic studies, including *Pre-Capitalist Modes of Production* (London: Routledge, 1975) and (along with A. Cutler and A. Hussain) *Marx's 'Capital' and Capitalism Today* (London: Routledge, 1977). But by pressing Althusser's own hostility to classical epistemology to a certain apparently logical limit, Hirst was led beyond Althusser and Marxism altogether into a 'post-Marxist' position. In this piece, first given as a talk in Cambridge in 1976, he summarises affirmatively some of Althusser's major theses on ideology.

The title of my talk today is 'Problems in the Marxist theory of ideology'. I am going to talk specifically about one set of discussions of Marxist theory of ideology, which is found in certain of the works of Louis Althusser. Now this may seem to some somewhat partisan, since there is a great deal of writing on the Marxist theory of ideology apart from Althusser's contribution. However, I think Althusser has made a number of significant advances in trying to deal with the problem of what is called 'ideology', and a number of important criticisms of previous theoretical positions. My talk will be an expositional one; its object will be to deal with what I think Althusser's advances are, and in doing this I want to try and say where Althusser has advanced over previous Marxist discussions of the problems of ideology. Previous discussions will be considered in that context.

---

*Reprinted from PAUL HIRST, *On Law and Ideology* (1976; London: Macmillan, 1979), pp. 22–39.

(1) Ideology as distorted representation

I want to deal with Althusser's theoretical advances in the form of a number of theses; for those who have read Althusser on the theory of ideology, these theses will be somewhat familiar. I would say that the general effect of Althusser's position is to attempt to combat the idea that ideology is falsity, and to challenge what I would call the sociological mode of interpretation of ideology, that is, to analyse ideology through the social positions of people who are conceived as embodying the 'outlook' of these positions. Let me start with the first Althusserian thesis: *Ideology is not a distorted representation of reality*. This I do not doubt will appear to some people to be scandalous. It will become clearer when we consider the concept of the imaginary relation. But for the moment let us see what criticisms Althusser makes of conceptions in which ideology is a distorted representation of the real world. These conceptions of ideology as a misrepresentation of reality involve certain important theoretical consequences, and I shall briefly dwell on these.

Firstly, this position involves a conception of knowledge as being formed through the consciousness or experience of human subjects; ideology is then a distorted perception of reality by these knowing subjects. But this is exactly the classical empiricist conception of knowledge, i.e. knowledge is derived from a subject's experience of an object which is exterior to it. So in order for the thesis that ideology is a distorted recognition of reality to be sustained, it must be argued that the process of knowledge described by empiricism is a real process, though it leads to 'false' results. This is the first basic theoretical consequence: Ideology is knowledge derived from experience. This is a position which many people, including 'structuralists' like Jacques-Alain Miller, in his paper 'The Function of Theoretical Training' and Jacques Rancière, in 'The Concept of "Critique" and the "Critique of Political Economy" ', have actually taken up.

The second theoretical consequence is that the experiences the subject has are mediated by the social position of the subject. In consequence society must be conceived as a system of places, points of perception, and these places have experience-effects: if one is a finance capitalist, one will see the world differently than if one is an artisan. To use a metaphor from astronomy we can regard this as being like the difference between one observer observing celestial phenomena given to experience while standing on the earth, and another observing from a position on the sun. Marx uses this metaphor once or twice in *Capital*. Ideology is therefore a function of the structure of reality itself; the places that are created by social relations generate the ideologies that follow from them, through the mechanism of experience. It follows that any system can only generate certain definite forms of ideology: any social formation like, for example, capitalism or feudalism can only create certain kinds of experience-effects because of the structure of 'places' in it, capitalist and worker, serf and lord, etc. These represent, as in the astronomical metaphor, different points of view of the totality.

From this position follows the reductionist or sociologistic mode of analysis of ideology. The key thing in this type of analysis of ideology is the determination of the position of the subject. This means that the practice of interpretation involves the analysis of looking at the subject's social position, because ideology is a form of misrepresentation of the real determined by the position of the subject in the real. Reality is the primary determinant of ideology, it is the origin of ideology because it creates the position from which the experience is generated, and because it determines it: it is the truth of ideology. It is the point of truth that contradicts the falsity that it itself creates. Ideology is an experience created by the real, so we must know how that experience is created by the real in order to understand it. The analysis of the origin, returning to the social position of the subject, is the primary form of analysis. And a return to the origin is a return to truth. Because we take the point of view of reality itself, we understand the limits in the forms of 'knowledge' generated by partial positions or standpoints subjects have inside reality. To use the astronomical metaphor again, we must as it were move from the point of view of the observer seeing apparent phenomena to the analysis of the structure of planetary spaces and their motions. You can see here that the reality or truth of ideology is outside it in the prior determination or the creation of a system of places. It follows that reductionism is a legitimate mode of analysis. The subject mediates the experience of the place – it is the structure of 'places' which generates experience-effects. To look for the social position of a subject is a legitimate means of analysis of the ideas subjects hold, whether those subjects be individual subjects or classes.

So, this reductionist mode of interpretation involves on the one hand sociologism; the subject is in effect reduced to its place. If one is a capitalist one is a personification of capital, an embodiment of a place. On the other hand it involves an essentialism, in that one crucial category *not* reducible to the system of places is that of experience. Experience is conceived as an essential attribute or faculty of the subject, who may be either an individual or a class. A system of places is presumed and then subjects are somehow parachuted into them; they just happen to land with all the faculties necessary for experience. In fact they land with their sociological recognition-apparatus all ready before they receive their social position. This recognition apparatus is the faculty of experience. So the notion that empiricism is a real process of knowledge and not merely a theory of knowledge is necessary to this position because you will note that, as in empiricism, you have to postulate the idea of a knowing subject with a capacity for experience and the faculty of experience.

I have presented this thesis at some length because I think it is central to reductionist theories of ideology. There are two basic variants of this thesis that ideology is a distorted representation of reality. One is what Althusser calls historicism. In considering historicism, we shall take the example of Lukács, for reasons of familiarity. In Lukács' *History and Class Consciousness* the key modulation of the argument is that the subjects of experience are class subject and that there is no 'disembodied' or 'objective' knowledge of reality independent of class standpoints. The subject who knows reality is actually the class subject which is dominant in the process of constructing history. This subject knows reality because it makes it, and it only knows it fully if it makes it in a non-alienated mode. So that the first subject really to know social relations will be the proletariat. This is because the proletariat, in the process of constructing socialism, will be the first class to make history without alienation. This subject will recognise the truth of social relations in so far as they can be comprehended at all. Here we have the position that there is a true consciousness, a subject whose knowledge is adequate to the social totality because this class subject is in the process of constructing and reconstructing the totality. It is the subject of history. This subject transcends alienation in a revolutionary praxis and therefore transcends the limitations of points of view, so that knowledge through the experience of this class subject is adequate to the totality it experiences.

The second variant of this position is what is often called 'structuralism'.

Two classic examples of the conception of ideology, assumed in the astronomical metaphor, are found in the works by Rancière and Miller mentioned before. As we have seen, this conception entails that there is a structure of places which have experience-effects, and that empiricism describes a real process of knowledge. But there is a key difference between the historicist position and the 'structuralist' position. The latter does not conceive of a 'true subject' of history, since it denies that there can be true knowledge through the experience of a subject. All knowledge by a subject is empiricist and therefore inadequate, ideological. All subjects whose knowledge of the social world is derived from experience are condemned to ideology (because experience is necessarily empiricist). To my mind, Rancière presents convincing arguments that this is the position adopted by Marx in sections of *Capital*.

One has to take Rancière's arguments about the theory of fetishism in *Capital* seriously, because if he is right, then Marx is also a 'structuralist', i.e. at least in those sections of *Capital* which Rancière deals with (the very parts of the work generally considered to be the most Hegelian), Marx had a structuralist theory of ideology.

What I have done here is to present the main criticism of the position that ideology is a distorted representation of reality, the criticism being that it presupposes that knowledge really is derived from the experience of a subject. In his philosophical work, Althusser argues that empiricism is an impossible epistemology, an inadequate conception of knowledge. For him, it cannot therefore designate a real process of knowledge.

(2) The materiality of ideology

The second thesis runs as follows: *Ideology is not ideal or spiritual*. There are no really good English substitutes for the words 'ideal' or 'spiritual' available for use in theoretical contexts. What Althusser is trying to do with this thesis is to displace the opposition or couple, ideas : matter. A great deal of the orthodox Marxist theory of ideology is the theoretical residue of a fight between idealist and materialist philosophies of history. It was a fight which Marx and Engels, in their break from Left Hegelianism and Feuerbachism, were forced to engage in. A classic example is *The German Ideology*. Recognising this, Marx said that *The German Ideology* was a labour he and Engels had to undertake, which they had gone beyond. No doubt it was necessary to fight the idealist–materialist battle in the philosophy of history; however, Marx later rejected the vulgar materialism of his initial positions in this struggle.

Althusser insists that ideology does not consist of 'ideas' as opposed to matter. For these categories return us to the classic dualist conception of the human subject as a combination of matter (body) and ideas (mind or consciousness). Materialism in these terms is simply the mirror image of idealism. Ideas are not to be counterposed to matter or reality. For Althusser, ideas are real and not 'ideal' because they are always inscribed in social practices and are expressed in objective social forms (languages, rituals, etc.). As such they have definite effects. Althusser asserts the materiality of ideology; in other words, he uses the thesis of materialism to upturn the matter : ideas opposition. Ideologies are not simply reflections in some realm of 'ideas' of social relations; they are part of social relations.

Ideology is what Althusser calls an instance of the social totality. What Althusser means by an 'instance' is that there is a specific practice involved in the instance and that the instance is the way in which this practice is articulated into the social totality. There are three main practices conceived in Althusser's work: economic practice (transformation of nature within social relations); political practice (the struggle to transform social relations themselves); and ideological practice (I shall explain what this is in a moment). Nevertheless ideology is a practice which is articulated in social formations in relation to the other practices, in a hierarchy of determinations. Ideology is a set of social practices and social representations and rituals. It is a structure of social relationships which is both determined by other social relations and which has a determining effect on them. So the analysis of ideology is the analysis of social relations, not of a reflection of social relations in some world of ideas. What Althusser tries to do here is to get away from the position that somehow reality is in your stomach or somewhere beyond the cosmos. 'Ideas' do not exist as spiritual entities. Ideologies are social relations, they are as real as the economy. The notion that somehow the economy is primary in the sense that it alone is the real foundation of everything else (it is 'matter') entails a retreat into philosophical materialism. Althusser argues that historical materialism conceives of the social totality as a hierarchy of instances and these are as real as one another; they merely have different relative weights in determining the whole. This thesis of being determined and determining is what Althusser means by the concept of overdetermination.

In essence Althusser's thesis that ideology is not spiritual is an attack on the kind of materialistic interpretation of history in which ideas are epiphenomenal. We should recall that it was this kind of vulgar materialism that led Marx to leave the 'Marxist' camp, in words at least. This Marxist camp wasn't Marx's camp. It was the camp of materialistic interpreters of history, who took 'matter' (a technicist conception of the economy) as a primary fact. When Marx said he was not a Marxist he was defending historical materialism against vulgar materialism.

(3) Ideology, history and the imaginary

The third thesis is a famous one and is probably the most misinterpreted of all Althusser's theses. The third thesis that Althusser puts forward is: *ideology has no history.* Surely this is a scandal; how can ideology have no history? Well, as with many scandals, scandalous words are being used to explain reasonable things. This thesis amounts to nothing more than a thesis of the universality of the ideological instance in the social totality. The theory of the social totality deals with three instances – economic, political, ideological – two of which are universal: economy and ideology. Politics is not universal because Althusser, being a Communist, believes in a communist society in which the domination of man by man gives way to the administration of things. So there is no mystery as to why the political disappears. Obviously, why ideology continues requires some argument. The reason why he argues this is so is because of the structure of all social totalities. There will never be a totality in which the human subjects who live in social relations can comprehend them through experience because social totalities do not exist in a form which is accessible to experience.

The subject is related to the totality through an 'imaginary' relation. This 'imaginary' relation of subjects to their conditions of existence is the foundation of ideology. We shall consider in a moment the concept of the imaginary. Before proceeding to this we shall make some remarks as to its status. It is the central concept in the Althusserian theory of ideology, and if one does not deal in detail with this concept one cannot comprehend the theory. Most of the critiques of Althusser's theory of ideology are based on the idea that it is a positivist theory of ideology in which ideology misrepresents the real. Hence it appears scandalous that Althusser asserts the universality of ideology. Critics of Althusser like Geras and Kolakowski, who make much of his theory of ideology and of the autonomy of science from the social formation, simply do not deal with the concept of the imaginary relation. Yet this is the central concept in Althusser's theory of ideology.

Althusser argues that there is no end to the imaginary relation by which men live their relations to their conditions of existence. The notion of the end of ideology involves the idea that it is possible for there to be a true consciousness of social relations, and in turn this involves the idea that social relations can exist in a form in which they can be known in experience. So that experience here corresponds to truth – it is the basis of an adequate knowledge of social relations. The classic argument for the notion of true consciousness, that is, that experience is adequate to its object (that object being manifest truth), is the *1844 Manuscripts*. In this text, Marx conceives the social relations of communism purely in terms of spontaneous human intersubjectivity. Marx calls communist society 'concrete sensuous human self-creation' and says that it is the solution to the 'riddle' of history. History ceases to be a riddle because it no longer exists. There is no history in communist society because there is concrete sensuous human activity which is 'immediate' to itself, i.e. not 'mediated' by alienated social relations. History is the process of man's realisation of his essence, and it proceeds through alienation. Experience is adequate to the social relations of communism because there is no longer alienation, and therefore there is no 'riddle'. The concept of immediacy is necessary in this case. Immediate social relations are ones which are spontaneous between human subjects. Under communism, social relations are dissolved into purely spontaneous intersubjective relations, spontaneous because not mediated by social forms which dominate human subjects and are outside their direct control. Only these immediate relations can be truly known through experience.

This thesis Althusser challenges as an historicist one. He argues that in historicist theories there is a correspondence between the knowledge of the subject and the object, through the mechanism of experience, because the subject is what he calls a constitutive subject. The subject constitutes what it knows, it is the origin of what it knows, and therefore experience is the return of the origin to itself. We must insist therefore that the subject is truly the origin of its social relations. Take the formula 'men make history'. If men 'make' history why does the 'falsity' of ideology distort their perceptions? Ideology represents the making of history in an alienated mode. Alienation is the displacement of immediacy, the creation of social relations which involve the mediation of the subject's product (history) to it in forms it does not recognise. Constitutivity is displaced, the subject is no longer constitutive of or to itself. Men are the authors of their social relations but the conditions under which they make them means that their product escapes them. Alienation is a necessary part of history. The end of alienation is the recognition by man of himself as origin of his social relations and true experience is the return of the origin to itself. Subject and object are one, and therefore there is a correspondence of knowledge with its object.

The thesis that one can dispense with ideology involves (if it is developed rigorously) the idea that social relations originate in the actions of human subjects who self-consciously know those actions and their consequences to be their own. The concept of a constitutive subject entails that the subject be an essence, a pure origin. The subject is origin – it can have no conditions of existence without ceasing to be constitutive. Constitutivity must further rely on the subject's experience as an adequate account of its nature (a super-subjective knowledge negates constitutivity). Because the subject is necessarily known through itself as knowing subject, historicism is committed either to an extreme idealism, or to the limits of knowledge entailed in empiricism. If the subject knows its essence through self-consciousness then this consciousness is the presence-to-itself of truth (this position is only credible with reference to God's knowledge; God is pure origin and questions as to the conditions of His existence are impertinent). If the subject simply experiences itself as object, it is caught in the classic empiricist 'problem of knowledge' (which Althusser considers to be a pseudo-problem). Self-consciousness is the subject's experience of itself as an object to itself. Even if it experiences itself as constitutive it has no knowledge of itself (of its nature and existence) other than this experience. The subject must either trust experience (Cartesian double-think) or collapse into scepticism. The subject ever-always exists as a given to itself and to knowledge. Historicism is forced to make the nature of its most important category (subject) a mystery, a given beyond knowledge.

(4) The concept of the imaginary relation

The fourth thesis is the most important one: *ideology is not false consciousness*. Althusser insists, and this takes us back to the first point, that ideology is not a distorted representation of reality. Althusser further insists that ideology is not a representation of reality at all. What ideology represents is men's lived relation to their conditions of existence. This lived relation is, Althusser insists, an 'imaginary' relation. Now what does it mean to say that the subject lives his relation to his conditions of existence in an 'imaginary' mode? This word 'imaginary' is a metaphor borrowed from psycho-analysis (from Jacques Lacan). I am not going to go into the source of the borrowing but rather into what Althusser makes of it.

The imaginary modality of living is necessary because men's conditions of existence can never be given to them in experience. Hence the importance of the attack on the theory of ideology as experience. There cannot be any true or false *consciousness* because there is no basis for a correspondence between the experience of the subject and his social relations. This requires us to introduce the Althusserian concept of the social totality somewhat more rigorously than we have done heretofore. The social totality is conceived as a 'process without a subject'. What does this mean? It means essentially that the social totality is not a process constituted by a subject, and that subjects occupy a place in it other than origin or author.

This fourth thesis involves the point that was made in relation to the intersubjective theories, i.e. social relations are not reducible to intersubjective relations. This means that the subject lives in relation to the totality of its social conditions of existence in such a way that the subject can never simply recognise these conditions. This is because there are no essential subjects involved. The forms of subjectivity are conceived as both effects of and supports of the process. The relation of subject to the process (what the subject is) is determined by the process and the subject as a support of this process becomes a part of the totality. The totality forms subjects (because it provides their conditions of existence) in such a way that they can never 'recognise' it. The imaginary is the form in which the subject 'lives' its relation both to the (absent) totality (its conditions of existence) and to its existence as a subject. The conditions of existence of the subject are both present and absent to it. They are present, in the sense that the structure of the totality determines the 'place' of the subject in it, and therefore the conditions the imaginary must articulate. They are absent, in that the totality is not an essential totality, united by some inner essence, its elements linked to one another in principle, but on the contrary, the totality is present in and as its effects. The 'imaginary' relation is a (relatively autonomous) element of the totality – determined and determining. The totality (the 'matrix' of the instances) determines the 'space' of the imaginary as one of its instances. The imaginary is a specific articulation of that space (it relates the supports to the process). Because there is no essential whole given in advance to the 'imaginary' and 'pictured' in it, the imaginary is what it is (it is a specific effectivity). The relation of the subjects to the process established in the imaginary is not given elsewhere: it is not a *pars totalis*, it does not reflect the relations it articulates. The whole is not present – i.e. manifest – in the imaginary; all that is present in the imaginary is the relation which the imaginary is and determines. As a consequence, the subject has a relation to the process which, although determined by the process, does not represent in an expressive form the totality of its determinations.

It is important to introduce the notion of 'as if' here. The imaginary essentially consists in the idea that the subject lives its relation to its conditions of existence *as if* it were a subject. It is a subject because it exists in the realm of the 'as if', but it lives these relations *as if* they were true. It would be too simple to say that subjects live in the supposition that they are constitutive. The 'as if' involves the position that subjectivity is both constitutive and non-constitutive. Subjects do not constitute their social relations, they are not the origin of their social relations. But they live them in a different mode to that, and they live them 'as if' they did do more than that. This means that they are subjects because they are constituted 'as if' they constituted themselves.

Let us say in relation to this concept of 'as if' that what the subject does in living things 'as if', really does have effects. So that if you will permit me a bit of dialectics . . . the subject lives 'as if' it were a subject, and through the 'as if' it really does have a determinate effect. So that although the subject is not a constitutive subject, and the imaginary is overdetermined by the totality of conditions of existence, the imaginary in turn overdetermines that totality and becomes part of it. So that we do not have a truth/falsity, illusion/reality opposition here. The imaginary relation is a relation of the totality (it is part of the totality) and has a determining effect in it. It is not determinant in the last instance but is effective as an instance. So the imaginary is not a reflection, it doesn't *reflect* the conditions of existence of men but *is* their relation to them. And it is not false, it is absolutely not falsity. The imaginary does not represent anything other than what it is, and it cannot be false since it is not an idea or conception of things, but it is a part of social relations which has a definite effect. In living 'as if', subjects do not live in illusion, this 'as if' is the *reality* of their existence as subjects.

With his concepts of the 'ideological instance' and the 'imaginary relation', Althusser opens up the possibility of a whole region of social relations relatively autonomous from the economy, and with a (potential) effect on the totality. Ideology in this conception has serious political implications since it raises the prospect of 'ideological struggle' as a distinct arena of political struggle. It raises the prospect of changes in the forms of the 'imaginary' producing changes in the relations of subjects to the totality. (It might be said that he also closes it again since the 'imaginary' is an effect of the totality, a product of the action of its structure: how is it to be changed since subjects are effects of the process?) The question whether ideological struggle is possible and does have an effect is a politically important one. If ideological struggle does have an effect on social relations we shall begin to think about what ideological practices there are, how they can be transformed, and what the conditions of doing so are. If ideology is a reflection of social position and falsity, or illusion, for all but the proletariat, then ideological struggle is limited to proclaiming a new world view, whose victory is pre-given. We should, therefore, return to Christopher Caudwell and take it from there, recognising along the way that Freud, Einstein and Joyce are bourgeois junk. These seem to be the choices; there is not a midway position. Those are the alternatives: either taking ideological struggle seriously, because 'ideology' is a relatively autonomous arena of social relations; or taking up a position that ideology is a reflection of social relations and, in its bourgeois forms, illusion. Reductionist analyses lead to a class essentialist and economistic practice in relation to ideology, a practice which is sectarian and self-defeating (ideological effects are given in class experience).

To many orthodox Marxists, it may well be the case, for example, that a great many of the things the Women's Movement do appear to be absurd. The practices in question have the ideological recognition effect of absurdity: 'Why do they do silly things like that? That won't solve "the real", economic and political, problems.' But though a great many campaigns in which the Women's Movement engages may not be terribly effective in promoting socialist politics directly, they may be important in creating the basis on which an important section of the population is prepared to take socialist agitation seriously. The struggles involved are for the removal of real 'ideological' obstacles, social practices not 'illusions'. Willingness to recognise that ideology is not a matter of 'consciousness' (false or otherwise) might change many Marxists' attitudes to struggles of this type. It might make it possible for the Left to offer such movements (badly needed) political leadership, rather than opportunist tolerance and sloganising. I think we must take seriously Althusser's case that forms of 'ideological struggle' may have positive political effects, and that there is an area of 'ideological social relations' which is relatively autonomous from the economic and political which is an area of specific political practices.

(5) The concept of the imaginary and the science/ideology distinction

The concept of the imaginary is an extremely problematic concept. I am not going to hide the fact that I think it is a metaphor and that a good deal of its substance evaporates when you look closely at it. I have examined the Althusserian theory of ideology as social relations and I have not dealt with Althusser's theory of ideology in relation to his theory of knowledge. Now I have done this quite deliberately because I think that what Althusser has to say about 'ideological social relations' is revolutionary in its implications, turning Marxism away from reductionist and sociologistic modes of handling ideology, whereas Althusser's theory of knowledge seems to me to be much more problematic. Although the two are connected I think that what Althusser has done in the theory of ideology can be considered relatively independently of his theory of knowledge. But as it were to subvert that, I will say that there is a very definite connection between the two, and that is in relation to the concept of the imaginary. The imaginary is vital for Althusser's conception of ideological and scientific knowledge. This is because ideology is always a form of the creation of recognition, i.e. the imaginary always creates forms of recognition, which are the basis of the lived relationship. The imaginary is a part of the totality. All recognition is necessarily coupled with misrecognition. Recognition is always a form of the imaginary relation, so that the analysis of ideology as a social relation provides a connection with the epistemological distinction between ideological and scientific knowledges. Ideological knowledges and theoretical ideologies are elaborations of what Althusser calls practical social ideologies (what we have been talking about so far). These ideological knowledges represent the elaboration or reflection of the forms of recognition that the subject has in the imaginary relation, so they elaborate the forms of recognition which form the imaginary relation in which the subject lives. Recognition entails misrecognition, it is a definite mode of the imaginary which does not reflect the totality to men. Ideological knowledges, as a consequence of this point of departure, are necessarily closed, and are condemned to repeat the closure which constitutes the recognition structure. They are condemned to repeat the forms of the imaginary in which the subject exists and lives as a subject. Sciences and ideologies are distinguished by the openness and closure of their discursive structures. That is, they are distinguished by the modes in which they develop and pose problems. The imaginary effects closure. Science, which comes into existence through the epistemological break, breaks the space of recognition. The epistemological break is a shattering of closure and hence creates the possibility of openness, because it breaks the forms of recognition. This entails the notion that science (and this is why Althusser insists on the autonomy of science in the social formation) is a process without a subject. This process begins with a critique of the forms of recognition, and goes beyond subjectivity and the imaginary, so that because it is a process without a subject it transcends the imaginary relation and therefore transcends closure. The autonomy of scientific knowledge from the social formation is argued in terms of the autonomy of scientific knowledge from the imaginary relation. This is the crucial point; Althusser does not believe that scientists sit on clouds. The autonomy involved is the autonomy from the imaginary, the critique breaking the imaginary space.

Science knows ideology to be ideological; it does not know it to be illusory or false. Science as Althusser tries to develop it is not an illusion/reality distinction. There are a lot of problems with that, and I do not subscribe to Althusserian epistemology. But I am prepared to put up the best possible case for Althusser. This is because his position is far more sophisticated than any of the critiques that have been produced of it. Ideology is not illusory for the reason we have given before; it is not illusion, it is not falsity, because how can something which has effects be false? It may derive from forms of the imaginary but it is not false. It would be like saying a black pudding is false, or a steamroller is false. Althusser argues that it is only because science transcends the imaginary relation that it can know what ideology is. How is it possible to defend this position? The answer is that it is not the theory of science which has discovered the imaginary, that somehow the epistemological searchlight has been switched on and we find ourselves living in a world of sophistry and illusion which we are about to commit to the flames. Althusser's position on his own epistemology is that it is possible only within Marxist philosophy. What it is that enables epistemology to deal with the theory of ideology is precisely a particular science, Marxism, and not simply any epistemological theory. This epistemological theory that Althusser advances has the concept of ideology it does, precisely because this epistemology is derived from Marxism.

Althusser would argue that the science/ideology distinction is a strong one, precisely because it rests on a particular science, Marxism, and particularly upon the Marxist theory of ideology. The distinction between science and ideology depends not simply on the concepts of Marxist philosophy, but upon those of historical materialism. A lot of the criticisms of Althusser's epistemology fail to recognise this. For example, how is it possible to reconcile the specificity of forms of proof employed in particular sciences with the claims of a general theory concerning the difference between scientific and ideological discourse? The answer is a relatively simple one – precisely because the general theory is derived from a particular science, namely historical materialism. The concept of ideology involved is a scientific, not a philosophical one. A major difficulty with a lot of this is that the way Althusser develops his argument involves a conjuring trick. He gives us to believe that the theory of ideology has always been there, i.e. that historical materialism contains an already elaborated theory of ideology. Whereas the theory of ideology he in fact depends on is his own.

(6) Conclusion

If one takes Althusser's epistemology and the defences that can be made of it seriously, one must take his theory of ideology seriously. It seems to me that this theory merits thorough analysis. It is, I would argue, the first significant advance in this area of Marxism since the early twentieth century; all the other basic positions have certainly been around since Lukács wrote *History and Class Consciousness*. What Althusser has done in criticising the earlier positions is absolutely central. He has challenged the reductionist and sociologistic mode of analysis of ideologies; challenged the notion of an 'end' to ideology in true consciousness: challenged the notion of ideology as false consciousness; and challenged the idea that ideology is an unreal or illusory reflection. He has generated the problem of the investigation of a definite area of social relations which is relatively independent of the economy and of politics and which has significant political consequences.

7   The Capitalist State and Ideologies*

NICOS POULANTZAS

Nicos Poulantzas was a Greek Marxist philosopher who worked closely with Louis Althusser in Paris during the period of his major influence. Among his most important works are *Political Power and Social Classes* (1973), *State, Power, Socialism* (London: New Left Books, 1978) and *Fascism and Dictatorship* (London: New left Books, 1979).

In this extract from the first of those volumes, Poulantzas criticises the 'historicist' conception of ideology, as exemplified by Lukács and Gramsci. For this theory, the 'essence' of the social formation is a dominant 'class subject', which survives in part by imbuing society as a whole with its own distinctive world vision. This conception, so Poulantzas argues, underrates the autonomy of ideology, and poses too simple and 'expressive' a relation between it, the dominant social class and the social totality. Ideologies are less forms of consciousness specific to a particular class than *relational* entities by which one social class 'lives' its relations to another. A dominant class may adopt the ideology of another class; and subordinated classes are often deeply impregnated with the ideology of their rulers. In all these ways, a reductive view of the relations between class, ideology and society is shown to be inadequate. A more 'structural' analysis of ideological formations is therefore necessary, which takes its starting-point from the material nature of class-conflict and the 'relative autonomy' of the ideological level in society as a whole.

The historicist conception of ideologies

The particular relation between the capitalist type of state and the dominated classes also manifests itself at the ideological level. In fact

---

*Reprinted from NICOS POULANTZAS, *Political Power and Social Classes* (London: New Left Books, 1973), pp. 195–210.

hegemonic class domination, as a particular type of class domination, marks the particular place and function of the ideological in its relations to the political in capitalist formations: in short, it marks the particular way in which *'bourgeois ideology'* functions politically. In fact, this particular feature of bourgeois ideology is merely the political aspect *vis-à-vis* the state of the specific operation of ideology as such, which Marx saw in *Capital* as the condition of existence of the CMP [Capitalist Mode of Production]. The question is all the more important in that it concerns one of the crucial problems of political science, that of *legitimacy*.

On this subject, Gramsci's analyses of class hegemony are very enlightening, especially on this point: on the one hand Gramsci, with amazing acuteness, perceived the problems posed by the political functioning of bourgeois ideology in a capitalist formation; on the other hand, though his analyses are distinct from the typical historicist conception of ideologies as presented for example by Lukács, because of the historicist problematic which essentially governs his work, they demonstrate very clearly the impasses and errors to which this problematic of ideology leads. This is why a radical critique of the historicist conception of ideologies is so important as a prior condition to the scientific posing of the question.

To do this we must first of all briefly mention the problematic of ideology as found in the young Marx, which was centred on the subject. Marx's conception of ideology, as well as of the superstructures in general, was based on the model: *'the subject/the real/alienation'*. The subject is deprived of its concrete essence in the 'real', this concept of the 'real' being constructed theoretically from the ontological objectification of the subject. Ideology is a projection in an imaginary world of the subject's mystified essence, i.e. the alienating 'ideal' reconstitution of its essence, objectified–alienated in the socio-economic real. Ideology, modelled according to the schema of alienation–abstraction, is identified with 'false consciousness'. Thus in the young Marx's elaboration of the concept of ideology there are the following oppositions characteristic of the historicist problematic: state/civil society, superstructures/base, ideology/real, alienation/essence, abstract/concrete.

This conception of ideology has remained alive in the historicist school of Marxism whose problematic is centred on the subject. It has had numerous consequences, including in the first place an inadequate analysis of ideologies in capitalist formations and of their current transformations. In fact, whether the subject is seen as the social class, the concrete individual, social work, praxis, etc., this problematic inevitably identifies *ideology* with *alienation* and results in an inadequate theoretical status being granted to ideologies: these are considered as the 'products' of consciousness (i.e. class consciousness) or of freedom (i.e. freedom of praxis), alienated from the subject. Hence this status of ideologies

presupposes that the 'subject' is at once both alienated and
not-totally-alienated in the 'real'. For example, in the case of a communist
society where the subject is supposed to have recovered his essence,
ideologies have disappeared and given way to a 'scientific' transparency of
consciousness to its objectified existence. But what is more interesting here
is the fact that this perspective dominates the contemporary theme of the
'end of ideology' which, according to some ideologists inspired by
Marxism, characterizes contemporary 'industrial societies'. In fact, in the
case of a total alienation of the subject in the real, ideologies are seen as
having swung 'into reality'; they have done this precisely in so far as
consciousness has been entirely ensnared in, and the subject entirely lost in
the real, and so any possibility of a projection of the essence on to an ideal
world, a projection which is 'alienating' yet in the sole case of the
proletariat (the privileged class in the real) 'liberating' and relatively
coherent, has disappeared. It is this precise invariant relation 'ideology/the
real/alienation' which governs the often implicit theme of the 'end of
ideology' in numerous authors from Marcuse[1] to Adorno[2] and Goldmann.[3]
They interpret contemporary developments of the capitalist formation
closely in accordance with the schema of a total reification–alienation of the
subject in the real in the industrial–technological society. Although there
are notable differences between these authors, the common conclusion
which they reach is, as Marcuse puts it, the 'absorption of ideology into
reality',[4] a claim that contemporary capitalist formations have been
de-ideologized, indeed, de-politicized.

However, the historicist conception of ideologies is even more clearly
expressed in the typical example of Lukács's theory of 'class consciousness'
and 'world-view' (*Weltanschauung*). It is important to dwell on this theory
for it poses clearly the whole problem of the epistemological
presuppositions of a historicist ideological perspective. More important
still, because of Gramsci's historicism as expressed in his views on
dialectical materialism and in particular in his concept of the 'historical
bloc', the majority of Marxist theorists use the concept of hegemony in a
sense relating it to Lukács's problematic. The most important part of my
following remarks is an exposition of the erroneous relation established by
this problematic between the politically dominant class and the dominant
ideology in a formation; and consequently, the relation between the
dominant ideology and the politically dominated classes: more specifically,
it is in this latter context that the extremely debatable consequences of
Gramsci's analysis are located.

In the Lukácsian problematic of the subject, the unity characterizing a
mode of production and a social formation is not that of a complex
ensemble with several specific levels and determined in the last instance by
the economic. In it this unity is reduced to a totality of the functionalist

type, composed of *gestalt* interactions, of which Hegel's concept of the concrete-universal is a good example: in other words it is an *expressive totality*. In this case, the unity of a formation is related to a central instance, originating and giving meaning to this unity. In Lukács, this 'totalizing' instance is represented by the class-subject of history: the unity of a social formation is referred back to the political organization of this class (itself reduced to the role of founding a 'world-view') which erects this world-view into a central principle in the unity of a determined formation. This world-view which encompasses *both ideology and science*,[5] expresses the unity of a formation within a linear and circular totality, in so far as it is related to the central principle of unity, the class-subject. This latter, through its world-view, constitutes the consciousness-will of the 'totality' of men 'who make their own history' through praxis. Thus the role assigned to ideology through the medium of the class-subject is that of the principle of totalizing a social formation, which is precisely the young Marx's position when he held that it is ideas that rule the world and the weapons of criticism that can change it.

This relation between ideology and the unity of a social formation is the more interesting because it governs the contemporary problematic of the 'functionalist' sociological school. It is implicit, as we shall see when discussing legitimacy, in many of the analyses of contemporary political science. In order to bring to light the links between Lukács's Hegelian totality and the functionalist totality, we need only refer to the direct filiation between Lukács and Max Weber. What links the theories of Weber to those of functionalism (as Parsons noted) is that the global structure is, in the last analysis, considered as the *product* of a society-subject which in its teleological becoming creates certain social values or ends. In functionalism, these determine the formal framework for an *integration* of the various particular and 'equivalent' structures in the social 'whole'. This integration is related to an 'equilibrium' based on certain regular and recurrent processes of *normative* elements, e.g., motivations of conduct,[6] which govern social 'action'. For Weber,[7] these social values are the crystallization of social actors' projects and are the elements out of which his ideal types are formed. In the case of the state, his conception leads to a typology exclusively of types of legitimacy, these types being constituted exactly out of the values of the agents–actors. Weber frequently relates the creation of these social values or ends to the action of social groups (the well-known 'status-groups' which he distinguishes from class situations, i.e., classes-in-themselves), which are the subjects of society and history: these considerations are at the basis of his conception of bureaucracy. But the theory of class consciousness of Lukács, whose explicit links with Weber are well known, looks like an attempt at a heavy-handed Marxization of Weber. It presupposes an expressive totality,[8] within which there is simply no role for a dominant factor (as Weber himself quite correctly saw), yet at the same time it attributes to ideology the role of dominant factor in the social whole.[9] Gramsci's historicist conception of dialectical materialism, coupled with the ambiguity of his formulations, has led several theorists to reduce his analyses of class hegemony to the Lukácsian problematic.[10] On such an interpretation, a hegemonic class becomes the class-subject of history which through its world-view manages to permeate a social formation with its unity and to lead, rather than dominate, by bringing about the 'active consent' of the dominated classes. This interpretation of Gramsci is for example very clear in the Marxist school of *New Left Review* which I have had the occasion to criticize elsewhere.[11] It appears in embryo in the following definition of hegemonic class by Perry Anderson, one of the most important representatives of this school: 'If a hegemonic class can be defined as one which imposes its own ends and its own vision on society as a whole, a corporate class is conversely one which pursues its own ends within a social totality whose global determination lies outside it.'[12] It is clear that the unity of a social formation, the social 'totality', is here related to a hegemonic class; its hegemony would consist in constituting a world-view which would establish that class as the unifying principle of a determinate formation: 'A hegemonic class seeks to transform society in its own image, inventing afresh its economic system, its political institutions, its cultural values, its whole "mode of insertion" into the world.'[13]

Moreover, Gramsci undeniably lays himself open to a misinterpretation of his analyses of historical materialism, particularly of his analyses of political domination, i.e. hegemonic class domination, because of his historicist conception of dialectical materialism. This historicism becomes clear in his treatment of the status of ideology, in Gramsci's concept of the 'historical bloc'. This concept allows Gramsci to think the unity of theory and practice, the unity of ideology, encompassing science ('organic intellectuals') and structure; i.e. the unity of a social formation in its ensemble at a historically determined instant. But this unity is precisely the expressive totality of the historicist type, which conflates the ideological and theoretical instances in the ensemble of the social structure. 'The analysis of these propositions tends to reinforce the conception of "historical bloc" in which precisely material forces are the content and ideologies are the form, though this distinction between form and content has purely didactic value.'[14] In this context the historical bloc is merely the theoretical formulation of the Hegelian historical 'present', the co-presence of instances in the expressive totality of linear becoming, with ideology conceived as the mere expression of history. This role of central principle of unity of a formation attributed to ideology/world-view is also manifest in the somewhat ambiguous metaphor, in Gramsci's context of ideology as the 'cement' of a formation: 'This problem is that of preserving the ideological unity of the entire social bloc which that ideology serves to cement and to unify . . . ' Or again: 'One might say "ideology" here, but on condition that the word is used in its highest sense of a conception of the world that is implicitly manifest in art, in law, in economic activity and in all manifestations of individual and collective life.'[15]

However, it is also true that we find several theoretical breaks in Gramsci's work, particularly in his analyses of dialectical and historical materialism: a *symptomal reading* of Gramsci, which is outside the scope of this work, would certainly reveal the scientific and original features contained (under the polemical cover of 'absolute historicism') in his conception of ideology. We may simply mention two of them here:

(a) Gramsci's metaphor of ideology as the 'cement' of a society poses the major problem of the relation between the dominant ideology and the unity of a social formation in an original manner.

(b) In the history of Marxist thought Gramsci is the first to break with the conception of ideology as a conceptual system, in the strict sense of these two terms.

Dominant ideology, dominant class and social formation

How can the Lukácsian problematic explain the Marxist tenet that the dominant ideology in a social formation is generally that of the dominant class? In other words, how does it explain the fact that the dominant ideology, possessing a unity of its own and thus reflecting in a relatively coherent universe the ensemble of the social formation which it permeates, is that of the dominant class? This is, in fact, *three series* of questions concerning the relation between the dominant ideology and the unity of a social formation:

(1) Concerning that specific unity and relative coherence (what the Lukácsian problematic happily terms 'totality of meaning') belonging to the ideological universe, i.e. to a formation's dominant ideology considered as a *regional structure* of instances.

(2) Concerning the fact that this coherent universe is a dominant ideology precisely in so far as it also permeates the dominated classes, and becomes their world-view also, i.e. in so far as its internal coherence corresponds to the ensemble of classes engaged in struggle in a formation.

(3) Concerning the fact that this dominant ideology is that of the dominant class.

It is useful to separate these three series of questions since their Lukácsian explanation depends precisely on conflating them, by reference to the generic principle of the class-subject of society and history. Once the unity of a formation is attributed to a class-subject and hence to the 'consciousness' of this class, the role of central determinant instance of the social whole will be attributed to that global world-view, which is the direct product of this class. So the answer to these questions will reside in the genetic relation between the dominant ideology and the class 'for itself', the subject of history. As Lukács says:

> For a class to be ripe for hegemony means that its interests and consciousness enable it to organize the whole of society in accordance with those interests. The crucial question in every class struggle is this: which class possesses this capacity and this consciousness at the decisive moment? . . . The question then becomes: how far does the class concerned perform the actions history has imposed on it 'consciously' or 'unconsciously'? And is that consciousness 'true' or 'false'?[16]

The dominant ideology both presents a unity and constitutes a characteristic world-view of the ensemble of a formation in so far as it is genetically related to the dominant class – or rather, to the rising class. This class, which is the subject of a historical becoming, progresses through broader and broader totalizations until it reaches the final coincidence of objectification and essence; it is always pregnant with the meaning of history and concretely incarnates the totality of meaning and unity of a social formation.

This conception of ideology leads to a whole series of errors of which I shall indicate only the more important.

(A) In general it leads to what can be termed an *over-politicization* of ideologies, the latter being considered as if they were political number-plates worn by social classes on their backs. The ideological structure is reduced to the political organization of a class and this political organization is constituted by its *own* world-view which establishes it as a class-for-itself, the subject of history. In this way, political class consciousness is identified with the function performed by the world-view. Consequently no specific autonomy can be attributed to the ideological instance. In particular, it is impossible in this conception to decipher the concrete relation between the dominant ideology and the politically dominant class or fraction. It leads to errors when we try to locate precisely the dominant class or fraction in a historically determined situation. In fact one of the indices permitting this location is to be found precisely in the relation between the dominant class or fraction and the structures of the dominant ideology: but this relation cannot be admitted in the Lukácsian problematic, except in the very rare cases in which the dominant ideology appears in the 'purity' of its relation to the dominant class or fraction. But in reality, the dominant ideology does not simply reflect the conditions of existence of the dominant class, the 'pure and simple' subject, but rather the concrete political relation between the dominant and the dominated classes in a social formation. It is often permeated by elements stemming from the 'way of life' of classes or fractions other than the dominant class or fraction. We have, for example, the classic case in which the dominant bourgeois ideology of capitalist formations receives 'elements' of petty-bourgeois ideology ('Jacobinism' and its successor 'radicalism'), and even of working-class ideology – the 'bourgeois socialism' described by Engels (e.g. Saint-Simonism during the Second Empire in France).[17]

Furthermore, owing to the specific autonomy of the ideological instance, and to the very status of the ideological in the structures, the relations between the dominant ideology and the dominant class or fractions are always masked. In the complex constitution of the ideological level, this ideology which (like all ideologies) hides its own principles from itself may appear closer to the way in which a class or fraction other than the dominant class or fraction experiences its conditions of existence. In short we can establish the possibility of a whole series of dislocations between the dominant ideology and the politically hegemonic class or fraction. These can be due to several factors: for example, to the concrete function of the caste of 'intellectuals'; or again to the uneven development of the various levels of the structures due to their specific rhythm and to their dislocation from the field of class practices. For example, a dominant ideology profoundly impregnated by the way of life of a class or fraction can continue to remain the dominant ideology even if this class or fraction is no longer dominant; in the latter case the ideology is not a mere 'survival' but is subject to a whole series of modifications with regard to its concrete political functioning. We can decipher these however only on condition that we break with the historicist problematic of ideology. The typical example of this case is Britain, where the displacement of the index of political dominance from the aristocracy to the bourgeoisie is characterized by the permanence of a dominant, though modified, aristocratic ideology. The Lukácsian problematic will mask the way in which this index has changed, since from the permanence of aristocratic ideology it will deduce the continuity of the domination of the feudal class.[18] In short, this problematic cannot establish an adequate relation between the series of questions indicated above; it only poses the question of the relation between the dominant ideology and the politically dominant class.

(B) Moreover it can lead to errors on the question of the relations between the dominant ideology and the *dominated classes*. This is demonstrated by one of Gramsci's own theses in which he incorrectly extends the concept of hegemony to the strategy of the working class. Though this thesis may appear to contradict the explicit conclusions of this problematic, it does however stem from the same theoretical principles and has to a large extent contributed to the falsification of the scientific content of the concept of hegemony, in the sense that hegemony is no longer considered as a type of class domination. Gramsci introduces a theoretical break between *hegemony* and *domination*. According to him, a class can and must become the leading[19] class *before* it becomes a politically dominant class; and it can win hegemony before the conquest of political power. In this context, the concept of hegemony effectively indicates the fact that a class imposes its own world-view on a formation and so (in this sense) gains ideological domination *before* the conquest of political power. But Gramsci applied this theoretical analysis to working-class strategy in opposition to Leninist theses. On many occasions Lenin insisted on the fact that in the case of a concrete conjuncture of transition from capitalism to socialism (as opposed to certain cases of transition from feudalism to capitalism, e.g. the case of the bourgeoisie in France), the working class cannot gain ideological domination before conquering political power. This analysis is at the root of Lenin's texts on the necessity of the ideological organization of the working class by its party. Gramsci's thesis is on the face of it opposed to the Lukácsian problematic in so far as it advocates a dislocation between the dominant ideology (which for Gramsci could be that of the dominated class) and the politically dominant class. Nevertheless, it flows from the same principles: the problem of the political organization of a class is apparently related to the elaboration of a world-view which it imposes on the ensemble of society.

In this case it is, however, impossible for a class not only to be politically dominant but even to have a strictly political organization without having gained the position of dominant ideology, since its ideological organization coincides with its emergence as class-subject of society and of history. Here we recognize Lukács's analyses of the proletariat's class consciousness, modelled on the general theme of the 'rising class', the bearer of the meaning of history. It is in this light that we can see in Gramsci's thesis the logical consequence of the Lukácsian thesis. Gramsci's dislocation between the ideologically dominant class (the hegemonic proletariat) and the politically dominant class (the bourgeoisie), i.e. the *historical* dislocation (which takes on the appearance of a *theoretical* dislocation in this thesis) between hegemony and domination, simply enables him to explain the facts by an inadequate theory, which provides an apparent contradiction to the Lukácsian conception. This also explains why Gramsci always thought that he had found this usage of the concept of hegemony in Lenin: Lenin indeed stressed the necessity for the autonomous ideological organization of the working class, but only as one of the aspects of its political organization. His theory differs importantly from Gramsci's in that according to it, (1) ideological organization has nothing to do with the proletariat's conquest of ideological domination before the taking of power, and (2) ideological organization is even systematically conceived as being directed against the dominant ideology: even after the conquest of power this dominant ideology continues for a long time to remain bourgeois and petty bourgeois.

(C) Finally, if ideologies were seen as number-plates carried on the backs of class-subjects (as in the historicist picture), it would be impossible (1) to establish the existence within the dominant ideology of elements belonging to the ideologies of classes other than the politically dominant class and (2) *to account for the permanent possibility of contamination of working-class ideology by the dominant and petty-bourgeois ideologies.* According to this conception of ideology there can be no *world over and beyond* the ideology of each class: these various ideologies each function as it were in a vacuum. Hence it is impossible to see the effects of ideological domination by the dominant ideology on working-class ideology. This leads directly to various forms of *spontaneism* and to its practical consequences: simply because it is the ideology of the proletariat–universal class, working-class ideology is considered to possess the keys to Marxist science. Yet numerous texts of Marx, Engels and Lenin show that the spontaneous ideology of the working class was at the root of anarcho-syndicalism and later of trade-unionism and of reformism: this is merely the effect of the permanent domination of working-class ideology by the dominant bourgeois and petty-bourgeois ideology. This conception is also at the base of Lenin's acceptance of the famous Kautskyist thesis according to which revolutionary ideology must be imported into the working class from outside. Whereas amongst the representatives of the leftist movement of the 1920s, some (Lukács, Korsch, etc.) propounded the thesis according to which the intellectuals should be rejected since the proletariat was its own intellectual, others (Rosa Luxemburg, etc.) failed to recognize the ideological role of the party. In short, the revolutionary ideology of the working class can exist only on the basis of a permanent critique of its spontaneous ideology by Marxist science. Such a critique presupposes a radical distinction between *ideology* and *science*, which cannot be made within the historicist conception.[20]

The Marxist conception of ideologies

In order to reveal the particular political function of ideologies in the case of hegemonic class domination, it is necessary to establish a scientific link between the three series of questions noted above, concerning the relation between the dominant ideology and the politically dominant class. To do this we must return to the status of the ideological.

Ideology consists of a specific objective level, of a *relatively coherent* ensemble of representations, values and beliefs: just as 'men', the agents within a formation, participate in an economic and political activity, they also participate in religious, moral, aesthetic and philosophical activities.[21] Ideology concerns the world in which men live, their relations to nature, to society, to other men and to their own activity including their own economic and political activity. The status of the ideological derives from the fact that it reflects the manner in which the agents of a formation, the bearers of its structures, live their conditions of existence; i.e. it reflects their relation to these conditions as it is 'lived' by them. Ideology is present to such an extent in all the agents' activities that it becomes indistinguishable from their *lived experience*. To this extent ideologies fix in a relatively coherent universe not only a real but also an *imaginary relation*: i.e. men's real relation to their conditions of existence in the form of an imaginary relation. This means that in the last analysis ideologies are related to human experience without being thereby reduced to a problematic of the subject-consciousness. This social-imaginary relation, which performs a real practical–social function, cannot be reduced to the problematic of alienation and false consciousness.

It follows that through its constitution ideology is involved in the functioning of this social-imaginary relation, and is therefore *necessarily* false; its social function is not to give agents a *true knowledge* of the social structure but simply to insert them as it were into their practical activities supporting this structure. Precisely because it is determined by its structure, at the level of experience the social whole remains *opaque* to the agents. In class-divided societies this opacity is over-determined by class exploitation and by the forms which this exploitation takes in order to be able to function in the social whole. Hence, even if it includes *elements* of knowledge, ideology necessarily manifests an adequation/inadequation *vis-à-vis* the real; it was this which Marx grasped under the term 'inversion'. It also follows that ideology is not itself visible to the agents in its internal action; like all levels of social reality ideology is determined by its own structure which remains opaque to the agents on the level of experience. This brings us to the problem of the specific unity of the ideological, i.e. of its *structure* and its relation to the dominant class. This unity of the ideological is not derived from some kind of genetic relation to a class-subject and its class consciousness. It is derived fundamentally from the relation between ideology and human experience in a formation, and to the imaginary form which this relation takes on. As opposed to science ideology has the precise function of hiding the real contradictions and of *reconstituting* on an imaginary level a relatively coherent discourse which serves as the horizon of agents' experience; it does this by moulding their representations of their real relations and inserting these in the overall unity of the relations of a formation. This is certainly the fundamental meaning of the ambiguous metaphor of '*cement*' used by Gramsci to designate the social function of ideology. Ideology, which slides into every level of the social structure, has the particular function of *cohesion*. It fulfils this function by establishing at the level of agents' experience relations which are obvious but false, and which allow their practical activities (division of labour, etc.) to function within the unity of a formation. Consequently this coherence specific to the ideological differs from that of science precisely because of their different social functions. As opposed to the scientific notion of system, ideology refuses to allow a contradiction within it, but attempts to resolve any contradiction by excluding it.[22] In other words the structures of ideological and scientific discourse are fundamentally different.

In this sense, if we abandon the conception of ideology as a *conceptual system* (in the strict sense of both of these terms) we can say that it encompasses what is often described as the 'culture' of a formation: provided, of course, that we do not fall into the mistake of ethnological culturalism which generally uses this term to cover a 'social formation' in its ensemble.[23] As Gramsci clearly realized, ideology encompasses not merely scattered elements of knowledge, notions etc., but also the whole process of symbolization, of mythical transposition, of 'taste', 'style', 'fashion', i.e. of the 'way of life' in general.

But the limits of this ambiguous metaphor of 'cement' must be pointed out. It must under no circumstances be applied to the agents of a formation, the bearers of structures, as the origin and central subject of these structures; nor must it be applied at the level of 'experience' to men as the producers of the unity of the ideology. This is because the coherence (unity) specific to ideological discourse, which is necessarily involved both in the imaginary form taken on by agents' experience and also in its function of masking real contradictions from scientific investigation, does not cause but rather presupposes the decentration of the subject at the level of supports. In fact the above considerations have demonstrated that it is necessary for the coherence of ideological discourse to be related to its social function, but they have not yet determined the principles of this coherence, i.e. of the *hidden structure* of the dominant ideology. Ideology, as a specific instance of a mode of production and social formation, is constituted within the limits fixed by this mode and this formation in that it offers an *imaginary coherence* to the unity governing the real contradictions of the ensemble of this formation. The structure of the ideological depends on the fact that it *reflects* the unity of a social formation. From this point of view, its specific, real role as unifier is not that of constituting the unity of a formation (as the historicist conception would have it) but that of reflecting that unity by *reconstituting* it on an imaginary plane. Hence, the dominant ideology of a social formation encompasses the 'totality' of this formation not because it constitutes the 'class consciousness' of a historico-social subject, but because it reflects (with those biases of *inversion* and *mystification* which are specific to it) the index of articulation of the instances which specifies the unity of this formation. As in the case of every other instance, the region of the ideological is fixed in its limits by the global structure of a mode of production and social formation.

We can thus determine the precise meaning of the relation between dominant ideology and politically dominant class in class-divided societies. In these societies the original function of ideology is over-determined by the class relations in which the structures distribute their agents. The correspondence between the dominant ideology and the politically dominant class is not due (any more than the specific internal coherence of the ideology is) to some kind of historico-genetic relation. It is due to the fact that the ideological (i.e. a given ideology) is constituted as regional instance within the unity of the structure; and this structure has the domination of a given class as its effect in the field of the class struggle. The dominant ideology, by assuring the practical insertion of agents in the social structure, aims at the maintenance (the cohesion) of this structure, and this means *above all* class domination and exploitation. It is precisely in this way that within a social formation ideology is dominated by the ensemble of representations, values, notions, beliefs, etc. by means of which class domination is perpetuated: in other words, it is dominated by what can be called the ideology of the dominant class.

In this way it can easily be understood that the structure (unity) of the dominant ideology cannot be deciphered from its relations with a class consciousness/world-view, considered in a vacuum, *but from the starting-point of the field of the class struggle,* i.e. from the concrete relation between the various classes in struggle, the relation within which class domination functions. Hence we can understand not only why the dominated classes necessarily experience their relation to their conditions of existence within the discourse of the dominant ideology, but also why this discourse often presents elements borrowed from ways of life other than that of the dominant class. Lenin points this out in an enlightening way: 'The *elements* of democratic and socialist culture are present, if only in a rudimentary form, in every national culture . . . But *every* nation also possesses a bourgeois culture, in the form, not merely of "elements" but of the dominant culture.'[24]

The dominant ideology contains features from ideologies other than that of the dominant class, incorporated as 'elements' in its own structure; but we also find in capitalist formations true *ideological sub-ensembles* which function with a relative autonomy *vis-à-vis* the dominant ideology within a formation: e.g. feudal and petty-bourgeois sub-ensembles. These sub-ensembles are dominated by the ideologies of the corresponding classes – feudal, petty bourgeois – but only to the extent that these ideologies which dominate the ideological sub-ensembles *are themselves*

dominated by the dominant ideology; we shall see below the form in which
this happens. Furthermore these ideological sub-ensembles themselves
contain elements stemming from ideologies other than those which
dominate them, or other than the dominant ideology of a formation. This is
characteristically the case in the recurring relations between the ideologies
of the petty bourgeoisie and the working class.

Notes

1. *One-Dimensional Man* (Boston, 1964) and 'Uber das Ideologieproblem in der
   Hochentwickelten Industriegesellschaft' in Kurt Lenk (ed.), *Ideologie* (Neuwied,
   1961), pp. 334ff.
2. *Prisms* (London, 1967).
3. *Pour une sociologie du roman* (Paris, 1964).
4. Op. cit., p. 11. It should be noticed that Marcuse refuses, explicitly, to reach the
   conclusion of the 'end of ideologies'.
5. This identification of ideology and science, or the conception of ideology as
   encompassing science, itself goes back to the relation between the subjective and
   the objective within the framework of a problematic of the subject. In fact, the
   subjective character of ideology as the expression of the subject encompasses the
   objectivity of science in the case in which a 'rising class's' subjective
   consciousness of the world takes in the totality of a social formation. This side of
   the argument, as applied by Lukács, Korsch, etc. to the proletariat and
   'proletarian science' is well known. According to it, the proletariat is in essence a
   universal class, so its subjectivity is universal; but a universal subjectivity can
   only be objective, therefore scientific. The consequence of this conception is also
   well known – spontaneism.
6. Motivations of conduct in the strict sense of the term. This leads exactly to
   Adorno's notion of 'political temperament' (see ADORNO and HORKHEIMER, *The
   Authoritarian Personality*, New York, 1950).
7. On the connections between Weber's and Lukács's theories of classes, which have
   been almost ignored in France, see WEBER, *Gesammelte politische Schriften*
   (Tübingen, 1958), pp. 294–431, especially 'Parlament und Regierung im
   neugeordneten Deutschland', written in 1918. As to the connections between
   Weber and Parsons, Parsons certainly misinterprets Weber's work in some
   respects: see *The Social System* (New York, 1964), pp. 100ff., 519ff., etc. However,
   the relation between Weber and functionalism which he establishes is in the last
   analysis correct. On the problem of Weber's historicism, it should be noted that
   Weber himself made an explicit critique of the historicist 'totality', particularly in
   his analyses of Eduard Meyer's work (see *Gesammelte Aufsätze zur
   Wissenschaftslehre*). However, despite his warnings, his theory may be considered
   as a 'typical' historicist theory. On the relations between Weber's 'ideal type' and
   Hegel's 'concrete-universal' concept, see especially K. LARENZ, *Methodenlehre der
   Rechtswissenschaft* (1960).
8. Weber's historicism goes hand in hand with the conception of an expressive
   totality of the social whole without a dominant instance, as is clear in his theory
   of *'factors'* and *'variables'*. It is also found in *The Protestant Ethic and the Spirit of*

Capitalism (London, 1930), and particularly in *Gesammelte Aufsätze zur Religionssoziologie.*

9. There is no better example of this perspective, applied to political analysis, than the work of Marcuse, although it leads him to different results. As long ago as 1935, for instance, he admitted that the unity of a social formation (as opposed to a purely 'functionalist' conception) lay in the 'dominance' of a certain element of this formation over the others. However, he saw this element as the consciousness-cum-world-view of a class which was ideologically dominant in this formation (*Kultur und Gesellschaft* (Frankfurt, 1965), pp. 34ff.). Marcuse now argues that a global de-ideologization characterizes industrial societies; from this he concludes that a social formation is an integrated Hegelian-functionalist 'totality', in the absence of an ideologically dominant class and in the absence of a proletarian 'class consciousness' which would 'countervail the whole' (*One Dimensional Man*, op. cit., pp. 51ff.).

10. A characteristic example is L. MAGRI, 'Problems of the Marxist theory of the revolutionary party' in *New Left Review*, **60** (March/April 1970).

11. N. POULANTZAS, 'Marxist Political Theory in Great Britain' in *New Left Review*, **43** (May/June 1967). I must however point out that this school's theoretical conceptions have in the meantime developed considerably.

12. P. ANDERSON, 'Origins of the Present Crisis' in *New Left Review*, **23** (January/February 1964), p. 41.

13. Ibid.

14. *Prison Notebooks* (London: Lawrence and Wishart, 1971), p. 377.

15. Ibid., p. 328.

16. *History and Class Consciousness* (London, 1971), pp. 52–3.

17. See C. WILLARD, *Socialisme et communisme français* (1967), pp. 18ff.

18. See N. POULANTZAS, 'Marxist Political Theory in Great Britain', op. cit.

19. Following the English translation of Gramsci's *Prison Notebooks*, *dirigente* is translated 'leading', in contrast to 'dominant' (trans.).

20. The fact that Gramsci always combated 'spontaneism' can be explained by the theoretical breaks in his own work.

21. See L. ALTHUSSER, 'Marxism and Humanism', *For Marx* (London, 1965).

22. Cf. MACHEREY, 'Lénine, Critique de Tolstoi', *Pour une théorie de la production littéraire* (Paris, 1966).

23. Cf. R. ESTABLET in *Démocratie Nouvelle* (June 1966).

24. 'Critical Notes on the National Question', *Collected Works*, Vol. 20, p. 24.

8 On the Theory of Ideology – Althusser's Politics*

JACQUES RANCIÈRE

Jacques Rancière is a political theorist who was a colleague of Louis Althusser during the 1960s and collaborated with him on his major work *Reading Capital* (London: New Left Books, 1969). The following essay, written in the wake of the political turbulence in Paris of May 1968, marks Rancière's decisive break with his mentor's theory of ideology. The theory, so Rancière claims, is excessively 'sociologistic', passing over the realities of ideological struggle for some more ahistorical concept of ideology as the 'cement' of the social formation as a whole, and its 'metaphysical' opposition of science and ideology is unable to come to terms with the class character of the universities, a character for Rancière dramatically exposed by the events of 1968.

> 'Certainly it is an interesting event we are dealing with: the putrescence of the absolute spirit'
>
> (Marx and Engels, *The German Ideology*, Part I)

'All the mysteries which lead theory into mysticism find their rational solution in human practice and in the understanding of that practice.' For a long time the main mystery as far as we were concerned was this sentence itself. We gave it a not unmystical solution: like the young theologians of Tübingen seminary, scouring the undergrowth to discover new 'faculties', we would multiply 'practices', each endowed with specific laws. In the forefront of course lay theoretical practice, containing the principles of its own verification. This was how we interpreted the question – the more so as its own opponents could only counter with a practice reduced, in the name of 'praxis', to the invocation of itself.

In May 1968 things were suddenly thrown into relief. When the class

*Reprinted from JACQUES RANCIÈRE, 'On the Theory of Ideology – Althusser's Politics' in R. Edgley and P. Osborne (eds), *Radical Philosophy Reader* (London: Verso, 1985), pp. 101–22.

struggle broke out openly in the universities, the status of the Theoretical came to be challenged, no longer by the endless verbiage of praxis and the concrete, but by the reality of a mass ideological revolt. No longer could any 'Marxist' discourse keep going on the mere affirmation of its own rigour. The class struggle, which put the bourgeois system of knowledge at issue, posed to all of us the question of our ultimate political significance, of our revolutionary or counter-revolutionary character.

In this conjuncture, the political significance of Althusserianism was shown to be quite different from what we had thought. Not only did the Althusserian theoretical presuppositions prevent us from understanding the political meaning of the student revolt. But further, within a year we saw Althusserianism serving the hacks of revisionism in a theoretical justification for the 'anti-leftist' offensive and the defence of academic knowledge. What we had previously chosen to ignore thus became clear: the link between the Althusserian interpretation of Marx and revisionist politics was not simply a dubious coexistence, but an effective political and theoretical solidarity.

The following remarks seek to indicate the point in the Althusserian reading where this interdependence is established: namely, the theory of ideology.

The analysis of ideology

The specificity of the Althusserian theory of ideology can be summarized in two basic theses:
  (1) In all societies – whether divided into classes or not – ideology has a common principal function: to assure the cohesion of the social whole by regulating the relation of individuals to their tasks.
  (2) Ideology is the opposite of science.

The critical function of thesis (1) is clear: it is directed against ideologies of 'de-alienation' according to which the end of capitalist alienation would be the end of the mystification of consciousness, the advent of a world where the relations of man to nature and of man to man would be perfectly transparent – in a certain sense, the Pauline transition from indistinct perception in the mirror to direct perception. Against these ideologies of transparency, Althusser sets the necessary opacity of every social structure to its agents. Ideology is present in every social totality by virtue of the determination of this totality by its structure. To this there corresponds a general function: that of supplying the system of representations which allow the agents of the social totality to accomplish the tasks determined by this structure. 'In a society without classes, just as in a class society, ideology has the function of securing the *bond* between men in the ensemble of the forms of their existence, the relation of individuals to their tasks fixed by the social structure.'[1]

So the concept of ideology can be defined in its generality before the concept of class struggle intervenes. To some extent, the class struggle will subsequently 'overdetermine'[2] the principal function of ideology.

We would like to examine how this thesis is established and how it is articulated with the second in a particularly explicit text:

> Ideology, in class societies, is a representation of the real, but a necessarily false one because it is necessarily aligned and tendentious – and it is tendentious because its goal is not to give men objective knowledge of the social system in which they live, but on the contrary to give them a mystified representation of this social system in order to keep them in their 'place' in the system of class exploitation. Of course, it is also necessary to pose the problem of ideology's function in a society without classes – and this would then be resolved by showing that the deformation of ideology is socially necessary as a function of the very nature of the social whole: more specifically, as a function of its determination by its structure which renders this social whole opaque to the individuals who occupy a place in it determined by this structure. The representation of the world indispensable to social cohesion is necessarily mystical, owing to the opacity of the social structure. In class societies, this principal function of ideology still exists, but is dominated by the additional social function imposed on it by the existence of class division. This additional function thus by far outweighs the first. If we want to be exhaustive, if we want to take these two principles of necessary deformation into account, we must say that in a class society ideology is necessarily distorting and mystifying, both because it is made distorting by the opacity of society's determination by the structure, and because it is made distorting by the existence of class division.[3]

Our first problem is the nature of the concepts put forward to define the general function of ideology: the notion of 'social cohesion' echoes the formula used above – 'the bond between men in the ensemble of the forms of their existence'. Is this 'bond' or 'cohesion' of the 'social whole' really the province of Marxist analysis? How, after having proclaimed that the whole history of mankind is that of the class struggle, can it define functions like: *securing social cohesion in general*? Is it not precisely because Marxist theory has nothing to say on this subject, that we have shifted our ground and moved on to that of a Comtean or Durkheimian type of sociology, which actually does concern itself with the systems of representation that secure or break up the cohesion of the social group? Is it not this phantasm of 'the social group' which is outlined here in Althusser's analysis? We can see an index of this displacement in the status Althusser here accords religion: 'In primitive societies where classes do not exist, one can already verify the existence of this bond, and it is no accident that its reality has been detected in the first general form of ideology, religion. (It is one of the possible etymologies of the word *religion*.)'[4]

By inverting the analysis we can pose this question: when ideology is conceived in general, before conceiving the class struggle, is it not necessarily conceived on the model of the traditional analysis of religion – that of a sociology which has inherited metaphysical discourse on society?[5] The *superimposition* of two functions of ideology (maintenance of social cohesion in general; and exercise of class domination) may thus signify for us the *coexistence* of two heterogeneous conceptual systems: that of historical materialism and that of a bourgeois sociology of the Durkheimian type. Althusser's special trick is to transform this coexistence into an articulation, which implies a double subversion.

First, ideology is defined not on the terrain of Marxism but on that of a general sociology (theory of the social whole in general). Marxist theory is then superimposed on this *sociological* theory of ideology as a theory of over-determination specific to class societies. The concepts defining the function of ideology in a class society will therefore depend on concepts from this general sociology.

But, secondly, the level of this general sociology is itself claimed to be a level of the Marxist theory of ideology, despite the fact that Marxism has nothing to say about it. This reverses the process: the analysis of the alleged general function of ideology will be made on the basis of the concepts and analyses by which Marxist theory has thought the function of ideology in class societies. Marxist concepts defining class societies will be used to define society in general.

The mechanics of this subversion are clearly revealed when Althusser describes the double determination of ideology in class societies: 'In a class society, ideology is necessarily distorting and mystifying, both because it is made distorting by the opacity of society's determination by the structure, and because it is made distorting by the existence of class division.'[6]

What is this structure, whose level is here distinguished from that of class division? In Marxist terms, the determination of a social totality by its structure means its determination by the *relations of production* characterizing a dominant mode of production. But 'relations of production' refers to the social forms of appropriation of the means of production, which are class forms of appropriation. Capitalist relations of production exhibit the class opposition between those who possess the means of production and those who sell their labour power. The distinction between the two levels disregards the fact that the level of the 'structure' is strictly the level of a class relation.[7]

The analysis of fetishism demonstrates this point very clearly. For it is not enough to say that fetishism is the manifestation-dissimulation of the relations of production (as I did in *Reading Capital*). What it specifically conceals is the *antagonistic* character of the relations of production: the Capital/Labour opposition disappears in the juxtaposition of the sources of revenue. The structure is not concealed because, like Heraclitan nature, it simply likes to hide. It disguises its *contradictory* nature, and this contradiction is a class contradiction. So the manifestation/dissimulation of the structure does not imply an opacity of the 'social structure in general': it is the effectivity of the relations of production; that is, of the class opposition 'labourers/non-labourers' which characterizes all class societies. Extended beyond class societies, this effectivity of the structure becomes a completely undetermined concept – or alternatively, it is determined by standing in for a traditional figure of metaphysics: the evil genie or the cunning of reason.

Ideology and struggle

The distinction between two levels of ideological disguise is thus highly problematic. It clearly functions by *analogy* with Marx's analysis of the two-fold nature of every production process (the labour-process in general, and the socially determined process of production). But the analogy is clearly illegitimate. By transferring the law of the last instance to the superstructures, by making the effects reproduce the law of the cause, it posits the social whole as a totality of levels each of which expresses the same law. It is easy to see the absurdity that would result from an application of the same principle to the political superstructure: one might then say that the 'social totality in general' requires the existence of a political superstructure and define the general functions of a State before touching on the class struggle. This comparison of ours is more than a mere joke: ideology for Althusser may well possess the same status as that conferred on the State by classical metaphysical thought. And it may well be that his analysis reinstates the myth of an ideological state of nature – a myth whose theoretical and political meaning we must now make clear.

First we have to appreciate the irrevocable consequence of the distinction between two levels. Ideology is not seen from the start as the site of a struggle. It is related not to two antagonists but to a totality of which it forms a natural element: 'It is as if human societies could not survive without these *specific formations*, these systems of representations (at various levels), their ideologies. Human societies secrete ideology as the very element and atmosphere indispensable to their historical respiration and life.'[8]

To put the myths of origins (or ends) in the restrictive form of 'as if' is a standard act of philosophical modesty, perfected in Kant; and this is not the only time we shall come across Althusser's Kantianism. In the traditional 'as if', ideas of origin preserve their political function of concealing division. Ideology will thus be established not as the site of a division, but as a totality unified by its relation to its referent (the social whole). At the same time, the analysis of the second level will focus not on the ideological forms of class struggle, but on the 'over-determination of Ideology' (in the singular) by class division. One will speak of the ideology of a class society, not of class ideologies. Only at the end of the analysis is the division of ideology into 'tendencies'[9] admitted. But at this stage its introduction is no longer of any use: ideology, not having been initially posited as the field of a struggle, will in the meantime have surreptitiously become one of *the participants in the struggle*. The class struggle in ideology, forgotten at the start, reappears in a chimerical, fetishized form as a class struggle between ideology (weapon of the dominant class) and science (weapon of the dominated class).

Before commenting on them in detail, let us indicate the stages in this logic of forgetfulness:

(1) Ideology is a system of representations controlling, in all societies, the relation of individuals to the tasks fixed by the structure of the social whole.

(2) This system of representations is thus not a system of knowledge. On the contrary, it is the system of illusions necessary to the historical subjects.

(3) In a class society, ideology acquires a supplementary function of keeping individuals in the place determined by class domination.

(4) The principle which undermines such domination therefore belongs to ideology's opposite, i.e. science.

The strategic move in this proof is that which articulates the function of ideology with the domination of a class. 'Ideology, in class societies, is a representation of the real, but a necessarily false one because it is necessarily aligned and tendentious – and it is tendentious because its goal is not to give men *objective* knowledge of the social system in which they live, but on the contrary, to give them a mystified representation of this social system in order to keep them in their "place" in the system of class exploitation.'[10]

By articulating two theses (ideology as the opposite of knowledge; ideology in the service of a class) which were previously only *juxtaposed*, Althusser sets forth the mechanism which, at a deeper level, ties them together: ideology is a false representation because it does not give knowledge. And it does not give knowledge because it is in the service of the ruling class. But what ideology is involved here? Would the ideology of the dominated class have the function of keeping the exploited 'in their place' in the system of class exploitation? What is defined here as a

function of *Ideology* is the function of the *dominant* ideology. To conceive of
a general function of ideology, Althusser has to present the domination of
an ideology as the domination of *ideology*. The trick has been played: the
general function of ideology will be said to be exercised to the profit of a
class domination, and the function of undermining this domination will be
conferred on the Other of Ideology, that is, on Science. The initial
suppression of the class struggle leads to a particularly interesting game of
theoretical hide-and-seek. The 'Ideology/Science' couple proceeds to
reintroduce the class struggle. But the latter also comes to the assistance of
the 'Science/Ideology' opposition – ideology had at first only been posited
as *other than science*; by being articulated with class domination, with the
radical opposition 'dominant class/dominating class', this *other than science*
has become the Other of Science. Difference has become contradiction.

What is this but the very process established by metaphysics and
consistently repeated throughout its history: the process which answers the
old problem of the *Sophist* – how, in the figure of the Other, to conceive
difference as contradiction?[11] That here Marxism serves to accomplish this
necessary yet impossible task of philosophy, is something to which we will
have to return. It is enough for the moment to point out the significance of
the displacement which has taken place in the conception of ideology.
Ideology is firstly an instance of the social whole. As such, it is *articulated*
with other instances, not confronted with any opposite. It is within
ideology itself that the oppositions that concern it are determined: above
all, that which opposes the ideology of one class to the ideology of another.
How then can the 'Ideology/Science' couple become the pertinent
opposition with which to grasp ideology? Only by a process which
detaches ideology from the system of instances, and erases the main
division of the ideological field to create a space in Marxist theory which it
then shares out between science and ideology. The functioning of the
'Science/Ideology' opposition depends on the re-establishment of a space
homologous to that of the whole metaphysical tradition: it supposes the
closure of a universe of discourse, divided into the realms of the true and
the false, into the world of Science and that of its Other (opinion, error,
illusion, etc.). If ideology is not fundamentally grasped as the site of a
struggle, of a class struggle, it immediately slips into this place determined
by the history of metaphysics: the place of the Other of Science.

Teachers and students

We have so far shown only the general form of this displacement. We will
now specify its functioning, by showing how the Science/Ideology couple
works in a *political* analysis. Two of Althusser's texts – the article

'Problèmes Etudiants' and the text 'Marxism and Humanism'[12] – are in fact devoted to the political consequences of the theory of ideology.

The article 'Problèmes Etudiants' was an intervention in the conflict that had arisen between the French Communist Party's (PCF) theses on the university, and the theses then dominant in the National Union of French Students (UNEF). The latter sought to oppose the simply 'quantitative' demands of the PCF (increase in the number of universities and academic staff, etc.) with a 'qualitative' questioning of the teaching relationship, conceived, through the concept of alienation, as analogous to a class relation. Althusser's intervention was meant to draw the real lines of demarcation for the political and trade union action of the student movement. It was therefore not so much a text on the situation of time, as an article drawing the strict consequences of the Althusserian theory of ideology. These have since provided the framework, whether admitted or not, of the revisionist analysis of the university.

The principle of the article is to shift the line of class division from the teacher/student relation (where it had been drawn by the UNEF theorists) to the content of the knowledge taught. The dividing line does not appear in the transmission of knowledge between teacher and student; it lies in the very content of knowledge, between science and ideology. Althusser's argument involves a whole system of implication which we think it useful to state explicitly at this point.

Althusser bases himself on the distinction between the technical and social division of labour: 'What are the Marxist theoretical principles which should and can intervene in scientific analysis of the University? . . . Above all the Marxist concepts of the *technical* division and the *social* division of labour. Marx applied these principles in the analysis of capitalist society. They are valid for the analysis of every human society (in the sense of a social formation based on a determinate mode of production). These principles are *a fortiori* valid for a particular social reality like the university, which, for various essential reasons, belongs to every modern society, whether capitalist, socialist or communist.'[13]

A first reading reveals the same mechanism that was at work in the analysis of Ideology: suppression of the class struggle, and its replacement by the generality of a function necessary to the social whole. But the concepts here require particular attention. Althusser says he is undertaking to *apply* the Marxist concepts of technical and social division of labour. But these are in no way given as such in Marx's analysis. Rather, he demonstrates the two-fold nature of every production process, depending on whether one considers it as the labour process in general, or as a socially defined process of production, reproducing the relations of production which determine it. While a distinction between 'technical division' and 'social division' of labour can be deduced from this analysis, it is not a real distinction but a merely *formal distinction* corresponding to two ways of conceptualizing the same process. Technical division and social division are two aspects of a *single division*. The functions which assure the technical reproduction of the process are the same as those which determine its social reproduction.

Now, in Althusser's analysis there is a real distinction of places and functions which correspond to one or other of the divisions. Thus 'the technical division of labour corresponds to all the "posts" of labour, whose existence is exclusively accounted for by the technical necessities defining a mode of production at a given moment of its development in a given society', while the social division 'has the function of ensuring that the labour process of this society continues in the same forms of class division and of the domination of one class over the others'.[14]

Technical and social division of labour

Formulated in this way, the distinction is enigmatic: how is one to define exclusively technical necessities in a mode of production? These would have to be independent of its social goals, of the reproduction of the social relations of production which determine them. And conversely, does not the 'technical' functioning of the process of production already imply the reproduction of the relations of production, and hence of the forms of class division and domination?

To resolve the enigma, we must once more reverse the argument. The technical division of labour is supposed to throw a light on the function of the university. But in point of fact, the status accorded to the university will enlighten us as to the function of the concept 'technical division of labour'. Althusser tells us that the university 'for various essential reasons, belongs to every modern society, whether capitalist, socialist or communist'. So the technical division of labour, which at first seemed to correspond to the requirements of a determinate mode of production, now corresponds to the technical necessities of a 'modern' society: i.e., in Marxist terms, of a society having reached a certain level of development of the productive forces. The distinction thus becomes somewhat clearer: the technical division of labour corresponds to a given level of development of the productive forces; the social division to the reproduction of the relations of production of a determinate mode of production.

It all works 'as if' a certain number of necessary places and functions of a modern society in general could be defined exclusively in terms of the level of development of the productive forces. This conclusion will not fail to surprise the reader of Althusser. Did he not elsewhere devote all his energy to freeing Marxist theory from every ideology that views history in terms of evolution and linear development? Does not his new concept of

'modernity' absolutely contradict such an attempt? To explain this
contradiction, we must ask what is at stake here politically. The
significance of Althusser's backsliding is clear: it leads one to attribute to
the technical division of labour – i.e., to the objective requirements of
science or 'modern' rationality – that which belongs to the social forms of
the capitalist mode of production.[15]

The concept of the technical division of labour appears, then, to be
merely the justification for revisionist slogans based on 'the real needs of
the nation', 'the real needs of the economy', 'modernization', and so forth.
We know that the PCF has replaced the Marxist dialectic with a type of
eclecticism resembling Proudhon's which distinguishes the good and the
bad side of things. The revolutionary necessity to destroy bourgeois
relations of production in order to free the productive forces, is reduced for
the PCF to the job of suppressing the bad (the domination of the
monopolies) to preserve and advance the good (the forms of the 'technical
division of labour' corresponding to the requirements of every 'modern'
society). But since Marx, we know that the 'real' needs of society always
serve to mask the interests of a class; in this case, they mask the interests of
the class which the PCF tends increasingly to represent: the labour
aristocracy and the intellectual cadres.[16] The functioning of the concept
'technical division of labour' succeeds in justifying revisionist ideology in
its two complementary aspects: a theory of 'objective needs' and a defence
of the hierarchy of 'skills'.

The backsliding and the contradictions are explained as follows:
Althusser has simply moved from the terrain of Marxist theory so that of
its opposite, the opportunist ideology of revisionism. This displacement of
Marxist analysis on to the eclectic ground of the good and the bad side is
not new to us: it describes the same movement as that which shifted the
theory of ideology towards the metaphysical relationship between Science
and its Other. The core of Althusserianism undoubtedly lies in this
articulation of the spontaneous discourse of metaphysics with revisionist
ideology – an articulation that is perfectly demonstrated in the
development of Althusser's argument. The distinction between the
technical division and the social division of labour is expressed in the
University as a distinction between science and ideology. In other words,
the theory of ideology, the foundations of which seemed problematic, is
now grounded on the theory of the two-fold division of labour. But as the
latter is but a scholarly justification for revisionism, the theory of ideology
here proclaims its political basis. Marxist theory at first acted as a solution
to a problem within metaphysics; this problematic, in its turn, acts in the
service of revisionist ideology. The analysis of knowledge will make this
trajectory explicit: 'It is in the knowledge taught in the university that the
permanent dividing-line of the technical division and the social division of
labour exists, the most reliable and profound line of class division.'[17]

The stratagem is here made perfectly plain: the science/ideology distinction is what allows the technical/social division to pass for a line of class division; which means that in Althusser's discourse, metaphysics arranges the promotion of revisionist ideology to the rank of Marxist theory. Only through this device does Althusser's thesis retain its 'obviousness'. For in fact it implies a double distortion: the first, already noted, concerns the status of ideology; the second bears on the effectivity of science, which is alleged to be automatically on the side of the revolution. 'It is not accidental if, in every matter, a reactionary or "technocratic" bourgeois government prefers half-truths, and if, on the other hand, the revolutionary cause is always indissolubly linked to rigorous knowledge, that is, to science.'[18]

We in turn will suggest that it is not accidental if Althusser's thesis appears here in its inverted form. It is both necessary for Althusser's argument – and impossible, without revealing what underlies it – to state in its direct form the thesis that scientific knowledge is intrinsically subversive of bourgeois domination. Such a problematic thesis is only comprehensible through a process which extends Marx's theses on scientific socialism outside their proper field. It is clear that the liberation of the proletariat is impossible without the theory of the conditions of its liberation; that is, without the Marxist science of social formations. The bond uniting the revolutionary cause and scientific knowledge is guaranteed in this case by their common object. But one has no right then to impute a revolutionary character to science in general. In any case, one has only to apply this thesis to the reality of the teaching of science in order to see its inanity. The bulk of the courses given in medical schools or the big Colleges of Science undoubtedly have a perfectly valid scientific content. If this education nevertheless has an obviously reactionary function, it is not simply because the sciences are taught there in a positivist way, but because of the very educational structure of determinate institutions, selection mechanisms, and relations between students and staff (in which the latter not only possess a certain knowledge but belong to a social hierarchy – cf. the role of consultants in medicine). The dominance of the bourgeoisie and of its ideology is expressed not in the content of the knowledge but in the structure of the environment in which it is transmitted. The scientific nature of the knowledge in no way affects the class content of the education. Science does not stand confronted by ideology as its other; it resides within institutions and in those forms of transmission where the ideological dominance of the bourgeoisie is manifested.

'At least', it will be said, 'the second element of the thesis is confirmed: ideology reinforces the power of the bourgeoisie – witness the role played by the "human sciences".' But the problem is badly posed. These disciplines owe their role to the fact that they constitute the place in the system of knowledge where the confrontations of the class struggle are most directly reflected. The problem is not their more or less 'ideological' nature, but the ideology which is transmitted in them. The psychology, sociology, law or political economy taught in higher education has a reactionary function not because it, wholly or in part, lacks scientificity, but because it spreads the ideology of the bourgeoisie. The point is not whether it falls under 'ideology', but whether it falls under *bourgeois* ideology. The task of revolutionaries is not to confront it with the requirements of scientificity, nor to appeal from these pseudo-sciences to the ideal scientificity of mathematics or physics. It is to oppose bourgeois ideologies with the proletarian ideology of Marxism–Leninism.

The most elementary concrete analysis of the university institution reveals the metaphysical nature of Althusser's division. The Science/Ideology couple is nowhere to be found in the analysis of the university, where we are concerned with the ideology of the dominant class, not with 'ideology'. And the ideology of the dominant class is not simply – let us even say, not essentially – expressed in such and such a content of knowledge, but in the very division of knowledge, the forms in which it is appropriated, the institution of the university as such. Bourgeois ideology has its existence not in the discourse of some ideologue, or in the system of the students' spontaneous notions, but in the division between disciplines, the examination system, the organization of departments – everything which embodies the bourgeois hierarchy of knowledge. Ideology is not in fact a collection of discourses or a system of ideas. It is not what Althusser, in a significant expression, calls an 'atmosphere'. The dominant ideology is a *power* organized in a number of institutions (the system of knowledge, the media system, etc.). Because Althusser thinks in the classic metaphysical terms of a theory of the *imaginary* (conceived as a system of notions separating the *subject* from the *truth*), he completely misses this point. The result is a complete distortion of ideological struggle, which comes to have the function of putting science where ideology was before. Bourgeois academic discourse is countered with a Marxist academic discourse; and the 'spontaneous, petty-bourgeois' ideology of the students is in turn countered with the scientific rigour of Marxism, incarnated in the wisdom of the Central Committee. The struggle of science against ideology is, in fact, a struggle in the service of bourgeois ideology, a struggle which reinforces two crucial bastions: the system of knowledge and revisionist ideology.

There is no ideology in the University which could be the Other of science. Nor is there a science which could be the Other of ideology. What the University teaches is not 'science' in the mythical purity of its essence, but a selection of scientific knowledges articulated into *objects of knowledge*. The transmission of scientific knowledges does not proceed from the concept of science. It forms part of the *forms of appropriation* of scientific knowledge, and these are *class* forms of appropriation. Scientific theories are transmitted through a system of discourses, traditions and institutions which constitute the very existence of bourgeois ideology. In other words, the relation of science to ideology is one not of rupture but of articulation. The dominant ideology is not the shadowy Other of the pure light of Science; it is the very space in which scientific knowledges are inscribed, and in which they are articulated as elements of a social formation's knowledge. It is in the forms of the dominant ideology that a scientific theory becomes an object of knowledge.[19]

The concept of knowledge, in fact, is not that of a content which can be either science or ideology. Knowledge is a system of which the 'contents' cannot be conceived outside their forms of appropriation (acquisition, transmission, control, utilization). The system is that of the ideological dominance of a class. It is not 'science' or 'ideology'. In it are articulated the class appropriation of science and the ideology of the dominant class. There is no more a class division in knowledge that there is in the State. Knowledge has no institutional existence other than as an instrument of class rule. It is not characterized by an interior division reproducing that which exists between the classes – on the contrary, its characteristics are determined by the dominance of a class. So the system of knowledge is, like State power, the stake in a class struggle, and, like State power, must be destroyed. The University is not the site of a class division, but the objective of a proletarian struggle. To transform this objective into the neutral site of a division, is quite simply to conceal the class struggle. Once it was finally grasped that there is not a bourgeois science and a proletarian science, it was thought possible to infer that science is intrinsically proletarian, or, at the very least, that it is an area of peaceful coexistence. But if science itself, at the level of its proof, cannot be bourgeois or proletarian, the constitution of objects of scientific knowledge, and the mode of their social appropriation, certainly can be. There is not a bourgeois science and a proletarian science. There is a bourgeois knowledge and a proletarian knowledge.

The function of teaching

The heart of Marxism is concrete analysis of a concrete situation. Now it is clear that the Science/Ideology opposition is unfit for such an analysis, class providing no more than a repetition of the classic dichotomy of metaphysics. It draws an imaginary line of class divisions for no other reason than to ignore class struggle as it really exists.[20] Althusser's misconception of the function of knowledge, and of the struggle which takes it as an objective, rests on this primary suppression. The position of the political having been misunderstood, it can only reappear in the wrong place; hidden in the alleged neutrality of the technical division of labour, or shifted into the hypothetically revolutionary function of science. We have already seen what the 'technical division of labour' represented. It remains to look more closely at the concept of science, at what gives it the specific function of concealing the class struggle.

To do this we must examine the second central thesis in Althusser's argument: 'The function of teaching is to transmit a determinate knowledge to subjects who do not possess this knowledge. The teaching situation thus rests on the absolute condition of *an inequality between a knowledge and a non-knowledge.*'[21]

One can see the logic which articulates this thesis with the previous one. The first indicated the real line of class division: science/ideology. The present thesis exposes the false dividing line: teaching/taught. The teaching relation has the function of transmitting knowledge to those who do not possess it. It is hence based exclusively on the technical division of labour. The two theses complement each other, but absolutely contradict each other as well. For the first presents knowledge as *determined* by the difference between science and ideology, whereas the second suppresses every determination other than the opposition of knowledge to non-knowledge, of the full to the empty. The dividing line had been drawn solely between the concepts 'science' and 'ideology'. It is obliterated as soon as the reality of the teaching function comes into play. Althusser declares that students 'very often risk alienating the good will of their teachers who are unjustly held in suspicion over the validity of their knowledge which is considered superfluous'.[22] But did not the science/ideology distinction precisely imply the deepest and most justifiable suspicion towards the knowledge of teachers? To remove that suspicion, it is necessary to give knowledge the status of science – to make the relation of science to non-science intervene a second time, not now in the shape of error (science/ideology) but in that of ignorance (knowledge/non-knowledge). The concept of science now appears in its true light: the science/ideology distinction ultimately had no other function than to justify the pure being of knowledge – more accurately, to justify the eminent dignity of the possessors of knowledge. To understand this reversal of quality into quantity, we must here again recognize the voice of the revisionist prompter: what is required is an education 'of quality', 'of a high cultural level'. As far as the teachers are concerned, in their double role of scholars and wage-earners they are objective allies of the working class. So in whose interest would it be to criticize them, if not that of provocateurs in the pay of the bourgeoisie? It is not accidental if etc., etc. . . .

But it would be wrong to see Althusser's discourse as a simple piece of hack-work in the service of revisionism. On the contrary, its interest lies in the fact that it reproduces the spontaneous discourse of metaphysics, the traditional position of philosophy with respect to knowledge. Althusser indicates this position, while at the same time concealing it, when he defines philosophy as follows: 'Philosophy represents politics in the domain of theory, or to be more precise: *with the sciences* – and *vice-versa*, philosophy represents scientificity in politics, with the classes engaged in the class struggle.'[23]

Althusser's thesis fails to recognize that this double representation – of the scientific with the political, and of the political with the scientific – already exists precisely in *knowledge*. Knowledge constitutes the system of appropriation of scientific conceptions to the profit of a class. It is a remarkable fact that philosophy has been established and developed in a definite relation to knowledge, but without ever recognizing its class nature. So when Plato attacks the Sophists, or Descartes scholasticism, their criticism functions largely as a critique of knowledge: that is, not simply of an erroneous discourse, but of a certain social and political power. But even when they grasp the properly political dimensions of this knowledge (Plato), they cannot attain to the level of the cause – that is to say, to the articulation of knowledge with the rule of a class. Unable to see knowledge as the system of the ideological dominance of a class, they are reduced to criticizing the effects of this system. Philosophy thus develops as a criticism of false knowledge in the name of true knowledge (Science), or of the empirical diversity of knowledge in the name of unity of science. The criticism of knowledge, failing to recognize its class function, is made in the name of an Ideal of Science, in a discourse which separates the realm of science from that of false knowledge (opinion, illusion, etc.). The opposition of Science and its Other has the function of misconceiving the class nature of knowledge. And the discourse of metaphysics propagates this misconception inasmuch as it presents itself as a *discourse on science*. What, it asks, constitutes the scientificity of science? The act of modesty characteristic of the 'epistemological' tradition to which Althusser returns, consists in believing that this question is produced at the very request of science. Thus for Althusser, a new science (Greek mathematics, Galilean physics, etc.). would call for a discourse defining the forms of its scientificity (Plato, Descartes, etc.). Is this not to play the question at its own game? In actual fact, the question may well exist *in order not to pose* the question: what is the basis of knowledge? It is produced not at the demand of Science (even if it voices this demand) but by knowledge's concealment of itself.[24]

Philosophy thus traditionally practises a critique of knowledge which is simultaneously a denegation[25] of knowledge (i.e. of the class struggle). Its position can be described as an *irony* with regard to knowledge, which it puts in question without ever touching its foundations. The questioning of knowledge in philosophy always ends in its restoration: a movement the great philosophers consistently expose in each other. Thus Hegel criticizes Cartesian doubt, which only results in re-establishing the authority of everything it pretended to reject. Feuerbach isolates the same pretence in the Hegelian 'path of despair'. 'The non-knowledge of the idea was only an ironic non-knowledge.' And this is what we rediscover in Althusser: the line of division is scarcely drawn before it is erased. Doubt about knowledge only existed the better to establish the authority of a knowledge elevated finally to the rank of science.

In repeating this manoeuvre, Althusser reveals its political significance, clearly showing that what is at issue is the status of the *possessors of knowledge*. Any serious doubt about the content of knowledge vanishes as soon as the question of its subject is raised, as soon as the very existence of a group possessing knowledge is at stake. Here again, there is an evident homology with that classic philosophical figure of which the Cartesian *cogito* provides a model illustration: the challenging of the object of knowledge aims at confirming its subject. Doubt about the object is only the obverse of the certainty of the subject. It is precisely this contradiction which gives philosophy its status: philosophy is constructed against the power of the false possessors of knowledge, or, more accurately, of the possessors of false knowledge (sophists, theologians, etc.). But it cannot go so far as to put at issue the very existence of knowledge as the instrument of a class. Against the object of false knowledge, it invokes the subject of true knowledge; which, in the final analysis, strengthens the grounds for dominance of those possessing (true) knowledge, and thereby justifies class domination. This passage from the object of false knowledge to the subject of true knowledge would consequently correspond to the political demand of a class excluded from power, lending this demand the form of universality. (The Cartesian 'good sense'.) This movement has ultimately no other end than to bolster the privileged position of the possessors of knowledge – a form of class domination.[26]

The Althusserian theory of ideology describes this same movement, and we now see how the spontaneous discourse of metaphysics comes to be articulated with revisionist ideology. Only one more mediation is required for this: Althusser's *academic ideology*. In it, the spontaneous discourse of metaphysics assumes the function of justifying the teachers, the possessors and purveyors of bourgeois knowledge (knowledge which includes academic Marxism). Speaking in their name, defending their authority, Althusser quite naturally adopts the class position expressed in revisionist ideology – that of the labour aristocracy and the cadres. The spontaneous discourse of metaphysics is thus the necessary mediation enabling Althusser to recognize his own class position in that expressed by revisionism. This convergence is located in the question of knowledge and the defence of academic authority. At this point, the Althusserian theory of ideology functions as the theory of an imaginary class struggle to the profit

of a real class collaboration, that of revisionism. The transformation of
Marxism into opportunism is complete.

Notes

1. Théorie, Pratique Théorique et Formation Théorique: Idéologie et Lutte
   Idéologique, p. 29.
2. N. POULANTZAS, *Political Power and Social Classes* (London, NLB 1973), p. 207.
3. Théorie, Pratique Théorique . . . , pp. 30–1.
4. Ibid., p. 26.
5. [Note added in February 1973:] The vague use of 'metaphysical discourse'
   subsequently inherited by sociology (social cohesion, the bond between men, etc.
   . . .) loses the specificity of the concepts involved here, the fact that they belong to
   a historically determined *political* problematic. It was this problematic which, in
   the second half of the 19th century, gave sociology its status and position in the
   ensemble of practices then introduced by the bourgeoisie to mould the men
   necessary to the reproduction of capitalist relations of production. It was a time
   when, after the establishment of those relations, the bourgeoisie had twice faced
   the possibility of its extinction as a result of the proletarian riposte. More astute
   than 'Marxist' scholars who prate endlessly about the 'spontaneously bourgeois'
   ideology of the proletariat, the bourgeoisie recognized in 1848 and 1871 that, even
   if they used the same words (order, republic, ownership, labour . . .), the workers
   were thinking *differently*. Hence the necessity for the bourgeoisie to strengthen
   the *ideological* weapons of its dictatorship. The political threat gave the new
   human sciences their place among the techniques for moulding the 'normal' man
   necessary to the system; a moulding which encompassed the detection of
   criminals or the prevention of suicides, as well as the selection of the cadres or
   parliamentary education of the masses (i.e. the parliamentary and electoral
   repression of the autonomous political practice of the masses). It also gave them
   their problematic as a science of the phenomena which consolidate or break up
   social cohesion. Its characteristic questions were: What principles strengthen the
   cohesion of a group? What criteria allow the most suitable ones to be chosen for
   such and such a position? Or, more crudely still: How can one identify in the
   physiognomy of a crowd, or in the dimensions of someone's skull, the danger
   that they represent for the social order? It is not difficult to spot behind the
   elaboration of the 'sociological method' the preoccupations of the detective
   Bertillon, author of anthropometry, or of the military doctor Lebon, theoretician
   of crowds and their 'ring-leaders'.
   The important thing here is that Althusser separates these concepts of the
   bourgeoisie's 'police-reason' from the political dangers and manoeuvrings of
   power which underlie them, in order to relate them to a function of the social
   whole in general. This is naturally complemented by a conception of science
   above and beyond classes, which reproduces precisely the 'scientistic' ideology
   that crowns the evidence of 'police-reason.' If a direct line leads from this abstract
   conception of ideology to the validation of Kautsky's thesis of 'the importation of
   Marxism into the working class', it is perhaps because this line reproduces in
   theory the historical collusion of social-democracy in the bourgeois attempt to

domesticate the working class, to wipe out its cultural identity. The pitiful bankruptcy of social-democracy must indeed have something to do with this 'importation of consciousness'. In practice, it has come to mean the containment of the working class by electoral parties which, while spreading parliamentary illusions, repress the political practices and pervert the organizational forms of the proletariat. At the same time a 'science' and a scientistic ideology are propagated which help to wipe out the traditions of autonomous popular expression, and so on. Conversely, the assertion that it is necessary to bring *consciousness* to a working class involuntarily trapped within bourgeois ideology, may really indicate the part played by social-democracy in the attempt to integrate the working class into bourgeois political life. If the working masses have been able to find the means to resist this kind of 'Marxism' in their practice, the intellectuals generally discover in it the form and substance of their 'Marxist' theoretical discourse.

6. Ibid., p. 31.
7. Naturally this class relation has to be carefully distinguished from the forms (political, economic, ideological) in which the class struggle is fought, which are its effects. It nonetheless remains that the relations of production can only be understood as class relations, unless they are transformed into a new 'backstage-world'. It is just such a transformation which results from the distinction made by Poulantzas (in *Political Power and Social Classes*) between the relations of production and 'social relations'. Starting from the correct idea that the relations of production are not 'human relations', Poulantzas falls into the dilemma indicated above: transparency or opacity. As a result, the relations of production appear withdrawn into that exteriority represented by the 'structure'. The analysis of Althusser and Poulantzas ultimately results in a truism: the structure is defined by no more than its own opacity, manifested in its effects. In a word, it is the opacity of the structure which renders the structure opaque. This quasi-Heideggerian withdrawal of the structure could in no way be politically innocent. The French Communist Party is happy to argue thus: the struggle of the students only concerns the effects of capitalist exploitation; the grass-roots struggles in the factories against the job hierarchy, automation and victimization also deal only with effects. It is necessary to come to grips with the very cause of exploitation, the capitalist relations of production. But to this dimension of the problem, only Science has access, i.e. the wisdom of the Central Committee. The withdrawal of the structure thus becomes a *focus imaginarius* in the Kantian manner, an inverted image, reduced to a point, of a future without limit: France's peaceful road to socialism.
8. *For Marx* (London: NLB, 1977), p. 232.
9. Théorie . . . etc., p. 32.
10. Ibid., p. 30.
11. A substitute conception for the contradiction which is based, of course, on the misunderstanding of the real contradiction.
12. 'Problèmes Etudiants', *Nouvelle Critique*, No. 152 (January 1964); 'Marxism and Humanism', in *For Marx*, op. cit.
13. 'Problèmes Etudiants', p. 83.
14. Ibid., p. 84.
15. Thus it is that in the same article, Althusser deduces the 'technical' necessity of the whole industrial hierarchy. As for the 'essential reasons' which necessitate the existence of the university in a socialist society, their discussion will have to be left for some other occasion.

16. [Note added in February 1973:] These brief remarks will lead one astray, should they be thought to trace revisionist ideology back to the interests of the intermediary strata. What this ideology basically represents is the ideology of a power structure which already contains the prefiguration of a social order to come. The reaction of the PCF and the CGT to the corpse of Pierre Overney [a Maoist militant shot dead by factory security guards] expresses less the cadres' terror or the condemnation by members of the professions, than how it appeared to the occupants of an alternative State apparatus, who, moreover, were already participating as such in the bourgeois State apparatus. At Renault, the cadres of the Party and the CGT do not defend the interests of an intermediary class, but their own participation in the power of the employers. By taking up the position it did, the PCF was representing not the interests of its electoral following, but its own interests as an apparatus sharing in the management of capitalist power in the factory.

17. 'Problèmes Étudiants', p. 89.

18. Ibid p. 94. It is not uninteresting to note the agreement, at the very level of rhetoric, between the metaphysical formulation 'as if' and the classic rhetorical figure employed in the PCF: 'It is not accidental if. . . . ' Popular common-sense is not mistaken when it says that chance does many things.

19. [Note added in February 1973:] The formulation of the problem seems to have gone astray, because it somewhat diplomatically restricts the question of 'class science' to what is clearly the safest ground – the *teaching* of scientific knowledges – in order to avoid the shifting sands of 'proletarian' geometry or genetics. Although laudable, this restraint has the drawback of failing to deal with precisely what is in question: namely, the place of a scientific practice which would only be affected by the class struggle at the level of the transmission of its *results*. It would be advisable therefore to look more closely at what is involved in this representation of a 'pure' scientific practice.

What is the 'rational kernel' in the idea of the university of scientific practice? It is that propositions exist whose modes of verification seem valid for all existing classes and social systems. Let us note in passing that this universality of the modes of verification does not, for all that, place the practice which produces these propositions *above classes*. (Such developments in arithmetic as took place in the 19th century can be universally acknowledged, but this does not eliminate the political problematic of *order* which supports them.) Above all, let us note that, except in the treatises of philosophers, no science is ever reduced solely to the ordering of universally verifiable propositions, nor any scientific practice solely to the process of their production. Scientific practice is never 'pure', as it has its forms of existence in a system of social relations of which propositions, formal proofs, experiments (on the basis of which the *ideal of science* is established) are only elements. The class struggle can manifest itself at different levels: present even in propositions, proofs, a field of application, the methods and occasion of their elaboration, and so on. One can see from this that scientific propositions and theories can, at one and the same time, keep their power of verifiability and yet belong to bourgeois science. The Chinese mathematicians who made their self-criticism during the Cultural Revolution were not accused of having produced false theorems, but of having practised in their ivory towers an academic's science, looking only for personal prestige. Similarly, they did not replace their 'bourgeois' theorems with 'proletarian' ones, but altered the relationship to the masses which had been implied in their practice. This is because the social nature of a science essentially depends on the two-fold question: *who* practises science and *for whom*? To conceal this double question is to vindicate, under cover of the universality of the modes of scientific verification, the universality of the bourgeois division of labour.

What was the basic flaw in the arguments about 'proletarian science' and 'bourgeois science' before the Cultural Revolution? Precisely that they neglected the question: who practises science? Not by accident, but because these arguments were based on a system of the division of labour which, keeping science out of the hands of the masses, entrusted the responsibility for judging its bourgeois or proletarian character to the functionaries of power and the experts on knowledge. Proletarian science will certainly never be created by a patent from the Academy of Proletarian Science and, as long as proletarian biology is the concern of Messieurs Besse, Garaudy et al., this science above classes will be in clover. As the Cultural Revolution has shown, proletarian science means essentially – and this can only be the work of a lengthy mass struggle – the suppression of a science which is the business of specialists beyond the reach of the masses. A proletarian science which distinguishes itself from the other not only by producing different propositions, but by virtue of the overthrow of the masses' age-old relation to knowledge and power.

20. The characteristic of a metaphysical conception is that it tries to draw a line of class division in realities (institution, social groups) which it views in a static way. Thus the revisionists list social groups in terms of whether they are revolutionary or not. The dialectic teaches that, on the contrary, there is knowable unity and division only in struggle. One cannot draw a line of class division in the university, but only in the struggle which puts it at stake.
21. 'Problèmes Étudiants', p. 90.
22. Ibid., p. 94.
23. *Lenin and Philosophy* (London: NLB, 1971), p. 65.
24. In his *Cours de Philosophie pour les Scientifiques* (a course run at the Ecole Normale Supérieure in 1967–68), Althusser develops the idea that philosophy is not concerned with Science – an ideological concept – but with *the sciences*. Balibar, in *L'Humanité* of 14.2.69, mocks those who talk about science as if it were a 'Speculative Holy Spirit' incarnated in the different sciences. But one might well ask what this strange concept of *the sciences* is. Can one say anything about it which does not pass through the mediation of the concept *Science*? The nature of a concept is not changed by putting it in the plural – it can be all the more hidden. This is just what is involved here: to replace science by the sciences, is to conceal the proper object of philosophy (Science) as produced by the denegation of knowledge. The proclaimed anti-speculative act of Althusser and Balibar has the sole effect of strengthening the philosophical denegation of knowledge.
25. Denegation is a word used by Freud to designate an unconscious denial masked by a conscious acceptance, or *vice versa*. It is used here in the sense of an ostensible criticism concealing a strengthened affirmation. The affirmation is *'misrecognized'* as criticism. (Translator's note.)
26. [Note added in February 1973:] This bird's-eye view of the history of philosophy will no doubt seem insubstantial. Let me briefly state:
    (1) It restricts itself to challenging, within his own terms of reference, Althusser's even more offhand interpretation of this history.
    (2) Nevertheless, I have no more intention of reproaching Althusser for his casualness than of excusing myself to the punctilious historians of philosophy. The day that these historians are as scrupulous in making the voice of the masses heard, as they are in establishing the sense of a line in

Plato it will be time to see, in their respect for the great philosophers, something other than simple respect for the *Great*. As far as I am concerned, Althusser's casual treatment of Plato or Descartes seems quite pardonable compared with his nonchalant endorsement of the official history of the labour movement (both social-democratic and revisionist), which adds the weight of its falsifications to the firing-squads and prison-sentences of the bourgeoisie.

9 Myth Today*

ROLAND BARTHES

Roland Barthes (1915–80) was a professor at the Collège de France in Paris and one of the leading intellectual celebrities of his day. In his early days he was a structuralist and political leftist, helping to found the newly-fledged science of semiology, or the study of signifying systems. In his later years he shifted to a form of post-structuralist libertarianism, savouring the pleasures of both body and text and producing a series of elegantly turned essays on a whole range of cultural topics from fashion to photography. Among his foremost works are *Writing Degree Zero* (1953; London: Jonathan Cape, 1967), *Critical Essays* (1964; Evanston: Northwestern University Press, 1972), *Mythologies* (1957; London: Jonathan Cape, 1972), *S/Z* (1970; London: Jonathan Cape, 1975) and *The Pleasure of the Text* (1973; London: Jonathan Cape, 1976).

In this extract from *Mythologies*, Barthes develops what could best be seen as a semiotic theory of ideology – a term which is roughly synonymous with his 'myth'. In a strikingly original commentary, he lays bare the mechanics by which certain privileged signifiers become 'naturalised', and thus produce an ideological effect.

Mythology, since it is the study of a type of speech, is but one fragment of this vast science of signs which Saussure postulated some forty years ago under the name of *semiology*. Semiology has not yet come into being. But since Saussure himself, and sometimes independently of him, a whole section of contemporary research has constantly been referred to the problem of meaning: psychoanalysis, structuralism, eidetic psychology, some new types of literary criticism of which Bachelard has given the first examples, are no longer concerned with facts except inasmuch as they are endowed with significance. Now to postulate a signification is to have recourse to semiology. I do not mean that semiology could account for all

*Reprinted from ROLAND BARTHES, *Mythologies* (1957; London: Paladin, 1973), pp. 111–24). Trans. Annette Lavers.

these aspects of research equally well: they have different contents. But they have a common status: they are all sciences dealing with values. They are not content with meeting the facts: they define and explore them as tokens for something else.

Semiology is a science of forms, since it studies significations apart from their content. I should like to say one word about the necessity and the limits of such a formal science. The necessity is that which applies in the case of any exact language. Zhdanov made fun of Alexandrov the philosopher, who spoke of '*the spherical structure of our planet*'. '*It was thought until now*', Zhdanov said, '*that form alone could be spherical.*' Zhdanov was right: one cannot speak about structures in terms of forms, and vice versa. It may well be that on the plane of 'life', there is but a totality where structures and forms cannot be separated. But science has no use for the ineffable: it must speak about 'life' if it wants to transform it. Against a certain quixotism of synthesis, quite platonic incidentally, all criticism must consent to the *ascesis*, to the artifice of analysis; and in analysis, it must match method and language. Less terrorized by the spectre of 'formalism', historical criticism might have been less sterile; it would have understood that the specific study of forms does not in any way contradict the necessary principles of totality and History. On the contrary: the more a system is specifically defined in its forms, the more amenable it is to historical criticism. To parody a well-known saying, I shall say that a little formalism turns one away from History, but that a lot brings one back to it. Is there a better example of total criticism than the description of saintliness, at once formal and historical, semiological and ideological, in Sartre's *Saint-Genet*? The danger, on the contrary, is to consider forms as ambiguous objects, half-form and half-substance, to endow form with a substance of form, as was done, for instance, by Zhdanovian realism. Semiology, once its limits are settled, is not a metaphysical trap: it is a science among others, necessary but not sufficient. The important thing is to see that the unity of an explanation cannot be based on the amputation of one or other of its approaches, but, as Engels said, on the dialectical co-ordination of the particular sciences it makes use of. This is the case with mythology: it is a part both of semiology inasmuch as it is a formal science, and of ideology inasmuch as it is an historical science: it studies ideas-in-form.[1]

Let me therefore restate that any semiology postulates a relation between two terms, a signifier and a signified. This relation concerns objects which belong to different categories, and this is why it is not one of equality but one of equivalence. We must here be on our guard for despite common parlance which simply says that the signifier *expresses* the signified, we are dealing, in any semiological system, not with two, but with three different terms. For what we grasp is not at all one term after the other, but the correlation which unites them: there are, therefore, the signifier, the signified and the sign, which is the associative total of the first two terms. Take a bunch of roses: I use it to *signify* my passion. Do we have here, then, only a signifier and a signified, the roses and my passion? Not even that: to put it accurately, there are here only 'passionified' roses. But on the plane of analysis, we do have three terms; for these roses weighted with passion perfectly and correctly allow themselves to be decomposed into roses and passion: the former and the latter existed before uniting and forming this third object, which is the sign. It is as true to say that on the plane of experience I cannot dissociate the roses from the message they carry, as to say that on the plane of analysis I cannot confuse the roses as signifier and the roses as sign: the signifier is empty, the sign is full, it is a meaning. Or take a black pebble: I can make it signify in several ways, it is a mere signifier; but if I weight it with a definite signified (a death sentence, for instance, in an anonymous vote), it will become a sign. Naturally, there are between the signifier, the signified and the sign, functional implications (such as that of the part to the whole) which are so close that to analyse them may seem futile; but we shall see in a moment that this distinction has a capital importance for the study of myth as semiological schema.

Naturally these three terms are purely formal, and different contents can be given to them. Here are a few examples: for Saussure, who worked on a particular but methodologically exemplary semiological system – the language or *langue* – the signified is the concept, the signifier is the acoustic image (which is mental) and the relation between concept and image is the sign (the word, for instance), which is a concrete entity.[2] For Freud, as is well known, the human psyche is a stratification of tokens or representatives. One term (I refrain from giving it any precedence) is constituted by the manifest meaning of behaviour, another, by its latent or real meaning (it is, for instance, the substratum of the dream); as for the third term, it is here also a correlation of the first two: it is the dream itself in its totality, the parapraxis (a mistake in speech or behaviour) or the neurosis, conceived as compromises, as economies effected thanks to the joining of a form (the first term) and an intentional function (the second term). We can see here how necessary it is to distinguish the sign from the signifier: a dream, to Freud, is no more its manifest datum than its latent content: it is the functional union of these two terms. In Sartrean criticism, finally (I shall keep to these three well-known examples), the signified is constituted by the original crisis in the subject (the separation from his mother for Baudelaire, the naming of the theft for Genet); Literature as discourse forms the signifier; and the relation between crisis and discourse defines the work, which is a signification. Of course, this tri-dimensional pattern, however constant in its form, is actualized in different ways: one cannot therefore say too often that semiology can have its unity only at the level of forms, not contents; its field is limited, it knows only one operation: reading, or deciphering.

In myth, we find again the tri-dimensional pattern which I have just described: the signifier, the signified and the sign. But myth is a peculiar system, in that it is constructed from a semiological chain which existed before it: it *is a second-order semiological system*. That which is a sign (namely the associative total of a concept and an image) in the first system, becomes a mere signifier in the second. We must here recall that the materials of mythical speech (the language itself, photography, painting, posters, rituals, objects, etc.), however different at the start, are reduced to a pure signifying function as soon as they are caught by myth. Myth sees in them only the same raw material; their unity is that they all come down to the status of a mere language. Whether it deals with alphabetical or pictorial writing, myth wants to see in them only a sum of signs, a global sign, the final term of a first semiological chain. And it is precisely this final term which will become the first term of the greater system which it builds and of which it is only a part. Everything happens as if myth shifted the formal system of the first significations sideways. As this lateral shift is essential for the analysis of myth, I shall represent it in the following way, it being understood, of course, that the spatialization of the pattern is here only a metaphor:

It can be seen that in myth there are two semiological systems, one of which is staggered in relation to the other: a linguistic system, the language (or the modes of representation which are assimilated to it), which I shall call the *language-object*, because it is the language which myth gets hold of in order to build its own system; and myth itself, which I shall call *metalanguage*, because it is a second language, *in which* one speaks about the first. When he reflects on a metalanguage, the semiologist no longer needs to ask himself questions about the composition of the language-object, he no longer has to take into account the details of the linguistic schema; he will only need to know its total term, or global sign, and only inasmuch as this term lends itself to myth. This is why the semiologist is entitled to treat in the same way writing and pictures: what he retains from them is the fact that they are both *signs*, that they both reach the threshold of myth endowed with the same signifying function, that they constitute, one just as much as the other, a language-object.

It is now time to give one or two examples of mythical speech. I shall borrow the first from an observation by Valéry.[3] I am a pupil in the second form in a French *lycée*. I open my Latin grammar, and I read a sentence, borrowed from Aesop or Phaedrus: *quia ego nominor leo*. I stop and think.

There is something ambiguous about this statement: on the one hand, the words in it do have a simple meaning: *because my name is lion*. And on the other hand, the sentence is evidently there in order to signify something else to me. Inasmuch as it is addressed to me, a pupil in the second form, it tells me clearly: I am a grammatical example meant to illustrate the rule about the agreement of the predicate. I am even forced to realize that the sentence in no way *signifies* its meaning to me, that it tries very little to tell me something about the lion and what sort of name he has; its true and fundamental signification is to impose itself on me as the presence of a certain agreement of the predicate. I conclude that I am faced with a particular, greater, semiological system, since it is co-extensive with the language: there is, indeed, a signifier, but this signifier is itself formed by a sum of signs, it is in itself a first semiological system (*my name is lion*). Thereafter, the formal pattern is correctly unfolded: there is a signified (*I am a grammatical example*) and there is a global signification, which is none other than the correlation of the signifier and the signified; for neither the naming of the lion nor the grammatical example are given separately.

And here is now another example: I am at the barber's, and a copy of *Paris-Match* is offered to me. On the cover, a young Negro in a French uniform is saluting, with his eyes uplifted, probably fixed on a fold of the tricolour. All this is the *meaning* of the picture. But, whether naively or not, I see very well what it signifies to me: that France is a great Empire, that all her sons, without any colour discrimination, faithfully serve under her flag, and that there is no better answer to the detractors of an alleged colonialism than the zeal shown by this Negro in serving his so-called oppressors. I am therefore again faced with a greater semiological system: there is a signifier, itself already formed with a previous system (*a black soldier is giving the French salute*); there is a signified (it is here a purposeful mixture of Frenchness and militariness); finally, there is a presence of the signified through the signifier.

Before tackling the analysis of each term of the mythical system, one must agree on terminology. We now know that the signifier can be looked at, in myth, from two points of view: as the final term of the linguistic system, or as the first term of the mythical system. We therefore need two names. On the plane of language, that is, as the final term of the first system, I shall call the signifier: *meaning* (*my name is lion, a Negro is giving the French salute*); on the plane of myth, I shall call it: *form*. In the case of the signified, no ambiguity is possible: we shall retain the name *concept*. The third term is the correlation of the first two: in the linguistic system, it is the *sign*; but it is not possible to use this word again without ambiguity, since in myth (and this is the chief peculiarity of the latter), the signifier is already formed by the *signs* of the language. I shall call the third term of myth the *signification*. This word is here all the better justified since myth has in fact a double function: it points out and it notifies, it makes us understand something and it imposes it on us.

The form and the concept

The signifier of myth presents itself in an ambiguous way: it is at the same time meaning and form, full on one side and empty on the other. As meaning, the signifier already postulates a reading, I grasp it through my eyes, it has a sensory reality (unlike the linguistic signifier, which is purely mental), there is a richness in it: the naming of the lion, the Negro's salute are credible wholes, they have at their disposal a sufficient rationality. As a total of linguistic signs, the meaning of the myth has its own value, it belongs to a history, that of the lion or that of the Negro: in the meaning, a signification is already built, and could very well be self-sufficient if myth did not take hold of it and did not turn it suddenly into an empty, parasitical form. The meaning is *already* complete, it postulates a kind of knowledge, a past, a memory, a comparative order of facts, ideas, decisions.

When it becomes form, the meaning leaves its contingency behind; it empties itself, it becomes impoverished, history evaporates, only the letter remains. There is here a paradoxical permutation in the reading operations, an abnormal regression from meaning to form, from the linguistic sign to the mythical signifier. If one encloses *quia ego nominor leo* in a purely linguistic system, the clause finds again there a fullness, a richness, a history: I am an animal, a lion, I live in a certain country, I have just been hunting, they would have me share my prey with a heifer, a cow and a goat; but being the stronger, I award myself all the shares for various reasons, the last of which is quite simply that *my name is lion*. But as the form of the myth, the clause hardly retains anything of this long story. The meaning contained a whole system of values: a history, a geography, a morality, a zoology, a Literature. The form has put all this richness at a distance: its newly acquired penury calls for a signification to fill it. The story of the lion must recede a great deal in order to make room for the grammatical example, one must put the biography of the Negro in parentheses if one wants to free the picture, and prepare it to receive its signified.

But the essential point in all this is that the form does not suppress the meaning, it only impoverishes it, it puts it at a distance, it holds it at one's disposal. One believes that the meaning is going to die, but it is a death with reprieve; the meaning loses its value, but keeps its life, from which the form of the myth will draw its nourishment. The meaning will be for the form like an instantaneous reserve of history, a tamed richness, which it is possible to call and dismiss in a sort of rapid alternation: the form must

constantly be able to be rooted again in the meaning and to get there what
nature it needs for its nutrient; above all, it must be able to hide there. It is
this constant game of hide-and-seek between the meaning and the form
which defines myth. The form of myth is not a symbol: the Negro who
salutes is not the symbol of the French Empire: he has too much presence,
he appears as a rich, fully experienced, spontaneous, innocent, *indisputable*
image. But at the same time this presence is tamed, put at a distance, made
almost transparent; it recedes a little, it becomes the accomplice of a
concept which comes to it fully armed, French imperiality: once made use
of, it becomes artificial.

Let us now look at the signified: this history which drains out of the
form will be wholly absorbed by the concept. As for the latter, it is
determined, it is at once historical and intentional; it is the motivation
which causes the myth to be uttered. Grammatical exemplarity, French
imperiality, are the very drives behind the myth. The concept reconstitutes
a chain of causes and effects, motives and intentions. Unlike the form, the
concept is in no way abstract: it is filled with a situation. Through the
concept, it is a whole new history which is implanted in the myth. Into the
naming of the lion, first drained of its contingency, the grammatical
example will attract my whole existence: Time, which caused me to be
born at a certain period when Latin grammar is taught; History, which sets
me apart, through a whole mechanism of social segregation, from the
children who do not learn Latin; paedagogic tradition, which caused this
example to be chosen from Aesop or Phaedrus; my own linguistic habits,
which see the agreement of the predicate as a fact worthy of notice and
illustration. The same goes for the Negro-giving-the-salute: as form, its
meaning is shallow, isolated, impoverished; as the concept of French
imperiality, here it is again tied to the totality of the world: to the general
History of France, to its colonial adventures, to its present difficulties.
Truth to tell, what is invested in the concept is less reality than a certain
knowledge of reality; in passing from the meaning to the form, the image
loses some knowledge: the better to receive the knowledge in the concept.
In actual fact, the knowledge contained in a mythical concept is confused,
made of yielding, shapeless associations. One must firmly stress this open
character of the concept; it is not at all an abstract, purified essence; it is a
formless, unstable, nebulous condensation, whose unity and coherence are
above all due to its function.

In this sense, we can say that the fundamental character of the mythical
concept is to be *appropriated*: grammatical exemplarity very precisely
concerns a given form of pupils, French imperiality must appeal to such
and such group of readers and not another. The concept closely
corresponds to a function, it is defined as a tendency. This cannot fail to
recall the signified in another semiological system, Freudianism. In Freud,
the second term of the system is the latent meaning (the content) of the

dream, of the parapraxis, of the neurosis. Now Freud does remark that the second-order meaning of behaviour is its real meaning, that which is appropriate to a complete situation, including its deeper level; it is, just like the mythical concept, the very intention of behaviour.

A signified can have several signifiers: this is indeed the case in linguistics and psychoanalysis. It is also the case in the mythical concept: it has at its disposal an unlimited mass of signifiers: I can find a thousand Latin sentences to actualize for me the agreement of the predicate, I can find a thousand images which signify to me French imperiality. This means that *quantitively*, the concept is much poorer than the signifier, it often does nothing but re-present itself. Poverty and richness are in reverse proportion in the form and the concept: to the qualitative poverty of the form, which is the repository of a rarefied meaning, there corresponds the richness of the concept which is open to the whole of History; and to the quantitative abundance of the forms there corresponds a small number of concepts. This repetition of the concept through different forms is precious to the mythologist, it allows him to decipher the myth: it is the insistence of a kind of behaviour which reveals its intention. This confirms that there is no regular ration between the volume of the signified and that of the signifier. In language, this ratio is proportionate, it hardly exceeds the word, or at least the concrete unit. In myth, on the contrary, the concept can spread over a very large expanse of signifier. For instance, a whole book may be the signifier of a single concept; and conversely, a minute form (a word, a gesture, even incidental, so long as it is noticed) can serve as signifier to a concept filled with a very rich history. Although unusual in language, this disproportion between signifier and signified is not specific to myth: in Freud, for instance, the parapraxis is a signifier whose thinness is out of proportion to the real meaning which it betrays.

As I said, there is no fixity in mythical concepts: they can come into being, alter, disintegrate, disappear completely. And it is precisely because they are historical that history can very easily suppress them. This instability forces the mythologist to use a terminology adapted to it, and about which I should now like to say a word, because it often is a cause for irony: I mean neologism. The concept is a constituting element of myth: if I want to decipher myths, I must somehow be able to name concepts. The dictionary supplies me with a few: Goodness, Kindness, Wholeness, Humaneness, etc. But by definition, since it is the dictionary which gives them to me, these particular concepts are not historical. Now what I need most often is ephemeral concepts, in connection with limited contingencies: neologism is then inevitable. China is one thing, the idea which a French petit-bourgeois could have of it not so long ago is another: for this peculiar mixture of bells, rickshaws and opium-dens, no other word possible but *Sininess*.[4] Unlovely? One should at least get some consolation from the fact that conceptual neologisms are never arbitrary: they are built according to a highly sensible proportional rule.

The signification

In semiology, the third term is nothing but the association of the first two, as we saw. It is the only one which is allowed to be seen in a full and satisfactory way, the only one which is consumed in actual fact. I have called it: the signification. We can see that the signification is the myth itself, just as the Saussurean sign is the word (or more accurately the concrete unit). But before listing the characters of the signification, one must reflect a little on the way in which it is prepared, that is, on the modes of correlation of the mythical concept and the mythical form.

First we must note that in myth, the first two terms are perfectly manifest (unlike what happens in other semiological systems): one of them is not 'hidden' behind the other, they are both given *here* (and not one here and the other there). However paradoxical it may seem, *myth hides nothing*: its function is to distort, not to make disappear. There is no latency of the concept in relation to the form: there is no need of an unconscious in order to explain myth. Of course, one is dealing with two different types of manifestation: form has a literal, immediate presence; moreover, it is extended. This stems – this cannot be repeated too often – from the nature of the mythical signifier, which is already linguistic: since it is constituted by a meaning which is already outlined, it can appear only through a given substance (whereas in language, the signifier remains mental). In the case of oral myth, this extension is linear (*for my name is lion*); in that of visual myth, it is multi-dimensional (in the centre, the Negro's uniform, at the top, the blackness of his face, on the left, the military salute, etc.). The elements of the form therefore are related as to place and proximity: the mode of presence of the form is spatial. The concept, on the contrary, appears in global fashion, it is a kind of nebula, the condensation, more or less hazy, of a certain knowledge. Its elements are linked by associative relations: it is supported not by an extension but by a depth (although this metaphor is perhaps still too spatial): its mode of presence is memorial.

The relation which unites the concept of the myth to its meaning is essentially a relation of *deformation*. We find here again a certain formal analogy with a complex semiological system such as that of the various types of psychoanalysis. Just as for Freud the manifest meaning of behaviour is distorted by its latent meaning, in myth the meaning is distorted by the concept. Of course, this distortion is possible only because the form of the myth is already constituted by a linguistic meaning. In a simple system like the language, the signified cannot distort anything at all because the signifier, being empty, arbitrary, offers no resistance to it. But here, everything is different: the signifier has, so to speak, two aspects: one full, which is the meaning (the history of the lion, of the Negro soldier), one empty, which is the form (*for my name is lion; Negro-French-soldier-saluting-the-tricolour*). What the concept distorts is of course what is full, the meaning: the lion and the Negro are deprived of their history, changed into gestures. What Latin exemplarity distorts is the naming of the lion, in all its contingency; and what French imperiality obscures is also a primary language, a factual discourse which was telling me about the salute of a Negro in uniform. But this distortion is not an obliteration: the lion and the Negro remain here, the concept needs them; they are half-amputated, they are deprived of memory, not of existence: they are at once stubborn, silently rooted there, and garrulous, a speech wholly at the service of the concept. The concept, literally, deforms, but does not abolish the meaning; a word can perfectly render this contradiction: it alienates it.

What must always be remembered is that myth is a double system; there occurs in it a sort of ubiquity: its point of departure is constituted by the arrival of a meaning. To keep a spatial metaphor, the approximative character of which I have already stressed, I shall say that the signification of the myth is constituted by a sort of constantly moving turnstile which presents alternately the meaning of the signifier and its form, a language-object and a metalanguage, a purely signifying and a purely imagining consciousness. This alternation is, so to speak, gathered up in the concept, which uses it like an ambiguous signifier, at once intellective and imaginary, arbitrary and natural.

I do not wish to prejudge the moral implications of such a mechanism, but I shall not exceed the limits of an objective analysis if I point out that the ubiquity of the signifier in myth exactly reproduces the physique of the *alibi* (which is, as one realizes, a spatial term): in the alibi too, there is a place which is full and one which is empty, linked by a relation of negative identity ('I am not where you think I am; I am where you think I am not'). But the ordinary alibi (for the police, for instance) has an end; reality stops the turnstile revolving at a certain point. Myth is a *value*, truth is no guarantee for it; nothing prevents it from being a perpetual alibi: it is enough that its signifier has two sides for it always to have an 'elsewhere' at its disposal. The meaning is always there to *present* the form; the form is always there to *outdistance* the meaning. And there never is any contradiction, conflict, or split between the meaning and the form: they are never at the same place. In the same way, if I am in a car and I look at the scenery through the window, I can at will focus on the scenery or on the window-pane. At one moment I grasp the presence of the glass and the distance of the landscape; at another, on the contrary, the transparence of the glass and the depth of the landscape; but the result of this alternation is constant: the glass is at once present and empty to me, and the landscape unreal and full. The same thing occurs in the mythical signifier: its form is empty but present, its meaning absent but full. To wonder at this contradiction I must voluntarily interrupt this turnstile of form and meaning, I must focus on each separately, and apply to myth a static method of deciphering; in short, I must go against its own dynamics: to sum up, I must pass from the state of reader to that of mythologist.

Notes

1. The development of publicity, of a national press, of radio, of illustrated news, not to speak of the survival of a myriad rites of communication which rule social appearances makes the development of semiological science more urgent than ever. In a single day, how many really non-signifying fields do we cross? Very few, sometimes none. Here I am, before the sea; it is truth that it bears no message. But on the beach, what material for semiology! Flags, slogans, signals, sign-boards, clothes, suntan even, which are so many messages to me.
2. The notion of *word* is one of the most controversial in linguistics. I keep it here for the sake of simplicity.
3. *Tel Quel*, II, p. 191.
4. Or perhaps *Sinity*? Just as if Latin/latinity = Basque/x, x = Basquity.

Part Three
Modern Debates

10 Ideology*

RAYMOND WILLIAMS

Raymond Williams (1921–88) was the foremost cultural thinker of postwar Britain. Born into a Welsh working-class family, he became Professor of Drama at Cambridge University, and produced numerous seminal studies of literature, culture and politics. Among his most influential works are *Culture and Society 1780–1950* (London: Chatto and Windus, 1958), *The Long Revolution* (London: Chatto and Windus, 1960), *The Country and the City* (London: Chatto and Windus, 1973) and *Politics and Letters* (London: Verso, 1979). Williams was never an orthodox Marxist, believing that Marxism had given too little weight to questions of culture and communication; and in this extract from *Marxism and Literature* (1977) he offers some perceptive comments on classical Marxist notions of ideology, as well as tracing a brief early history of the concept.

The concept of 'ideology' did not originate in Marxism and is still in no way confined to it. Yet it is evidently an important concept in almost all Marxist thinking about culture, and especially about literature and ideas. The difficulty then is that we have to distinguish three common versions of the concept, which are all common in Marxist writing. These are, broadly:
  (1) a system of beliefs characteristic of a particular class or group;
  (2) a system of illusory beliefs – false ideas or false consciousness – which can be contrasted with true or scientific knowledge;
  (3) the general process of the production of meanings and ideas.

In one variant of Marxism, senses (1) and (2) can be effectively combined. In a class society, all beliefs are founded on class position, and the systems of belief of all classes – or, quite commonly, of all classes preceding, and other than, the proletariat, whose formation is the project of the abolition of class society – are then in part or wholly false (illusory). The specific

---

*Reprinted from RAYMOND WILLIAMS, *Marxism and Literature* (Oxford: Oxford University Press, 1977), pp. 55–71.

problems in this powerful general proposition have led to intense controversy within Marxist thought. It is not unusual to find some form of the proposition alongside uses of the simple sense (1), as in the characterization, for example by Lenin, of 'socialist ideology'. Another way of broadly retaining but distinguishing senses (1) and (2) is to use sense (1) for systems of belief founded on class position, including that of the proletariat within class society, and sense (2) for contrast with (in a broad sense) *scientific* knowledge of all kinds, which is based on reality rather than illusions. Sense (3) undercuts most of these associations and distinctions, for the ideological process – the production of meanings and ideas – is then seen as general and universal, and ideology is either this process itself or the area of its study. Positions associated with senses (1) and (2) are then brought to bear in Marxist ideological studies.

In this situation there can be no question of establishing, except in polemics, a single 'correct' Marxist definition of ideology. It is more to the point to return the term and its variations to the issues within which it and these were formed; and specifically, first, to the historical development. We can then return to the issues as they now present themselves, and to the important controversies which the term and its variations reveal and conceal.

'Ideology' was coined as a term in the late eighteenth century, by the French philosopher Destutt de Tracy. It was intended to be a philosophical term for the 'science of ideas'. Its use depended on a particular understanding of the nature of 'ideas', which was broadly that of Locke and the empiricist tradition. Thus ideas were not to be and could not be understood in any of the older 'metaphysical' or 'idealist' senses. The science of ideas must be a natural science, since all ideas originate in man's experience of the world. Specifically, in Destutt, ideology is part of zoology: 'We have only an incomplete knowledge of an animal if we do not know his intellectual faculties. Ideology is a part of Zoology, and it is especially in man that this part is important and deserves to be more deeply understood' (*Éléments d'idéologie* (1801), Preface). The description is characteristic of scientific empiricism. The 'real elements' of ideology are 'our intellectual faculties, their principal phenomena and their most evident circumstances'. The critical aspect of this emphasis was at once realized by one kind of opponent, the reactionary de Bonald: 'Ideology has replaced metaphysics . . . because modern philosophy sees no other ideas in the world but those of men.' De Bonald correctly related the scientific sense of ideology to the empiricist tradition which had passed from Locke through Condillac, pointing out its preoccupation with 'signs and their influence on thought' and summarizing its 'sad system' as a reduction of 'our thoughts' to 'transformed sensations'. 'All the characteristics of intelligence', de Bonald added, 'disappeared under the scalpel of this ideological dissection.'

The initial bearings of the concept of ideology are then very complex. It was indeed an assertion against metaphysics that there are 'no ideas in the world but those of men'. At the same time, intended as a branch of empirical science, 'ideology' was limited, by its philosophical assumptions, to a version of ideas as 'transformed sensations' and to a version of language as a 'system of signs' (based, as in Condillac, on an ultimately mathematical model). These limitations, with their characteristic abstraction of 'man' and 'the world', and with their reliance on the passive 'reception' and 'systematic association' of 'sensations', were not only 'scientific' and 'empirical' but were elements of a basically bourgeois view of human existence. The rejection of metaphysics was a characteristic gain, confirmed by the development of precise and systematic empirical enquiry. At the same time the effective exclusion of any social dimension – both the practical exclusion of social relationships implied in the model of 'man' and 'the world', and the characteristic displacement of necessary social relationships to a formal system, whether the 'laws of psychology' or language as a 'system of signs' – was a deep and apparently irrecoverable loss and distortion.

It is significant that the initial objection to the exclusion of any active conception of intelligence was made from generally reactionary positions, which sought to retain the sense of activity in its old metaphysical forms. It is even more significant, in the next stage of the development, that a derogatory sense of 'ideology' as 'impractical theory' or 'abstract illusion', first introduced from an evidently reactionary position by Napoleon, was taken over, though from a new position, by Marx.

Napoleon said:

> It is to the doctrine of the ideologies – to this diffuse metaphysics, which in a contrived manner seeks to find the primary causes and on this foundation would erect the legislation of peoples, instead of adapting the laws to a knowledge of the human heart and of the lessons of history – to which one must attribute all the misfortunes which have befallen our beautiful France.[1]

Scott (*Napoleon*, VI (1827), p. 251) summarized: 'Ideology, by which nickname the French ruler used to distinguish every species of theory, which, resting in no respect upon the basis of self-interest, could, he thought, prevail with none save hot-brained boys and crazed enthusiasts.'

Each element of this condemnation of 'ideology' – which became very well known and was often repeated in Europe and North America during the first half of the nineteenth century – was taken up and applied by Marx and Engels, in their early writings. It is the substantial content of their attack on their German contemporaries in *The German Ideology* (*GI*: 1846). To find 'primary causes' in 'ideas' was seen as the basic error. There is even the same tone of contemptuous practicality in the anecdote in Marx's Preface:

> Once upon a time an honest fellow had the idea that men were drowned in water only because they were possessed with the idea of gravity. If they were to knock this idea out of their heads, say by stating it to be a superstition, a religious idea, they would be sublimely proof against any danger from water.
>
> (*GI*, p. 2).

Abstract theories, separated from the 'basis of self-interest', were then beside the point.

Of course the argument could not be left at this stage. In place of Napoleon's conservative (and suitably vague) standard of 'knowledge of the human heart and of the lessons of history', Marx and Engels introduced 'the real ground of history' – the process of production and self-production – from which the 'origins and growth' of 'different theoretical products' could be traced. The simple cynicism of the appeal to 'self-interest' became a critical diagnosis of the real basis of all ideas: 'the ruling ideas are nothing more than the ideal expression of the dominant material relationships, the dominant material relationships grasped as ideas' (*GI*, p. 39).

Yet already at this stage there were obvious complications. 'Ideology' became a polemical nickname for kinds of thinking which neglected or ignored the material social process of which 'consciousness' was always a part:

> Consciousness can never be anything else than conscious existence, and the existence of men is their actual life-process. If in all ideology men and their circumstances appear upside down as in a *camera obscura*, this phenomenon arises just as much from their historical life-process as the inversion of objects on the retina does from their physical life-process.
>
> (*GI*, p. 14).

The emphasis is clear but the analogy is difficult. The physical processes of the retina cannot reasonably be separated from the physical processes of the brain, which, *as a necessarily connected activity*, control and 'rectify' the inversion. The *camera obscura* was a conscious device for discerning proportions; the inversion had in fact been corrected by adding another lens. In one sense the analogies are no more than incidental, but they probably relate to (though in fact, as examples, they work against) an underlying criterion of 'direct positive knowledge'. They are in a way very like the use of 'the idea of gravity' to refute the notion of the controlling power of ideas. If the idea had been not a practical and scientific understanding of a natural force but, say, an idea of 'racial superiority' or of 'the inferior wisdom of women', but the argument might in the end have come out the same way but it would have had to pass through many more significant stages and difficulties.

This is also true even of the more positive definition:

> We do not set out from what men say, imagine, conceive, nor from men as narrated, thought of, imagined, conceived, in order to arrive at men in the flesh. We set out from real, active men, and on the basis of their real life-process we demonstrate the development of the ideological reflexes and echoes of this life-process. The phantoms formed in the human brain are also, necessarily, sublimates of their material life-process, which is empirically verifiable and bound to material premises. Morality, religion, metaphysics, all the rest of ideology and their corresponding forms of consciousness, thus no longer retain the semblance of independence.
>
> (*GI*, p. 14)

That 'ideology' should be deprived of its 'semblance of independence' is entirely reasonable. But the language of 'reflexes', 'echoes', 'phantoms', and 'sublimates' is simplistic, and has in repetition been disastrous. It belongs to the naive dualism of 'mechanical materialism', in which the idealist separation of 'ideas' and 'material reality' had been repeated, but with its priorities reversed. The emphasis on consciousness as inseparable from conscious existence, and then on conscious existence as inseparable from material social processes, is in effect lost in the use of this deliberately degrading vocabulary. The damage can be realized if we compare it for a moment with Marx's description of 'human labour' in *Capital* (I, pp. 185–6):

> We presuppose labour in a form that stamps it as exclusively human . . . What distinguishes the worst architect from the best of bees is this, that the architect raises his structure in imagination before he erects it in reality. At the end of every labour-process, we get a result that already existed in the imagination of the labourer at its commencement.

This goes perhaps even too much the other way, but its difference from the world of 'reflexes', 'echoes', 'phantoms', and 'sublimates' hardly needs to be stressed. Consciousness is seen from the beginning as part of the human material social process, and its products in 'ideas' are then as much part of this process as material products themselves. This, centrally, was the thrust of Marx's whole argument, but the point was lost, in this crucial area, by a temporary surrender to the cynicism of 'practical men' and, even more, to the abstract empiricism of a version of 'natural science'.

What had really been introduced, as a corrective to abstract empiricism, was the sense of material and social history as the real relationship between 'man' and 'nature'. But it is then very curious of Marx and Engels to abstract, in turn, the persuasive 'men in the flesh', at whom we 'arrive'. To begin by presupposing them, as the necessary starting-point, is right while we remember that they are therefore also conscious men. The decision not to set out from 'what men say, imagine, conceive, nor from men as narrated, thought of, imagined, conceived' is then at best a corrective reminder that there is other and sometimes harder evidence of what they have done. But it is also at its worst an objectivist fantasy: that the whole 'real life-process' can be known independently of language ('what men say') and of its records ('men as narrated'). For the very notion of history would become absurd if we did not look at 'men as narrated' (when, having died, they are hardly likely to be accessible 'in the flesh', and on which, inevitably, Marx and Engels extensively and repeatedly relied) as well as at that 'history of industry . . . as it objectively exists . . . an *open book of the human faculties* . . . a human *psychology* which can be directly apprehended' (p. 121), which they had decisively introduced against the exclusions of other historians. What they were centrally arguing was a new way of seeing the total relationships between this 'open book' and 'what men say' and 'men as narrated'. In a polemical response to the abstract history of ideas or of consciousness they made their main point but in one decisive area lost it again. This confusion is the source of the naive reduction, in much subsequent Marxist thinking, of consciousness, imagination, art, and ideas to 'reflexes', 'echoes', 'phantoms', and 'sublimates', and then of a profound confusion in the concept of 'ideology'.

We can trace further elements of this failure if we examine those definitions of ideology which gain most of their force by contrast with what is not ideology. The most common of these contrasts is with what is called 'science'. For example:

> Where speculation ends – in real life – there real, positive science begins: the representation of the practical activity, of the practical process of development of men. Empty talk about consciousness ceases, and real knowledge has to take its place. When reality is depicted, philosophy as an independent branch of activity loses its medium of existence.
>
> (*GI*, p. 17)

There are several difficulties here. The uses of 'consciousness' and 'philosophy' depend almost entirely on the main argument about the futility of separating consciousness and thought from the material social process. It is the separation that makes such consciousness and thought into ideology. But it is easy to see how the point could be taken, and has often been taken, in a quite different way. In a new kind of abstraction, 'consciousness' and 'philosophy' are separated, in their turn, from 'real knowledge' and from the 'practical process'. This is especially easy to do with the available language of 'reflexes', 'echoes', 'phantoms', and 'sublimates'. The result of this separation, against the original conception of an *indissoluble* process, is the farcical exclusion of consciousness from the 'development of men' and from 'real knowledge' of this development. But the former, at least, is impossible by any standard. All that can then be done to mask its absurdity is elaboration of the familiar two-state model (the mechanical materialist reversal of the idealist dualism), in which there is *first* material social life and *then*, at some temporal or spatial distance, consciousness and 'its' products. This leads directly to simple reductionism: 'consciousness' and 'its' products can be nothing but 'reflections' of what has already occurred in the material social process.

It can of course be said from experience (that experience which produced the later anxious warnings and qualifications) that this is a poor practical way of trying to understand 'consciousness and its products': that these continually escape so simple a reductive equation. But this is a marginal point. The real point is that the separation and abstraction of 'consciousness and its products' as a 'reflective' or 'second-stage' process results in an ironic idealization of 'consciousness and its products' at this secondary level.

For 'consciousness and its products' are always, though in variable forms, parts of the material social process itself: whether as what Marx called the necessary element of 'imagination' in the labour process; or as the necessary conditions of associated labour, in language and in practical ideas of relationship; or, which is so often and significantly forgotten, in the real processes – all of them physical and material, most of them manifestly so – which are masked and idealized as 'consciousness and its products' but which, when seen without illusions, are themselves necessarily social material activities. What is in fact idealized, in the ordinary reductive view, is 'thinking' or 'imagining', and the only materialization of these abstracted processes is by a general reference back to the whole (and because abstracted then in effect complete) material social process. And what this version of Marxism especially overlooks is that 'thinking' and 'imagining' are from the beginning social processes (of course including that capacity for 'internalization' which is a necessary part of any social process between actual individuals) and that they become accessible only in unarguably physical and material ways: in voices, in sounds made by instruments, in penned or printed writing, in arranged pigments on canvas or plaster, in worked marble or stone. To exclude these material social processes from the material social process is the same error as to reduce all material social processes to mere technical means for some other abstracted 'life'. The 'practical process' of the 'development of men' necessarily includes them from the beginning, and as more than the technical means for some quite separate 'thinking' and 'imagining'.

What can then be said to be 'ideology', in its received negative form? It

can, of course be said that these processes, or some of them, come in
variable forms (which is as undeniable as the variable forms of any
production), and that some of these forms are 'ideology' while others are
not. This is a tempting path, but it is usually not followed far, because there
is a fool's beacon erected just a little way along it. This is the difficult
concept of 'science'. We have to notice first a problem of translation. The
German *Wissenschaft*, like the French *science*, has a much broader meaning
than English science has had since the early nineteenth century. The
broader meaning is in the area of 'systematic knowledge' or 'organized
learning'. In English this has been largely specialized to such knowledge
based on observation of the 'real world' (at first, and still persistently,
within the categories of 'man' and 'the world') and on the significant
distinction (and even opposition) between the formerly interchangeable
words *experience* and *experiment*, the latter attracting, in the course of
development, new senses of *empirical* and *positive*. It is then very difficult
for any English reader to take the translated phrase of Marx and Engels –
'real, positive science' – in anything other than this specialized sense. But
two qualifications have then at once to be made. First, that the Marxist
definition of the 'real world', by moving beyond the separated categories of
'man' and 'the world' and including, as central, the active material social
process, had made any such simple transfer impossible:

> If industry is conceived as an exoteric form of the realization of the
> *essential human faculties*, one is able to grasp also the *human* essence of
> Nature or the *natural* essence of man. The natural sciences will then
> abandon their abstract materialist, or rather, idealist, orientation, and
> will become the basis of a *human* science . . . One basis for life and
> another for science is *a priori* a falsehood.
>
> (*EPM*, p. 122).

This is an argument precisely against the categories of the English
specialization of 'science'. But then, second, the actual progress of scientific
rationality, especially in its rejection of metaphysics and in its triumphant
escape from a limitation to observation, experiment, and inquiry within
received religious and philosophical systems, was immensely attractive as
a model for understanding society. Though the object of inquiry had been
radically changed – from 'man' and 'the world' to an active, interactive,
and in a key sense self-creating material social process – it was supposed,
or rather hoped, that the methods, or at least the mood, could be carried
over.

This sense of getting free of the ordinary assumptions of social inquiry,
which usually began where it should have ended, with the forms and
categories of a particular historical *phase* of society, is immensely important
and was radically demonstrated in most of Marx's work. But it is very

different from the uncritical use of 'science' and 'scientific', with deliberate references to and analogies from 'natural science', to describe the essentially *critical and historical* work which was actually undertaken. Engels, it is true, used these references and analogies much more often than Marx. 'Scientific socialism' became, under his influence, a polemical catchword. In practice it depends almost equally on a (justifiable) sense of systematic knowledge of society, based on observation and analysis of its processes of development (as distinct, say, from 'utopian' socialism, which projected a desirable future without close consideration of the past and present processes within which it had to be attained); and on a (false) association with the 'fundamental' or 'universal' 'laws' of natural science, which, even when they turned out to be 'laws' rather than effective working generalizations or hypotheses, were of a different kind because their objects of study were radically different.

The notion of 'science' has had a crucial effect, negatively, on the concept of 'ideology'. If 'ideology' is contrasted with 'real, positive science', in the sense of detailed and connected knowledge of 'the practical process of development of men', then the distinction may have significance as an indication of the received assumptions, concepts/and points of view which can be shown to prevent or distort such detailed and connected knowledge. We can often feel that this is all that was really intended. But the contrast is of course less simple than it may look, since its confident application depends on a knowable distinction between 'detailed and connected knowledge of the practical process of development' and other kinds of 'knowledge' which may often closely resemble it. One way of applying the distinguishing criterion would be by examining the 'assumptions, concepts, and points of view', whether received or not, by which any knowledge has been gained and organized. But it is just this kind of analysis which is prevented by the *a priori* assumption of a 'positive' method which is not subject to such scrutiny: an assumption based in fact on the received (and unexamined) assumptions of 'positive, scientific knowledge', freed of the 'ideological bias' of all other observers. This position, which has been often repeated in orthodox Marxism, is either a circular demonstration or a familiar partisan claim (of the kind made by almost all parties) that others are biased but that, by definition, we are not.

That indeed was the fool's way out of the very difficult problem which was now being confronted, within historical materialism. Its symptomatic importance at the level of dogma has to be noted and then set aside if we are to see, clearly, a very different and much more interesting proposition, which leads to a quite different (though not often theoretically distinguished) definition of ideology. This begins from the main point of the attack on the Young Hegelians, who were said to 'consider conceptions, thoughts, ideas, in fact all the products of consciousness, to which they attribute an independent existence, as the real chains of men'. Social liberation would then come through a 'change of consciousness'. Everything then turns, of course, on the definition of 'consciousness'. The definition adopted, polemically, by Marx and Engels, is in effect their definition of ideology: not 'practical consciousness' but 'self-dependent theory'. Hence 'really it is only a question of explaining this theoretical talk from the actual existing conditions. The real, practical dissolution of these phrases, the removal of these notions from the consciousness of men, will . . . be effected by altered circumstances, not by theoretical deductions' (*GI*, p. 15). In this task the proletariat has an advantage, since 'for the mass of men . . . these theoretical notions do not exist'.

If we can take this seriously we are left with a much more limited and in that respect more plausible definition of ideology. Since 'consciousness', including 'conceptions, thoughts, ideas', can hardly be asserted to be non-existent in the 'mass of men', the definition falls back to a kind of consciousness, and certain *kinds* of conceptions, thoughts and ideas, which are specifically 'ideological'. Engels later sought to clarify this position:

> Every ideology . . . once it has arisen, develops in connection with the given concept-material, and develops this material further; otherwise it would cease to be ideology, that is, occupation with thoughts as with independent entities, developing independently and subject only to their own laws. That the material life conditions of the persons inside whose heads this thought process goes on, in the last resort determines the course of this process, remains of necessity unknown to these persons, for otherwise there would be an end to all ideology.
>
> (*Feuerbach*, pp. 65–6)

> Ideology is a process accomplished by the so-called thinker, consciously indeed but with a false consciousness. The real motives impelling him remain unknown to him, otherwise it would not be an ideological process at all. Hence he imagines false or apparent motives. Because it is a process of thought he derives both its form and its content from pure thought, either his own or that of his predecessors.[2]

Taken on their own, these statements can appear virtually psychological. They are structurally very similar to the Freudian concept of 'rationalization' in such phrases as 'inside whose heads'; 'real motives . . . unknown to him'; 'imagines false or apparent motives'. In this form a version of 'ideology' is readily accepted in modern bourgeois thought, which has its own concepts of the 'real' – material or psychological – to undercut either ideology or rationalization. But it had once been a more serious position. Ideology was specifically identified as a consequence of the division of labour:

Division of labour only becomes truly such from the moment when a division of material and mental labour appears. . . . From this moment onwards consciousness can really flatter itself that it is something other than consciousness of existing practice, that it *really* represents something without representing something real; from now on consciousness is in a position to emancipate itself from the world and to proceed to the formation of 'pure' theory, theology, philosophy, ethics, etc.

(*GI*, p. 51).

Ideology is then 'separated theory', and its analysis must involve restoration of its 'real' connections.

The division of labour . . . manifests itself also in the ruling class as the division of mental and material labour, so that inside this class one part appears as the thinkers of the class (its active, conceptive ideologists, who make the perfecting of the illusion of the class about itself their chief source of livelihood) while the other's attitude to these ideas and illusions is more passive and receptive, because they are in reality the active members of this class and have less time to make up illusions and ideas about themselves.

(*GI*, pp. 39–40).

This is shrewd enough, as is the later observation that 'each new class . . . is compelled . . . to represent its interest as the common interest of all the members of society, put in an ideal form; it will give its ideas the form of universality, and represent them as the only rational, universally valid ones' (*GI*, pp. 40–1). But 'ideology' then hovers between 'a system of beliefs characteristic of a certain class' and 'a system of illusory beliefs – false ideas or false consciousness – which can be contrasted with true or scientific knowledge'.

This uncertainty was never really resolved. Ideology as 'separated theory' – the natural home of illusions and false consciousness – is itself separated from the (intrinsically limited) 'practical consciousness of a class'. This separation, however, is very much easier to carry out in theory than in practice. The immense body of direct class-consciousness, directly expressed and again and again directly imposed, can appear to escape the taint of 'ideology', which would be limited to the 'universalizing' philosophers. But then what name is to be found for these powerful direct systems? Surely not 'true' or 'scientific' knowledge, except by an extraordinary sleight-of-hand with the description 'practical'. For most ruling classes have not needed to be 'unmasked'; they have usually proclaimed their existence and the 'conceptions, thoughts, ideas' which ratify it. To overthrow them is ordinarily to overthrow their conscious practice, and this is always very much harder than overthrowing their 'abstract' and 'universalizing' ideas, which also, in real terms, have a much more complicated and interactive relationship with the dominant 'practical consciousness' than any merely dependent or illusory concepts could ever have. Or again, 'the existence of revolutionary ideas in a particular period presupposes the existence of a revolutionary class'. But this may or may not be true, since all the difficult questions are about the development of a pre-revolutionary or potentially revolutionary or briefly revolutionary into a sustained revolutionary class, and the same difficult questions necessarily arise about pre-revolutionary, potentially revolutionary, or briefly revolutionary ideas. Marx and Engels's own complicated relations to the (in itself very complicated) revolutionary character of the European proletariat is an intensely practical example of just this difficulty, as is also their complicated and acknowledged relationship (including the relationship implied by critique) to their intellectual predecessors.

What really happened, in temporary but influential substitution for just this detailed and connected knowledge, was, first, an abstraction of 'ideology', as a category of illusions and false consciousness (an abstraction which as they had best reason to know would prevent examination, not of the abstracted ideas, which is relatively easy, but of the material social process in which 'conceptions, thoughts, ideas', of course in different degrees, become practical). Second, in relation to this, the abstraction was given a categorical rigidity, an *epochal* rather than a genuinely historical consciousness of ideas, which could then be mechanically separated into forms of successive and unified stages of – but which? – both knowledge and illusion. Each stage of the abstraction is radically different, in both theory and practice, from Marx's emphasis on a necessary conflict of real interests, in the material social process, and on the 'legal, political, religious, aesthetic, or philosophical – in short ideological – forms in which men become conscious of this conflict and fight it out'. The infection from categorical argument against specialists in categories has here been burned out, by a practical recognition of the whole and indissoluble material and social process. 'Ideology' then reverts to a specific and practical dimension: the complicated process within which men 'become' (are) conscious of their interests and their conflicts. The categorical short-cut to an (abstract) distinction between 'true' and 'false' consciousness is then effectively abandoned, as in all practice it has to be.

All these varying uses of 'ideology' have persisted within the general development of Marxism. There has been a convenient dogmatic retention, at some levels, of ideology as 'false consciousness'. This has often prevented the more specific analysis of operative distinctions of 'true' and 'false' consciousness at the practical level, which is always that of social relationships, and of the part played in these relationships by 'conceptions, thoughts, ideas'. There was a late attempt, by Lukács, to clarify this analysis by a distinction between 'actual consciousness' and 'imputed' or 'potential' consciousness (a full and 'true' understanding of a real social position). This has the merit of avoiding the reduction of all 'actual consciousness' to ideology, but the category is speculative, and indeed *as a category* cannot easily be sustained. In *History and Class Consciousness* it depended on a last abstract attempt to identify truth with the idea of the proletariat, but in this Hegelian form it is no more convincing than the earlier positivist identification of a category of 'scientific knowledge'. A more interesting but equally difficult attempt to define 'true' consciousness was the elaboration of Marx's point about changing the world rather than interpreting it. What became known as the 'test of practice' was offered as a criterion of truth and as the essential distinction from ideology. In certain general ways this is a wholly consistent projection from the idea of 'practical consciousness', but it is easy to see how its application to specific theories, formulations, and programmes can result either in a vulgar 'success' ethic, masquerading as 'historical truth', or in numbness or confusion when there are practical defeats and deformations. The 'test of practice', that is to say, cannot be applied to 'scientific theory' and 'ideology' taken as abstract categories. The real point of the definition of 'practical consciousness' was indeed to undercut these abstractions, which nevertheless have continued to be reproduced as 'Marxist theory'.

Three other tendencies in twentieth-century concepts of ideology may be briefly noted. First, the concept has been commonly used, within Marxism and outside it, in the relatively neutral sense of 'a system of beliefs characteristic of a particular class or group' (without implications of 'truth' or 'illusion' but with positive reference to a social situation and interest and its defining or constitutive system of meanings and values). It is thus possible to speak neutrally or even approvingly of 'socialist ideology'. A curious example here is that of Lenin:

> Socialism, in so far as it is the ideology of struggle of the proletarian class, undergoes the general conditions of birth, development and consolidation of any ideology, that is to say it is founded on all the material of human knowledge, it presupposes a high level of science, scientific work, etc. . . . In the class struggle of the proletariat which develops spontaneously, as an elemental force, on the basis of capitalist relations, socialism is introduced by the ideologists.[3]

Obviously 'ideology' here is not intended as 'false consciousness'. The distinction between a class and its ideologists can be related to the distinction made by Marx and Engels, but one crucial clause of this – active, conceptive ideologists, who make the perfecting of the illusion of the class about itself their chief source of livelihood' – has then to be tacitly dropped, unless the reference to a 'ruling class' can be dressed up as a saving clause. More significantly, perhaps, 'ideology' in its now neutral or approving sense is seen as 'introduced' on the foundation of 'all . . . human knowledge . . . science . . . etc', of course brought to bear from a class point of view. The position is clearly that ideology is theory and that theory is at once secondary and necessary; 'practical consciousness', as here of the proletariat, will not itself produce it. This is radically different from Marx's thinking, where all 'separate' theory is ideology, and where genuine theory – 'real, positive knowledge' – is, by contrast, the articulation of 'practical consciousness'. But Lenin's model corresponds to one orthodox sociological formulation, in which there is 'social situation' and there is also 'ideology', their relations variable but certainly neither dependent nor 'determined', thus allowing both their separate and their comparative history and analysis. Lenin's formulation also echoes, from a quite opposite political position, Napoleon's identification of 'the ideologists', who bring ideas to 'the people', for their liberation or destruction according to point of view. The Napoleonic definition, in an unaltered form, has of course also persisted, as a popular form of criticism of political struggles which are defined by ideas or even by principles. 'Ideology' (the product of 'doctrinaires') is then contrasted with 'practical experience', 'practical politics', and what is known as pragmatism. This general sense of 'ideology' as not only 'doctrinaire' and 'dogmatic' but as *a priori* and abstract has co-existed uneasily with the equally general (neutral or approving) descriptive sense.

Finally there is an obvious need for a general term to describe not only the products but the processes of all signification, including the signification of values. It is interesting that 'ideology' and 'ideological' have been widely used in this sense. Vološinov, for example, uses 'ideological' to describe the process of the production of meaning through signs, and 'ideology' is taken as the dimension of social experience in which meanings and values are produced. The difficult relation of so wide a sense to the other senses which we have seen to be active hardly needs stressing. Yet, however, far the term itself may be compromised, some form of this emphasis on signification as a central social process is necessary. In Marx, in Engels, and in much of the Marxist tradition the central argument about 'practical consciousness' was limited and frequently distorted by failures to see that the fundamental processes of social signification are intrinsic to 'practical consciousness' and intrinsic also to the 'conceptions, thoughts, and ideas' which are recognizable as its products. The limiting condition within 'ideology' as a concept, from its beginning in Destutt, was the tendency to limit processes of meaning and valuation to formed, separable 'ideas' or 'theories'. To attempt to take these back to 'a world of sensations' or, on the other hand, to a 'practical consciousness' or a 'material social process' which has been so defined as to exclude these fundamental signifying processes, or to make them essentially secondary, is the persistent thread of error. For the practical links between 'ideas' and 'theories' and the 'production of real life' are all in this material social process of signification itself.

Moreover, when this is realized, those 'products' which are not ideas or theories, but which are the very different works we call 'art' and 'literature', and which are normal elements of the very general processes we call 'culture' and 'language', can be approached in ways other than reduction, abstraction, or assimilation. This is the argument that has now to be taken into cultural and literary studies, and especially into the Marxist contribution to them, which, in spite of appearances, is then likely to be even more controversial than hitherto. But it is then an open question whether 'ideology' and 'ideological', with their senses of 'abstraction' and 'illusion', or their senses of 'ideas' and 'theories', or even their senses of a 'system' of beliefs or of meanings and values, are sufficiently precise and practicable terms for so far-reaching and radical a redefinition.

Notes

1. Cited in A. NAESS, *Democracy, Ideology, and Objectivity* (Oslo, 1956), p. 151.
2. Letter to F. Mehring, 14 July 1893: *Marx and Engels: Selected Correspondence* (New York, 1935).
3. LENIN, *What is to be Done?* II (Oxford).

11 'Ideology'*

JÜRGEN HABERMAS

The most prominent modern-day heir of the Frankfurt School, Jürgen Habermas (b. 1929) teaches at the Johann Wolfgang Goethe University in Frankfurt. A versatile and prolific thinker, his work spans sociology, psychology, ethics, aesthetics, philosophy and political theory; among his major works have been *Knowledge and Human Interests* (1968), *The Theory of Communicative Action* (Boston: Beacon Press, 1981) and *The Philosophical Discourse of Modernity* (1985).

The kernel of Habermas's work has been an attempt to ground the idea of the just society in a particular model of human communicative rationality. But Habermas has been also much preoccupied with what he sees as the fundamental changes which industrial capitalist societies have undergone, as state intervention, bureaucracy and technological development erode the possibility of a public sphere of democratic discourse. In this essay, he considers the effect of these changes on the classical concept of ideology, and argues for a significant revision of the traditional Marxist view of the topic in the light of a new social order where economic 'base' and political 'superstructure' can be seen increasingly to interpenetrate.

By the middle of the nineteenth century the capitalist mode of production had developed so fully in England and France that Marx was able to identify the locus of the institutional framework of society in the relations of production and at the same time criticize the legitimating basis constituted by the exchange of equivalents. He carried out the critique of bourgeois ideology in the form of *political economy*. His labour theory of value destroyed the semblance of freedom, by means of which the legal institution of the free labour contract had made unrecognizable the relationship of social force that underlay the wage–labour relationship. Marcuse's criticism of Weber is that the latter, disregarding this Marxian

*Reprinted from Tom Bottomore (ed.), *Interpretations of Marx* (1968; Oxford: Basil Blackwell, 1988), pp. 299–309.

insight, upholds an abstract concept of rationalization, which not merely fails to express the specific class content of the adaptation of the institutional framework to the developing systems of purposive-rational action, but conceals it. Marcuse knows that the Marxian analysis can no longer be applied as it stands to advanced capitalist society, with which Weber was already confronted. But he wants to show through the example of Weber that the evolution of modern society in the framework of state-regulated capitalism cannot be conceptualized if liberal capitalism has not been analysed adequately.

Since the last quarter of the nineteenth century two developmental tendencies have become noticeable in the most advanced capitalist countries: an increase in state intervention in order to secure the system's stability, and a growing interdependence of research and technology, which has turned the sciences into the leading productive force. Both tendencies have destroyed the particular constellation of institutional framework and sub-systems of purposive-rational action which characterized liberal capitalism, thereby eliminating the conditions relevant for the application of political economy in the version correctly formulated by Marx for liberal capitalism. I believe that Marcuse's basic thesis, according to which technology and science today also take on the function of legitimating political power, is the key to analysing the changed constellation.

The permanent regulation of the economic process by means of state intervention arose as a defence mechanism against the dysfunctional tendencies which threaten the system, that capitalism generates when left to itself. Capitalism's actual development manifestly contradicted the capitalist idea of a bourgeois society, emancipated from domination, in which power is neutralized. The root ideology of just exchange, which Marx unmasked in theory, collapsed in practice. The form of capital utilization through private ownership could only be maintained by the governmental corrective of a social and economic policy that stabilized the business cycle. The institutional framework of society was repoliticized. It no longer coincides immediately with the relations of production, i.e. with an order of private law that secures capitalist economic activity and the corresponding general guarantees of order provided by the bourgeois state. But this means a change in the relation of the economy to the political system: politics is no longer *only* a phenomenon of the superstructure. If society no longer 'autonomously' perpetuates itself through self-regulation as a sphere preceding and lying at the basis of the state – and its ability to do so was the really novel feature of the capitalist mode of production – then society and the state are no longer in the relationship that Marxian theory had defined as that of base and superstructure. Then, however, a critical theory of society can no longer be constructed in the exclusive from of a critique of political economy. A point of view that methodically isolates the economic laws of motion of society can claim to grasp the overall structure of social life in its essential categories only as long as politics depends on the economic base. It becomes inapplicable when the 'base' has to be comprehended as in itself a function of governmental activity and political conflicts. According to Marx, the critique of political economy was the theory of bourgeois society only as *critique of ideology*. If, however, the ideology of just exchange disintegrates, then the power structure can no longer be criticized *immediately* at the level of the relations of production.

With the collapse of this ideology, political power requires a new legitimation. Now since the power indirectly exercised over the exchange process is itself operating under political control and state regulation, legitimation can no longer be derived from the unpolitical order constituted by the relations of production. To this extent the requirement for direct legitimation, which exists in precapitalist societies, reappears. On the other hand, the resuscitation of immediate political domination (in the traditional form of legitimation on the basis of cosmological world views) has become impossible. For traditions have already been disempowered. Moreover, in industrially developed societies the results of bourgeois emancipation from immediate political domination (civil and political rights and the mechanism of general elections) can be fully ignored only in periods of reaction. Formally democratic government in systems of state-regulated capitalism is subject to a need for legitimation which cannot be met by a return to a pre-bourgeois form. Hence the ideology of free exchange is replaced by a substitute programme. The latter is oriented not to the social results of the institution of the market but to those of government action designed to compensate for the dysfunctions of free exchange. This policy combines the element of the bourgeois ideology of achievement (which, however, displaces assignment of status according to the standard of individual achievement from the market to the school system) with a guaranteed minimum level of welfare, which offers secure employment and a stable income. This substitute programme obliges the political system to maintain stabilizing conditions for an economy that guards against risks to growth and guarantees social security and the chance for individual upward mobility. What is needed to this end is latitude for manipulation by state interventions that, at the cost of limiting the institutions of private law, secure the private form of capital utilization *and bind the masses' loyalty to this form*.

In so far as government action is directed toward the economic system's stability and growth, politics now takes on a peculiarly negative character. For it is oriented toward the elimination of dysfunctions and the avoidance of risks that threaten the system: not, in other words, toward the *realization of practical goals* but toward the *solution of technical problems*. Claus Offe pointed this out in his paper at the 1968 Frankfurt Sociological Conference:

In this structure of the relation of economy and the state, 'politics' degenerates into action that follows numerous and continually emerging 'avoidance imperatives': the mass of differentiated social-scientific information that flows into the political system allows both the early identification of risk zones and the treatment of actual dangers. What is new about this structure is . . . that the risks to stability built into the mechanism of private capital utilization in highly organized markets, risks that can be manipulated, prescribe preventive actions and measures that *must* be accepted as long as they are to accord with the existing legitimation resources (i.e., substitute programme).[1]

Offe perceives that through these preventive action-orientations, government activity is restricted to administratively soluble technical problems, so that practical questions evaporate, so to speak. *Practical substance is eliminated.*

Old-style politics was forced, merely through its traditional form of legitimation, to define itself in relation to practical goals: the 'good life' was interpreted in a context defined by interaction relations. The same still held for the ideology of bourgeois society. The substitute programme prevailing today, in contrast, is aimed exclusively at the functioning of a manipulated system. It eliminates practical questions and therewith precludes discussion about the adoption of standards; the latter could emerge only from a democratic decision-making process. The solution of technical problems is not dependent on public discussion. Rather, public discussion could render problematic the framework within which the tasks of government action present themselves as technical ones. Therefore the new politics of state interventionism requires a depoliticization of the mass of the population. To the extent that practical questions are eliminated, the public realm also loses its political function. At the same time, the institutional framework of society is still distinct from the systems of purposive-rational action themselves. Its organization continues to be a problem of *practice* linked to communication, not one of *technology*, no matter how scientifically guided. Hence, the bracketing out of practice associated with the new kind of politics is not automatic. The substitute programme, which legitimates power today, leaves unfilled a vital need for legitimation: how will the depoliticization of the masses be made plausible to them? Marcuse would be able to answer: by having technology and science *also* take on the role of an ideology.

Since the end of the nineteenth century the other developmental tendency characteristic of advanced capitalism has become increasingly momentous: the scientization of technology. The institutional pressure to augment the productivity of labour through the introduction of new technology has always existed under capitalism. But innovations depended on sporadic inventions, which, while economically motivated, were still fortuitous in character. This changed as technical development entered into a feedback relation with the progress of the modern sciences. With the advent of large-scale industrial research, science, technology and industrial utilization were fused into a system. Since then, industrial research has been linked up with research under government contract, which primarily promotes scientific and technical progress in the military sector. From there information flows back into the sectors of civilian production. Thus technology and science become a leading productive force, rendering inoperative the conditions for Marx's labour theory of value. It is no longer meaningful to calculate the amount of capital investment in research and development on the basis of the value of unskilled (simple) labour power, when scientific-technical progress has become an independent source of surplus-value, in relation to which the only source of surplus-value considered by Marx, namely the labour power of the immediate producers, plays an ever smaller role.[2]

As long as the productive forces were visibly linked to the rational decisions and instrumental action of men engaged in social production, they could be understood as the potential for a growing power of technical control and not be confused with the institutional framework in which they are embedded. However, with the institutionalization of scientific-technical progress, the potential of the productive forces has assumed a form owing to which men lose consciousness of the dualism of work and interaction.

It is true that social interests still determine the direction, functions and pace of technical progress. But these interests define the social system so much as a whole that they coincide with the interest in maintaining the system. *As such* the private form of capital utilization and a distribution mechanism for social rewards that guarantees the loyalty of the masses are removed from discussion. The quasi-autonomous progress of science and technology then appears as an independent variable on which the most important single system variable, namely economic growth, depends. Thus arises a perspective in which the development of the social system *seems* to be determined by the logic of scientific-technical progress. The immanent law of this progress seems to produce objective exigencies, which must be obeyed by any politics oriented toward functional needs. But when this semblance has taken root effectively, then propaganda can refer to the role of technology and science in order to explain and legitimate why in modern societies the process of democratic decision-making about practical problems loses its function and 'must' be replaced by plebiscitary decisions about alternative sets of leaders of administrative personnel. This technocracy thesis has been worked out in several versions on the intellectual level.[3] What seems to me more important is that it can also become a background ideology that penetrates into the consciousness of the depoliticized mass of the population, where it can take on legitimating power.[4] It is a singular achievement of this ideology to detach society's self-understanding from the frame of reference of communicative action and from the concepts of symbolic interaction and replace it with a scientific model. Accordingly the culturally defined self-understanding of a social life-world is replaced by the self-reification of men under categories of purposive-rational action and adaptive behaviour.

The model according to which the planned reconstruction of society is to proceed is taken from systems analysis. It is possible in principle to comprehend and analyse individual enterprises and organizations, even political or economic sub-systems and social systems as a whole, according to the pattern of self-regulated systems. It makes a difference, of course, whether we use a cybernetic frame of reference for analytic purposes or *organize* a given social system in accordance with this pattern as a man-machine system. But the transferral of the analytic model to the level of social organization is implied by the very approach taken by systems analysis. Carrying out this intention of an instinct-like self-stabilization of social systems yields the peculiar perspective that the structure of one of the two types of action, namely the behavioural system of purposive-rational action, not only predominates over the institutional framework but gradually absorbs communicative action as such. If, with Arnold Gehlen, one were to see the inner logic of technical development as the step-by-step disconnection of the behavioural system of purposive-rational action from the human organism and its transferral to machines, then the technocratic intention could be understood as the last stage of this development. For the first time man can not only, as *homo faber*, completely objectify himself and confront the achievements that have taken on independent life in his products; he can in addition, as *homo fabricatus*, be integrated into his technical apparatus if the structure of purposive-rational action can be successfully reproduced on the level of social systems. According to this idea the institutional framework of society – which previously was rooted in a different type of action – would now, in a fundamental reversal, be *absorbed* by the sub-systems of purposive-rational action, which were embedded in it.

Of course this technocratic intention has not been realized anywhere even in its beginnings. But it serves as an ideology for the new politics, which is adapted to technical problems and brackets out practical questions. Furthermore it does correspond to certain developmental tendencies that could lead to a creeping erosion of what we have called the institutional framework. The manifest domination of the authoritarian state gives way to the manipulative compulsions of technical-operational administration. The moral realization of a normative order is a function of communicative action oriented to shared cultural meaning and presupposing the internalization of values. It is increasingly supplanted by conditioned behaviour, while large organizations as such are increasingly patterned after the structure of purposive-rational action. The industrially most advanced societies seem to approximate the model of behavioural control steered by external stimuli rather than guided by norms. Indirect control through fabricated stimuli has increased, especially in areas of putative subjective freedom (such as electoral, consumer, and leisure behaviour). Socio-psychologically, the era is typified less by the authoritarian personality than by the destructuring of the superego. The increase in *adaptive behaviour* is, however, only the obverse of the dissolution of the sphere of linguistically mediated interaction by the structure of purposive-rational action. This is paralleled subjectively by the disappearance of the difference between purposive-rational action and interaction from the consciousness not only of the sciences of man, but of men themselves. The concealment of this difference proves the ideological power of the technocratic consciousness.

In consequence of the two tendencies that have been discussed, capitalist society has changed to the point where two key categories of Marxian theory, namely class struggle and ideology, can no longer be employed as they stand.

It was on the basis of the capitalist mode of production that the struggle of social classes as such was constituted, thereby creating an objective situation from which the class structure of traditional society, with its immediately political constitution, could be *recognized* in retrospect. State-regulated capitalism, which emerged from a reaction against the dangers to the system produced by open class antagonism, suspends class conflict. The system of advanced capitalism is so defined by a policy of securing the loyalty of the wage-earning masses through rewards, that is, by avoiding conflict, that the conflict still built into the structure of society in virtue of the private mode of capital utilization is the very area of conflict which has the greatest probability of remaining latent. It recedes behind others, which, while conditioned by the mode of production, can no longer assume the form of class conflicts. In the paper cited, Claus Offe has analysed this paradoxical state of affairs, showing that open conflicts about social interests break out with greater probability the less their frustration has dangerous consequences for the system. The needs with the greatest conflict potential are those on the periphery of the area of state intervention. They are far from the central conflict being kept in a state of latency, and therefore they are not seen as having priority among dangers to be warded off. Conflicts are set off by these needs to the extent that disproportionately scattered state interventions produce backward areas of development and corresponding disparity tensions:

> The disparity between areas of life grows above all in view of the differential state of development obtaining between the actually institutionalized and the possible level of technical and social progress.

The disproportion between the most modern apparatuses for industrial and military purposes and the stagnating organization of the transport, health and educational systems is just as well known an example of this disparity between areas of life as is the contradiction between rational planning and regulation in taxation and finance policy and the unplanned, haphazard development of cities and regions. Such contradictions can no longer be designated accurately as antagonisms between classes, yet they can still be interpreted as results of the still dominant process of the private utilization of capital and of a specifically capitalist power structure. In this process the prevailing interests are those which, without being clearly localizable, are in a position, on the basis of the established mechanism of the capitalist economy, to react to disturbances of the conditions of their stability by producing risks relevant to the system as a whole.[5]

The interests bearing on the maintenance of the mode of production can no longer be 'clearly localized' in the social system as class interests. For the power structure, aimed as it is at avoiding dangers to the system, precisely excludes 'domination' (as immediate political or economically mediated social force) exercised in such a manner that one class subject *confronts* another as an identifiable group.

This means not that class antagonisms have been abolished but that they have become *latent*. Class distinctions persist in the form of sub-cultural traditions and corresponding differences not only in the standard of living and life-style but also in political attitude. The social structure also makes it probable that the class of wage earners will be hit harder than other groups by social disparities. And finally, the generalized interest in perpetuating the system is still anchored today, on the level of immediate life chances, in a structure of privilege. The concept of an interest that has become *completely* independent of living subjects would cancel itself out. But with the deflection of dangers to the system in state-regulated capitalism, the political system has incorporated an interest – which transcends latent class boundaries – in preserving the compensatory distribution façade.

Furthermore, the displacement of the conflict zone from the class boundary to the underprivileged regions of life does not mean at all that serious conflict potential has been disposed of. As the extreme example of racial conflict in the United States shows, so many consequences of disparity can accumulate in certain areas and groups that explosions resembling civil war can occur. But unless they are connected with protest potential from other sectors of society no conflicts arising from such underprivilege can really overturn the system – they can only provoke it to sharp reactions incompatible with formal democracy. For underprivileged groups are not social classes, nor do they ever even potentially represent

197

the mass of the population. Their *disfranchisement* and pauperization no longer coincide with *exploitation*, because the system does not live off their labour. They can represent at most a past phase of exploitation. But they cannot through the withdrawal of cooperation attain the demands that they legitimately put forward. That is why these demands retain an appellative character. In the case of long-term non-consideration of their legitimate demands underprivileged groups can in extreme situations react with desperate destruction and self-destruction. But as long as no coalitions are made with privileged groups, such a civil war lacks the chance of revolutionary success that class struggle possesses.

With a series of restrictions this model seems applicable even to the relations between the industrially advanced nations and the formerly colonial areas of the Third World. Here, too, growing disparity leads to a form of underprivilege that in the future surely will be increasingly less comprehensible through categories of exploitation. Economic interests are replaced on this level, however, with immediately military ones.

Be that as it may, in advanced capitalist society deprived and privileged groups no longer confront each other *as* socio-economic classes – and to some extent the boundaries of underprivilege are no longer even specific to groups and instead run across population categories. Thus the fundamental relation that existed in all traditional societies and that came to the fore under liberal capitalism is mediatized, namely the class antagonism between partners who stand in an institutionalized relationship of force, economic exploitation and political oppression to one another, and in which communication is so distorted and restricted that the legitimations serving as an ideological veil cannot be called into question. Hegel's concept of the ethical totality of a living relationship which is sundered because one subject does not reciprocally satisfy the needs of the other is no longer an appropriate model for the mediatized class structure of organized, advanced capitalism. The suspended dialectic of the ethical generates the peculiar semblance of *post-histoire*. The reason is that relative growth of the productive forces no longer represents *eo ipso* a potential that points beyond the existing framework with emancipatory consequences, in view of which legitimations of an existing power structure become enfeebled. For the leading productive force – controlled for scientific-technical progress itself – has now become the basis of legitimation. Yet this new form of legitimation has cast off the old shape of *ideology*.

Technocratic consciousness is, on the one hand, 'less ideological' than all previous ideologies. For it does not have the opaque force of a delusion that only transfigures the implementation of interests. On the other hand today's dominant, rather glassy background ideology, which makes a fetish of science, is more irresistible and farther-reaching than ideologies of the old type. For with the veiling of practical problems it not only justifies a *particular class's* interest in domination and represses *another class's* partial need for emancipation, but affects the human race's emancipatory interest as such.

Technocratic consciousness is not a rationalized, wish-fulfilling fantasy, not an 'illusion' in Freud's sense, in which a system of interaction is either represented or interpreted and grounded. Even bourgeois ideologies could be traced back to a basic pattern of just interactions, free of domination and mutually satisfactory. It was these ideologies which met the criteria of wish-fulfilment and substitute gratification; the communication on which they were based was so limited by repressions that the relation of force once institutionalized as the capital – labour relation could not even be called by name. But the technocratic consciousness is not based in the same way on the causality of dissociated symbols and unconscious motives, which generates both false consciousness and the power of reflection to which the critique of ideology is indebted. It is less vulnerable to reflection, because it is no longer *only* ideology. For it does not, in the manner of ideology, express a projection of the 'good life' (which even if not identifiable with a bad reality, can at least be brought into virtually satisfactory accord with it). Of course the new ideology, like the old, serves to impede making the foundations of society the object of thought and reflection. Previously, social force lay at the basis of the relation between capitalist and wage labourers. Today the basis is provided by structural conditions which predefine the tasks of system maintenance: the private form of capital utilization and a political form of distributing social rewards that guarantees mass loyalty. However, the old and new ideology differ in two ways.

First, the capital–labour relation today, because of its linkage to a loyalty-ensuring political distribution mechanism, no longer engenders uncorrected exploitation and oppression. The process through which the persisting class antagonism has been made virtual presupposes that the repression on which the latter is based first came to consciousness in history and *only then* was stabilized in a modified form as a property of the system. Technocratic consciousness, therefore, cannot rest in the same way on collective repression as did earlier ideologies. Second, mass loyalty today is created only with the aid of rewards for *privatized needs*. The achievements in virtue of which the system justifies itself may not in principle be interpreted politically. The acceptable interpretation is immediately in terms of allocations of money and leisure time (neutral with regard to their use), and mediately in terms of the technocratic justification of the occlusion of practical questions. Hence the new ideology is distinguished from its predecessor in that it severs the criteria for justifying the organization of social life from any normative regulation of interaction, thus depoliticizing them. It anchors them instead in functions of a putative system of purposive-rational action.

Technocratic consciousness reflects not the sundering of an ethical situation but the repression of 'ethics' as such as a category of life. The common, positivist way of thinking renders inert the frame of reference of interaction in ordinary language, in which domination and ideology both arise under conditions of distorted communication and can be reflectively detected and broken down. The depoliticization of the mass of the population, which is legitimated through technocratic consciousness, is at the same time men's self-objectification in categories equally of both purposive-rational action and adaptive behaviour. The reified models of the sciences migrate into the socio-cultural life-world and gain objective power over the latter's self-understanding. The ideological nucleus of this consciousness is *the elimination of the distinction between the practical and the technical*. It reflects, but does not objectively account for, the new constellation of a disempowered institutional framework and systems of purposive-rational action that have taken on a life of their own.

The new ideology consequently violates an interest grounded in one of the two fundamental conditions of our cultural existence: in language, or more precisely, in the form of socialization and individuation determined by communication in ordinary language. This interest extends to the maintenance of intersubjectivity of mutual understanding as well as to the creation of communication without domination. Technocratic consciousness makes this practical interest disappear behind the interest in the expansion of our power of technical control. Thus the reflection that the new ideology calls for must penetrate beyond the level of particular historical class interests to disclose the fundamental interests of mankind as such, engaged in the process of self-constitution.[6]

If the relativization of the field of application of the concept of ideology and the theory of class be confirmed, then the category framework developed by Marx in the basic assumptions of historical materialism requires a new formulation. The model of forces of production and relations of production would have to be replaced by the more abstract one of work and interaction. The relations of production designate a level on which the institutional framework was anchored only during the phase of the development of liberal capitalism, and not either before or after. To be sure, the productive forces, in which the learning processes organized in the sub-systems of purposive-rational action accumulate, have been from the very beginning the motive force of social evolution. But, they do not appear, as Marx supposed, *under all circumstances* to be a potential for liberation and to set off emancipatory movements – at least not once the continual growth of the productive forces has become dependent on scientific-technical progress that has *also* taken on functions of *legitimating political power*. I suspect that the frame of reference developed in terms of the analogous, but more general relation of institutional framework (interaction) and sub-systems of purposive-rational action ('work' in the broad sense of instrumental and strategic action) is more suited to reconstructing the socio-cultural phases of the history of mankind.

Notes

1. CLAUS OFFE, 'Politische Herrschaft und Klassenstrukturen', in Gisela Kress and Dieter Senghaas (eds), *Politikwissenschaft*. The quotation in the text is from the original manuscript, which differs in formulation from the published text.
2. The most recent explication of this is EUGEN LÖBL, *Geistige Arbeit – die wahre Quelle des Reichtums*, translated from the Czech by Leopold Grünwald.
3. See HELMUT SCHELSKY, *Der Mensch in der wissenschaftlichen Zivilisation*; JACQUES ELLUL, *The Technological Society*; and ARNOLD GEHELN, 'Uber kulturelle Kristallisationen', in *Studien zur Anthropologie und Soziologie*; and 'Über kulturelle Evolution', in *Die Philosophie und die Frage nach dem Fortschritt*, M. Hahn and F. Wiedmann (eds).
4. To my knowledge there are no empirical studies concerned specifically with the propagation of this background ideology. We are dependent on extrapolations from the findings of other investigations.
5. OFFE, 'Politische Herrschaft und Klassenstrukturen'.
6. See my essay 'Erkenntnis und Interesse' in *Technik und Wissenschaft als 'Ideologie'*. It will appear in English as an appendix to *Knowledge and Human Interests*.

12 Ideological Discourse as Rationality and False Consciousness*

ALVIN GOULDNER

Alvin Gouldner was an American sociologist who had been prominent among those for whom ideology is a distinctive *modern* term, sharply distinguishable from the myth and religion of 'traditional' societies. In contrast to these essentially 'closed' universes, Gouldner saw ideology as a practical, rational discourse whose point is to mobilise men and women for particular political projects, and whose rhetoric is open to argument and debate. Ideology thus belongs to the public sphere of a secularised, modernised world, and for Gouldner is especially bound up with the predominance of the 'word', of discursive persuasion and mass communication, in such modern social orders.

Ideology premises the existence of 'normal' participants or normal speakers; of normal situations in which they conduct their discourse; of the rules admitting them to the discourse, and governing their conduct during it. This is as true of ideological discourse as of others. In ordinary language it is significant that we do not usually speak of *children* as having an ideology. Commonly, ideology is taken to imply a normal speaker beyond a certain minimum age, of a certain imputed maturity and linguistic competence. In short, reference is made to a responsible and potent subject.

But it is not just because children are defined as immature intellectually that they are *not* commonly seen as having ideologies. For the normal expression of ideological adherence is an act in the public sphere, to which children have only limited access. Ideologies entail discourse among members of different families, not just within them; discourse among strangers, not just among friends.

Ideologies may organize social action and social solidarities in ways irrelevant to, or cutting across, the traditional structures of society – family, neighborhood, or church. Ideologies can bind men who may have little in

*Reprinted from ALVIN GOULDNER, *The Dialectic of Ideology and Technology* (London: Macmillan, 1976), pp. 23–31.

common except a shared idea. Ideologies thus premise the possibility of powerful affinities, of claims and obligations among persons bound only by common belief. In some part, it is possible for them to do so because of the deterioration of traditional social structures in the transition from old regime society to modern bourgeois societies.

1

The ideological mobilization of masses (like the use of ideology as a basis of social solidarities) premises a detraditionalization of society and of communication, of what is allowed to be brought into open discussion, to be sought and claimed. In traditional societies only relatively fixed and limited claims might be made; and these were already known and established, for the legitimate in traditional societies is the What Has Been, the Old; only fairly fixed, limited, and stereotyped claims may be made under traditionalism. The manner in which claims could be justified was correspondingly limited. Speech was, more typically, authorized by the authority or social position of the speaker.

The emergence of ideology, however, premises that new kinds of claims and new kinds of legitimations (for them) are now possible and, at the same time, that the old stereotyped limits on what is claimable have been removed. Now, almost anything might be claimed. In this limitlessness of possibility some begin to experience themselves as potent Prometheans or, from another standpoint, as anomically insatiable. As Lucien Goldmann puts it, '. . . once the possibility of supernatural interference was destroyed, everything became both natural and possible.' Everything: including both man's terror and his reification.

An intact traditional society, then, leaves little room for the play and appeal of ideologies. But, at the same time, ideologies have their own reciprocally deteriorating impact upon traditional structures and on people's involvement in them.

1.1

Ideologies weaken traditional structures by refocusing the vision of everyday life and, specifically, by calling to mind things that are not in normal evidence, not directly viewable by the senses, not in the circumference of the immediate – they make reference to things not 'at hand.' One cannot, for example, *see* a 'class,' or a 'nation,' or a 'free market,' but the ideologies of socialism, nationalism, and liberalism bring these structures to *mind*. In doing so, they provide a language that enables interpretations to be made of some things that *may* be seen or heard within the immediate. Ideologies permit some of the seen-but-unnoticed aspects of everyday life to be seen *and* newly noticed. Ideologies permit interpretations of the everyday life that are not possible within the terms of everyday life's *ordinary* language: an argument between workers and foreman may now, for example, be interpreted as an intensifying 'class struggle.' Ideologies become the self-consciousness of ordinary language; they are a metalanguage.

The tradition-dissolving consequences of ideology arise, in part, because they enable actors to acquire distance from the at-hand immediacies of everyday life, to begin to see the world in ways that go beyond the limits of ordinary language; and they may create new solidarities that distance persons from traditional involvements, from family and neighbors. Ideologies, then, enable people more effectively to pursue interests without being restricted by particularistic ties and by the conventional bonds of sentiment or loyalty that kinsmen and neighbors owe one another. Ideology serves to uproot people; to further uproot the already uprooted, to extricate them from immediate and traditional social structures; to elude the limits of the 'common sense' and the limiting perspective of ordinary language, thus enabling persons to pursue projects they have *chosen*. Ideologies thus clearly contribute, at least in these ways, both to rational discourse and rational politics, but to a rationality that is both activated and limited by anxieties exacerbated by an uprooting from at-hand, everyday life. Ideologies capture and refocus energies involved in free-floating anxieties. Anxiety liquidates old symbolic commitments, allowing men to seek new ones and to judge them in new ways; but anxiety also means that this must be done urgently.

1.2

Eric Hobsbawm's discussion of the transition from the older traditionalism to the newer age of ideologies quite properly stresses that it is a passage from the dominance of religious thought systems to more secular ones: 'For most of history and over most of the world . . . the terms in which all but a handful of educated and emancipated men thought about the world were those of traditional religion. . . . At some stage before 1848, this ceased to be so in part of Europe. . . . Religion stopped being something like the sky . . . became something like a bank of clouds. . . . Of all the ideological changes this is by far the most profound. . . . At all events, it is the most unprecedented. What was unprecedented was the secularization of the masses. . . . In the ideologies of the American and French . . . Christianity is irrelevant. . . . The general trend of the period from 1789 to 1848 was therefore one of emphatic secularization.'[1]

If men like de Maistre, de Bonald, or Burke spoke well of religion and tradition, they spoke with a rationality and awareness that manifested that these were no longer the things they had once been, but something quite new. Most great and articulate defenses of traditionalism are, and can only be, made from a standpoint outside of it. Outside of the time when it was a viable and uncontested force, as de Maistre and de Bonald wrote *following* the French Revolution; or outside of the membership boundaries that the tradition had marked out, as Edmund Burke was. An Irishman seeking his fortune in England, Burke embraced its cracking traditions with the fervor of the new convert and with the ability to see it as a boundaried whole possible only to someone not born to it. In like manner, it was only the sharp crisis of established religion that could then enable Madame de Stäel to speak of the need to believe *something,* and which led Georg Brandes to speak of men looking at eighteenth-century religion 'pathetically, gazing at it from the outside, as one looks at an object in a museum.' As Karl Mannheim observed, tradition was being transformed into *conservatism* via this self-awareness and via the justification of rational discussion. Tradition was, in short, being modernized into an 'ideology.'

1.3

Like conventional religion, ideology too seeks to shape men's behavior. Religion, however, focuses on the *everyday life* and on its proper conduct. Ideology, by contrast, is concerned not so much with the routine immediacies of the everyday, but with achieving especially mobilized projects. Ideology seeks to gather, assemble, husband, defer, and control the *discharge* of political energies. Religion, however, is ultimately concerned with the round of daily existence and the recurrent crises of the life cycle. Ideologies assemble scarce *energies* for focused concentrated discharge in the public sphere. Religion constantly monitors, disciplines, and inhibits discharges of energy into the everyday life. Birth, puberty, marriage, death, and grief are its central concerns. Ideology functions to change institutions by mobilizing energies and concerting public projects freely undertaken, which are justified by world-referencing rational discourse. Ideology seeks earthly reaction, reform, or revolution, not transcendental reconciliation. Religions are concerned with the sacred and thus those powers within whose limits, or under whose governance, men act. Religions thus see men as limited, created, or other-grounded beings and foster a sense of men's limitedness; ideologies, by contrast, focus on men as sources of authority and as sites of energy and power. If religions and ideologies are thus disposed to a different ontology of man, they are also, correspondingly, disposed to different epistemologies, religion making knowledge (or *part* of it) a phenomenon that is *bestowed* on men and vouchsafed by higher powers and authorities, while ideologies give greater emphasis to the self-groundedness of men's knowledge, involving his reason and his experience: *cogito ergo sum.*

Yet if ideologies (conceived in their modern historical uniqueness) are secularized and rational belief-systems, they embody and rest upon a unique secularization that is linked in the West to the last great revival of religious zeal, the emergence of Protestantism. Auguste Comte's instinct here was correct, especially in his tacit linking of Protestantism to the proliferation of ideologies, which he offered to transcend via his positivism. When Comte deplored the 'anarchy' brought by the modern 'liberty of conscience' he tacitly contended that this ideological diversity had a *religious* root. Certainly, modern ideological diversity was partly grounded in Protestantism's insistence on liberty of conscience. More than that, this liberty of conscience goes to the core of modern ideology's tacit but characteristic insistence on the individual's right to make his own judgment about the truth of claims and, correspondingly, on the importance of persuading him of that truth in its own, new ways. Modern ideology is grounded in Protestantism's conception of the rights and, as I shall stress later, of the *powers*, of individuals.

The age of ideology premised the prior experience of the band of emerging protest-ants; it is grounded in the diffusion of this concrete historical experience into a *tacit*, secularized paradigm for a broader politics of protest. Modern ideology premised Protestantism's this-worldly ascetic activism and, on a different level, modern ideology premised the activistic inclinations with which this religious transformation – among other forces – had sedimented the modern character.

1.4

Ideology also premises the deritualization of public communication so characteristic of the Puritan revolution. In this, the sermon exhorting men to abide by the Word was substituted for the ritualized Mass.[2] Through the sermon, men were called to a unity of theory and practice and to a conforming enactment with the Word in *everyday* life and in all their deeds, rather than in the occasional Sunday ritual set apart from men's everyday life. Unlike the Mass, which tranquilized anxieties, the sermon probed and proded them. In the sermon, the age of ideology could find a paradigm of righteous and energetic persuasion, the paradigm of a rhetoric that could mobilize men to deeds. Ideologists assume that words matter, that they have a power that can change men and their worlds, sometimes dropping the scales from their eyes or the shackles from their hands. Ideologists, in brief, believe in the power of the idea as vested in the word.

Protestantism commonly encourages a pattern of coping with anxiety by work, rather than by ritual or magic. Resting on a sublimated Protestantism that survives the 'death of God' at the level of character structure, grounded in activistic and ascetic this-worldly impulses, modern ideological politics comes to be defined as a kind of *work*.[3] From this standpoint, both work and worklike politics are expected to be performed diligently and methodically, with a scrupulous surmounting of self, precisely because it is defined as pursuing a higher moral obligation that is all the more binding because it is freely chosen. Sedimented with Protestantism on the level of character structure, ideology was the Gospel of Labor in Politics.

In much the same way, Protestantism had undermined Renaissance magic and alchemy by linking control of the environment to the conduct of disciplined, routine work, thereby laying the cultural infrastructure for modern technology and and science. Science and technology arise when the will to know is grounded in an impulse to *control, and* when this control is felt to be possible through routine *work*. Both modern ideology, on the one side, and modern science and technology, on the other, have a certain affinity because both in part rest on Protestantism's assumption that work is anxiety relieving.

Michael Walzer tells us of Calvin: as he

> firmly believed that the terrors of contemporary life could be politically controlled, he became an activist and ecclesiastical politician. . . . In his political as in his religious thought, Calvin sought a cure for anxiety not in reconciliation but in obedience . . . he promptly engaged in sharp polemic against the Anabaptists, whose goal was not so much reconstruction as the dissolution of the political world. . . . Calvinism was thus anchored in this worldly endeavor; it appropriated worldly means and usages. . . .[4]

1.5

It was in this manner that Protestant-grounded modern ideology premised the doctrine of the unity of theory and (worldly) practice and thereby unleashed a vast political force in the modern world, a force still powerful and far from spent. This great political power also premises that great importance is attributed to ideas. It supposes that people can have an obligation by reason of having an idea or a theory. It premises the capacity and duty of men to commit themselves to the logic of an idea, to endure its implications, despite its costs to other interests: family, friends, or neighbors.

Obedience to the word is here defined as a supreme value and as a decisive test of character. Ideologies premise that the word can lay binding obligations on persons. This is one important basis enabling ideology, as *address*, to counter the effect of conventional duties and institutions. It is thus that ideologies can serve as a counterweight to the 'heaviness' of interests. Ideology thus implies a view of rational discourse as a potent source of world change, on the one hand, and, on the other, as a source of tension with conduct grounded in interest. Ideologies foster the suppression and repression of some interests, even as they give expression to others.

In fighting for his ideas (or 'principles'), the ideologue now experiences himself as engaged in a new, purified kind of politics. He understands and

presents himself as not just engaged in politics for the old, selfish reason –
to further his own interests or to advance himself 'materially.' Ideological
politics now claims to be a historically new and higher form of politics; a
kind of selfless work. It thereby authorizes itself to make the highest claims
upon its adherents. It obliges them to pursue their goals with zealous
determination, while authorizing them to inflict the severest penalties on
those opposing such goals.

Moreover, as politics is transformed into a sacred labor, there is greater
pressure for practitioners to conceal, from themselves as well as others, any
'base' motives they may have for their political activity; they thus become
dulled by that distinct kind of false consciousness called 'piety.' They may
come to believe that, unlike others, they are disinterested in personal
perquisites. One specific way this is done is to define the power they seek
(or exercise) solely from the standpoint of the functions it has for the group
interests, rather than as an enjoyable privilege that its possessors may
consume privately. More generally, their claim is that when *they* seek
office, power, living, tenures, or income, they do not seek them as private
enjoyments but only because they advance collective interests. Ideology
thus serves, on the one hand, to permit ruthlessness to others in the name
of high values, and, on the other, to present oneself as having a selfless
ambition, that nonpartisanship which legitimates any claim to power.
Ideology thereby permits the mobilization of power and, at the same time,
allows its full and unrestrained discharge.

Ideology fosters a politic that may be set off, radically and profoundly,
from prosaic bourgeois society with its moral flabbiness, its humdrum
acceptance of venality, and its egoism. The conservative ideologist, no less
than the radical, is in tension with a bourgeois society that is unashamedly
self-seeking and egoistic. The ideologue, by contrast with the bourgeois,
claims to be altruistic, never seeking his private interest but speaking only
in behalf of 'the Word.' In this tension between the normal corruptness of
bourgeois society and the abnormal altruism of the ideologist, political
conflict emerges as a higher dramaturgy in which one side presents itself
as acting out the impersonal pursuit of an idea. The vulgar venality of the
bourgeois thus finds its match in the unembarrassed righteousness of the
ideologist.

2

Ideologies entail projects of public reconstruction and require that believers
support actively the accomplishment of the project and oppose whoever
rejects it. This call for support is now justified by formulating a conception
of the social world, or a part or process in it. In short, each ideology
presents a map of 'what is' in society; a 'report' of how it is working, how it
is failing, and also of how it could be changed. Ideology is thus a call to

action – a 'command' grounded in a social theory – in a world-referencing discourse that presumably justifies that call. Granted that it does not pursue 'knowledge for its own sake'; nonetheless, ideology offers reports or imputes knowledge of the social world; its claims and its calls-to-action are grounded in that imputed knowledge.

Note: I am not saying that a specific view of the social world offered by ideology is necessarily 'correct'; I am saying merely that ideology is a rational mode of discourse. (Thus a Socrates might use rational discourse to argue for the immortality of the soul.)

2.1

Ideology thus entailed the emergence of a new mode of political discourse; discourse that sought action but did not merely seek it by invoking authority or tradition, or by emotive rhetoric alone. It was discourse predicated on the idea of grounding political action in secular and rational theory. A fundamental rule of the grammar of all modern ideology, tacit or explicitly affirmed, was the principle of the *unity of theory and practice* mediated by rational discourse. Ideology separated itself from the mythical and religious consciousness; it justified the course of action it proposed, by the logic and evidence it summoned on behalf of its views of the social world, rather than by invoking faith, tradition, revelation or the authority of the speaker. Ideology, then, premised policies shaped by rational discourse in the public sphere, and premised that support can be mobilized for them by the rhetoric of rationality.

This is no new view, but is offered by a surprising variety of modern theories and ideologists. Thus Irving Kristol remarks: 'Ideologies are religions of a sort, but they differ from the older kinds in that they argue from information instead of ultimately from ignorance. . . . Ideology presupposes an antecedent "enlightenment"; before it can do its special job of work, facts must be widely available, and curiosity about the facts quickened. Men must be more interested in the news from this world than in the tidings from another. The most obdurate enemy of ideology is illiteracy. . . .'[5]

Much the same view is affirmed by Stephen Rousseas and James Farganis, although from an ideological position opposed to Kristol's: ideology's 'major function,' they affirm, 'is to apply intelligence – the fusion of passion and critical reason – to the problem of the modern world.'[6] Erik Erikson also makes the same point from the standpoint of his psychohistory: ideology, he holds, is an unconscious tendency underlying religious and scientific as well as political thought; the tendency to 'make the facts amenable to ideas, and ideas to facts, in order,' he adds, 'to create a world image convincing enough to support the collective and individual sense of identity.'[7] The unspoken point here, however, is that what makes a

Ideology

'world image' *credible* differs under different historical conditions. Erikson, however, is essentially correct about the construction of world views in the *modern* epoch.

Ideology makes a diagnosis of the social world and claims that it is true. It alleges an accurate picture of society and claims (or implies) that its political policies are grounded in that picture. To that extent, ideology is a very special sort of rational discourse by reason of its world-referring claims. It defends its policies neither by traditionalistic legitimation nor by invoking faith or revelation. As a historical object, then, ideology differs from both religion and metaphysics in that it is concerned to make 'what is' in society a basis of action.

In Jürgen Habermas' terms: ' . . . what Weber termed "secularization" has two aspects. First, traditional world views and objectivations lose their power and validity as myth, as public religion, as customary ritual, as justifying metaphysics, as unquestionable tradition. Instead, they are reshaped into subjective belief systems and ethics which ensure the private cogency of modern value-orientations (the "Protestant Ethic"). Second, they are transformed into constructions to do both at once: criticize tradition and reorganize the released material of tradition . . . existing legitimations are replaced by new ones. The latter emerge from the critique of dogmatism of traditional interpretations of the world and claim a scientific character. Yet they retain legitimating functions, thereby keeping actual power relations inaccessible to analysis and to public consciousness. It is in this way that ideologies in the restricted sense first came into being. They replace traditional legitimations of power by appearing in the mantle of modern science and by deriving their justification from the critique of ideology. Ideologies are coeval with the critique of ideology. In this sense there can be no prebourgeois "ideologies." '[8]

Notes

1. ERIC J. HOBSBAWM, *The Age of Revolution* (London: Weidenfeld and Nicolson, 1962), pp. 217, 222.
2. Cf. P. MILLER, *The New England Mind* (Boston: Beacon Press, 1961).
3. Cf. MICHAEL WALZER, *The Revolution of the Saints* (Cambridge, Mass: Harvard University Press, 1965).
4. MICHAEL WALZER, ibid., p. 28.
5. CHAIM WAXMAN, ibid., p. 108.
6. Ibid., p. 216.
7. DAVID APTER, ibid., cited by APTER, p. 20.
8. JÜRGEN HABERMAS, *Toward a Rational Society* (Boston: Beacon Press, 1970; German volume, 1968), pp. 98–9.

13　The Theory of Ideology in *Capital**

JOHN MEPHAM

John Mepham taught philosophy at the University of Sussex and since then has been a freelance writer, editor and translator. He has been closely associated with the Radical Philosophy movement, and in this early article follows the work of the later Marx in arguing for an understanding of ideology as based upon the real conditions and relations of capitalist society. Ideology is less the product of a dominant social class, than of the social formation as a whole; and its particular discourses are generated by categories which have their roots in the material operations of capitalist society.

> 'There must be some way out of here'
> Said the joker to the thief
> 'There's too much confusion
> I can't get no relief'
>
> (Dylan)

Where do incorrect ideas come from?
In *What is to be Done?* Lenin argues that 'the spontaneous development of the working-class movement leads to its subordination to bourgeois ideology'.[1] It is the necessity of going beyond the spontaneous development of the movement that is the basis of his argument for a three-fold struggle, theoretical, political and economic. It is in the same context that he makes the famous statement that 'without revolutionary theory there can be no revolutionary movement'.[2] What are the epistemological bases of these interconnected necessities, the spontaneous dominance of bourgeois ideology and the need for theory? Standing behind such analyses there must be a theory of the conditions for the production of knowledge and of effective practice and also a theory of the

---

*Reprinted from JOHN MEPHAM, 'The Theory of Ideology in Capital', in John Mepham and D-H. Ruben (eds), *Issues in Marxist Philosophy, vol. 3: Epistemology, Science, Ideology* (Hemel Hempstead: Harvester Press, 1979), pp. 141–69.

production of mystification. In *What is to be Done?*, which is not intended as a work on the theory of knowledge, Lenin only offers a passing remark about the origins of mystification.

> But why, the reader will ask, does the spontaneous movement, the movement along the line of least resistance, lead to the domination of bourgeois ideology? For the simple reason that bourgeois ideology is far older in origin than socialist ideology, that it is more fully developed, and that it has at its disposal immeasurably more means of dissemination.[3]

Now I think that this statement is, not surprisingly given its context, incomplete, and is open to misinterpretation. It may suggest a view that is very common but which is, in my opinion, fundamentally mistaken. This view, which is an ideology of ideology, is that the dominance of bourgeois ideology has its basis in the dominance of the bourgeoisie as a class only in the sense that this dominance as a class allows the bourgeoisie to have a monopoly on the production and dissemination of ideas. Thus, from the point of view of the workers ideas have their origin in the means of the dissemination of ideas produced originally elsewhere. Ideas are transmitted, via cultural and educational institutions, public communications systems and so on, into the otherwise empty minds of the working class. It could be that conditions in mid-twentieth-century bourgeois society are such as to spontaneously suggest this view. There is no doubt that mid-twentieth-century capitalism does generate a formidable semic pollution to a degree and of kinds quite unimaginable one hundred or even fifty years ago. The very forms and modern technological means of the production and dissemination of ideas (the 'advertising industry', the 'public' television and radio systems, political campaigns designed around the production of 'images' of politicians etc., etc.) do seem to suggest a social division between the producers of ideas (advertising copy writers, press agents, speech writers etc.) and the consumers of ideas ('the public').[4] And some writers who have attempted to diagnose our contemporary condition ('one-dimensional man') do, perhaps because of this, stumble sometimes into the error of mislocating the source of mystification in the way defined above. Marcuse, for example, in his essay 'Repressive Tolerance' tends to identify the conditions under which people live and think, and which thereby determine *what* they think, with the 'prevailing indoctrination' by the 'media', advertisements and so on, to which they are exposed. He says 'The people exposed to this impartiality are no *tabulae rasae*, they are indoctrinated by the conditions under which they live and think and which they do not transcend. To enable them to become autonomous, to find by themselves what is true and what is false for man in the existing society, they would have to be freed from the prevailing indoctrination. . . . ' And 'different opinions and "philosophies" can no longer compete peacefully for adherence and persuasion on rational grounds: the "market-place of ideas" is organized and delimited by those who determine the national and the individual interest'.[5] Perhaps if it were only Marcuse who made this mistake it would not deserve so much emphasis here. I believe, however, that it is a mistake very commonly made by, for example, the students that I teach, and it is perhaps what Marx would call a 'natural and spontaneous mode of thought' in contemporary capitalist society. If this is so then this view is self-refuting because it would itself be ideology which has its origins in something other than the indoctrination which it identifies as the origins of ideology.

In what follows I do not, of course, intend to deny for one moment that the bourgeoisie *do* control the means for the dissemination of ideas in Lenin's sense, nor that they do use this control as a powerful weapon in the defence of their class-interests. But my view is that the bourgeois class is the producer of ideas only in the sense that sleep is the producer of dreams. To say that the bourgeoisie produces ideas is to ignore the conditions that make this possible, to ignore that which determines *which* ideas are thus produced, and to conceal the real nature and origins of ideology. It is not the bourgeois *class* that produces ideas but bourgeois *society*. And the effective dissemination of ideas is only possible because, or to the extent that, the ideas thus disseminated are ideas which, for quite different reasons, do have a sufficient degree of effectiveness both in rendering social reality intelligible and in guiding practice within it for them to be apparently acceptable. It is the relation between ideology and reality that is the key to its dominance. To show this one would have to explore the relation between the 'representations in men's brains' and the reality of which these are representations both as a cognitive and as a practical relation. In what follows I will for the most part be concerned with the cognitive aspect of this relation.

The theory of ideology in *The German Ideology*

The obvious place to begin is with those passages in *The German Ideology* in which Marx discusses the epistemology of mystification. But my claim will be that, in fact, Marx has not, in such early works on which discussions of ideology are usually based, achieved a clear theoretical position on the origin of ideology, and that the metaphors in terms of which he discusses the problem have to be drastically modified in the light of what he says in his later works. I claim that on this epistemological question of the origin of incorrect ideas *Capital* is a great advance on *The German Ideology*.

In a familiar and typical passage from *The German Ideology* Marx says:

If in all ideology men and their circumstances appear upside down as in a *camera obscura*, this phenomenon arises just as much from their historical life process as the inversion of objects on the retina does from their physical life process. . . . We set out from real, active men, and on the basis of their real life process we demonstrate the development of the ideological reflexes and echoes of this life process. The phantoms formed in the human brain are also, necessarily, sublimates of their material life process, which is empirically verifiable and bound to material premises. . . .[6]

Now this is not a clear statement. Marx is here struggling to discover an adequate language and the result is a series of metaphors which are the symptoms of his failure (not that metaphors as such are a symptom of failure in philosophy. Here it is the profusion of them which suggests that none of them alone satisfies the author – *camera obscura*, reflexes, echoes, phantoms, sublimates . . .). Also the passage is open to many different interpretations. Perhaps most unfortunately the words 'empirically verifiable' and 'material premises' taken together with the word 'phantom' suggest a positivist interpretation. This would be that ideology arises from the tendency to be taken in by phantoms in such a way that the victim simply overlooks or is distracted from 'empirically verifiable facts' that would otherwise be obvious and clear.

As a way of focusing later on the model of relations involved in the production of ideology which I will extract from *Capital* it will be useful at this point to make explicit some of the features involved in the use of the *camera obscura* metaphor. This metaphor involves the following representations of the relations between reality and ideas.

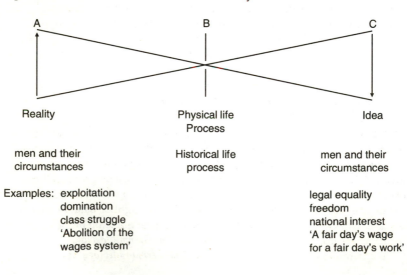

A	B	C
Reality	Physical life Process	Idea
men and their circumstances	Historical life process	men and their circumstances

| Examples: | exploitation domination class struggle 'Abolition of the wages system' | | legal equality freedom national interest 'A fair day's wage for a fair day's work' |

This metaphor suggests that in the production of ideology there are the following aspects:

(1) Three independent entities: the real object A, the representation C, and the mediating entity (light) B which effects the production of the latter from the former. Each idea is the distorted representation of some one 'thing' in reality to which it corresponds in a one-to-one manner.

(2) The relation between A and C is one of inversion. The transformation A to C preserves all internal relations.

(3) The metaphor not only suggests the independence of the entity reflected, A (it does not need C in order to exist) and denies the independence of C (ideas are not themselves among the conditions for the production of ideas), but also suggests that representations are in some sense 'mere illusions' (an epistemological thesis) and 'mere epiphenomena' or 'phantoms' (an ontological thesis).

It seems to follow that they (the representations) can therefore have no element of either truth or practical effectiveness. These suggestions amount to a thesis of crude materialism with which Marx certainly disagreed. Why then is Marx so fascinated with this metaphor which is very frequent throughout his work and which has led to gross misinterpretations of his views?

The structure of ideology and its relation to reality

I shall now state three theses concerning the structure of ideology and its relation to reality. These are stated in such a way as to make it clear that they are different from views on ideology mentioned above. I shall in the following sections show how these theses amount to a part of a theory of ideology that is implicit in *Capital*.

Thesis I: Ideology is structured discourse. It is, directly or indirectly, based on or generated by a set of mutually interdependent categories. The view that ideology is made up of *ideas* is itself misleading to the extent that this has been taken in philosophy to suggest that the units of which ideology is composed, or out of which it is constructed, are independent of one another, and that they can be traced back to atomistic ideas which are derived from reality 'one at a time', or on a one-to-one basis (as for example in the relation A to C in the *camera obscura* metaphor). One cannot understand ideological concepts or ideological propositions as standing in some such one-to-one relation with non-ideological, non-distorted, factual or scientific concepts, propositions or facts. The translation of ideology (or manifest text) into the true, under-lying (latent) text cannot be performed on a word-to-word or proposition-to-proposition basis. The 'true text' is reconstructed not by a process of piecemeal decoding but by the identification of the generative set of ideological categories and its replacement by a different set. This different set will be differently constituted in its internal relations. And one must discover the transformational mechanism whereby the distorted matrix is, in the historical life process substituted for the undistorted one.

Thesis 2: The relation between reality and ideology (which produces 'inversion') is the cognitive relation. That is to say that mystification has its basis in the perception of the apparently intelligible order of social reality by a process of 'misrecognition'. An implication of this second thesis is that ideology does not derive fundamentally from the intention to deceive others, from self-deception, or in the perversion of cognition by its being infected with values (for example the value of self- or class-interests). Nor does ideology derive fundamentally from the cognitive function being overwhelmed by non-cognitive functions such as the emotions, feelings or passions. I am not denying that ideology does have the effect of, or does constitute mystification or deception, and that it does function as a defence of class-interests, and does have the result that what *appears* to be objective, positive, scientific discourse is not in fact 'value-free'.

I will try to clarify this second thesis and its implications by reference to some analogies. This will also help to locate this discussion in a broader context. I am thinking of the problem of ideology in relation to the general questions, 'What are the conditions for the production of knowledge and what are the conditions for the production of various systems of mystificatory belief?'. These questions have been raised not only in relation to ideology but also, for example, in relation to the history of science and to the problem of myth in anthropology.[7] As one aspect (but only one; there are many others) of such enquiries progress has been achieved I think by the rediscovery, paradoxical as it may seem, of the cognitive basis of some systems of mystificatory belief. The history of science makes great strides to the extent that it rejects the view that 'pre-scientific' systems of belief and practice such as alchemy or natural magic resulted from simple lack of interest in the empirical facts, or from ignorance of the importance of empirical study, or from simple empirical mistakes or oversights; and also rejects the view that such systems were essentially the result of enterprises that were overwhelmed entirely by non-cognitive subjective forces (for example greed or 'mysticism'). One might claim in fact that such systems were possible by virtue of the fact that they were too firmly established on the basis of the 'immediately perceivable' forms of empirical reality (such as for example the occurrence of the transformation of apparently elemental substances, systems of perceivable relations of analogy, sympathy and antipathy and so on).[8] Similarly anthropological study of myth has progressed to the extent that it has refused the ethnocentric prejudice that myth is pure 'superstition' satisfying only affective demands or that it is infantile proto-science which paid insufficient attention to detailed empirical facts. This is clearly one of the main themes of Lévi-Strauss in *La Pensée Sauvage*. Elsewhere Lévi-Strauss identifies the main mistake in the work of Lévi-Bruhl by saying that 'he denied to "primitive mentality" the cognitive character which he had initially conceded to it, and cast it back entirely into the realm of affectivity'.[9]

Thesis 3: Ideology arises from the opacity of reality, where the opacity of reality is the fact that the forms in which reality 'presents itself' to men, or the forms of its appearance, conceal those real relations which themselves produce the appearances. This thesis involves the introduction of the concepts *phenomenal form, real relation* and *opacity*. It is stated explicitly by Marx, for example in vol. I, Chapter 19, which is called 'The Transformation of the Value of Labour-Power into Wages'. 'Value of Labour-Power' is the name of a real relation, and 'Wages' (or the wage-form) is a phenomenal form. The selling of the commodity labour-power is the real relation of exchange which is transformed, in experience, into the mystifying phenomenal form Wages or wage-contract, thus disguising the real nature of the social relations involved in transactions between capitalist and labourer in bourgeois society. In political economy the mystified form 'value of labour' (as distinct from the 'value of labour-power') is identified with wages.[10]

> Hence, we may understand the decisive importance of the transformation of value and price of labour-power into the form of wages, or into the value and price of labour itself. This phenomenal form, which makes the actual relation invisible, and, indeed, shows the direct opposite of that relation, forms the basis of all the juridical notions of both labourer and capitalist, of all the mystifications of the capitalist mode of production, of all its illusions as to liberty, of all the apologetic shifts of the vulgar economists.
>
> (p. 540)

This third thesis involves an important aspect of Marx's epistemology, namely his distinction between 'phenomenal forms' (or appearances) and 'real relations' as developed in *Capital* in the context of a critique of the categories of political economy. Marx himself thought his most fundamental theoretical break-through the discovery of the true concept of surplus-value which enabled him to penetrate in a rigorous way to the secret and hidden realities of capitalism. It is this theoretical advance that also allows Marx to make a decisive move beyond the ambiguities of his earlier remarks on ideology. Marx's claim is then that it is the importance of the phenomenal forms that they render invisible real relations and hence give rise to bourgeois ideology. Here is another example of Marx's use of these concepts.

> . . . in respect to the *phenomenal form*, 'value and price of labour', or
> 'wages', as contrasted with the *essential relation* manifested therein, viz.
> the value and price of labour-power, the same difference holds in
> respect to all *phenomena* and their *hidden substratum*. The former *appear*
> *directly and spontaneously* as current modes of thought; the latter must
> first be discovered by science. Classical Political Economy nearly
> touches the *true relation of things*, without, however, consciously
> formulating it. This it cannot so long as it sticks in its bourgeois skin.
>
> (p. 542: my emphases)

Notice that here Marx is making a *general* point ('the same difference holds
in respect to all phenomena and their hidden substratum'), and is not
limiting his remarks to this particular categorical transformation and
mystification. And second it should be noted that Marx is here providing
us with an answer to the question with which we started 'Why does the
spontaneous movement lead to the domination of bourgeois ideology?',
namely that phenomenal forms appear 'directly and spontaneously as
current modes of thought'.

These three theses stated in this section can be summed up in a remark
by Henri Lefebvre,[11]

> Social reality, that is interacting human individuals and groups,
> produces *appearances* which are something more and else than mere
> illusions. Such appearances are the modes in which human activities
> manifest themselves within the whole they constitute at any given
> moment – call them modalities of consciousness. They have far greater
> consistency, let alone coherence, than mere illusions or ordinary lies.
> Appearances have reality, and reality involves appearances.

I think that, if true, these theses necessitate drastic and illuminating
modifications to the *camera obscura* metaphor in ways which I will explain
later.

Phenomenal forms and real relations

Before going on to give a detailed account of Marx's use of this distinction
in relation to his analysis of the categories of political economy I will give
in this section further clarification and elaboration of Marx's general thesis.
The distinction is referred to in *Capital* by a variety of interchangeable
terms. Phenomenal forms are called semblances, appearances, estranged
outward appearances, illusions, forms, forms of manifestation. Real
relations are called essences, real nature, actual relations, secret or hidden

substratum, content, inner connections. And the distinction is a systematic one in Marx's later writings. That is to say it is not invoked in an *ad hoc* fashion nor is it appealed to only infrequently. It is involved systematically at each point where the problem of mystification arises, and this in connection with the discussion of many different categories (not *only* in connection with the famous fetishism of commodities). Norman Geras has listed some of its occurrences.[12] His examples, and those given elsewhere in this paper, mostly relate to a discussion of basic socio-economic formations, but it is important to notice that the distinction is also used in relation, for example, to the theory of the state and of the class struggle.

> . . . the different states of the different civilized countries, in spite of their manifold *diversity of form*, all have this in common, that they are based on modern bourgeois society, only one more or less capitalistically developed. They have, therefore, also certain *essential features* in common. In this sense it is possible to speak of the 'present-day state' . . .[13]

> It is altogether self-evident that, to be able to fight at all the working class must organize itself at home as a class and that its own country is the immediate arena of its struggle. In so far its class struggle is national, not *in substance*, but as the *Communist Manifesto* says, '*in form*'.[14]

And note that in such cases as these Marx is also, as in the cases I will be analysing later, discussing the origin or basis of *ideology* (the ideology of the independence of the state and society in the first case, and that of nationalism in the second).

This distinction between phenomenal form and real relation is applied both to the order of reality and to the order of language and thought ('phenomenal forms appear as modes of thought'). Wages, for example, are an aspect of social reality, namely its phenomenal aspect. And the category 'wages' or 'price of labour' is a conceptual category. One thinks about and talks about social relations in these terms *because* these categories have the same form that reality has, because this is the form in which reality 'is presented to us'. 'Value of labour-power' is both a real relation, the exchange relation between the worker and the capitalist and it is a scientific category in terms of which one understands that real relation. This means that the distinction is not a superficial one, a simple rewording of some such commonsense distinctions as those between 'superficial' and 'profound' or 'confused' and 'clear'. It is a distinction that contains a substantial epistemological theory about the relation between thought and reality and about the origins of illusions about reality. This theory is that the origin of ideological illusions is in the phenomenal forms of reality itself.

This theory is also presented by Marx using the concepts 'imperceptibility', 'invisibility' and related notions. In these terms the

theory says that it is a feature of social life, and in particular the life of
social production, that it is so structured as to render that social reality
sometimes opaque to its participants. The invisibility of real relations
derives from the visibility of outward appearances or forms. The apparent
immediacy of these forms obscures their mystificatory character. For
example, of the commodity-form and of the systematic illusion of
individual freedom Marx says

> It is, however, *just this ultimate money-form* of the world of commodities
> that actually *conceals, instead of disclosing*, the social character of private
> labour, and the social relations between individual producers.
>
> (p. 76)

> A commodity is therefore a mysterious thing, simply because in it the
> social character of men's labour appears to them as an objective
> character stamped upon the product of that labour; because the relation
> of the producers to the sum total of their own labour is *presented to them*
> as a social relation, existing not between themselves, but between the
> products of their labour. *This is the reason* why the products of labour
> become commodities, social things whose qualities are at the same time
> *perceptible and imperceptible by the senses*.
>
> (p. 72)

> The Roman slave was held by fetters: the wage-labourer is bound to his
> owner by *invisible threads*. The *appearance* of independence *is kept up by
> means of* a constant change of employers, and by the *fictio juris* of a
> contract.
>
> (p. 574: my emphases throughout)

In Geras's words then Marx is providing us with an analysis of 'the
mechanisms by which capitalist society necessarily appears to its agents as
something other than it really is. . . . It is because there exists, at the interior
of capitalist society, a kind of internal rupture between the social relations
which obtain and the manner in which they are experienced.'[15] The
function of ideology is to keep hidden the real social relations. But the
possibility of performing this function is not given in the possibility of
some individual wishing to perform this function, or deliberately
designing a language, or using a discourse in which it may be performed.
Ideological language does not just distract attention away from real social
relations, nor does it explain them away, nor even does it directly deny
them. It structurally excludes them from thought. And this is because the
phenomenal forms of social life constitute not merely a realm of
appearances of particulars, but appearances articulated upon a semantic
field. Social life is a domain of meanings with which men 'spontaneously'

think their relations to other men and to nature. It is therefore not accurately captured in the idealist notion of a 'world-view'.[16] Social life is structured like a language; or rather the conditions that make it possible for social life to be of a particular kind (a particular mode of production) are also conditions for the possibility of a particular language. These conditions are material conditions and are the social practices which constitute a particular mode of production. The 'natural self-understood' meanings encountered in social life form a text which one needs to decipher to discover its true meaning. 'The characters that stamp products as commodities, and whose establishment is a necessary preliminary to the circulation of commodities, have already acquired the stability of natural, self-understood forms of social life before man seeks to decipher . . . their meaning' (p. 75).

I think that the theory of ideology which I have been presenting can only be clear if it is examined in its application in detailed analyses.[17] Lack of space here means that I will only be able to present sketches of Marx's analyses. I will give four sketches using each as a way of making a general point. I will deal mostly with the wage-form and the money-form but it is important to note that Marx's treatment follows exactly the same lines in relation to all the categories (commodity-form, value-form, etc.). I use mainly the wage-form partly for ease of exposition and partly because of its clear and direct connection with the problem of the dominance of bourgeois ideology in trade union practice.

The mystification of the wage-form

The wage payment seems to involve a fair exchange of equivalents.

> If history took a long time to get at the bottom of the mystery of wages, nothing, on the other hand, is more easy to understand than the necessity, the *raison d'être*, of this phenomenon. The exchange between capital and labour at first presents itself to the mind in the same guise as the buying and selling of all other commodities. The buyer gives a certain sum of money, the seller an article of a nature different from money.
>
> (p. 540)

Marx's argument here depends on his distinction between labour and labour-power. That which is sold by the worker is his labour-power; the capitalist buys the labourer's capacity to work for a certain period of time. The labour performed in that period creates value. It creates as much value as is paid back to the worker as his wage, and it creates value over and above this amount, it creates surplus-value which is retained by the capitalist.[18] Labour itself does not have value.

> Labour is the substance and the immanent measure of value, but has itself no value. In the expression 'value of labour', the idea of value is not only completely obliterated, but actually reversed. It is an expression as imaginary as the value of the earth. These imaginary expressions, arise, however, from the relations of production themselves. They are categories for the phenomenal forms of essential relations.
>
> (p. 537)

Imaginary expressions have their home in the ordinary language of everyday life. 'Classical Political Economy borrowed from every-day life the category "price of labour" without further criticism . . . ' (p. 537). 'On the surface of bourgeois society the wage of the labourer appears as the price of labour, a certain quantity of money that is paid for a certain quantity of labour. Thus people speak of the value of labour' (p. 535). For Marx the fact that people speak of the value of labour, that this is a 'spontaneous, natural' mode of speech under capitalism, shows that 'ordinary language', far from being something to which one should appeal in theoretical discussion, is something which one has good grounds for suspecting of distortion. Ordinary language is the repository of category mistakes. Theoretical discourse corrects ordinary language, tells one what one *should* say. Ordinary language, and the philosophy which makes a fetish of it, has, as Marx says, things standing on their heads.

The fact that the wage-form has the form of an exchange of equivalents, then, disguises the reality which is that wage-labour contains unpaid labour and is the source of surplus-value. One can consider the working day as divided into that period in which the labourer works to create value equivalent to his own needs of means of subsistence, and another period in which he works to create value given *gratis* to the capitalist. One of Marx's criticisms of the Gotha programme was that it had fallen back into the modes of thought of bourgeois ideology on this point and he restates, in his *Critique*, his analysis of the real relations involved.[19]

> . . . wages are not what they *appear* to be, namely, the *value*, or *price, of labour*, but only a masked form for the *value*, or *price, of labour-power* . . . it was made clear that the wage-worker has permission to work for his own subsistence, that is *to live*, only in so far as he works for a certain time *gratis* for the capitalist . . . the system of wage-labour is a system of slavery . . . whether the worker receives better or worse payment.

It is for this reason that the notion of a 'fair wage', another of the imaginary expressions of everyday life, is an absurd one. The very meaning of wages which is now deciphered is the extraction of unpaid labour. Therefore wages are unfair as such.[20]

This particular mystification illustrates a general point, namely that the transformation from real relations to phenomenal forms is a transformation in which a complex relation (or a relation of relations, as in the complex wages-money-value-commodities, etc.) is presented as a simple relation or is presented as a thing or the property of a thing.[21] Thus here an apparent relation of exchange of equivalents is in reality a compound of an exchange of equivalents plus an extraction of surplus-value; and this compound is itself ultimately analysable into a complex set of relations between relations.[22] Also what appears as a fair and free exchange (a contract) is in reality a relation of exploitation and domination.

At this point one can begin (but only begin) to see the connection between ideological categories and ideology in the broader sense, that whole range of discourse and practices structured by these categories. In this familiar case one can see some of the connections between the wage-form and the ideological concept of a fair wage. On the basis of complex comparisons the workers, or the organizations which defend their interests, negotiate wage agreements. The political party which is thought of as that which represents the workers' interests, has as one of its slogans 'a fair day's wage for a fair day's work'; and has attempted to enact an 'incomes policy', a machinery for defending both 'employers' and 'employed' against 'unfairness', thus also defending 'the national interest'. In difficult cases (for example 'special cases') a court of inquiry is empowered to arbitrate and suggest ways of reaching a 'just settlement' which is then 'freely' agreed to by all parties.[23] Now all of this is *necessary*. It is no good ever losing sight of the fact that the workers' fight to defend themselves in such ways is a necessary response to those forces in capitalist society which systematically tend to sacrifice their interest. But it is also true that this historically elaborated complex of institutions and practices is a mystification because it systematically excludes an understanding of real social relations.

Now if it is necessary for the working class to conduct an economic, trade-union struggle in self-defence, and if the spontaneous language in which this struggle is conducted is structured by the wage-form and other 'natural, self-understood' bourgeois categories, and if these categories and their embodiments in practice *systematically exclude* the categories of real relations, then what is the point of saying that the workers *ought not* to be *'exclusively* absorbed' in this struggle?[24]

[The workers] ought not to be exclusively absorbed in these unavoidable guerrilla fights [against the tendency to decrease real wages, to reduce the working day, etc.] incessantly springing up from the never-ceasing encroachments of capital or changes of the market. They ought to understand that, with all the miseries it imposes upon them, the present system simultaneously engenders the *material conditions* and the *social forms* necessary for an economic reconstruction of society. Instead of the *conservative* motto '*A fair day's wage for a fair day's work!*' they ought to inscribe on their banner the revolutionary watchword '*Abolition of the wages system!*'

If this is not to be a purely idealist moral exhortation there must be some sense in which it is possible to conduct the struggle on the three fronts mentioned at the beginning of this paper, the theoretical, the political and the economic, for it is this that is involved in this passage from Marx. It would be impossible to clarify the issues involved here without a very long detour. I am only concerned to make the point that Marx's theory of ideological categories does not contradict the demand for a three-fold struggle and in fact may actually help to reveal its theoretical basis. How is one to understand the double thesis of Lenin; 'the spontaneous struggle is dominated by bourgeois ideology' *and* 'the working class spontaneously gravitates towards socialism'?[25] And how is it possible in practice to *both* conduct the necessary defence of workers' economic interests and simultaneously struggle for 'economic reconstruction of society'? These problems have been the central theoretical and practical problems for the workers' movement since the debates on reformism in the SDP to the current debates on the alleged reformism of the continental communist parties.

There are two points which would need to be taken into account in this debate which spring directly from Marx's theory of ideology. First, the present system 'engenders the material conditions and the social forms necessary for an economic reconstruction of society'. The system 'real relations/phenomenal forms' is a dynamic one and is not unchanging any more than is the mode of production of which it is an aspect. Second, it does not follow from the fact that the categories of bourgeois ideology exclude socialist categories that the reverse of this is also true. There is a sense in which the wage-form, etc. is included in or assimilated into the categories of *Capital*. I can only indicate here that Marx attempts an explanation of this inclusion in the 1857 Introduction, in the section 'The Method of Political Economy'.[26]

The interdependence of categories

Notice also about the wage-form that it conceals not only the real relation involved in the exchange transaction, but that it also conceals the real nature of the labour-fund, or variable capital, from which the labourer is paid. This particular mystification is analysed by Marx in the section of *Capital* on 'The Accumulation of Capital'. 'The simple fundamental form of the process of accumulation is *obscured by* the incident of the circulation which brings it about, and by the splitting up of surplus-value. An exact analysis of the process, therefore, demands that we should, for a time, disregard all *phenomena that hide the play of its inner mechanism*' (p. 565: my emphases). It is worth noting the particular forms of concealment involved here because they illustrate another general point that I want to make explicit, namely that the various appearance-forms are not independent. They support each other. Each form can appear as an element in the composition of any other form; and each element is itself a form constructed out of other elements. It is this that defines the categories as a *structure* of appearances.

In this case one has the following particular combinations. How is it that the source of the wage is obscured? It is because it is paid in the form of *money*. But,

> this money is merely the transmuted form of the product of his labour. While he is converting a portion of the means of production into products, a portion of his former product is being turned into money. It is his labour of last week, or of last year, that pays for his labour-power this week or this year. The illusion begotten by the intervention of money vanishes immediately, if, instead of taking a single capitalist and a single labourer, we take the class of capitalists and the class of labourers as a whole. The capitalist class is constantly giving to the labouring class order-notes, in the form of money, on a portion of the commodities produced by the latter and appropriated by the former. The labourers give these order-notes back just as constantly to the capitalist class, and in this way get their share of their own product. *The transaction is veiled by the commodity-form of the product and the money-form of the commodity.*
>
> (p. 568: my emphases)

This example illustrates the point that whichever category one starts with in the immediate problem (in this case Marx is discussing the simple reproduction of capital) this inevitably leads to an analysis in which all the central categories are employed. Their systematic relations in reality are reproduced in their systematic relations in thought. Thus the analysis of the simple reproduction of capital involves the recognition that the capitalist pays the labourer by returning to him only a portion of that which is produced by him. This is obscured by the intervention of money, which makes it seem as if the capitalist has some other source of wealth than the expropriation of unpaid labour. And this intervention of money is an aspect of the commodity-form of production. And the commodity-form of production is that form in which use-values are produced for exchange, and are exchanged in relation to their values. As Marx says, 'the transaction is veiled by the commodity-form of the product and the money-form of the commodity'. Thus the real process is veiled not by some single element but by the whole system of related elements. The bourgeois economist cannot see through the concept of capital as source of the labour-fund because the concept is not the name for a simple empirical relation which can be examined independently. He is caught up in a system of categories which generates 'solutions' to each particular analytic problem in a way like that in which a particular calculation in arithmetic is generated by the whole of arithmetic.

Historical specificity of phenomenal forms

Taking Marx's analysis one step further will demonstrate a third and extremely important point about the forms of opacity, namely that they differ under different modes of production, they are historically specific. Marx often reveals a real, but hidden, relation in capitalism by reference to other modes of production in which this particular relation or its equivalent is transparent. Mystification can occur, especially at the level of theory (for example political economy) when a correct analysis of some aspect of social relations goes together with the assumption that that form of the relation is a natural one and not an historically specific one. Consider, for example, the fact mentioned above that the labour-fund appears in the form of capital. This is specific to the capitalist mode of production. 'The bourgeois economist whose narrow mind is unable to separate the form of appearance from the thing that appears, shuts his eyes to the fact that it is but here and there on the face of the earth, that even now-a-days the labour-fund crops up in the form of capital' (p. 569). But notice that this 'shutting of the eyes' is not simply a wilful refusal to see a fact. The secret of the labour-fund, namely that it is accumulated surplus-value, *cannot be thought* within the categories of bourgeois political economy.[27] The 'narrow mind' of the bourgeois economist is thus not simply the narrow mind of the bigot or the fool but is, as Marx says, the narrowness of the mind 'which is unable to separate the form of appearance from the thing that appears'.

In order to demonstrate the correctness of his own analysis Marx has simply to refer to an historical example the relation of which to its equivalent under capitalism is made clear *by Marx's categories*; that is it is not made clear by simply referring to the facts in an empiricist sense.[28] Thus,

Let us take a peasant liable to do compulsory service for his lord. He works on his own land, with his own means of production, for, say, 3 days a week. The 3 other days he does forced work on the lord's domain. He constantly reproduces his own labour-fund, which never, in his case, takes the form of a money payment for his labour, advanced by another person. But in return, his unpaid forced labour for the lord, on its side, never acquires the character of voluntary paid labour. If one fine morning the lord appropriates to himself the land, the cattle, the seed, in a word, the means of production of this peasant, the latter will thenceforth be obliged to sell his labour-power to the lord. He will, *caeteris paribus*, labour 6 days a week as before, 3 for himself, 3 for his lord, who thenceforth becomes a wages-paying capitalist . . . from that moment the labour-fund, which the peasant himself continues as before to produce and reproduce, takes the form of a capital advanced in the form of wages by the lord.

(p. 568).

Money, commodities and language

The conditions for the production of ideology are the conditions for the production of a language, and can only be understood by reference to the structure of forms and social practices which systematically enter into the production of particular concepts and propositions in that language. Ideology is not a collection of discreet falsehoods but a matrix of thought firmly grounded in the forms of our social life and organized within a set of interdependent categories. We are not aware of these systematically generative interconnections because our awareness is organized through them.

Whenever, by an exchange, we equate as values our different products, by that very act, we also equate, as human labour, the different kinds of labour expended upon them. *We are not aware of this, nevertheless we do it.* Value, therefore, does not stalk about with a label describing what it is. It is *value, rather, that converts every product into a social hieroglyphic.* Later on, we try to decipher the hieroglyphic, to get behind the secret of our own social products [that is, the value-form]; for to stamp an object of utility as a value, is just as much a social product as language.

(p. 74: my emphases)

The puzzle of *money* is especially like the puzzle of language. Each element, taken by itself (a word, a coin) seems to have the power to function in an efficacious act (of reference, of exchange) by virtue of having a particular property (a meaning, a value). In each case the puzzle derives from the contrast between the efficacy of the element on the one hand, and the arbitrariness of its substance (sounds, inscriptions, bits of metal or paper) on the other. How is it possible to breathe life into a sign?[29] How is it possible to conjure value into a coin? The fetishism of commodities (of the value-system and of the money-form) has its equivalent in the fetishism of names (of the concept-system and the reference-form). This is why it is not just a joke to say that just as money is the universal medium of exchange of labour-power and commodities so logic is the universal medium of exchange of concepts and propositions. And just as political economy cannot take the money-form for granted but must explain it, similarly philosophy cannot take logic for granted but must explain it.

The arbitrariness of the money-substance (like that of the sign-substance in linguistics), that is the fact that there is no necessary or natural connection between the physical properties and the monetary properties of a coin, has given rise to the mistaken notion that money is a *mere symbol*.

> In this sense every commodity is a symbol, since, in so far as it is value, it is only the material envelope of the human labour spent upon it. But if it be declared that the social characters assumed by objects, or the material forms assumed by the social qualities of labour under the regime of a definite mode of production, are mere symbols, it is in the same breath also declared that these characteristics are arbitrary fictions sanctioned by the so-called universal consent of mankind. This suited the mode of explanation in favour during the eighteenth century. Unable to account for the origin of the puzzling forms assumed by social relations between man and man, people sought to denude them of their strange appearance by ascribing to them a conventional origin.
>
> (p. 91)

The parallels between philosophical theories of meaning and economic theories of value should be no surprise because the structural feature that the phenomena have in common is the dislocation between the invisibility of the social life which makes them possible and the visibility of the individual acts in which they enter into social practice.

Ideology and dialectic

I will recapitulate some of the points that I have been making by returning to the *camera obscura* metaphor. The relation between reality and the representation of reality in men's brains is not a relation involving three independent entities (two entities and a mediating entity between them) as is suggested by the *camera obscura* and the mirror-image metaphors. Marx's metaphor of 'inversion' is notoriously difficult to understand and has suggested many different interpretations. The metaphor continues to occur throughout his later works. It is worth remembering that this very same metaphor of inversion, plus that of reflection, mixed with that of the kernel and its shell, all occur together in the very famous passage in the Afterword to the second German edition of *Capital* in which Marx struggled to explain the difference between Hegel's dialectical method and his own.[30] Hegel's dialectic was the mystified form of the dialectic and was an aspect of the famous 'German Ideology'. Marx's discussion of it is both an attempt to identify his own dialectical method and an attempt to explain the relation between a mystified form of thought and its nondistorted equivalent. But the multitude of interpretations of this passage, and its obvious inadequacy as a theoretical statement (how does one conceive of turning something 'right side up again' in order to discover 'the rational kernel within the mystical shell'?) has led to an ambitious attempt by Louis Althusser to analyse the specific problem that Marx was struggling with and which led him back again and again to this metaphor.[31] Althusser's analysis focuses particularly on the problem of Marx's dialectical method. I think that since the metaphors in question are invoked by Marx most often in relation to the general problem of mystification (and not only mystification in its specifically Hegelian form) it would be worth trying to think beyond them here also.

The difference between Marxian categories and the ideological categories of, for example, political economy, is that where the latter designate things and their properties the former designate internal relations and their transformations; and where the latter designate relations between things the former designate relations between relations.[32] This is the most general form of what Marx calls 'fetishism'. For example,

> Whence arose the illusions of the monetary system? To it gold and silver, when serving as money, did not represent a social relation between producers, but mere natural objects with strange social properties. And modern economy, which looks down with such disdain on the monetary system, does not *its* superstition come out as clear as noonday, whenever it treats of capital? How long is it since economy discarded the physiocratic illusion, that rents grow out of the soil and not out of society?
>
> (p. 82)

Similarly I think the difference between Marx's theory of ideology and the ideology of ideology is that whereas the latter thinks of it in terms of two elements and a relation between them (or one element, reality, and its property of creating another element, an idea) Marx's theory is dialectical.

It is a theory of a totality. Both the nature of the components and that of the relations between them are thus drastically different. It can be represented as below although it should be remembered that this is presented as merely a helpful graphical device and should not be taken too seriously especially inasmuch as it can give no account of the relations within the totality.

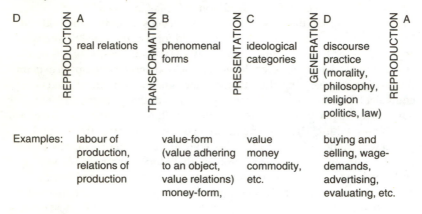

D	REPRODUCTION	A	TRANSFORMATION	B	PRESENTATION	C	GENERATION	D	REPRODUCTION	A
		real relations		phenomenal forms		ideological categories		discourse practice (morality, philosophy, religion politics, law)		

Examples:	labour of production, relations of production	value-form (value adhering to an object, value relations) money-form,	value money commodity, etc.	buying and selling, wage-demands, advertising, evaluating, etc.

The properties of this system are complex. I can only make a few comments here by way of highlighting some of its differences from the *camera obscura* model. I have said that this model differs from the earlier one both in the nature of its components (A,B,C, etc.) and in the relations between them. In both these respects we can only understand the model by reference to some concept of a structured totality. As Balibar points out[33] the notion of the structural complexity of a totality was introduced by Althusser in order to clarify the relations within the totality base-superstructure, that is the social structure as a whole, as an articulation of several relatively autonomous levels. But it is also true that each of these 'levels' is itself a structured totality. I have given some indication of this above in discussing the interdependence of ideological categories, and below I note briefly a similar feature in relation to the level D, discourse and practice. It is equally true that 'real relation' names (for example social-labour, capital, interest, surplus-value, property) are not the names of things, nor even of relations between things, but of structured functions. In his attempt to grasp this Ollman quotes Marx on 'fixed capital':[34] 'It is not a question of a definition which things must be made to fit. We are dealing here with definite functions which must be expressed in definite categories.'

Thus, relations *within* A, B, etc. are not easy to describe. But it is clear that the relations within A are not the same as those within C (the relation between labour and value for example) and that the inversion metaphor, with its preservation of internal relations in the transformation from real to ideological categories, is therefore incorrect. As for the relations *between* A, B, etc., it is again clear that, however difficult to describe they may be, certain indications of difference from the earlier model can be made. The problem would be to spell out the properties of the new model in such a way as to preserve certain of Marx's central tenets; in particular the interpretation would have to be compatible with some notion of historical materialism and with the doctrine of the determination in the last instance by the 'economic'. However this is done at least it is clear that, unlike the earlier model, this later one shows that each of the elements A, B, etc., is a necessary condition for each of the others. In particular D is necessary for A (which removes the most blatant problem of the 'phantom' metaphor, its suggestion that social reality is independent of 'ideas'). The way in which D relates to A is suggestively analysed by Althusser in his theory that ideology, as 'materialized' in the Ideological State Apparatuses, secures the reproduction of the relations of production.[35]

Discourse, practice and institutions

What is the relation between C and D, that is between ideological categories and ideological discourse and practices? The massive, powerful presence of mystification secreted by man in the course of his social production and consumption, in its extremely diverse visual, linguistic and institutional forms, is ultimately constructed upon (determined in the penultimate instance by?) the spontaneous categories of the forms of representation of social life. But clearly many mediations and many local specificities would have to be taken into account in any convincingly detailed analysis of some of the more elaborate or bizarre forms of ideological discourse (religions, moralities, philosophical systems etc.). Also one would have to know how to distinguish in any particular case between superficial, apparent, manifest semantic content, and deeper, more revealing, latent, formative principles of discourse. At the surface level ideology is infinitely flexible and a determined ideologist can plunder even the least likely sources for sentences, images, phrases, words, with which to forge effective weapons (think of Watney's beer and the 'Red Revolution'; or of Nixon at a banquet in Peking invoking the image of the Long March). Such curiosities remind one that meaning is not a matter of words, images, phrases, etc. taken in isolation, but of an order of discourse and practices within which particular words, phrases, or images can take on a variety of meanings. It should also remind one of the problem that discourse is over-determined, so that there may well be levels of relative coherence and intelligibility autonomous from that of any particular set of generative categories. Thus the theory of ideology outlined here is clearly very incomplete inasmuch as it would have to be expanded to include a theory of mediations and over-determination to make of it a useful tool of analysis for cases which are less directly grounded in the particular categories discussed in *Capital* than are those related to the wage-form discussed above.

It must also be remembered that ideology is present in history not as disembodied thought, nor merely in the form of the thought, speech and behaviour of individuals, but in social organizations of various kinds. (See Althusser's concept of Ideological State Apparatus mentioned above.) Since I have been mainly concerned with the cognitive basis of ideology I have no doubt been using rather abstract concepts which may have suggested that phenomenal forms and their corresponding ideological categories exist only as aspects of the cognitive acts of individuals, for example the experience of the individual worker of his wage-transactions and of his production and consumption of commodities. But of course it is not this that is involved at all. The worker's experience is mediated not only by language and culture but also by social institutions. The worker not only reads newspapers and watches television, but is also a member of a family, has been to school, belongs to a union, has perhaps been in the army, and in a football club, is perhaps a member of a church. The conditions for the production of mystification are not abstract but are material and historical.

Keeping this in mind one can get a firmer grip on the problem of the domination of the workers' movement by bourgeois ideology that has been a continuing theme of this paper. Bourgeois ideology dominates because, within serious limits, *it works*, both cognitively and in practice. It provides intelligibility and is embodied in effective working-class organizations. This is the point made by E.P. Thompson in his argument against some of the abstractions of Perry Anderson's analysis of the 'peculiarities of the English'.[36] The main peculiarity diagnosed by Engels was the dominance of unionism over politics, 'the indifference to all theory which is one of the main reasons why the English working-class movement crawls along so slowly in spite of the splendid organization of the individual unions'.[37] Thompson's explanation of this absence of a socialist political and theoretical counterbalance to the spontaneously bourgeois union movement in England consists in locating this absence in the context of the history of the labour movement's success.[38]

> . . . the workers, having failed to overthrow capitalist society, proceeded to warren it from end to end. This 'caesura' [between the defeat of Chartism and the appearance of strong unions and eventually the Labour Party] is exactly the period in which the characteristic class institutions of the Labour movement were built up – trade unions, trades councils, TUC, co-ops, and the rest – which have endured to this

day. It was part of the logic of this new direction that each advance within the framework of capitalism simultaneously involved the working class far more deeply in the status quo. As they improved their position by organization within the workshop, so they became more reluctant to engage in quixotic outbreaks which might jeopardize gains accumulated at such cost. Each assertion of working-class influence within the bourgeois-democratic state machinery, simultaneously involved them as partners (even if antagonistic partners) in the running of the machine . . . reformist pressures from secure organizational bases, bring evident returns . . . British reformism is strong because, within very serious limits, it has worked.

Conclusion

It would not be possible to account further for the nature of the relation between the subject and the reality that Marx describes in ideological discourse without entering further into the theory of language and the theory of consciousness. But it should be clear that from Marx's thesis some negative points about this relation do emerge, points which are criticisms of other possible theories of ideology. It is not necessary to postulate that any basic role in the generation of ideological discourse is played by subjective and individual agencies such as the desire to deceive, or the deliberate intention to manipulate the beliefs of others in such a way as to protect one's own interests. Nor is it necessary to postulate that ideology need be believed only by the aid of some process of self-deception or refusal or bad-faith. Such existentialist concepts are invoked in order to explain how it can come about that a person believes things which are manifestly contradictory, or believes things which he is in a good position to know are false. But Marx's theory postulates that ideology arises from the fact that the situation might be such as to provide a person with reasons for thinking in terms of categories which necessarily generate falsehood and illusion.

Marx's theory does not assert a merely causal relation between socio-economic reality and ideology. This is the trouble with some of his early formulae, such as the famous 'religion is the opium of the people', inasmuch as they can be interpreted as meaning that ideology functions as a sort of drug which acting on a person's cognitive and perceptual equipment would somehow causally prevent him from seeing what was there to be seen. This is at variance with the *Capital* theory which asserts that the basis of ideology is precisely in its apparent justification by the perceived forms of empirical social reality. So, one must reject the view that ideology has its basis in some sort of defective perception of clearly perceptible facts. For Marx understanding comes not from making good the oversights of others, nor from merely noticing what they had not noticed, but from discovering that which is concealed by the apparent facts, or more accurately by the form of the facts that are directly perceptible in social life. It is the forms of social relations with which one is apparently directly acquainted in experience (value, wages, money, commodities, etc.) that are deceptive. Scientific advance is not so much a matter of discovery as of penetration. And this is achieved by systematic conceptual innovation, that is by theory, which allows us to grasp the hidden coherence of the object.

I am not, of course, denying the reality of self-deception. Nor am I denying that there have been and are many who believe what they believe about social relations because they are aware of the connection between such beliefs and the advancement of their own interests. That is to say that in some way or other beliefs which they regard as justified are fortified or are denied criticism because it is in the interests of that person or group of persons that such beliefs be held. Nor am I denying the obvious truth that there are many who attempt to manipulate others into believing things which they know to be false or into thinking in ways that they know to be mystifying or which simply blunt people's critical faculties in such a way as indirectly to prevent them from arriving at the truth. I have no doubt that such methods of attempted manipulation of people's beliefs are very common, that for example the present (1972) President of the United States and many members of his administration are liars, that they and many others not only lie but use their enormous power and wealth to make as certain as possible that their lies fill the media and penetrate into every corner of the language and of people's minds. But I think Marx's theory is an attempt to account for much more puzzling phenomena than this. Namely that at least in certain historical conditions ideological forms of thought are the 'natural self-understood modes of thought'. The bourgeois ideology that has dominated not only the thought of the bourgeoisie but also the theory and practice for example of the British Labour movement for over a century has clearly not had its origins in the methods or instruments that are now available to and used by the cynical élite of crisis-torn America. Such methods have not normally been necessary. If everyone has been brain-washed then it is by the very forms of social reality itself. It is they, Marx says, that are impressed on our brains. Of course this is not an unchanging or unchangeable state of affairs. But just what Marx's theory of the conditions for the production of mystification can teach us about the conditions for the production of knowledge, and for the production of a non-mystifying social reality, are not questions which I have attempted to answer in this paper.

Notes

1. LENIN, *What is to be Done?* (Moscow, 1969), p. 41.
2. Ibid., p. 25.
3. Ibid., p. 42.
4. For some exhilarating analyses, based on structuralist linguistics, of some of these semiological phenomena see ROLAND BARTHES, *Mythologies* (London, 1972).
5. HERBERT MARCUSE, 'Repressive tolerance' in *A Critique of Pure Tolerance*, by Marcuse et al. (New York, 1965), pp. 98, 110.
6. *The German Ideology*, given for example in Lewis Feuer (ed.), *Marx and Engels, Basic Writings on Politics and Philosophy* (New York, 1959), p. 247.
7. One might have added here 'also in relation to the problem of madness' with reference to the work of FOUCAULT, *Histoire de la Folie*.
8. See M. FOUCAULT, 'The prose of the world', in *The Order of Things*, Chapter 2.
9. C. LÉVI-STRAUSS, *The Scope of Anthropology* (London, 1967), p. 41.
10. All quotes from *Capital* are from vol. I of the Moore and Aveling translation (Moscow, 1961), and the page references are given in the text after each quote.
11. HENRI LEFEBVRE *The Sociology of Marx* (Harmondsworth, 1968), p. 62.
12. NORMAN GERAS, 'Essence and appearance; aspects of fetishism in Marx's *Capital*', *New Left Review*, LXV (Jan.–Feb. 1971), p. 69.
13. *Critique of the Gotha Programme* in Marx and Engels, *Selected Works* II (Moscow, 1962), p. 32 (my emphasis).
14. *Critique of the Gotha Programme*, p. 27 (my emphasis).
15. GERAS, art. cit. p. 71.
16. The notion of 'world-views' tends to be explained on the model of Gestalt switch experiences of visual perception. Marx's view clearly differs from this in at least this basic respect. The difference between the one 'language' and the other is one which can be explained in terms of appearance and reality, or in terms of the aspect of reality which is its appearance and that which is its hidden substratum. Thus the difference is explained by reference to properties of the object and not solely of the subject and his idiosyncracies. No doubt these considerations would form the basis for an explanation of the way in which Marx's epistemology escapes the problems of idealism and relativism with which I do not deal in this essay.
17. I also think that a full treatment of these problems would require a close examination or Marx's theory of categories given in the 1857 Introduction to the *Critique of Political Economy*, especially the section 'The method of political economy'. This is now available in DAVID MCLELLAN, *Marx's Grundrisse* (London, 1971), pp. 33–43.
18. This presentation of the concept of surplus-value is certainly fetishistic in as much as it says of various things (labour-power, commodities) that they *have* value. The relation between labour and value cannot be presented here more accurately for lack of space – it would involve noting at least two movements of totalization (a) the labour of the individual does not *in itself* have a relation to value or surplus-value, but only as a component of the aggregate of social labour; (b) the value of the products of labour is correctly understood only in relation to their multiple appearance both as products and as commodities, and hence their location in the spheres both of production and of consumption. The 1857 Introduction (see note 17) is invaluable in its discussion of the semantic and logical problems involved here. A fuller presentation of these relations would be

too complex given the space available but would only strengthen and further support the points I am making in the text. Marx himself often appeals, in passing, to such over-simplified examples for ease of presentation.

19. *Critique of the Gotha Programme, Selected Works*, II, p. 29 (Marx's emphases).
20. Marx points out that wages take a *variety of forms* 'a fact not recognizable in the ordinary economic treatises which, *exclusively interested in the material side of the question,* neglect every difference of form' (p. 543). Marx, being interested also in the practical and cognitive (and hence ideological, political, etc.) sides of capitalism, systematically considers forms as well as contents throughout *Capital*. In Chapters 20 and 21 he considers some varieties of the wage-form (time-wages, piece-wages), showing how each conceals real relations and how 'difference of form in the payment of wages alters in no way their essential nature' (p. 552).
21. This is most clearly spelt out by Marx in relation to the commodity-form; see Chapter 1, section 4, 'The fetishism of commodities and the secret thereof'.
22. See note 18.
23. Some of the connections between ideological categories and ideological moral principles are discussed by MARCUSE, *Reason and Revolution*, pp. 280–1 for example:

    If wages . . . express the value of labour, exploitation is at best a subjective and personal judgment. If capital were nothing other than an aggregate of wealth employed in commodity production, then capital would appear to be the cumulative result of productive skill and diligence. If the creation of profits were the peculiar quality of utilized capital, such profits might represent a reward for the work of the entrepreneur.

24. MARX, *Wages, Price and Profit* in *Selected Works* I, p. 446 (Marx's emphases).
25. *What is to be Done?*, p. 42.
26. See Introduction 'The anatomy of the human being is the key to the anatomy of the ape.' I think a clear exposition of the theory in this Introduction would be invaluable. It would show, for example, just how different Marx's theory of categories and of ideology is from, for example, the relativist, idealist Kuhnian theory of 'paradigms' in which two competing paradigms, in a revolutionary period, *do exclude* one another. It would also show how Marx would be able to give an account of 'justification' in terms of his theory of inclusion and hence escape the irrationalism of Kuhn and the retreat to methodology of Lakatos.
27. See ENGELS, 'Preface to the second volume of *Capital*' (also in *Selected Works*, I, pp. 470ff., where Engels, using an interesting parallel between Marx's theoretical achievement and that of Lavoisier in chemistry, describes how economists had 'remained in thrall to the economic categories as they had found them' thus making it impossible for them to understand surplus-value. 'Then Marx came forward. And he did so in direct opposition to all his predecessors. Where they had seen a *solution*, he saw only a *problem*.' I think the philosophy of science has a lot to learn from such passages.
28. Since this is such a frequent and powerful aspect of Marx's analyses, and since I have dealt with it so briefly, it may be worth referring to perhaps the most extraordinary occurrences of it – in the chapter on 'The Fetishism of Commodities' Marx goes through a series of five distinct historical variations in the relation between the labour of an individual producer and aggregate of social production, to demonstrate the peculiarities of commodity-production (*Capital*, I, pp. 75–9). Or see pp. 539–42 on slavery (' . . . in the system of slavery, where frankly, and *openly, without any circumlocution*, labour-power itself is sold . . . ').

29. See WITTGENSTEIN, *Philosophical Investigations*, para. 432 'Every sign *by itself* seems dead. What gives it life? – In use it is *alive*. Is life breathed into it there? – or is the *use* its life?'.

30. *Capital*, p. 19.

> My dialectic method is not only different from the Hegelian, but is its *direct opposite*. To Hegel, the life-process of the human brain, that is the process of thinking, which, under the name of 'the Idea', he even transforms into an independent subject, is the demiurgos of *the real world, and the real world is only the external, phenomenal form of 'the idea'*. With me, on the contrary, the ideal is nothing else than *the material world reflected by the human mind, and translated into forms of thought*. . . . The mystification which dialectic suffers in Hegel's hands, by no means prevents him from being the first to present its general form of working in a comprehensive and conscious manner. With him it is *standing on its head*. It must be turned right side up again, if you would discover *the rational kernel within the mystical shell* [My emphases].

31. L. ALTHUSSER, *For Marx* (Harmondsworth, 1969), especially Part 3, 'Contradiction and Overdetermination'.

32. A brave effort to explain the peculiarities of a 'philosophy of internal relations' and the consequent difficulties in the interpretation of Marx is made by BERTELL OLLMAN, *Alienation: Marx's Conception of Man in Capitalist Society* (Cambridge, 1971).

33. ETIENNE BALIBAR, 'The basic concepts of historical materialism' in *Reading Capital*, by L. ALTHUSSER and E. BALIBAR (London, 1970), p. 215.

34. B. OLLMAN, *Alienation*, p. 23. The quote is from *Capital*, II, p. 226. This conception of categories and its elaboration in relation to the basic categories of historical materialism is probably most usefully discussed in BALIBAR, op. cit.

35. L. ALTHUSSER, 'Ideology and ideological state apparatuses' in *Lenin and Philosophy and other Essays* (London, 1971).

36. E.P. THOMPSON, 'The peculiarities of the English' in *Socialist Register* (1965). PERRY ANDERSON 'Origins of the present crisis' in *New Left Review*, XXIII.

37. Quoted in LENIN, *What is to be Done?*, p. 27.

38. E.P. THOMPSON, art. cit., p. 343. See also p. 342.

> Let us look at history *as* history – men placed in actual contexts which they have not chosen, and confronted by indivertable forces, with an overwhelming immediacy of relations and duties and with only a scanty opportunity for inserting their own agency. . . . An interpretation of British Labourism which attributes all to Fabianism and intellectual default is as valueless as an account of Russia between 1924 and 1953 which attributes all to the vices of Marxism, or of Stalin himself. And one thing which it lacks is any sociological dimension. . . .

14 Belief, Bias and Ideology*

Jon Elster

Jon Elster is Associate Professor in Social and Historical Philosophy at the University of Oslo, and also holds a professorial appointment in the United States. His many publications on political philosophy include *Logic and Society* (Chichester: Wiley, 1978), *Ulysses and the Sirens* (Cambridge: Cambridge University Press, 1979) and *Explaining Technical Change* (Cambridge: Cambridge University Press, 1983). Elster belongs to the school of so-called Rational Choice Marxism, which seeks to revise Marxist thought in the light of modern-day analytical philosophy; and in this extract he brings a sceptical, analytic mind to bear on certain problems of belief and cognition.

An ideology is a set of beliefs or values that can be explained through the (non-cognitive) interest or position of some social group. I shall mainly discuss ideological beliefs, though at some points reference is also made to ideological value systems. Ideological beliefs belong to the more general class of biased beliefs, and the distinction between interest and position explanations corresponds to the more general distinction between distortion and illusion as forms of bias. In recent work in social psychology the distinction has also been captured by the opposition between 'hot' and 'cold' causation of beliefs, or between 'psychodynamics' and 'psychologic'.[1]

The goal of my essay is to provide micro-foundations for the Marxist theory of ideological belief. I believe that this theory is potentially of great importance, and that its underdeveloped state is mainly due to misguided notions of what kinds of evidence and explanation it requires. Some have been content to impute causal connection between beliefs and social structure on the basis of 'structural homologies', a solemn name for whatever arbitrary similarities the writer in question can think of.[2] Others have explained beliefs through their accordance with class interest, without pausing to define the terms (long-term or short-term interest?,

*Reprinted from Martin Hollis and Steven Lukes (eds), *Rationality and Relativism* (Oxford: Basil Blackwell, 1982), pp. 123–48.

interest of the class members or of the class as a whole?) or to sketch plausible mechanisms by which the interests can bring about their own fulfilment. Against these approaches I would like to insist on the need for an understanding of the psychological mechanisms by which ideological beliefs are formed and entrenched. This in turn is part of a broader argument that Marxist theory will prove incapable of fruitful development without an explicit espousal of methodological individualism.[3]

I should briefly mention the two traditions that I draw most heavily on in the following pages. First, there is the recent work in cognitive psychology by Amos Tversky and others, recently and admirably synthetized by Richard Nisbett and Lee Ross. I shall have some critical remarks to offer on the more speculative of their arguments, but these do not detract from the solid achievements of their empirical work. These advocates of the 'cool' approach to irrational beliefs have set a standard for theoretical and experimental rigour that their 'hot' opponents should certainly try to emulate, even though by the nature of the case this may prove more difficult.

Secondly, I have learned much from some outstanding case studies in intellectual and political history. Joseph Levenson's analysis of China's confrontation with the West shows unforgettably how varied and subtle are the reactions of the human mind to a state of acute dissonance, in this case traditional Chinese assumption of superiority set on collision course with perceived military inferiority. And Paul Veyne's study of civic giving in classical antiquity argues convincingly that the subjects' ideological adaptation to their state of submission was endogenous, and not only did not require, but would have been incompatible with, deliberate ideological manipulation by the rulers. He thus provides a theoretical alternative to Gramsci's notion of hegemony that for a generation has dominated Marxist thought on the subject. In fact, Veyne's study offers a whole system of philosophical anthropology, inspired in approximately equal parts by Hegel, Focqueville and Festinger. As I have argued elsewhere, his is a path-breaking contribution to the theory of micro-foundations of political institutions that all social theorists henceforward ignore at their peril.[4]

In the first part below, I sketch in broad outline a view of human irrationality, including irrational beliefs. In the second part I deal with the illusionary beliefs that are faulty because shaped by defective cognitive processes. The third part then looks at the distorted beliefs that arise when belief-formation is shaped by wants or preferences. The discussion is largely typological and conceptual, not because I do not value causal analysis, but because I believe there is a need to find out which way the grain runs before you cut.

Ideology

I

It is generally agreed that in the genesis of human behaviour both beliefs and values (which I shall call interchangeably also desires, wants and preferences) are involved. I shall follow Donald Davidson and assume that beliefs and wants are causes of actions. This implies that action may be irrational in two cases: either it is caused in a wrong way by the desires and beliefs causing it, or it is caused by beliefs and desires that have themselves been caused in a wrong manner. Davidson has mostly studied the first variety of irrational behaviour.[5] Here I shall survey some mechanisms of the second kind, with the purpose of locating bias and ideology on the map of irrational mental phenomena.

Some cases of irrational formation of mental states are also formation of irrational mental states. In some cases, that is, we can tell from the desires and beliefs alone that they are irrational, without any need to study their genesis. If there is such a thing as self-deception, it must be detectable independently of the past mental history, but this need not be the case for wishful thinking. Similarly, we can tell that intransitive preferences are irrational from their structure alone, but to be able to say the same about what I elsewhere have called adaptive preferences ('sour grapes')[6] we typically need to know how they were shaped. In this survey I am mainly concerned with beliefs that do not have irrationality written on them for all to read. I am concerned with beliefs that satisfy the Hintikka criterion for defensibility, i.e. beliefs such as there exists a possible world in which they are true and also believed.[7] In fact, the belief may be true in the actual world and still be irrational, if it is not well grounded in the available evidence. Even more important, they may be well grounded (false or true, it does not matter) and still be irrational, because shaped in an irrational way. This will prove of central importance in Part III.

I have distinguished between two varieties of mental states, cognitive and affective. Similarly we may distinguish between two ways in which irrational mental states may be brought about, by a faulty cognitive structure or by some affective drive. This gives us altogether four possibilities. Let me explain them through some examples, not intended to be exhaustive of the respective classes (which themselves are not thought to be exhaustive of the larger universe of irrational mental processes).[8]

Adaptive preference is the adjustment of wants to possibilities, not the deliberate adaptation favoured by Stoic, Spinozistic or Buddhist philosophy, but a causal process taking place 'behind the back' of the individual concerned. The driving force between such adaptation is the often intolerable tension and frustration ('cognitive dissonance') of having wants that one cannot possibly satisfy. I use the term 'drive' rather than 'desire' of this force, to convey that it is not a question of something that guides your choice, but of something that shapes what guides your choice.[9]

Preference change by framing means that the relative attractiveness of options changes when the choice situation is reframed in a way that rationally should have no impact on the preferences. It has been extensively studied by Amos Tversky and Daniel Kahneman, who cite an example from L.J. Savage of 'a customer who is willing to add £X to the total cost of a new car to acquire a fancy car radio, but realizes that he would not be willing to add £X for the radio after purchasing the car at its regular price'. And the authors add: 'Many readers will recognize the temporary devaluation of money that makes new acquisitions unusually attractive in the context of buying a house.'[10] They refer to such phenomena as akin to perceptual illusions.

Wishful thinking is the shaping of beliefs by wants so as to produce a belief that a desired state actually obtains or will obtain. A desire for promotion may bring about the belief that promotion is imminent. Like adaptive preference formation this is a 'hot' rather than a 'cold' process, but unlike adaptive preference formation the end-result is a set of beliefs, not of desires.

Inferential error is the cold way to irrational beliefs. The varieties of such errors have been extensively surveyed by Nisbett and Ross, who conclude that the 'intuitive scientist' is prone to a depressingly large number of unfounded judgements and inferences stemming from defects in the cognitive apparatus. Such errors are like framing shifts in preferences with respect to their causes, and like wishful thinking with respect to their effects. A typical example is that 'an individual judged *very* likely to be a Republican but rather *unlikely* to be a lawyer would be judged *moderately* likely to be a *Republican lawyer*'[11] as if the probabilities were additive and not multiplicative.

There is no need here to discuss the relative importance of cold versus hot factors in the formation of irrational desires and beliefs. Common sense tells us that both must be important, and science presumably will be able to tell us when the one or the other mechanism is at work. Let me make a polemical remark, however, that may bring out some important conceptual points. This remark is addressed to Nisbett and Ross, who argue that the hot motivational factors have been over-stressed in the analysis of bias, and the cold cognitive factors underestimated. Two of their arguments go as follows. First, they say that 'self-serving motivational factors need not be introduced to explain most of the fundamental inferential or judgmental biases discussed in this book. In fact, as we shall see, the erroneous judgments, predictions and causal assessments reached by the intuitive psychologist – far from being self-serving – often undermine self-esteem and limit the individual's capacity to satisfy personal needs.'[12] This I read as an argument that since beliefs shaped by interests typically also serve them, beliefs that undermine interests cannot have been shaped by them. But the premise of this inference is wrong, as I argue below. Beliefs born of passion tend to betray it, not to serve it.

Secondly, towards the end of the book the authors seem to recognize this fact, when they write that the '*costs* of willy-nilly distortions in perception are simply too high to make them a cure-all for the disappointed or threatened perceiver'.[13] But then, curiously, they seem to reverse their earlier reasoning and use this observation as an argument against the motivational theory of bias. They invoke in passing natural selection, which 'must surely deal harshly with such unrestrained subservience of reality to wishes'.[14] They do not, however, ask the analogous question about inferential error, except for some brief references to the idea that such error may be an inevitable by-product of rational meta-strategies for problem-solving.[15] Whatever may be the value of this approach,[16] I cannot see why it might not work as well for such hot phenomena as self-deception and weakness of will.[17] There does not seem to be any difference between hot and cold errors in that (i) they are likely to get you into trouble, and (ii) that they may turn out to be lesser evils compared to the lack of the meta-strategies of which they are by-products.

Often, in a state of dissonance, there are two functionally equivalent ways of achieving consonance, by adaptive preferences or by wishful thinking. This is reflected in the way in which we talk about these phenomena. Thus in the original French version the fox disliked the grapes because they were too *green*, a perceptual distortion, not because they were too sour. Similarly, a well-known self-destructive mechanism is proverbially rendered either by 'Forbidden fruit is sweet' or by 'The grass is always greener on the other side of the fence'. The first achieves dissonance by changing the preferences, the second by changing the perception. In such cases the distinction between beliefs and values is tenuous. In other cases the two mechanisms, while equivalent, can be clearly distinguished from each other. Thus Levenson explains how the spectrum of Chinese reaction to Western superiority included both wishful thinking, through the belief that China could adopt Western techniques while retaining the Chinese essence; and 'sour grapes' through the argument that Western techniques were not worth having anyway, and that they in fact represented an option that China had rejected long ago.[18] In complex ideological phenomena the two strands of distorted beliefs and of adaptive preferences are nearly always found together, but we know little of the mechanisms that determine the relative importance of the one and the other. The practical difference between the two is enormous, for through adaptive preference change some durable peace may be found, whereas wishful thinking more often than not only postpones the confrontation.

II

I first explore some of the modes of ideological thought that are due to cognitive sources: illusions that stem from the position of the observer in the social structure. Let me state at the outset the first of a series of negative propositions that form an important part of my argument:

> *First proposition*: There is no reason to suppose that beliefs shaped by a social position tend to serve the interests of the persons in that position.

In particular, ideas shaped by class position need not serve class interest. This insight is also formulated by Leszek Kolakowski:

> [When] Engels says that the Calvinistic theory of predestination was a religious expression of the fact that commercial success or bankruptcy does not depend on the businessman's intention but on economic forces, then, whether we agree with his statement or not, we must regard it as asserting a merely causal connection: for the idea of absolute dependence on an external power (viz. the market in the 'mystified' shape of Providence) does not seem to further the businessman's interest, but rather to set the seal on his impotence.[19]

The context shows that Kolakowski is not quite clear in his mind on this point, as he only makes a distinction between causal and teleological determination of beliefs, and not the further distinction between hot and cold causation. He seems to believe, wrongly in my opinion, that the phrases 'beliefs are caused by the interests of the class in question' and 'beliefs are what they are because of the situation of the class' are synonymous. In fact, the two distinctions between causal and teleological explanations of beliefs and between position and interest explanations cut across each other, giving a total of three rather than two possible cases: causal position explanations, causal interest explanations and the teleological interest explanations (or functional, as I shall say here).

This ambiguity means that Kolakowski's observation could also be seen as an instance of my third proposition (Part III). But the example he cites from Engels clearly falls under the first proposition. The example is of interest also from a substantial point of view. It says, roughly, that agents in a competitive market tend to generalize the economic fact that their behaviour cannot influence prices, so as to believe that they are equally powerless with respect to non-material elements that are important to them. (Weber, on the other hand, stressed that his analysis of the relation between capitalism and Calvinism was valid only for the early stage of capitalism, when religion had to provide the element of compulsion that later was realized through the competitive market.[20] A corollary would be that imperfectly competitive capitalism should foster an 'illusion of control', so that agents that are more than quantity-adjusting price-takers should also come to believe that their actions make a difference for their salvation. This may or may not be the case: it could be interesting to find out. More generally, perfect, imperfect and strategic markets might tend to develop, respectively, attitudes of dependence, control and interdependence that might be less justified in other arenas.

A particularly important case backing the first proposition is the tendency of the oppressed and exploited classes in a society to believe in the justice of the social order that oppresses them. This belief, perhaps, is mainly due to distortion, i.e. to such affective mechanisms as rationalization. But there is also an element of illusion, of bias stemming from purely cognitive sources. As brilliantly explained by Paul Veyne, it was obvious to any dependent man in classical antiquity that he owed his living and his security to his master: 'c'est à ce patron de droit divin que je dois de manger et d'exister, car que deviendrais-je, si lui-même n'existait pas, ni ce vaste domaine où je vis et dont il est le propriétaire?'[21] This may be called a micro-political illusion, corresponding to what Veyne elsewhere calls the micro-economic illusion and which is the belief that the economic mechanisms that are valid for the individual, at the margin, also are valid for the whole.[22] Since I would be worse off without my master, it follows that a society without masters would be intolerable, for who would then provide employment and protection? A similar optical illusion may account for the theories that explain feudalism as a voluntary exchange between the serfs and the lord, the latter providing protection and receiving goods and labour services in return.[23] The illusion of a voluntary and rational arrangement disappears when one observes that the lord provided protection mainly against other lords, much as a gangster can justify his protection racket by pointing to the threat from rival gangsters. Feudalism may have been a Nash equilibrium, in the sense that for each agent feudal behaviour was optimal given that everybody else behaved feudally. But there may have been other Nash equilibria as well, and in any case a Nash equilibrium may well be severely sub-optimal. And even a Pareto-optimal Nash equilibrium may be unjust on criteria of distributive justice.

The same illusion, I believe, underlies the neoclassical theory of exploitation under capitalism[24] and, more generally, all theories that argue that workers should be paid according to what each of them produces in circumstances that, logically, have no place for all of them. Neoclassical theory says that labour is not exploited if paid according to marginal product, i.e. if each worker is paid as if he were the last to be hired, or, more to the point, the first to be fired. With individual wage negotiations, each worker can be made to see himself in this light, but of course each cannot be the last. Similarly Marx argued that the capitalist could reap the profit from co-operation by paying each worker according to what he could make by himself before entering into co-operation with other workers:

> Being independent of each other, the labourers are isolated persons, who enter into relations with the capitalist, but not with each other. . . . Because [the productive power developed by the labourer when working in co-operation] costs capital nothing, and because, on the other hand, the labourer himself does not develop it before his labour belongs to capital, it appears as a power with which capital is endowed by Nature.[25]

These examples have shown that because of their place in the social and economic structure, the dependent, oppressed and exploited may have beliefs that do not serve their interests. But, correspondingly, these beliefs certainly serve the interests of their masters. And there is indeed an important strand in the theory of ideology that argues for a systematic correlation between the belief systems in a society and the interest of the ruling classes. Against this I advance my

> *Second proposition*: There is no reason to suppose that beliefs shaped by a social position tend to serve the interest of the ruling or dominant group.

In particular, there is no reason to believe that ideas shaped by the position of the dominant class itself serve the interest of that class. The example from Engels cited by Kolakowski illustrates this point. Another example shows that the capitalist can fall victim to an optical illusion similar to the worker's. Marx argues that the confusion between money and capital, characteristic of mercantilist economic thought, is explained by the equivalence of the two for the practical capitalist: 'He has the choice of making use of his capital by lending it out as interest-bearing capital, or of expanding its value on his own by using it as productive capital, regardless of whether it exists as money-capital from the very first, or whether it still has to be converted into money-capital. But to apply [this argument] to the total capital of society, as some vulgar economists do, is of course preposterous.'[26] And of course this preposterous argument, which was the theoretical foundation of many mercantilist policies and according to Heckscher was still employed by German economists during the First World War,[27] was in no way favourable to the interest of the dominant class out of whose position it emerged. For a third example consider George Katona's argument that a manufacturer, when asked about the probable incidence of a general tax increase on the general price level, may answer wrongly that prices will rise, because in his limited sphere of experience a tax increase is just like a wage increase in the effect on cost and pricing.[28] But if this view of the practical capitalist was made into a policy foundation, it would certainly have bad consequences for the capitalist class. In fact, no extended arguments are needed for the case that an illusionary perception of reality will in general not be conducive to an efficient manipulation of reality.

Another kind of backing for the second proposition would be provided by cases, if such could be found, in which the social position of an oppressed class generated illusions that actually served its interest, and therefore went counter to that of the dominant class. But, as just observed, this is not likely to happen. Nisbett and Ross point out, however, that 'unrealistically positive self-schemas or other illusions about the self, together with the processing biases they can engender, may be more socially adaptive than are totally accurate self-perceptions'.[29] Similarly, Kolakowski writes of Lenin:

> After 1917 he expected a European revolution any day, and thought he could run the Russian economy by means of terror. But all his misjudgements were in the direction of expecting the revolutionary movement to be stronger and to manifest itself earlier, than it actually did. They were fortunate errors from his point of view, since it was only on the basis of false estimates that he decided on an armed insurrection in October 1917. His mistakes enabled him to exploit the possibilities of revolution to the full, and were thus the cause of his success.[30]

In other words, 'fortunate errors' of perception may raise the level of aspiration and mobilize energy that would have lain dormant with a more realistic understanding of the situation. Such errors need not stem from a cognitive bias. They are perhaps more likely to arise out of wishful thinking, or even be deliberately nurtured by some agent manipulating the situation.[31] But on the abstract level one may well imagine that an oppressed class can be led by its situation to form illusionary beliefs that also serve its interests in some way. Still there is, I believe, a *presumption* that illusions are inefficient, and therefore the second proposition is false if we restrict ourselves to the positions of the oppressed classes.

I want to dwell somewhat on the notion of illusions that are either useful or conducive to truth. Nisbett and Ross offer some interesting, though partly ambiguous, observations on this 'dangerous notion'. First, as already mentioned, they stress that illusions may actually benefit the individual having them, by the effect on motivation. Secondly they observe, but without distinguishing this case from the preceding one, that such illusions may be good from the overall social point of view: 'We probably would have few novelists, actors or scientists if all potential aspirants to these careers took action based on a normatively justifiable subjective probability of success.'[32] Observe that this way of 'rationalizing the irrational' – a favourite pastime of the modern social scientist – differs from the alternative way, already referred to, which is that of seeing illusions as inevitable by-products of the rational allocation of time to problem-solving. Saying that illusions are actually conducive to success differs from saying that they are the necessary cost of success, just as saying that luxury is an indispensable means to welfare (through the effect on employment) differs from saying that luxury is an inevitable but regrettable side-product of welfare.[33]

Thirdly, and passing now from utility to truth, the authors observe that some illusions may even be conducive to truth, either by correcting another illusion or by substituting for correct inference. For example, people seem to have great difficulties in understanding or applying the simple notion of regression to the mean, e.g. in seeing that extreme observations are likely to prove atypical. This defect can lead to such harmful practical conclusions that punishment is more effective than reward in training, because on the average good performances (even when rewarded) will be followed by less good, while bad performances (even when not punished) will be followed by less bad.[34] Nisbett and Ross then point to no less than three mechanisms that, by compensation or substitution, may enable us to make correct predictions. (1) By diluting the information that leads to wrong predictions with additional *irrelevant* information, subjects are enabled to improve their score. (2) The irrational gambler's fallacy, when interacting with the equally irrational 'fundamental attribution error', may give a net result of rational regression. (3) As in other cases,[35] a causal interpretation of what is essentially a sampling effect may give a correct result, as when the baseball trainer argues that the brilliant first-year player will be spoiled by all the attention he gets and not live up to his performance in the next season.

The important question here is whether the beneficial consequences of the illusions can serve to *explain* them. No one, I believe, would argue that all illusions are beneficial and to be explained by their benefits, though some might want to say that they are part of an optimal meta-strategy in the sense indicated above. But one might want to argue that when an illusion is systematically beneficial, the question should at least be raised whether it cannot be explained as a compensating or substituting device. Both natural selection and psychological reinforcement might conceivably serve as mechanisms underlying this functional explanation.[36] This holds for the cases in which the illusions are beneficial for the person having them. Much more controversial is the idea that illusions could be explained by consequences beneficial for other persons. I find it hard to imagine a mechanism by which the illusions of an oppressed class could be explained by their beneficial consequences for the ruling class. There are good reasons for thinking that the oppressed classes often will be victims of a kind of myopia that prevent them from seeing the injustice of their situation – and it is clear that this is good for the ruling class; but even a systematic correlation would not by itself warrant an explanatory statement. And it is even less plausible that illusions could be explained, as suggested by Nisbett and Ross, by their good effects on 'society', because this does not give us the kind of actor required for the monitoring of a feedback process. If beneficial consequences of an illusion shall serve to explain it, they must be, I think, beneficial for the individual subject to the illusion (or for his close relatives through kin selection). Some additional considerations on functional explanations of ideologies are offered in Part III.

A final remark on the topic of illusions answers a question that some readers may have put to themselves: Is there not an inconsistency when I attribute illusions both to features of the situation and to the cognitive apparatus of the subject? In the Marxist theory of ideologies class position is central, but in cognitive psychology the stress is laid on the internal psychic mechanism of the subject, and so it might seem strange to seek in the latter micro-foundations for the former. This, however, is an artificial opposition. For illusions to occur both the external situation and the internal processing must come into play. It is consistent with cognitive psychology to assume that individuals differ systematically, e.g. in a class-related way, in the extent to which their external situation lends itself to certain kinds of fallacies, inferential errors and illusions. And one could also speculate, though I would be more sceptical as to the value of the outcome, that differences in social origin generate differences in the internal apparatus and thus in the liability to illusions (keeping the external situation constant).

III

Beliefs often are distorted by interest, mainly perhaps through wishful thinking (of which rationalization is a subspecies), but also by pessimism, conformism and related mechanisms. I shall here limit my attention to wishful thinking, the tendency to form beliefs when, and because, I prefer the state of the world in which they are true to states in which they are false. Let me sharply distinguish this phenomenon from that of believing at will, a deliberate choice rather than a causal process. Believing at will, supposing it to be at all possible,[37] is related to wishful thinking, as is deliberate character-planning to adaptive preferences.[38] The decision to believe is guided by a conscious desire, wishful thinking is shaped by a non-conscious drive. Or perhaps (I have little confidence in my ability to see clear in these muddy waters) we should argue that in wishful thinking my conscious desire is the cause of my belief, with the proviso that it causes the belief in a wrong or non-standard way. (And if I am right in thinking that believing at will is impossible, there is no right way.)[39]

Similarly, wishful thinking should be distinguished clearly from self-deception, supposing the latter to be at all possible. Many writers use these terms interchangeably, and 'rationalization' as synonymous with both.[40] But I believe that the notion of self-deception as commonly understood involves paradoxes that are absent from that of wishful thinking. Self-deception or bad faith involves two inconsistent beliefs, a fact that in itself does not make it impossible.[41] But there is also the peculiar feature that the self-deceiver intentionally hides one of his beliefs from himself and professes the other as his official view. The idea of (successful) self-deception therefore raises two closely related questions: How do you manage to *forget intentionally* what you really know or believe? And how can you *believe at will* something which you know that there are inadequate grounds for believing? The decision to forget is in itself paradoxical and inconsistent, in that the harder you try to carry it out, the harder it is to succeed; it is like an attempt to create darkness by light. And I have already suggested that believing at will may be a feat beyond human abilities.

However, as in the related case of weakness of will, the theoretical objections simply seem to evaporate in the case of massive clinical, fictional and everyday experience attesting to the reality of the phenomenon. And so there is a need for a theoretical analysis of self-deception: *wie ist es überhaupt möglich*? Among the better-known attempts to provide an answer are those of Freud, Sartre, Fingarette and Schafer.[42] In my view none of them are convincing, as they all tend to reproduce the basic paradox in ever-subtler forms. I would rather suggest a diversified strategy, explaining different cases of what is usually called self-deception along different lines.[43] First, some cases may be unsuccessful *attempts* at self-deception, and so no more paradoxical than other attempts to realize contradictory goals. Secondly, some cases can be understood through a distinction between higher-level and lower-level beliefs that would give substance to my higher-level belief and thus make it less tolerable. ('I do not want to know the details.') Thirdly, some cases may be understood as unsuccessful attempts at character-modification, when I exploit the leeway in the description of my character in order to change it. ('I am *not* afraid.') Fourthly, I may now bring it about that I believe something at a later time, if I can also bring about forgetfulness of the process itself. And fifthly, there is wishful thinking.

The argument for a distinction between wishful thinking and self-deception is that the former, unlike the latter, can arrive at beliefs that are not only true (which is irrelevant) but well grounded in the available evidence. Consider again the man who wishes to be promoted. We might speak of self-deception if he 'really' (somehow, somewhere) believes that he is not going to be promoted, but nevertheless hides this knowledge from himself and believes promotion to be imminent. But it might also be the case that the man had very good grounds for believing himself about to be promoted, but that he arrived at this belief in another way, viz. through wishful thinking. Here there is no duality, no opposition between the reality principle and the pleasure principle. There is no question here of hiding from oneself an unpleasant truth or well-grounded belief, for the well-grounded belief is also the one which the believer wants to be true and indeed believes because he wants it to be true. He has good reasons for believing it, but does not believe it for those reasons.[44]

I believe, moreover, that this abstract possibility has many embodiments in everyday life. Surely we have all met persons basking in self-satisfaction that seems both to be justified and not to be justified: justified because they have good reasons for being satisfied with themselves, and not justified because we sense that they would be just as satisfied were the reasons to disappear. In other words, distortion is not like a 'force', because it cannot be measured by its effects. There may be a strong tendency to distort, and yet zero distortion. The point is well made by Levenson: 'To speak of apologetics is not to suggest that Chinese thinkers, in vindicating the worth of Chinese culture against Western pretensions, were saying anything untrue. What is true is no less true because apologists insist on it. But apologists are no less apologetic because what they insist upon is true; it is the insistence that counts.'[45] In other words, wishful thinking cannot be detected simply by looking at the ideas involved, nor by comparing the beliefs with the evidence available. We have to get knowledge about the way in which the belief was actually shaped.

I believe this shows irrefutably that in some cases at least wishful thinking does not involve self-deception: the cases, namely, in which the belief born of desire is also borne out by the evidence. But then, why should not the same be true in other cases? Why could it not be the case that the wishful believer goes directly for the pleasant belief, instead of going through the four-step process of (1) arriving at the well-grounded belief, (2) deciding that it is unpalatable, (3) suppressing it, and only then (4) adhering to another and more tolerable belief? Or again, why should the repellent force of an unpleasant belief have explanatory privilege over the attracting force of a pleasant belief? I suggest that in the absence of specific arguments to the contrary, wishful thinking is a more parsimonious explanation than self-deception. Indeed, I believe that the substitution of wishful thinking for self-deception is a major step towards the elimination of Freudian unconscious as a theoretical entity – an elimination that is highly desirable not only because of the paradoxes of self-deception (defence and repression), but also because of the incoherence of the notion of unconscious intentions.[46] My own half-shaped view is that in order to understand the irrational side of human behaviour we shall do better by appealing to *inconsistent intentions backed by wishful thinking* than by invoking unconscious intentions backed by self-deception.

Paralleling the first proposition above, I now argue for a

Third proposition: There is no reason to suppose that beliefs shaped by interests tend to serve these interests.

On general grounds, distorted beliefs cannot be expected, any more than illusionary beliefs, to be very helpful for goal achievement. If out of wishful thinking I form a belief that I am about to be promoted, my subsequent display of unwarranted self-confidence may destroy once and for all my chances of promotion. The Lysenko affair showed how disastrous may be the result when scientific beliefs are formed by wishful thinking, an attitude unforgettably captured in *The First Circle*. Blatant apologetics, while often shaped by interest, do not serve them very well, precisely because they are so blatant.[47] And, referring again to Paul Veyne,[48] the exploited and oppressed classes may be led by rationalization into believing that their fate is just and proper – a belief that may indeed give short-term gratification, but cannot be said to serve the interest of these classes well at all.

Let us make some distinctions here, as not all the examples just cited can be reduced to a single formula. First, the tendency to engage in wishful thinking is in itself liable to get you into trouble, independently of the actual beliefs. The promotion example can be modified to include the previously used assumption that the belief in promotion is well-grounded, and yet the chances for promotion may be destroyed if the good reasons for believing in it are not what causes the belief. ('He would be promoted were he not so infernally confident that he will be promoted.') Secondly, it may be the actual belief that is relevant for the question of interest. A belief about instrumental means–end relationship, if true, is no less efficient because it is arrived at by wishful thinking. But of course instrumental beliefs shaped by interest will serve interest only by a fluke. Thirdly, the relevant question may be whether the belief is generally accepted rather than whether it is true. A belief system that, if accepted, would have the consequence of legitimating a system of social inequality, may not be accepted by the lower classes if it is too obviously tailor-made to, and shaped by, the interest of the upper classes. Self-serving theories of the need for inequality are rarely self-serving. The interest of the upper class is better served by the lower classes spontaneously inventing an ideology justifying their inferior status. This ideology, while stemming from the interest of the lower classes in the sense of leading to dissonance reduction, is contrary to their interest because of a tendency to overshoot, resulting in excessive rather than in proper meekness.[49] And in addition what is proper meekness in the short run may well be excessive in the long, and therefore contrary to interest in another sense as well.[50]

But lucidity about self may also be contrary to interest. In his study of Chinese reactions to Western superiority, Levenson discusses at some length what he calls the '*t'i-yung* rationalizers', a group of thinkers who thought it possible to reconcile Chinese *t'i* (essence or substance) with Western *yung* (function). But of course, 'Chinese learning had come to be prized as substance because of its function, and when its function was usurped, the learning withered.'[51] The reactionary traditionalists, as may be imagined, had no difficulty in denouncing the fallacy. 'Nevertheless, although the reactionaries might well plume themselves for sensing the logical inadequacies of that particular rationalization for innovation, their conclusion – that the innovation must be stopped, rather than the rationalization changed – was unsound. For they were obscurantist in failing to realize that innovation was inevitable, and that some rationalization, logical or not, was a psychological necessity.'[52] Wishful thinking, that is, may be as efficient as illusionary beliefs in setting up a bootstrap operation by which something becomes possible because it is thought to be possible. But as in the case of illusionary beliefs, self-serving wishful thinking must be the exception.

Conversely, I would like to argue for a

Fourth proposition: There is no reason to suppose that beliefs that serve certain interests are also to be explained by those interests.

I deliberately use the language of explanation instead of that of causation, because interest may explain beliefs in other than causal ways. In a straightforward causal explanation, interest shapes belief and thereby explains it. It follows from what has already been said that there is no reason to suppose that a belief serving a given interest will also have been shaped by that interest, although this may happen by fluke. But there is also a possible functional explanation, to the effect that a belief may be explained by the interest it serves. When Marx says that the social principles of Christianity, among many other things, 'preach the necessity of a ruling and an oppressed class, and for the latter all they have to offer is the pious wish that the former may be charitable',[53] we may well wonder whether this is not also offered as an *explanation* of Christianity in class societies. The phrase 'opium of the people' has similar explanatory overtones. As observed above, for a consequence to explain its cause there must be some underlying feedback mechanism, which in the present case is hard to imagine. But in other cases it is not difficult to conceive of ways in which beliefs persist because they serve certain interests. Theories in the social sciences often are hard to falsify by testing, and so there is some scope for interest to determine which of several contending theories shall receive economic support and be enabled to survive.[54] But the mere fact that a belief system has beneficial effects for some social class, e.g. by legitimating its rule, does not in itself create a presumption that these effects can explain the persistence of the system.

Two additional remarks on this point may be in order. First, I think it is important to stress that the ambiguities of the notion of an ideology are in fact common to the whole Marxist notion of the superstructure. For example, when Marxists argue that the state in capitalist society is also a capitalist state, i.e. is to be explained by the interest of the capitalist class, they can and do mean two radically different things. Some political institutions are to be explained (*à la* Cohen) through their stabilizing *effect on* the economic structure, others as *effects of* that structure. An example of the first according to Marx is nineteenth-century England, in which property was distributed so that capitalists had much, landowners had some and workers had none, while political power was distributed so that the capitalists had little, landowners virtually all and workers none. Marx argued that the second distribution had to be explained in terms of its stabilizing consequences for the first, because the political struggle of the workers against the government would then weaken their economic struggle against the capitalists.[55] Accepting for the sake of argument that this explanation is correct, it does not follow that the power structure was an effect of the economic structure. More plausibly the power structure was a remnant from feudalism that was retained because it had these effects on the structure. An example of the second explanation-type would be Marx's analysis in the *18 Brumaire* of the naked class rule of the bourgeoisie before Bonaparte's *coup d'état*. This regime represented an unequal distribution of power that directly grew out of, and was causally explainable in terms of, the unequal distribution of property, and yet it had a destabilizing effect on the property structure.[56] Political regimes shaped by economic interest may turn out to be disastrous for those interests.

The second observation concerns some theoretical problems of scientific explanation. To my argument that the subjects spontaneously invent an ideology justifying their oppression, so that there is no need to explain the ideology in terms of the interest of the ruling class which it in fact serves, two objections may be raised. The first[57] is that the ruling class, being in control of the means of education, could have corrected the distorted (and illusionary) beliefs of the subjects had it so chosen; therefore the fact that it did not so choose makes it co-responsible for the ideology. To this I have three brief replies. First, moral responsibility cannot be used as grounds for imputing causal responsibility (one cannot infer 'is' from 'ought'), and it is with the latter exclusively that I deal here. Secondly, acts of omission cannot normally serve as causes (though they may serve as a basis for ascribing moral responsibility). And thirdly, the objection presupposes that the ruling class does not share the distorted beliefs, e.g. that the Roman emperors did not themselves believe in their divine nature. But this, as argued by Veyne, is a total misunderstanding of religious psychology. The subjects will believe only in the superiority of rulers who never stoop to prove their superiority. (Which is why no Soviet citizens believe in the superiority of the Soviet leadership.)

The second objection[58] is the following. Given that the legitimation was spontaneously invented by the oppressed, can we not reasonably assert that in the absence of such an ideology (e.g. in the presence of a rebellious ideology) the rulers would have cracked down on the subjects by violent repression? (In fact, Veyne does not assert that the spontaneous ideologies are indispensable for the stability of class rule, and again we may look to the Soviet Union to see that they are not.) And if this is granted, can we not then argue that in class societies the rule of the dominant class will be stabilized *by some mechanism*, be it an endogenous and spontaneous belief in the natural superiority of the superiors, or a harshly repressive system? And from this, does it not follow that we can explain functionally, at high level of generality, the presence of such mechanisms? That there is *some* mechanism can be explained in terms of the stabilizing effect, even though other arguments may be needed to explain why this or that mechanism is realized. I have not made up my mind as to the general validity of this somewhat counter-intuitive idea, that when asked 'Why is it there?' one may answer: 'Because if it had not been there, something else with the same consequences would have been there.' For the present purposes, however, it suffices to observe that if we are trying to explain *ideologies*, the explanation must not be at a level of abstraction at which it is impossible to distinguish between ideological and political facts. Whatever the relevance of the functional explanation for whatever it is trying to explain, it seems obvious that the purely causal explanation of belief formation does indeed have explanatory force.

The four propositions argued above have been directed towards a facile Marxist theory of ideologies, that concludes unthinkingly from the fact that an idea is shaped by class position to the proposition that it also serves class interest; or that assumes that class interests served by an idea automatically also explain it. More generally, there has been in Marxist thought an obsession with the social significance of ideas and institutions – a tendency to impose arbitrary patterns on events so as to make them guided by the invisible hand of history. (Actually two hands have been postulated, each of which can be invoked when the other will not do – one that makes everything come out in the interest of the capitalist class, and one that makes everything into a precondition for the communist revolution.) To say this is not to advocate that we abandon Marxism, but that we firmly retain the causal mode of Marxist explanation and equally firmly reject the functional mode. Even if Cohen's attempt to salvage functionalist Marxism proved to be successful, his criteria for a valid functional explanation are so strict that almost no actual theories would satisfy them.[59] If, then, we retain Marxism together with methodological individualism and causal explanation, the foundation is laid for a satisfactory theory of socially grounded belief. The scope of this theory is much wider than has been argued by some recent writers, who have focused exclusively on the relation between beliefs and evidence. Against this I would like to advance a

> *Fifth proposition*: There is no reason to believe that if a belief is rationally grounded in the available evidence, the search for a genetic explanation is misguided.

In particular, this goes against what Larry Laudan has called the *arationality assumption*: 'whenever a belief can be explained by adequate reasons, there is no need for, and little promise in, seeking out an alternative explanation in terms of social causes'.[60] We have seen repeatedly that this is not correct. A belief may be illusionary, and yet be well grounded in the available evidence, if it stems from the two compensatory errors or from an error that in some type of context can substitute for correct inference; or justified belief and wishful thinking may coincide simply by fluke. Why did Malthus believe that unproductive consumption was required for economic growth? Because good economic reasons made him think so (Keynes)? Or because he had a desire to justify the existence of the unproductive classes to which he himself belonged (Marx)? The mere fact that there were adequate reasons for the belief is not sufficient to decide in favour of the first answer. Whatever the apparent rationality of the belief, a genetic explanation may show that it was not in fact held for those good reasons. Since epistemology deals with the rationality of beliefs, and since the rationality of a belief can neither be read off it straight away nor be assessed by comparing the belief with the evidence, we must conclude that epistemology needs history.[61]

Notes

I am grateful to G.A. Cohen and Martin Hollis for their comments on an earlier draft of this essay.

1. For the first opposition, see R.P. ABELSON, 'Computer simulation of hot cognition', in S. Tomkins and S. Messick (eds), *Computer Simulation of Personality* (New York: Wiley, 1963), pp. 277–98. For the second, see R. NISBETT and L. ROSS, *Human Inference: Strategies and Shortcomings of Social Judgment* (Englewood Cliffs, NJ: Prentice-Hall, 1980), Chapter 10.
2. See J. ELSTER, *Leibniz et la Formation de l'Esprit Capitaliste* (Paris: Aubier-Montaigne, 1975), Chapter 1, for a comment on the methodological problems of this structuralist approach to the history of ideas.
3. See my forthcoming 'Marxism, functionalism and game theory', *Theory and Society* (1982), for a more sustained argument to this effect.
4. See J. ELSTER, 'Un historien devant l'irrationnel: Lecture de Paul Veyne', *Social Science Information*, 19 (1980): 773–804, for an introduction to Veyne's thought. My 'Sour grapes', in A.K. Sen and B. Williams (eds), *Utilitarianism and Beyond*

(Cambridge: Cambridge University Press, 1982), is a companion-piece to the present essay, in which I attempt to spell out some of the broader implications of Veyne's theory of preference formation, paralleling the ideas offered here on belief formation.

5. Thus weakness of will occurs when a reason is a cause of an action without being a reason for it: D. DAVIDSON, 'How is weakness of the will possible?' in J. Feinberg (ed.), *Moral Concepts* (Oxford: Oxford University Press, 1969), pp. 93–113. Davidson also explains elsewhere how non-standard internal causal chains may lead to a reason causing the action for which it is a reason, but causing it in the wrong way: 'Freedom to act', in T. Honderich (ed.), *Essays on Freedom of Action* (London: Routledge & Kegan Paul, 1973), pp. 136–56.

6. See my 'Sour grapes'.

7. J. HINTIKKA, *Knowledge and Belief* (Ithaca, N.Y.: Cornell University Press, 1961). Why not simply say that a belief-system is consistent if there is some possible world in which it is true? Hintikka shows that the presence of higher-order beliefs imposes the need for a more complex criterion. See also ELSTER, *Logic and Society* (Chichester: Wiley, 1978), Chapter 4.

8. In particular, irrational emotions and their formation falls outside the scope of the present typology. For some comments on this intriguing problem see A. RORTY, 'Explaining the emotions', *Journal of Philosophy*, 75 (1978), pp. 139–61; and R. DE SOUSA, 'The rationality of emotions', in A. Rorty (ed.), *Explaining the Emotions* (Berkeley and Los Angeles: University of California Press, 1980), pp. 127–52.

9. Need I say that this is a nebulous and difficult opposition? The reality of, and the need for, some such distinction can be brought out by considering the case of 'counter-adaptive preferences', as when a person prefers living in Paris over London when in London and vice versa. Here there is a self-destructive *drive* that shapes the person's *desire* so that it is never satisfied. By contrast, it is harder to distinguish the drive from the desire when the drive is for the satisfaction of the desire. In my 'Sour grapes' I discuss some criteria that may help us distinguish drives from meta-desires.

10. A. TVERSKY and D. KAHNEMAN, 'The framing of decisions and the rationality of choice', *Science* (1981). See also D. KAHNEMAN and A. TVERSKY, 'Prospect theory', *Econometrica*, 47 (1979): 263–91.

11. NISBET and ROSS, *Human Inference*, p. 146.

12. Ibid., p. 13.

13. Ibid., p. 234.

14. Ibid.

15. The authors refer to A. GOLDMAN, 'Epistemics: the regulative theory of cognition', *Journal of Philosophy*, 75 (1978): 509–24; but the idea has been current among economists for some time. D. North actually argued that ideologies may be a rational response to the problem of costly information: 'Institutional change and economic growth', *Journal of Economic History*, 31 (1971): 118–25.

16. The idea obviously has some attractions, but it could be vindicated only by showing that the actual amount of error is close to the optimal one (i.e. part of an optimal package). And I cannot see how one could even make a start at this demonstration.

17. Rorty offers an argument to this effect, relying on the idea that *habit* is the important feature of human life that both makes for integrity *and* for self-deception and weakness of will: 'Self-deception, akrasia and irrationality', *Social Science Information*, 19 (1980).

18. J. LEVENSON, *Confucian China and its Modern Fate* (Berkeley and Los Angeles: University of California Press, 1968), vol. 1, Ch. 4, and *passim*.

19. L. KOLAKOWSKI, *Main Currents of Marxism* (Oxford University Press, 1978), vol. I, p. 342.

20. M. WEBER, 'Die protestantische Ethik und der Geist des Kapitalismus', in *Gesammelte Aufsätze zur Religionssoziologie* (Tübingen: Mohr, 1920), vol. I, p. 203. It might prove worth while to pursue this comparison between causal and functional theories of the relation between Calvinism and capitalism. See also ELSTER, *Leibniz*, Chapter 5.

21. P. VEYNE, *Le Pain et le Cirque* (Paris: Seuil, 1976), p. 554.

22. Ibid., pp. 148ff. For the logical structure of this fallacy, see also ELSTER, *Logic and Society*, pp. 97ff.

23. D. NORTH and R. THOMAS, 'The rise and fall of the manorial system: a theoretical model', *Journal of Economic History*, **31** (1971).

24. See, for a brief exposition and references, ELSTER, 'Exploring exploitation', *Journal of Peace Research*, **15** (1978), pp. 3–17.

25. K. MARX, *Capital*, vol. I (1867) (New York: International Publishers), p. 333.

26. MARX, *Capital*, vol. III (1894) (New York: International Publishers), p. 377.

27. E. HECKSCHER, *Mercantilism* (London: Allen and Unwin, 1954), rev. edn, vol. II, p. 202; also ELSTER, *Leibniz*, pp. 115ff., 169ff.

28. G. KATONA, *Psychological Analysis of Economic Behavior* (New York: McGraw-Hill, 1951), pp. 45ff. The classical example of this line of reasoning is Adam Smith's statement: 'What is prudence in the conduct of every private family can hardly be folly in that of a great kingdom.'

29. NISBETT and Ross, *Human Inference*, pp. 189–99.

30. KOLAKOWSKI, *Main Currents of Marxism*, vol. II, p. 525.

31. As in the notion of 'optimal tautness of plans', see, e.g., M. KEREN, 'On the tautness of plans', *Review of Economic Studies*, 39 (1972): 469–86.

32. NISBETT and Ross, *Human Inference*, p. 271.

33. Cf. ELSTER, *Leibniz*, pp. 194–5, for brief remarks on the historical antecedents of these two rationalizations of the irrational, corresponding on the theological level to Leibniz and Malebranche respectively and on the secular level to Mandeville and Leibniz respectively.

34. See A. TVERSKY and D. KAHNEMAN, 'Judgment under uncertainty', *Science*, 185 (1974): 1124–30.

35. See W. FELLER, *An Introduction to Probability Theory and its Applications* (New York: Wiley, 1968), 3rd edn, vol. 1, p. 122, for the distinction between real after-effects and effects of sampling. But even though the two procedures may give roughly similar predictions, they may lead to very different evaluations. Given the statistical observation that the longer a person has been unemployed the greater the chances that he will not find employment in the next period, it may not make much difference for prediction whether the underlying mechanism is taken to be mover–stayer or cumulative inertia – see R. BOUDON, *Mathematical Structures of Social Mobility* (Amsterdam: Elsevier, 1973) – but in the former case we may consider the unemployed as inherently lazy and in the latter as unfortunate victims of a process that hits them. Bias is seldom totally innocent.

36. P. VAN PARIJS makes a persuasive case for reinforcement as one mechanism capable of sustaining functional explanations in 'Functional explanation and the linguistic analogy', *Philosophy of the Social Sciences*, 9, (1979): pp. 525–43.

37. For various arguments to the effect that it is not possible to believe at will, in

various senses of that phrase, see: B.A.O. WILLIAMS, 'Deciding to believe', in his *Problems of the Self* (Cambridge: Cambridge University Press, 1973), pp. 136–51; J. ELSTER, *Ulysses and the Sirens* (Cambridge: Cambridge University Press, 1979), Chapter 2.3; B. WINTERS, 'Willing to believe', *Journal of Philosophy*, 76 (1979): 243–56.

38. For the relation between adaptive preferences and character planning, see my 'Sour grapes'.

39. Wishful thinking would be even more irrational than weakness of will if this account is accepted. In weakness of will, on Davidson's argument, the action is caused by reasons that *are* reasons for acting that way, and it is irrational only because these reasons defeat the stronger reasons for acting differently. But given the premises of the text, a desire could *never* rationalize a belief.

40. E.G. KOLAKOWSKI, *Main Currents of Marxism*, vol. III, pp. 89, 116, 82; LEVENSON, *Confucian China*, vol. 1, pp. 59ff., 70.

41. ELSTER, *Logic and Society*, Chapter 4.

42. H. FINGARETTE, *Self-Deception* (London: Routledge & Kegan Paul, 1969) also includes useful accounts of Freud and Sartre. ELSTER, *Ulysses and the Sirens*, Chapter 4.4, has a brief discussion of R. SCHAFER, *A New Language for Psychoanalysis* (New Haven, Conn.: Yale University Press, 1976).

43. The following is a brief résumé of ELSTER, *Ulysses and the Sirens*, Chapter 4.4, itself an excessively brief and programmatic account that cannot claim to have solved the problem of self-deception or given an adequate refutation of rival views.

44. The Davidsonian flavour of this phrase is obvious, but see note 39 for a difference between this case and the non-standard causal chains in DAVIDSON, 'Freedom to act'.

45. LEVENSON, *Confucian China*, vol. 1, pp. 73–4.

46. Very briefly put, the notion is incoherent because intentional action is action conducted in terms of something physically absent, viz. a future, as yet unrealized goal. But for the absent to make a difference for action in the present, it must be re-presented in some way, and I believe that consciousness is nothing but a medium for such re-presentation of the absent. The unconscious would at most be capable of some local climbing along a pleasure gradient.

47. See E. GENOVESE, *The World the Slaveholders Made* (New York: Pantheon, 1969), on George Fitzhugh's attempt in 1857 to justify Southern slavery by a series of arguments that may have done more harm than good to the cause he defended: G. FITZHUGH, *Cannibals All* (Cambridge, Mass.: Harvard University Press, 1960).

48. VEYNE, *Le Pain et le Cirque*, pp. 298ff.

49. Ibid., p. 313; also my forthcoming 'Sour grapes' for a tentative explanation of this overshooting.

50. See ELSTER, *Logic and Society*, pp. 119ff., for an analysis of the temporal Prisoner's Dilemma involved here.

51. LEVENSON, *Confucian China*, vol. 1, p. 61.

52. Ibid., p. 77.

53. K. MARX, 'The Communism of the *Rheinischer Beobachter*' (1847) in K. MARX and F. ENGELS, *Collected Works* (London: Lawrence and Wishart), vol. 6, p. 231.

54. T. STANG-DAHL, *Barnevern og Sammfunnsvern* (Oslo: Pax, 1977), shows how the contrast between French and Italian criminology was decided not on scientific grounds (both were essentially worthless), but because the Italian school was too deterministic to appeal to the judges and penologists whose co-operation was needed. Punishment requires a modicum of free will to make sense.

55. See Marx's article 'The Chartists', *New York Daily Tribune*, 10 August 1852.
56. K. MARX, *The Eighteenth Brumaire of Louis Bonaparte* (1852) in MARX and ENGELS, *Collected Works* (London: Lawrence and Wishart), vol. 11, pp. 142–3.
57. This objection was raised both by G.A. Cohen and by Martin Hollis in their comments on an earlier draft of this essay.
58. This objection was raised by G.A. Cohen in his comment on the earlier draft.
59. Let me briefly sum up some salient aspects of the problem. We are dealing with cases in which there is no known feedback mechanism from consequence to cause. With such a mechanism the functional explanation is explicitly reduced to a causal one, and so the problem disappears. Cohen then argues that even without the knowledge of a feedback mechanism, we can back the functional explanation by a consequence law, mirroring the ordinary causal laws used to back causal explanations: *Karl Marx's Theory of History: A Defence* (Oxford: Oxford University Press, 1978), Chapter 9. One objection then is that such consequence laws would not distinguish between real and spurious correlation. To this Cohen replies that one could in principle do this by suitable experiments and comparisons. To this I counter that in practice, and perhaps in principle as well, such corrective procedures could not dispense with knowledge of the mechanism. There may be more to be said about the problem, but it is at any rate clear that there has perhaps not been a single example in the history satisfying the austere criteria that Cohen lays down for a successful functional explanation backed exclusively by consequence laws. More detailed discussion of these issues is found in the exchanges between Cohen and myself in *Political Studies* (1980) and in *Theory and Society* (1982), and in my review of his book in *Annales: Economies, Sociétés, Civilisations* (1981).
60. L. LAUDAN, *Progress and its Problems* (Berkeley and Los Angeles: University of California Press, 1977), p. 203.
61. This conclusion parallels the conclusion of my 'Sour grapes': 'Adaptive preference formation is relevant for ethics, and it is not always reflected in the preferences themselves, and so it follows that ethics needs history.'

15 Ideology*

RAYMOND GEUSS

Raymond Geuss is a philosopher who teaches in the Faculty of Social and Political Science at the University of Cambridge. His major work, *The Idea of a Critical Theory* (1981), is largely devoted to a critique of the Frankfurt School, but it contains some suggestive reflections on the concept of ideology in general. In particular, Geuss distinguishes between what he terms 'descriptive', 'pejorative' and 'positive' meanings of ideology, along with a distinction between 'epistemic', 'functional' and 'genetic' types of ideological distortion. A body of ideological beliefs may be actually untrue; or they may be true, but functional for the maintenance of some unjust political power; or they may spring from some discreditable political motive of which those who hold the beliefs are unaware. His book contains much interesting material on such key issues in the theory of ideology as rationalisation, self-deception and the relation of beliefs and desires.

1 Ideology in the descriptive sense

The term 'ideology' is used in many different ways; this is at least partly due to the fact that social theorists have propounded theories of ideology in the course of trying to answer very different questions. I will try to distinguish three different research contexts within which theories of ideology have been developed; corresponding to each of these three research programs there will be a family of ways in which the term 'ideology' is used.[1]

The first of the three research programs I wish to distinguish is the program of an empirical study of human groups – call it 'anthropology.' There are various things one might wish to study about a given human

---

*Reprinted from RAYMOND GEUSS, *The Idea of a Critical Theory* (Cambridge: Cambridge University Press, 1981), pp. 4–22.

group. One might study the biological and quasi-biological properties of the group – the birth-rate, the distribution of blood-type or human phenotype among the subgroups, the resistance to or incidence of various kinds of diseases, etc. Or one might wish to study the cultural or socio-cultural features of the group – the kinship system, pattern of land-tenure, artistic traditions, religious and scientific beliefs, legal institutions, values, agricultural technology, etc. Although this distinction between the biological properties of a group and its 'culture' or 'socio-cultural system' is rough and imprecise,[2] let us suppose that we know clearly enough what a 'culture' or a 'socio-cultural system' is that we can make it an object of empirical investigation. Thus, for any given human group we can undertake to describe the salient features of its socio-cultural system and how they change over time. If we have at our disposal descriptions of several human groups, we may begin to look for universal or invariant features which all cultures exhibit or for relations of concomitance among apparently distinct socio-cultural features; we may try to elaborate a typology of human cultures, classifying them according to their similarities and differences; if we are bold, we may hazard hypotheses about why certain features are found in certain societies or why certain historical changes take place.

In the course of this kind of empirical inquiry we may subdivide the socio-cultural sphere into different 'parts' for further study. Thus, vulgar Marxists distinguish between (economic) base and (ideological) superstructure. Many twentieth-century anthropologists seem to prefer a tripartite scheme which distinguishes technology (or technology/economy), social structure, and ideology, and even more complicated schemes have been suggested.[3] A theory of ideology, then, can arise in the course of pursuing the project of describing and explaining certain features of or facts about human social groups; 'ideology' in the first sense will just refer to one of the 'parts' into which the socio-cultural system of a human group can be divided for convenient study. Depending on how the particular division is made, the 'ideology' of the group will be more or less extensive, but typically it will include such things as the beliefs the members of the group hold, the concepts they use, the attitudes and psychological dispositions they exhibit, their motives, desires, values, predilections, works of art, religious rituals, gestures, etc.[4] I will call 'ideology' in this very broad sense (including at least all of the above listed elements) 'ideology in the purely descriptive sense.' In this broad and rather unspecific sense of 'ideology' every human group has an ideology – the agents of any group will have some psychological dispositions, use some concepts, and have some beliefs. In particular 'ideology' in this sense does *not* comprise *only* those beliefs, habits, attitudes, traits, etc. *all* the members of a group share. Human groups contain variety, diversity, and conflict. The more detailed and complete we wish our account of a given group to be, the more it will have to contain descriptions of such differences of belief, motivation, preference, attitude, etc. Furthermore, this sense of 'ideology' is non-evaluative and 'non-judgmental'[5] – one isn't praising or blaming a group by asserting that its members 'have an ideology' in this sense.

An ideology in this merely descriptive sense will contain both discursive and non-discursive elements. By 'discursive' (or 'conceptual' or 'propositional') elements I mean such things as concepts, ideas, beliefs, and by 'non-discursive' elements such things as characteristic gestures, rituals, attitudes, forms of artistic activity, etc.[6] This distinction between discursive and non-discursive elements is not the same as the distinction sometimes made (by Plamenatz, for instance) between explicit and implicit elements.[7] Clearly, discursive elements can be either explicit or implicit – agents can hold a particular belief explicitly or merely tacitly – but the distinction between 'explicit' and 'implicit' would seem to have no clear application to most non-discursive elements. It is hard to see what could be meant by calling a particular melody or gesture 'implicit' or 'explicit' in the sense under consideration here. Nevertheless, I would like to leave open the possibility of distinguishing between explicit and implicit non-discursive elements at least in *some* cases. It doesn't seem so odd to speak of attitudes, for instance, as being explicit or implicit.[8]

Finally neither of the two distinctions made above is identical with Plamenatz's distinction between unsophisticated and sophisticated elements of an ideology.[9] A belief can be quite explicit but unsophisticated, as can a taste or preference.

Since I don't want to try to give definitions of the terms used in these distinctions, perhaps an examination of an example will clarify their use. If one examines the religion of a group, one might discover that the performance of a particular ritual plays an important role – one might think here, for instance, of the role Baptism or the Eucharist play in Christianity. Of course, if the ritual is particularly important, it is unlikely that the agents who perform it will lack a term for it, but still a ritual is a set of actions, of things done, not itself a concept or belief.[10] The religion is part of the ideology of the group; the ritual is a non-discursive element of the ideology. Given that rituals can have a long life – baptism and eucharist in some recognizable form have been around for at least a couple of millennia, and, even if one takes stricter criteria of identity, the particular form of the rituals defined for the Catholic Church by the Council of Trent standardized a practice that remained more or less unchanged for half a millennium – it is likely that at different historical periods the ritual will have been associated with quite different sets of implicit beliefs and attitudes. Peasants in the Abruzzi in 1600 and English Catholics in Toronto in 1950 both participated in the 'same' ritual of baptism, but, given the enormous other differences between these two groups, it would be amazing if the members of the two groups had the same implicit attitudes toward the ritual, beliefs about it, etc. Again what sorts of beliefs and attitudes most people in the society naively associate with the ritual, or 'express' by participating in it, may be very different from the conflicting theological interpretations conceptually sophisticated members of the society give to the ritual. So at one extreme one has a set of ritual actions, a 'non-discursive element' in the ideology, and at the other a perhaps very sophisticated, explicit theology – a body of systematically interconnected propositions – and in between varying kinds of more or less explicit and more or less sophisticated beliefs, attitudes, habits, etc.

For certain purposes it may be useful or desirable to single out for further study certain subsets of the set of all the beliefs, attitudes, concepts, etc. a group of agents has or uses. Since there doesn't seem to be any uniquely legitimate way to subdivide what I have called the 'ideology in a purely descriptive sense,' there will be a plurality of such divisions, and, corresponding to each distinguished part, a narrower, but perfectly legitimate descriptive sense of 'ideology.'[11] Thus, I may decide that I would like to retain a close connection between 'ideology' and 'idea,' and hence use the term 'ideology' to refer only to the beliefs of the agents in the society, i.e. only to the 'discursive elements' of the ideology (in the purely descriptive sense).

Habermas, in strong contrast to the earlier members of the Frankfurt School, does seem to use the term 'ideology' to refer in the first instance to the beliefs the agents in a society hold. The obvious next step, then, is to try to divide the set of all the beliefs the agents in the society hold into more or less 'natural' parts. One might then start to use the term 'ideology' yet more narrowly to refer to some subset of the set of all the discursive elements. Habermas' discussion of ideology suggests that he countenances two major ways of subdividing the set of all the agents' beliefs, and hence of distinguishing between kinds of ideologies in the very narrow sense: (1) One can distinguish between 'ideologies' (i.e. subsets of the set of all beliefs) on the basis of differences in their 'manifest content,'[12] i.e. by reference to differences in what the beliefs are beliefs *about*. So a set of beliefs about superhuman entities who are thought to supervise and enforce standards of human behavior may be called a 'religious ideology,' while a set of concepts for talking about economic transactions is an 'economic ideology.' (2) One can distinguish between ideologies in this very narrow sense in terms of their functional properties. By 'functional properties' I mean the way the elements of the ideology influence action.[13] So in this sense a set of beliefs of no matter *what* manifest content which significantly influences economic behavior could be called an 'economic ideology,' a set of beliefs and attitudes which significantly influences religious practices a 'religious ideology.'

In many cases there will be a close connection between the two senses of 'ideology' – or at least between concrete ideologies in the two senses. Thus a 'religious ideology' can be either a set of beliefs ostensibly about superhuman entities, i.e. a set of beliefs with a religious 'manifest content' or a set of beliefs and attitudes which in fact function to regulate or otherwise influence religious behavior or practices. There is the obvious difficulty with this second sense of 'ideology' that there isn't any such thing as 'specifically religious behavior' (except perhaps for some ritual behavior) or 'purely economic behavior' or what have you; actions and institutions don't come neatly boxed into well-defined and easily identifiable types. Often one may not know how to classify a particular bit of behavior or an institution – is it a religious ceremony, an economic institution, a political institution, or some combination of all three? Furthermore there may be differences between the classification the participating agents would prefer to give and the classification we, as outside observers, might prefer. Even if there aren't difficulties in principle about the basic classification of a certain bit of behavior as a 'religious ritual', it may also have political or economic aspects, overtones, or implications. The more indeterminate the notion of 'religious behavior' is allowed to become, the less well-defined will be the beliefs which might influence such behavior.

But despite the generally close connection between ideologies in the two senses, it is important to retain the distinction because some of the most interesting cases will be ones in which there are significant differences between the manifest content of the beliefs in an ideology and their functional properties – a set of 'religious and philosophical' beliefs about the nature of the gods may actually serve to regulate economic and political transactions. It will in general be an important fact about a given society how the various kinds of acts and institutions are individuated, how large a class of acts are considered to be 'purely economic transactions' or acts to which religious beliefs are directly relevant,[14] in other words, what kinds of beliefs, beliefs of what kind of manifest content, will be able to function as ideologies for what domains of action.

In these senses, then, the group may have more than one ideology – it may have a religious ideology *and* an economic ideology, and the two may not appreciably overlap. 'Ideologies' in these narrower senses are different from 'ideology in a purely descriptive sense' in an important way: Every human group is composed of members who have *some* beliefs, and so every human group has an 'ideology in the descriptive sense,' but not every group will have an ideology in each of the possible narrower senses – since hunting-and-gathering bands have no state, and, *a fortiori*, no state-finances, they won't have a 'fiscal ideology' either.

In addition to speaking of 'the political ideology' of the group or 'the ideology for economic behavior' social theorists and others often speak of '*the*' ideology of the group simpliciter. Sometimes 'the' ideology of the group seems to mean nothing more than:

(a) the set of all those concepts and beliefs which do *not* contribute to production 'in virtue of the material character of production'[15]
(b) the set of all the moral and normative beliefs[16]
(c) the set of beliefs the agents have about themselves as social agents.[17]

But often 'the' ideology of a group seems to mean the world-view or 'world-picture' of the group. This notion of ideology as world-view is *not* identical with our original 'ideology in a purely descriptive sense.' The 'ideology of a group in the purely descriptive sense' comprises *all* the beliefs members of the group hold (or perhaps – if this notion seems too all-encompassing and too indiscriminate to be of any use at all – it includes the characteristic beliefs widely shared among the members of the group), but of course not all the beliefs the members of a group hold belong to their world-view. Even beliefs which are widely shared and quite distinctive of members of the group need not belong to the world-view in the most normal sense of 'world-view.'

The intuition which motivates the introduction of a concept of 'ideology as world-view' is that individuals and groups don't just 'have' randomly collected bundles of beliefs, attitudes, life-goals, forms of artistic activity, etc. The bundles generally have some coherency – although it is very hard to say in general in what this coherency consists – the elements in the bundle are complexly related to each other, they all somehow 'fit,' and the whole bundle has a characteristic structure which is often discernible even to an outside observer. By an 'ideology in the sense of "world-view"' then is meant a subset of the beliefs which constitute the ideology of the group (in a purely descriptive sense) which has the following properties:

(a) the elements in the subset are widely shared among the agents in the group
(b) the elements in this subset are systematically interconnected
(c) they are 'central to the agents' conceptual scheme' in Quine's sense, i.e. the agents won't easily give them up[18]
(d) the elements in the subset have a wide and deep influence on the agents' behavior or on some particularly important or central sphere of action
(e) the beliefs in the subset are 'central' in that they deal with central issues of human life (i.e. they give interpretations of such things as death, the need to work, sexuality, etc.) or central metaphysical issues.[19]

These properties are no more than very loosely defined, and whether or not any purported 'world-view' has any one of them is a question of degree – just how wide an influence on the agents' actual behavior must a set of elements have in order to qualify as part of the world-view of those agents? Also there is no canonical principle of ordering or weighting the various properties. So even if there were to be agreement that these five properties specify what we mean by the 'world-view' of a group, there would still be much room for disagreement in particular cases about what should count as 'the' world-view or 'the' ideology of this particular group. Whether or not every human group will have a world-view (in the way that every group has an ideology in the purely descriptive sense) will depend partly on how strictly one construes the five properties, but also partly on how one decides to pick out human groups. Up to now we have tacitly allowed groups to be picked out any way at all. Of course it would not be correct to assume that any group of agents individuated by some biological, ethnic, economic, social, political, or linguistic criterion will share the same, one world-view. This, of course, is quite a strong (and quite an implausible) empirical assumption.

The last descriptive sense of 'ideology' I would like to consider is what I will call 'ideology in the programmatic sense.' This sense is related to the sense in which the term 'ideology' is used by Daniel Bell and other proponents of the 'end of ideology' thesis. Bell calls an ideology 'a way of translating ideas into action'[20] and defines a *total* ideology' as an 'all-inclusive system of comprehensive reality, it is a set of beliefs, infused with passion, and seeks to transform the whole of a way of life.'[21] So a 'total ideology' is

(a) a program or plan of action[22]
(b) based on an explicit, systematic model or theory of how the society works
(c) aimed at radical transformation or reconstruction of the society as a whole
(d) held with more confidence ('passion') than the evidence for the theory or model warrants.[23]

The addition of '(d)' makes this no longer a descriptive or non-judgmental use of the term 'ideology' but rather a pejorative use. Even without '(d)' however, the definition is still rather tendentious in that the presence of '(c)' makes it artificially easy for Bell-style liberals to deny that they have an 'ideology' (because, presumably, liberals are not at present in the US and the Western European countries in favor of 'radical transformation of society as a whole'). I will call '(a)' and '(b)' of Bell's 'total ideology' (*without* '(c)' and '(d)' as *necessary* components) an 'ideology in the programmatic sense.'[24]

2 Ideology in the pejorative sense

The second research program within which a theory of ideology may arise is a program of criticism of the beliefs, attitudes, and wants of the agents in a particular society. This research program is initiated by the observation that agents in the society are deluded about themselves, their position, their society, or their interests. The aim of the project is to demonstrate to them *that* they are so deluded. It might turn out that one can only convince them that they are deluded if one can explain to them *why* they hold the beliefs and attitudes they do, or one might have an independent theoretical interest in understanding and explaining how it came about that the agents developed this delusion, and why they continue to suffer from it – the theoretical interest will be all the greater, the more the delusion seems to have the result that the agents act contrary to what is manifestly in their own true interest. Still, in essence this is *not* an explanatory project like the first research program in section 1. Rather the point is to free the agents from a particular kind of delusion. In most of the interesting cases the ideological delusion to be rooted out (it is claimed) is not an empirical error even of a very sophisticated kind, but something quite different.

The basic use of the term 'ideology' in this program is a negative, pejorative, or critical one. 'Ideology' is (ideological) delusion' or '(ideologically) false consciousness.'[25] I will use the term 'form of consciousness' to refer to a particular constellation of beliefs, attitudes, dispositions, etc.[26] So the basic question posed in this research program is: In what sense or in virtue of what properties can a form of consciousness be ideologically false, i.e. can it be an ideology in the pejorative sense? I will consider three kinds of answers to this question:

    (a) a form of consciousness is ideologically false in virtue of some *epistemic* properties of the beliefs which are its constituents;

    (b) a form of consciousness is ideologically false in virtue of its *functional* properties;

    (c) a form of consciousness is ideologically false in virtue of some of its *genetic* properties.

In the next few pages I will try to explain what I mean by each of these three ways of answering the question: What makes a form of consciousness an ideology?

(I) By the 'epistemic properties' of a form of consciousness I mean such things as whether or not the descriptive beliefs contained in the form of consciousness are supported by the available empirical evidence, or whether or not the form of consciousness is one in which beliefs of different epistemic type (e.g. descriptive beliefs and normative beliefs) are confused. I will now consider four ways of using the term 'ideology'; in each case a form of consciousness will be considered to be ideological in virtue of some epistemic properties.

(1) A form of consciousness is an ideology if it is essentially dependent on mistaking the epistemic status of some of its apparently constituent beliefs. As an example of what I mean by 'mistaking the epistemic status of a belief' consider the early positivist view that a proposition has cognitive content or is cognitively meaningful if and only if it is empirically

verifiable, that is, if and only if it has some kind of observational content. To take a belief which is *not* empirically verifiable as being cognitively meaningful is to make a mistake about its epistemic status. Thus, on this view, all theological forms of consciousness are to be rejected as ideological because a theological form of consciousness is presumably a structured set of beliefs, attitudes, etc. which depends essentially on the assumption that there can be cognitively significant discourse about gods. Since beliefs about gods are not empirically verifiable – they don't have cognitive content – a theological form of consciousness is based on a mistake about the epistemic standing of one of its central constitutive beliefs. Note that to say that all *theological* forms of consciousness are 'ideology' for the positivist is not to say that all forms of religious belief are 'ideology' (in the pejorative sense); the positivist can have no objection to religious beliefs as long as they don't pretend to be forms of knowledge.

This usage of 'ideology' is not dependent on accepting the verification theory of meaning. I might well reject the verification theory of meaning and still, for instance, think that value judgments had very different conditions of verification from descriptive beliefs, and hence a very different 'epistemic standing.' I might then want to call forms of consciousness 'ideological' if they presented value judgments as statements of fact.[27]

(2) A form of consciousness is ideological if it contains essentially an 'objectification' mistake, i.e. if it contains a false belief to the effect that some social phenomenon is a natural phenomenon, or, to put it another way, human agents or 'subjects' are suffering from ideologically false consciousness if they falsely 'objectify' their own activity, i.e. if they are deceived into taking that activity to be something 'foreign' to them,[28] especially if they take that activity to be a natural process outside their control.

(3) A form of consciousness is ideologically false if it contains a false belief to the effect that the particular interest of some subgroup is the general interest of the group as a whole.[29]

(4) A form of consciousness is ideologically false if it mistakes self-validating or self-fulfilling beliefs for beliefs which are not self-validating or self-fulfilling. The notion of a 'self-validating or self-fulfilling belief' is modelled on Merton's notion of a 'self-fulfilling prophecy.'[30] If we think members of a subgroup G are lazy, unreliable, and unintelligent, and hence act toward them in ways which make them become lazy, unreliable, and unintelligent, the belief that the members of G are lazy etc. is self-fulfilling. There is nothing *inherently* wrong with holding self-fulfilling beliefs, as long as one *knows* that they are self-fulfilling. What is objectionable is the *use* of self-fulfilling beliefs in a context of justification of action where their justificatory force depends on misconstruing them as non-self-fulfilling, i.e. depends on mistaking their epistemic standing.[31]

(II) The second kind of answer to the question, What makes a form of consciousness an ideology?, was: A form of consciousness is an ideology in virtue of some of its functional properties. I will consider three specific versions of this functional approach.

(1) A form of consciousness is an ideology in virtue of the function or role it plays in supporting, stabilizing, or legitimizing certain kinds of social institutions or practices. Habermas regularly speaks of an ideology as a 'world-picture' which stabilizes or legitimizes domination or hegemony (Herrschaft).[32] It is in virtue of the fact that it supports or justifies reprehensible social institutions, unjust social practices, relations of exploitation, hegemony, or domination that a form of consciousness is an ideology.

But, of course, the above isn't yet an unambiguous view. One must distinguish between the function of supporting, fostering, or stabilizing hegemony and the function of justifying or legitimizing hegemony. Any set of beliefs which legitimizes or justifies a social practice will thereby tend to support it, but the converse is not the case: a belief that a given ruling class is strong and ruthless, so that any resistance to the dominant social order is futile, may well be a belief, the acceptance of which by large segments of the population will have the effect of stabilizing the existing relations of dominance, but it is unlikely that such a belief could be used to *justify* these relations.[33] So 'herrschaftsstabilisierendes Bewußtsein' is not identical with 'herrschaftslegitimierendes Bewußtsein.'

Note further that neither of these two kinds of 'consciousness' is identical with the kind of consciousness intended in the famous slogan definition of ideology as 'socially necessary illusion.' The statement 'Form of consciousness *f* "stabilizes" hegemony' can be interpreted in two different ways: (a) 'Form of consciousness *f* contributes to the stability of hegemony (but it is an open question whether or not this contribution is sufficient to insure that the hegemony remains intact)' – 'stabilize' is used here as an 'attempt-verb.' (b) 'Form of consciousness *f* is successful in causing the hegemony to remain intact' – 'stabilize' is used here as a 'success-verb.' So at best (namely, if 'stabilize' is interpreted as a 'success-verb') 'Form of consciousness *f* stabilizes hegemony' means that form of consciousness *f* is a *sufficient* condition for the continued existence of given relations of dominance, not that it is *necessary* for the functioning or reproduction of the society. Similarly, the fact that some beliefs in a form of consciousness are used to legitimate some social practice or institution in no way implies that those beliefs are the *only* ones which could be used, much less that the practice in question would cease to exist if they could not longer be used to legitimize it.

We also require further clarification of the notion of 'Herrschaft.' I will distinguish several 'semantic components' in the notion of 'Herrschaft.'[34]

(A) 'Herrschaft' means the power to repress, i.e. to enforce frustration of some given human preferences. But this is clearly not an adequate or sufficient characterization of 'Herrschaft.' What is at issue here is the *critical* use of the term 'ideology.' But that means that to show that something is an ideology should be to show that we ought somehow to try to eliminate it. It seems unrealistic under the present conditions of human life to assume that any and every preference human agents might have can be satisfied, or to assume that all conflict between the preferences of different agents will be peacefully and rationally resolved. *Some* frustration – even some imposed frustration – of *some* human preferences must be legitimate and unexceptionable. But then to show that a form of consciousness is an ideology in the sense that it functions to support 'Herrschaft' is not yet to give any reason at all to eliminate it.

(B) 'Herrschaft' is the exercise of power within a political order and is linked with some kind of *claim* to legitimacy. If a group of invaders simply ransacks a country, doing and taking what they want by sheer force, they will clearly be frustrating the preferences of the agents on whom they act, but they are not exercising 'Herrschaft' in the sense intended here. 'Normative repression' is frustration of agents' preferences which makes a claim to legitimacy that is accepted by those agents because of certain normative beliefs they hold.[35] 'Herrschaft' is power to exercise normative repression. This, too, is not yet an adequate account of 'Herrschaft' for the obvious reasons: There is nothing wrong with 'supporting or legitimizing Herrschaft' if the claim the 'Herrschaft' makes to legitimacy is valid.

(C) 'Herrschaft' is normally unequally distributed; it is the domination *of* one group *over* another. So, in general, a society in which 'Herrschaft' is exercised will be one in which some groups have a much higher level of frustration of their preferences than others do. The society may be extraordinarily repressive, as many egalitarian communities are, but, as long as the power to repress is equally distributed, it would be odd to speak of 'Herrschaft' being exercised.

But this concept of 'Herrschaft' is not adequate for use in our account of ideology, either. Unless unequal distribution of the power to exercise normative repression were *always* illegitimate, showing that a form of consciousness supported or legitimized this distribution of power would in no way imply that the form of consciousness was to be rejected. Marxists at least don't think that questions of the 'legitimacy' of social institutions can be answered 'abstractly,' that is, apart from consideration of the actual historical situation in which such questions arise. Marxists are also committed to the view that at certain levels of development of the material forces of production an unequal distribution of repressive normative power is historically necessary, i.e. necessary for the society to maintain and reproduce itself. If a certain distribution of power is 'necessary' there seems no point in questioning its legitimacy.

We probably *would* like to call unequal distribution of power to exercise normative repression 'Herrschaft.' Feudal lords *do* exercise 'Herrschaft' over their serfs, even if such 'Herrschaft' is historically necessary (at some particular moment in history). Showing that a form of consciousness supports unequal distribution of power does not in itself give us reason to reject the form of consciousness – unless we *also* know that this distribution of power is not at present necessary.

(D) To say that a society imposes 'surplus repression' on its members is to say that it frustrates their preferences to a greater extent than is necessary for it to maintain and reproduce itself.[36] So 'surplus repression' refers to the total amount of aggregate repression in the society without reference to how this repression is distributed among the members. If 'Herrschaft' is defined as above in (C), let 'surplus Herrschaft' mean more 'Herrschaft' than is needed for the society to maintain and reproduce itself.[37] We could then define 'ideology' as 'a form of consciousness which supports or legitimizes surplus Herrschaft.' But why should we reject a form of consciousness if we discover that it supports or legitimizes surplus Herrschaft? Is surplus Herrschaft always illegitimate? Why?[38]

(2) The second kind of functional definition takes 'ideology' to be any form of consciousness which hinders or obstructs the maximal development of the forces of material production. This view is usually associated with a reading of Marx which takes him as positing the development of the forces of material production as an inherent goal of human societies.[39] It isn't hard to see a connection between this notion and 'surplus repression' – if a form of consciousness hinders the development of the forces of production it will obviously impose on the agents in the society more repression than they need suffer – but any connection with surplus Herrschaft is harder to see. Perhaps one could make an argument from the plausible motivation of agents – no agents in the society would have a motivation to impose more repression than necessary unless the surplus repression differentially benefited some group in the society more than others. Then the members of the privileged group would have such a motivation.

(3) Finally we might call a form of consciousness which served to 'mask social contradictions'[40] an 'ideology.' Since 'masking social contradictions' might include such things as diverting attention from them, a form of consciousness might successfully mask social contradictions without containing any false beliefs. The concept of a 'social contradiction' is too complex and obscure to be adequately treated here. Note however, that if we take the 'major' contradiction in a social formation to be the contradiction between the relations of production and the forces of production, and if we take this 'contradiction' to consist in the fact that the relations of production fetter the development of the forces, it is not difficult to see how one might move from this third functional approach to ideology to the second.[41]

Ideology in the pejorative or critical sense was to be some kind of delusion or *false* consciousness. Granted that an ideology in one or another of the above 'functional' senses would be something eminently worthy of being rejected by the members of any known human society, would such an ideology be rejected *because* it is a delusion or because it is in some sense *false*? A form of consciousness may contain all kinds of non-discursive elements; it isn't clear how such elements *could* be false. Even the beliefs in a form of consciousness might be worthy of being rejected or given up on all kinds of grounds other than that they are delusions – they may be obnoxious, insensitive, immoral, nasty, ugly, etc. If I know that a form of consciousness I hold contributes to more massive frustration of my own preferences than necessary I may feel that I have grounds to give it up or change it, but does that mean that I think it is 'false' or some kind of delusion? The sense in which it is a delusion must be one which depends on a claim that, *if* I were to come to know something about the functional properties of this form of consciousness, I would no longer retain it. The form of consciousness qualifies as 'false' or a delusion because my retaining it depends in some way on my being in ignorance of or having false beliefs about its functional properties.

(III) The third major way to answer the question, In virtue of what is a form of consciousness an ideology?, is: In virtue of some of its genetic properties, that is, by virtue of some facts about its origin, genesis, or history, about how it arises or comes to be acquired or held by agents, or in virtue of the motives agents have for adopting and acting on it.

Thus, Runciman claims that for the later Engels a form of consciousness is ideologically false in virtue of the fact that the 'beliefs and attitudes' which compose it are 'related in a causal sense to the social situation and thereby to the interests of the believer.'[42] So, presumably, a form of consciousness is an ideology in virtue of something about its causal history. Karl Mannheim holds a similar view, that forms of consciousness are ideological because they are 'expressions' of the class position of those who hold them, that is, because their origin can be traced to the particular experiences of a particular class in society with its characteristic perceptions, interests, and values.[43] Finally, the analogy between psychoanalysis and social theory which is so dominant in much of the work of the members of the Frankfurt School suggests that ideologies might be construed as 'collective rationalizations,' i.e. as systems of beliefs and attitudes accepted by the agents for reasons which they could not acknowledge.[44] But what does 'could not' mean here?

This genetic approach seems to pose more problems for the understanding than did the functional approach.[45] Why should anything we might learn about the origin, motivation, or causal history of a form of consciousness give us (rational) grounds for rejecting it, much less for rejecting it as 'false consciousness' or as a 'delusion?' Of course, if the form of consciousness has an unsavory causal history this might make us very *suspicious* of it – we may examine the beliefs it contains with more than our usual care and may think twice about the implications of adopting the attitudes – but that doesn't in itself give us good grounds to reject the form of consciousness. Also if a form of consciousness is an 'expression' of the class-position of a group in society not merely in the sense that it 'arose out of their experience' but also in the sense that it is *appropriate only* to those who share that class-position, e.g. if it speaks only to their particular needs, problems, and values, then it may be irrelevant to those of us who do not share that class-position. But to say that it is irrelevant to us is not to say that it is a delusion – it certainly wouldn't seem to be any kind of delusion for *them*; if we *do* reject it, it is because it is 'not appropriate' for us and that is something we may determine without any knowledge of its causal history. The causal history may explain *why* it is inappropriate, but the causal history isn't itself the grounds for rejecting it; its inappropriateness is.

By now there is a long history of criticism of the 'genetic fallacy' – one hasn't shown anything about the truth or falsity of a belief by showing how it arose, one must clearly distinguish 'context of discovery' from 'context of justification.' If the genetic approach to ideology in the pejorative sense is to get off the ground, it must somehow show that the 'genetic fallacy,' granted its validity for scientific statements, is *not* necessarily a fallacy for forms of consciousness.

I have already tipped my hand as to how this argument might proceed. When speaking of the analogy between psychoanalysis and social theory above, I said that ideologies might be understood as systems of beliefs and attitudes accepted by the agents for reasons or motives which those agents *could* not acknowledge. Suppose I have a belief, attitude, or habit of action which I have adopted and cultivate for unacknowledged and unacceptable motives; perhaps I have adopted and cultivate a habit of virtuous action of a certain sort for completely narcissistic reasons which I don't acknowledge and which I would find unacceptable. Even though my motives or reasons for acting in the way I do may be unacceptable, the habit of action may be a habit of virtuous action, i.e. I may consistently do the right thing for the wrong reasons. In this case, coming to acknowledge and recognize my own motives may in fact bring *me* to stop cultivating the habit of action, but then again it may not, and in either case the habit of action may remain the right habit of action for me to cultivate, and I may still recognize that it is the right habit (although I may cease to have the strong motivation I had to continue to cultivate it). But in the case of 'ideologies' it isn't just that they are said to have been adopted for *unacknowledged* motives or reasons, but for motives which *could* not be acknowledged by the agents. This presumably means that *if* the agents had to recognize and acknowledge that *these* were their motives, they would thereby not only no longer be motivated as strongly as they were to continue to accept the ideology, but they would see that there is *no* reason for them to accept it.

One might wonder whether cases like this really exist – cases in which the *only* motive or reason for adopting a form of consciousness is a motive which *cannot* be acknowledged – and one might also legitimately ask for further clarification of the sense in which a motive 'cannot' be acknowledged. Finally one might wonder whether this kind of analysis can be extended to other cases involving the 'causal history' or 'origin and genesis' of a form of consciousness. But *if* these potential objections can be deflected, there might be a chance of showing that the genetic approach to ideology can yield a sense of ideology as delusion or false consciousness. The form of consciousness is false in that it requires ignorance or false belief on the part of the agents of their true motives for accepting it.

So the term 'ideology' is used in a pejorative sense to criticize a form of consciousness because it incorporates beliefs which are false, or because it functions in a reprehensible way, or because it has a tainted origin. I will call these three kinds of criticism: criticism along the epistemic, the functional, and the genetic dimensions respectively.[46] It is extremely important to determine which of these three modes of criticism is basic to a theory of ideology – does the theory start with an epistemology, with a theory of the proper functioning of society and of which forms of social organization are reprehensible, or with a theory of which 'origins' of forms of consciousness are acceptable and which unacceptable? Still, although one or another of these three modes of criticism may be basic, interesting theories of ideology will be ones which assert some connection between two or more of the three modes. One of the senses in which the Critical Theory is said by its proponents to be 'dialectical' (and hence superior to its rivals) is just in that it explicitly connects questions about the 'inherent' truth or falsity of a form of consciousness with questions about its history, origin, and function in society.

Notes

1. Needless to say, the following discussion makes no claim to exhaust the various senses in which the term 'ideology' and its derivatives have been used. Vide LICHTHEIM (1967); BARTH (1975); and LARRAIN (1979).
2. KROEBER and KLUCKHOHN (1952) distinguish over a hundred senses of 'culture'. Vide also D. KAPLAN and R. MANNERS (1972).
3. SAHLINS distinguishes technology, social structure, and ideology (1968, pp. 14ff.) Service has: technology, economy, society, polity, and ideology (1966). KAPLAN and MANNERS give: ideology, social structure, technoeconomics, personality (1972, p. 89). Probably there is no canonical division of the society into parts

which would be applicable to all societies; in fact it is often claimed that a criterion of the 'primitiveness' of a society is the extent to which it lacks division between economy, society, kinship system, etc.

4. Vide KAPLAN and MANNERS (pp. 112f.).
5. Vide KAPLAN and MANNERS (p. 113).
6. On p. 345 of ZR Habermas speaks of 'die nichtpropositionalen Zeichensysteme der Literatur, der Kunst, und der Musik.' This is another one of those distinctions which are easier to see than to formulate exactly. One might want to claim that *all* the elements of an ideology are symbolically organized – certainly paintings, pieces of music, dances etc. are highly organized, but the organization is not conceptual; a piece of music may have a meaning, even if one wishes to speak this way (I don't particularly) a 'grammar,' but that meaning is not a proposition. Naturally, too, by 'beliefs' I don't mean just simple empirical beliefs, but also normative beliefs, metaphysical beliefs etc.
7. PLAMENATZ, pp. 17f., 21ff.
8. Tastes, preferences, and predilections, too, can be either explicit or implicit. Certain of my tastes and preferences may simply express themselves in my customary mode of behavior. I may show no tendency to make much of them; I may in fact not even realize that I have them. We may wish to contrast this kind of case in which my tastes and preferences are 'merely implicit' with other cases in which I recognize, articulate, and cultivate a particular taste or preference. That in this second case I may be able to glory in my predilections only if I have certain beliefs does not imply that the predilections, tastes, or preferences themselves *are* beliefs.
9. PLAMENATZ, pp. 18ff.
10. Vide BURKERT, esp. Ch. 11.
11. Of course, certain divisions may be more useful or illuminating than others. My general 'purely descriptive sense' of ideology corresponds roughly to Mannheim's 'total sense' (cf. MANNHEIM, pp. 54ff.); my 'narrower version' of ideology to his 'special sense' (p. 77).
12. TW 160 [T1 311]. Habermas speaks of 'der manifeste Gehalt von Aussagen.' Some of the essays in TW are translated in T5, but the one cited here is translated as an appendix to T1.
13. Non-discursive elements cannot be 'about' anything in the way in which propositions can, but they can have functional properties, so the 'religious ideology' in this functional sense might well be taken to include pictures, chants, etc.
14. GEERTZ (1971), gives examples of the way in which the sphere of what is identified as 'religious behavior' can vary even within the 'same' religious tradition.
15. COHEN, pp. 47; 33f., 45–7, 88ff. McMURTRY, pp. 125f., 128, 130ff., 140.
16. PLAMENATZ, pp. 323ff. For a related use vide Barry, p. 39.
17. In the *Deutsche Ideologie* Marx speaks of ideology as the agents' 'Illusionen und Gedanken über sich selbst,' MARX, vol. 3, pp. 46f., 13.
18. W.V.O. QUINE, 1963, pp. 42ff.
19. At KK 391 Habermas calls 'world-pictures' 'Interpretationen der Welt, der Natur, und der Geschichte im Ganzen.'
20. BELL in WAXMAN, p. 88.
21. BELL in WAXMAN, p. 96. Bell is not very careful in attributing this notion to Mannheim. This is not the definition Mannheim gives of 'total ideology' when he

introduces it in *Ideology and Utopia* (pp. 55f.); there is no implication that a 'total ideology' (for Mannheim) is a program of action for the transformation of a whole way of life.

22. Vide FRIEDRICH and BRZEZINSKI, p. 75: 'Ideologies are essentially action-related systems of ideas. They typically contain a program and a strategy for its realization.'

23. I may be reading more into the phrase 'infused with passion' than is intended. I'm obviously trying to assimilate Bell's view here with that of e.g. Popper, who seems to think that a theory of the society as a whole can have so little evidentiary support that *any* degree of confidence in it as a guide to radical transformation of society is more than is warranted. Vide POPPER, 1971, Chapter 9; POPPER, 1964, sections 21ff.

24. Clearly if 'ideology' means 'ideology in the programmatic sense' liberals do have an ideology – they have a general view of society and how it works, and, more important, a general view about how it ought to work. Part of that general view is that certain kinds of decisions should be decentralized. This might seem to make the notion of a programmatic ideology vacuous: that is, the 'program for action' may be the 'action' of *not* interfering with certain parts of the economy and society. Still it seems to me not just a quibble to distinguish between cases like those of perhaps certain hunting-and-gathering societies in which people just don't make and implement certain kinds of plans for social action at all, and cases in which people espouse laissez-faire as a doctrine, and act on the theory that society is best run when certain possible kinds of centralized planning are avoided.

25. WL 73, 95, 104 [T6 71, 90, 99], TP 435ff.

26. LS 48 [T2]. So a 'form of consciousness' is an ideology in one of the narrower descriptive senses, i.e. a particular systematically interconnected subset of the set of all the beliefs, attitudes, etc. the agents of a group hold. I will henceforth use this term 'form of consciousness' because I would like to reserve 'ideology' to mean 'ideology in the pejorative sense', i.e. *'false* consciousness.' So from now on, 'ideology' unless further specified means 'ideology in the pejorative sense.' Also KK 334, TP 310 [T4 257], EI 16 [T1 8], WL 96, 105 [T6 90f., 100]. [Note that in this last passage 'Bewußtseinsformationen' ('forms of consciousness') is mistranslated as 'information of consciousness.']

27. Gustave Bergmann uses 'ideology' in this sense: 'a value judgment disguised as or mistaken for a statement of fact I shall call an "ideological statement" ' (BRODBECK, p. 129).

28. N2 400f. and TG 246 where Habermas claims that Marx develops the notion of ideology 'als Gegenbegriff zu einer Reflexion . . . durch die falsches Bewußtsein, nämlich die notwendigen Täuschungen eines Subjekts über seine eigenen, ihm fremd gewordenen Objektivationen zerstört werden kann.' The classic Marx passage is the chapter on the fetishism of commodity production in the first volume of *Kapital*, MARX, vol. 23, pp. 85ff.

29. TG 289; KK 336, 391; and the discussion in Part III of LS. Standard loci from Marx are vol. 3, pp. 359ff., 374ff.

30. MERTON, pp. 421ff.

31. Note that most self-fulfilling beliefs are beliefs which embody an objectification mistake.

32. An ideology for Habermas is 'herrschaftslegitimierendes Weltbild' or a 'herrschaftsstabilisierendes Weltbild.' TG 120f, 239ff., 246f., 258; TW 72 [T5 99];

LS 34 [T2 19]; etc. ZR 53; TG 257ff., 279, 289.

33. Although it might be used by an individual to justify some action, e.g. refusal to join an abortive uprising.
34. The following discussion is based primarily on TG 246f., 254, 285ff., ZR 336.
35. TG 254.
36. This is Habermas' sense of 'surplus repression' (vide EI 80 [T1 57f.], TG 290) which is probably not the same as Marcuse's, p. 32, where 'surplus repression' means 'restrictions required by social domination.' If 'social domination' means 'unequal distribution of normative power,' then there can be repression 'required by social domination' which is *not* 'surplus' in Habermas' sense. Thus in a 'hydraulic' society, the priests as a class may have more normative power than the peasants, and the priests may typically impose a certain amount of repression on the peasants in order to insure their continued domination – this repression is 'surplus' on Marcuse's view. *If* this drastically unequal distribution of normative power is the only way in which a society which has a very low level of productivity and depends on large-scale irrigation can function and reproduce itself, the 'repression' extracted by the priests to maintain their position is not 'surplus' in Habermas' sense.
37. In most normal cases, where there is surplus repression, there will also be surplus 'Herrschaft,' for what could motivate agents collectively to impose upon themselves more repression than is needed, unless the 'fruits' of that surplus repression are distributed unequally? In that case the beneficiaries of the unequal distribution will have a stake in its continuance.
38. The question is whether 'illegitimate repression' is a separate category. Might there not be Herrschaft, surplus repression, etc. which is not illegitimate? Might there not also be kinds of illegitimate repression which are not either surplus or instances of Herrschaft? This question will become important in Chapter 3.
39. Vide COHEN (1978). The members of the Frankfurt School recognize this strand in Marx, but think it is a mistake, WL 73 [T6 70f.].
40. LARRAIN, pp. 45ff.
41. Vide COHEN, Chs. VI, X, XI.
42. RUNCIMAN, p. 212. The Engels passage on which this is based is one in a letter to Mehring from 1893 (translated in TUCKER, p. 648) which states: 'Ideology is a process accomplished by the so-called thinker consciously, but with false consciousness. The real motive forces impelling him remain unknown to him; otherwise it simply would not be an ideological process.'
43. MANNHEIM, pp. 55ff., 77ff.
44. TW 159f. [T1 311].
45. MANNHEIM, pp. 271ff., 283ff., 286f., 291ff.
46. NIKLAS LUHMANN sums up some of the standard views about ideology (before dismissing them all) thus: 'Nicht in der kausalen Berwirktheit liegt das Wesen der Ideologie, auch nicht in der instrumentellen Verwendbarkeit bei der es nicht um Wahrheit, sondern um Wirkungen geht, und schließlich auch nicht darin, daß sie die eigentlichen Motive verbirgt' (p. 57). Of these the first and third refer to the 'genetic' dimension, and the second to the 'functional.' Habermas criticizes Luhmann because his functionalist theory of ideology leaves no room for a sense in which ideology could be 'false,' i.e. for lacking an analysis of the 'epistemic dimension' (TG 239ff.). As will become clearer later, the reason Habermas insists that it must be possible to call an ideology 'false' is that he thinks this is the only way to avoid a kind of pernicious relativism.

Works cited

BARTH, HANS, *Wahrheit und Ideologie* (Frankfurt: Suhrkamp, 1975).

BRODBECK, MAY, *Readings in Philosophy of Social Science* (New York: Macmillan, 1968).

BURKERT, WALTER, *Structure and History in Greek Mythology and Ritual* (Berkeley and Los Angeles: University of California Press, 1979).

COHEN, G. A., *Karl Marx's Theory of History: A Defense* (Princeton: Princeton University Press, 1978).

FRIEDRICH, C. J. and BRZEZINSKI, Z., *Totalitarian Dictatorship and Autocracy* (Cambridge, Mass.: Harvard University Press, 1956).

GEERTZ, CLIFFORD, *Islam Observed* (Chicago: University of Chicago Press, 1971).

KAPLAN, DAVID and MANNERS, ROBERT, *Culture Theory* (Englewood Cliffs, NJ: Prentice-Hall, 1972).

KROEBER, ALFRED and KLUCKHOHN, CLYDE, 'Culture: A Critical Review of Concepts and Definitions,' Papers of the Peabody Museum of American Archaeology and Ethnology, vol. 47 (Cambridge, Mass., 1952).

LARRAIN, JORGE, *The Concept of Ideology* (Athens, Georgia: University of Georgia Press, 1979).

LICHTHEIM, GEORGE, *The Concept of Ideology* (New York: Random House, 1967).

LUHMANN, NIKLAS, *Soziologische Aufklärung* (Köln und Opladen, 1979).

MANNHEIM, KARL, *Ideology and Utopia* (New York: Harcourt, Brace and World, 1936).

MARX, KARL and ENGELS, FRIEDRICH, *Werke* (Berlin: Dietz Verlag, 1956–)

MERTON, ROBERT, *Social Theory and Social Structure* (Glencoe: Free Press, 1957).

PLAMENATZ, JOHN, *Ideology* (London, 1979).

POPPER, KARL, *The Poverty of Historicism* (New York: Harper and Row, 1964).

POPPER, KARL, *The Open Society and its Enemies* (Princeton: Princeton University Press, 1971).

QUINE, W. V. O., *From a Logical Point of View* (New York: Harper, 1963).

QUINE, W. V. O., *Ontological Relativity and Other Essays* (New York: Columbia, 1969).

RUNCIMAN, W.G., *Sociology in its Place* (Cambridge: Cambridge University Press, 1970).

SAHLINS, MARSHALL, *Culture and Practical Reason* (Chicago: University of Chicago Press, 1976).

SAHLINS, MARSHALL, *Tribesmen* (Englewood Cliffs, NJ: Prentice-Hall, 1968).

SERVICE, ELMAN, *The Hunters* (Englewood Cliffs, NJ: Prentice-Hall, 1966).

TUCKER, R. (ed.), *Marx–Engels Reader* (New York: Norton, 1971).

WAXMAN, CHAIM (ed.), *The End of Ideology Debate* (New York: Simon and Schuster, 1968).

16 Ideology as a Cultural System*

Clifford Geertz

Clifford Geertz is a distinguished American social anthropologist and Professor of Social Science at the Institute for Advanced Study, Princeton University. His many works include *Islam Observed* (New York: Basic Books, 1968), *The Interpretation of Cultures* (London: Hutchinson, 1973) and *Local Knowledge* (New York: Basic Books, 1983). In this essay, he implicitly dismisses a Marxist conception of ideology as false consciousness or the expression of political interests, and argues instead for a broad understanding of ideology as a symbolic system which allows individuals to orientate themselves in relation to their social world. Ideology for Geertz is a form of cognitive mapping which emerges into being at the point where traditional or taken-for-granted values and motives break down or come under challenge; and at such points of historical crisis, ideology is at hand as a set of rhetorical or suasive discourses to provide men and women with an alternative, more conscious understanding of the social order and their place within it.

It is of singular interest . . . that, although the general stream of social scientific theory has been deeply influenced by almost every major intellectual movement of the last century and a half – Marxism, Darwinism, Utilitarianism, Idealism, Freudianism, Behaviorism, Positivism, Operationalism – and has attempted to capitalize on virtually every important field of methodological innovation from ecology, ethology, and comparative psychology to game theory, cybernetics, and statistics, it has, with very few exceptions, been virtually untouched by one of the most important trends in recent thought: the effort to construct an independent science of what Kenneth Burke has called 'symbolic action'.[1] Neither the work of such philosophers as Peirce, Wittgenstein, Cassirer, Langer, Ryle, or Morris nor of such literary critics as Coleridge, Eliot,

*Reprinted from Clifford Geertz, *The Interpretation of Cultures* (1973; London: Fontana, 1993), pp. 208–20, 230–3.

Burke, Empson, Blackmur, Brooks, or Auerbach seems to have had any
appreciable impact on the general pattern of social scientific analysis.[2]
Aside from a few more venturesome (and largely programmatic) linguists
– a Whorf or a Sapir – the question of how symbols symbolize, how they
function to mediate meanings has simply been bypassed. 'The
embarrassing fact', the physician *cum* novelist Walker Percy has written, 'is
that there does not exist today – a natural empirical science of symbolic
behavior *as such* . . . Sapir's gentle chiding about the lack of a science of
symbolic behavior and the need of such a science is more conspicuously
true today than it was thirty-five years ago.'[3]

It is the absence of such a theory and in particular the absence of any
analytical framework within which to deal with figurative language that
have reduced sociologists to viewing ideologies as elaborate cries of pain.
With no notion of how metaphor, analogy, irony, ambiguity, pun, paradox,
hyperbole, rhythm, and all the other elements of what we lamely call 'style'
operate – even, in a majority of cases, with no recognition that these
devices are of any importance in casting personal attitudes into public
form, sociologists lack the symbolic resources out of which to construct a
more incisive formulation. At the same time that the arts have been
establishing the cognitive power of 'distortion' and philosophy has been
undermining the adequacy of an emotivist theory of meaning, social
scientists have been rejecting the first and embracing the second. It is not
therefore surprising that they evade the problem of construing the import
of ideological assertions by simply failing to recognize it as a problem.[4]

In order to make explicit what I mean, let me take an example that is, I
hope, so thoroughly trivial in itself as both to still any suspicions that I
have a hidden concern with the substance of the political issue involved
and, more important, to bring home the point that concepts developed for
the analysis of the more elevated aspects of culture – poetry, for example –
are applicable to the more lowly ones without in any way blurring the
enormous qualitative distinctions between the two. In discussing the
cognitive inadequacies by which ideology is defined for them, Sutton et al.
use as an example of the ideologist's tendency to 'oversimplify' the
denomination by organized labor of the Taft-Hartley Act as a 'slave labor
law':

> Ideology tends to be simple and clear-cut, even where its simplicity and
> clarity do less than justice to the subject under discussion. The
> ideological picture uses sharp lines and contrasting blacks and whites.
> The ideologist exaggerates and caricatures in the fashion of the
> cartoonist. In contrast, a scientific description of social phenomena is
> likely to be fuzzy and indistinct. In recent labor ideology the
> Taft-Hartley Act has been a 'slave labor act'. By no dispassionate
> examination does the Act merit this label. Any detached assessment of

the Act would have to consider its many provisions individually. On any set of values, even those of trade unions themselves, such an assessment would yield a mixed verdict. But mixed verdicts are not the stuff of ideology. They are too complicated, too fuzzy. Ideology must categorize the Act as a whole with a symbol to rally workers, voters and legislators to action.[5]

Leaving aside the merely empirical question of whether or not it is in fact true that ideological formulations of a given set of social phenomena are inevitably 'simpler' than scientific formulations of the same phenomena, there is in this argument a curiously depreciatory – one might even say 'oversimple' – view of the thought processes of labor-union leaders on the one hand and 'workers, voters and legislators' on the other. It is rather hard to believe that either those who coined and disseminated the slogan themselves believed or expected anyone else to believe that the law would actually reduce (or was intended to reduce) the American worker to the status of a slave or that the segment of the public for whom the slogan had meaning perceived it in any such terms. Yet it is precisely this flattened view of other people's mentalities that leaves the sociologist with only two interpretations, both inadequate, of whatever effectiveness the symbol has: either it deceives the uninformed (according to interest theory), or it excites the unreflective (according to strain theory). That it might in fact draw its power from its capacity to grasp, formulate, and communicate social realities that elude the tempered language of science, that it may mediate more complex meanings than its literal reading suggests, is not even considered. 'Slave labor act' may be, after all, not a label but a trope.

More exactly, it appears to be a metaphor or at least an attempted metaphor. Although very few social scientists seem to have read much of it, the literature on metaphor – 'the power whereby language, even with a small vocabulary, manages to embrace a multi-million things' – is vast and by now in reasonable agreement.[6] In metaphor one has, of course, a stratification of meaning, in which an incongruity of sense on one level produces an influx of significance on another. As Percy has pointed out, the feature of metaphor that has most troubled philosophers (and, he might have added, scientists) is that it is 'wrong': 'It asserts of one thing that it is something else.' And, worse yet, it tends to be most effective when most 'wrong'.[7] The power of a metaphor derives precisely from the interplay between the discordant meanings it symbolically coerces into a unitary conceptual framework and from the degree to which that coercion is successful in overcoming the psychic resistance such semantic tension inevitably generates in anyone in a position to perceive it. When it works, a metaphor transforms a false identification (for example, of the labor policies of the Republican Party and of those of the Bolsheviks) into an apt analogy; when it misfires, it is a mere extravagance.

That for most people the 'slave labor law' figure was, in fact, pretty much a misfire (and therefore never served with any effectiveness as 'a symbol to rally workers, voters and legislators to action') seems evident enough, and it is this failure, rather than its supposed clear-cut simplicity, that makes it seem no more than a cartoon. The semantic tension between the image of a conservative Congress outlawing the closed shop and of the prison camps of Siberia was – apparently – too great to be resolved into a single conception, at least by means of so rudimentary a stylistic device as the slogan. Except (perhaps) for a few enthusiasts, the analogy did not appear; the false identification remained false. But failure is not inevitable, even on such an elementary level. Although, a most unmixed verdict, Sherman's 'War is hell' is no social-science proposition, even Sutton and his associates would probably not regard it as either an exaggeration or a caricature.

More important, however, than any assessment of the adequacy of the two tropes as such is the fact that, as the meanings they attempt to spark against one another are after all socially rooted, the success or failure of the attempt is relative not only to the power of the stylistic mechanisms employed but also to precisely those sorts of factors upon which strain theory concentrates its attention. The tensions of the Cold War, the fears of a labor movement only recently emerged from a bitter struggle for existence, and the threatened eclipse of New Deal liberalism after two decades of dominance set the sociopsychological stage both for the appearance of the 'slave labor' figure and – when it proved unable to work them into a cogent analogy – for its miscarriage. The militarists of 1934 Japan who opened their pamphlet on *Basic Theory of National Defense and Suggestions for Its Strengthening* with the resounding familial metaphor, 'War is the father of creation and the mother of culture', would no doubt have found Sherman's maxim as unconvincing as he would have found theirs.[8] They were energetically preparing for an imperialist war in an ancient nation seeking its footing in the modern world; he was wearily pursuing a civil war in an unrealized nation torn by domestic hatreds. It is thus not truth that varies with social, psychological, and cultural contexts but the symbols we construct in our unequally effective attempts to grasp it. War *is* hell and *not* the mother of culture, as the Japanese eventually discovered – although no doubt they express the fact in a grander idiom.

The sociology of knowledge ought to be called the sociology of meaning, for what is socially determined is not the nature of conception but the vehicles of conception. In a community that drinks its coffee black, Henle remarks, to praise a girl with 'You're the cream in my coffee' would give entirely the wrong impression; and, if omnivorousness were regarded as a more significant characteristic of bears than their clumsy roughness, to call a man 'an old bear' might mean not that he was crude, but that he had catholic tastes.[9] Or, to take an example from Burke, since in Japan people smile on mentioning the death of a close friend, the semantic equivalent (behaviorally as well as verbally) in American English is not 'He smiled', but 'His face fell'; for, with such a rendering, we are 'translating the accepted social usage of Japan into the corresponding accepted social usage of the West'.[10] And, closer to the ideological realm, Sapir has pointed out that the chairmanship of a committee has the figurative force we give it only because we hold that 'administrative functions somehow stamp a person as superior to those who are being directed'; 'should people come to feel that administrative functions are little more than symbolic automatisms, the chairmanship of a committee would be recognized as little more than a petrified symbol and the particular value that is now felt to inhere in it would tend to disappear'.[11] The case is no different for 'slave labor law'. If forced labor camps come, for whatever reasons, to play a less prominent role in the American image of the Soviet Union, it will not be the symbol's veracity that has dissolved but its very meaning, its capacity to be *either* true or false. One must simply frame the argument – that the Taft-Hartley Act is a mortal threat to organized labor – in some other way.

In short, between an ideological figure like 'slave labor act' and the social realities of American life in the midst of which it appears, there exists a subtlety of interplay, which concepts like 'distortion', 'selectivity', or 'oversimplification' are simply incompetent to formulate.[12] Not only is the semantic structure of the figure a good deal more complex than it appears on the surface, but an analysis of that structure forces one into tracing a multiplicity of referential connections between it and social reality, so that the final picture is one of a configuration of dissimilar meanings out of whose interworking both the expressive power and the rhetorical force of the final symbol derive. This interworking is itself a social process, an occurrence not 'in the head' but in that public world where 'people talk together, name things, make assertions, and to a degree understand each other'.[13] The study of symbolic action is no less a sociological discipline than the study of small groups, bureaucracies, or the changing role of the American woman; it is only a good deal less developed.

Asking the question that most students of ideology fail to ask – what, precisely, do we mean when we assert that sociopsychological strains are 'expressed' in symbolic forms? – gets one, therefore, very quickly into quite deep water indeed; into, in fact, a somewhat untraditional and apparently paradoxical theory of the nature of human thought as a public and not, or at least not fundamentally, a private activity.[14] The details of such a theory cannot be pursued any distance here, nor can any significant amount of evidence be marshaled to support it. But at least its general outlines must be sketched if we are to find our way back from the elusive world of symbols and semantic process to the (apparently) more solid one of sentiments and institutions, if we are to trace with some circumstantiality the modes of interpenetration of culture, personality, and social system.

The defining proposition of this sort of approach to thought *en plein air* –
what, following Galanter and Gerstenhaber, we may call 'the extrinsic
theory' – is that thought consists of the construction and manipulation of
symbol systems, which are employed as models of other systems, physical,
organic, social, psychological, and so forth, in such a way that the structure
of these other systems – and, in the favorable case, how they may therefore
be expected to behave – is, as we say, 'understood'.[15] Thinking,
conceptualization, formulation, comprehension, understanding, or
what-have-you, consists not of ghostly happenings in the head but of a
matching of the states and processes of symbolic models against the states
and processes of the wider world:

> Imaginal thinking is neither more nor less than constructing an image of
> the environment, running the model faster than the environment, and
> predicting that the environment will behave as the model does. . . . The
> first step in the solution of a problem consists in the construction of a
> model or image of the 'relevant features' of the [environment]. These
> models can be constructed from many things, including parts of the
> organic tissue of the body and, by man, paper and pencil or actual
> artifacts. Once a model has been constructed it can be manipulated
> under various hypothetical conditions and constraints. The organism is
> then able to 'observe' the outcome of these manipulations, and to project
> them onto the environment so that prediction is possible. According to
> this view, an aeronautical engineer is thinking when he manipulates a
> model of a new airplane in a wind tunnel. The motorist is thinking
> when he runs his finger over a line on a map, the finger serving as a
> model of the relevant aspects of the automobile, the map as a model of
> the road. External models of this kind are often used in thinking about
> complex [environments]. Images used in covert thinking depend upon
> the availability of the physico-chemical events of the organism which
> must be used to form models.[16]

This view does not, of course, deny consciousness: it defines it. Every
conscious perception is, as Percy has argued, an act of recognition, a
pairing in which an object (or an event, an act, an emotion) is identified by
placing it against the background of an appropriate symbol:

> It is not enough to say that one is conscious *of* something; one is also
> conscious of something being something. There is a difference between
> the apprehension of a gestalt (a chicken perceived the Jastrow effect as
> well as a human) and the grasping of it under its symbolic vehicle. As I
> gaze about the room, I am aware of a series of almost effortless acts of
> *matching:* seeing an object and knowing what it is. If my eye falls upon

an unfamiliar something, I am immediately aware that one term of the match is missing, I ask what [the object] is – an exceedingly mysterious question.[17]

What is missing and what is being asked for are an applicable symbolic model under which to subsume the 'unfamiliar something' and so render it familiar:

> If I see an object at some distance and do not quite recognize it, I may see it, actually see it, as a succession of different things, each rejected by the criterion of fit as I come closer, until one is positively certified. A patch of sunlight in a field I may actually see as a rabbit – a seeing which goes much further than the guess that it may be a rabbit; no, the perceptual gestalt is so construed, actually stamped by the essence of rabbitness: I could have sworn it was a rabbit. On coming closer, the sunlight pattern changes enough so that the rabbit-cast is disallowed. The rabbit vanishes and I make another cast: it is a paper bag, and so on. But most significant of all, even the last, the 'correct' recognition is quite as mediate an apprehension as the incorrect ones; it is also a cast, a pairing, an approximation. And let us note in passing that even though it is correct, even though it is borne out by all indices, it may operate quite as effectively to conceal as to discover. When I recognize a strange bird as a sparrow, I tend to dispose of the bird under its appropriate formulation: it is only a sparrow.[18]

Despite the somewhat intellectualist tone of these various examples, the extrinsic theory of thought is extendable to the affective side of human mentality as well.[19] As a road map transforms mere physical locations into 'places', connected by numbered routes and separated by measured distances, and so enables us to find our way from where we are to where we want to go, so a poem like, for example, Hopkins's 'Felix Randal' provides, through the evocative power of its charged language, a symbolic model of the emotional impact of premature death, which, if we are as impressed with its penetration as with the road map's, transforms physical sensations into sentiments and attitudes and enables us to react to such a tragedy not 'blindly' but 'intelligently'. The central rituals of religion – a mass, a pilgrimage, a corroboree – are symbolic models (here more in the form of activities than of words) of a particular sense of the divine, a certain sort of devotional mood, which their continual re-enactment tends to produce in their participants. Of course, as most acts of what is usually called 'cognition' are more on the level of identifying a rabbit than operating a wind tunnel, so most of what is usually called 'expression' (the dichotomy is often overdrawn and almost universally misconstrued) is mediated more by models drawn from popular culture than from high art and formal religious ritual. But the point is that the development, maintenance, and dissolution of 'moods', 'attitudes', 'sentiments', and so forth are no more 'a ghostly process occurring in streams of consciousness we are debarred from visiting' than is the discrimination of objects, events, structures, processes, and so forth in our environment. Here, too, 'we are describing the ways in which . . . people conduct parts of their predominantly public behavior'.[20]

Whatever their other differences, both so-called cognitive and so-called expressive symbols or symbol-systems have, then, at least one thing in common: they are extrinsic sources of information in terms of which human life can be patterned – extrapersonal mechanisms for the perception, understanding, judgment, and manipulation of the world. Culture patterns – religious, philosophical, aesthetic, scientific, ideological – are 'programs'; they provide a template or blueprint for the organization of social and psychological processes, much as genetic systems provide such a template for the organization of organic processes:

> These considerations define the terms in which we approach the problem of 'reductionism' in psychology and social science. The levels we have tentatively discriminated [organism, personality, social system, culture] . . . are . . . levels of organization and control. The lower levels 'condition', and thus in a sense 'determine' the structures into which they enter, in the same sense that the stability of a building depends on the properties of the materials out of which it is constructed. But the physical properties of the materials do not determine the *plan* of the building; this is a factor of another order, one of *organization*. And the organization controls the *relations* of the materials to each other, the *ways* in which they are utilized in the building by virtue of which it constitutes an ordered system of a particular type – looking 'downward' in the series, we can always investigate and discover sets of 'conditions' in which the function of a higher order of organization is dependent. There is, thus, an immensely complicated set of physiological conditions on which psychological functioning is dependent, etc. Properly understood and evaluated, these conditions are always authentic determinants of process in the organized systems at the next higher levels. We may, however, also look 'upward' in the series. In this direction we see 'structures', organization patterns, patterns of meaning, 'programs', etc., which are the focus of the organization of the system at the level on which we have concentrated our attention.[21]

The reason such symbolic templates are necessary is that, as has been often remarked, human behavior is inherently extremely plastic. Not strictly but only very broadly controlled by genetic programs or models – intrinsic sources of information – such behavior must, if it is to have any effective form at all, be controlled to a significant extent by extrinsic ones. Birds learn how to fly without wind tunnels, and whatever reactions lower animals have to death are in great part innate, physiologically preformed.[22] The extreme generality, diffuseness, and variability of man's innate response capacities mean that the particular pattern his behavior takes is guided predominantly by cultural rather than genetic templates, the latter setting the overall psychophysical context within which precise activity sequences are organized by the former. The tool-making, laughing, or lying animal, man, is also the incomplete – or, more accurately, self-completing – animal. The agent of his own realization, he creates out of his general capacity for the construction of symbolic models the specific capabilities that define him. Or – to return at last to our subject – it is through the construction of ideologies, schematic images of social order, that man makes himself for better or worse a political animal.

Further, as the various sorts of cultural symbol-systems are extrinsic sources of information, templates for the organization of social and psychological processes, they come most crucially into play in situations where the particular kind of information they contain is lacking, where institutionalized guides for behavior, thought, or feeling are weak or absent. It is in country unfamiliar emotionally or topographically that one needs poems and road maps.

So too with ideology. In polities firmly embedded in Edmund Burke's golden assemblage of 'ancient opinions and rules of life', the role of ideology, in any explicit sense, is marginal. In such truly traditional political systems the participants act as (to use another Burkean phrase) men of untaught feelings; they are guided both emotionally and intellectually in their judgments and activities by unexamined prejudices, which do not leave them 'hesitating in the moment of decision, sceptical, puzzled and unresolved'. But when, as in the revolutionary France Burke was indicting and in fact in the shaken England from which, as perhaps his nation's greatest ideologue, he was indicting it, those hallowed opinions and rules of life come into question, the search for systematic ideological formulations, either to reinforce them or to replace them, flourishes. The function of ideology is to make an autonomous politics possible by providing the authoritative concepts that render it meaningful, the suasive images by means of which it can be sensibly grasped.[23] It is, in fact, precisely at the point at which a political system begins to free itself from the immediate governance of received tradition, from the direct and detailed guidance of religious or philosophical canons on the one hand and from the unreflective precepts of conventional moralism on the other, that formal ideologies tend first to emerge and take hold.[24] The differentiation of an autonomous polity implies the differentiation, too, of a separate and distinct cultural model of political action, for the older, unspecialized models are either too comprehensive or too concrete to provide the sort of guidance such a political system demands. Either they trammel political behavior by encumbering it with transcendental significance, or they stifle political imagination by binding it to the blank realism of habitual judgment. It is when neither a society's most general cultural orientations nor its most down-to-earth, 'pragmatic' ones suffice any longer to provide an adequate image of political process that ideologies begin to become crucial as sources of sociopolitical meanings and attitudes.

In one sense, this statement is but another way of saying that ideology is a response to strain. But now we are including *cultural* as well as social and psychological strain. It is a loss of orientation that most directly gives rise to ideological activity, an inability, for lack of usable models, to comprehend the universe of civic rights and responsibilities in which one finds oneself located. The development of a differentiated polity (or of greater internal differentiation within such a polity) may and commonly does bring with it severe social dislocation and psychological tension. But it also brings with it conceptual confusion, as the established images of political order fade into irrelevance or are driven into disrepute. The reason why the French Revolution was, at least up to its time, the greatest incubator of extremist ideologies, 'progressive' and 'reactionary' alike, in human history was not that either personal insecurity or social disequilibrium were deeper and more pervasive than at many earlier periods – though they were deep and pervasive enough – but because the central organizing principle of political life, the divine right of kings, was destroyed.[25] It is a confluence of sociopsychological strain and an absence of cultural resources by means of which to make sense of the strain, each exacerbating the other, that sets the stage for the rise of systematic (political, moral, or economic) ideologies.

And it is, in turn, the attempt of ideologies to render otherwise incomprehensible social situations meaningful, to so construe them as to make it possible to act purposefully within them, that accounts both for the ideologies' highly figurative nature and for the intensity with which, once accepted, they are held. As metaphor extends language by broadening its semantic range, enabling it to express meanings it cannot or at least cannot yet express literally, so the head-on clash of literal meanings in ideology – the irony, the hyperbole, the overdrawn antithesis – provides novel symbolic frames against which to match the myriad 'unfamiliar somethings' that, like a journey to a strange country, are produced by a transformation in political life. Whatever else ideologies may be – projections of unacknowledged fears, disguises for ulterior motives, phatic expressions of group solidarity – they are, most distinctively, maps of problematic social reality and matrices for the creation of collective conscience. Whether, in any particular case, the map is accurate or the conscience creditable is a separate question to which one can hardly give

the same answer for Nazism and Zionism, for the nationalisms of
McCarthy and of Churchill, for the defenders of segregation and its
opponents.

> Critical and imaginative works are answers to questions posed by the
> situation in which they arose. They are not merely answers, they are
> *strategic* answers, *stylized* answers. For there is a difference in style or
> strategy, if one says 'yes' in tonalities that imply 'thank God!' or in
> tonalities that imply 'alas!' So I should propose an initial working
> distinction between 'strategies' and 'situations' whereby we think of
> . . . any work of critical or imaginative cast . . . as the adopting of
> various strategies for the encompassing of situations. These
> strategies size up the situations, name their structure and outstanding
> ingredients, and name them in a way that contains an attitude toward
> them.
>   This point of view does not, by any means, vow us to personal or
> historical subjectivism. The situations are real; the strategies for
> handling them have public content; in so far as situations overlap from
> individual to individual, or from one historical period to another, the
> strategies possess universal relevance.
>
> (Kenneth Burke, *The Philosophy of Literary Form*)

As both science and ideology are critical and imaginative 'works' (that is
symbolic structures), an objective formulation both of the marked
differences between them and of the nature of their relationship to one
another seems more likely to be achieved by proceeding from such a
concept of stylistic strategies than from a nervous concern with
comparative epistemological or axiological status of the two forms of
thought. No more than scientific studies of religion ought to begin with
unnecessary questions about the legitimacy of the substantive claims of
their subject matter ought scientific studies of ideology to begin with such
questions. The best way to deal with Mannheim's, as with any true
paradox, is to circumvent it by reformulating one's theoretical approach so
as to avoid setting off yet once more down the well-worn path of argument
that led to it in the first place.

The differentiae of science and ideology as cultural systems are to be
sought in the sorts of symbolic strategy for encompassing situations that
they respectively represent. Science names the structure of situations in
such a way that the attitude contained toward them is one of
disinterestedness. Its style is restrained, spare, resolutely analytic: by
shunning the semantic devices that most effectively formulate moral
sentiment, it seeks to maximize intellectual clarity. But ideology names the
structure of situations in such a way that the attitude contained toward
them is one of commitment. Its style is ornate, vivid, deliberately

suggestive: by objectifying moral sentiment through the same devices that
science shuns, it seeks to motivate action. Both are concerned with the
definition of a problematic situation and are responses to a felt lack of
needed information. But the information needed is quite different, even in
cases where the situation is the same. An ideologist is no more a poor social
scientist than a social scientist is a poor ideologist. The two are – or at least
they ought to be – in quite different lines of work, lines so different that
little is gained and much obscured by measuring the activities of the one
against the aims of the other.[26]

Where science is the diagnostic, the critical, dimension of culture,
ideology is the justificatory, the apologetic one – it refers 'to that part of
culture which is actively concerned with the establishment and defense of
patterns of belief and value'.[27] That there is natural tendency for the two
to clash, particularly when they are directed to the interpretation of the
same range of situations, is thus clear; but that the clash is inevitable and
that the findings of (social) science necessarily will undermine the validity
of the beliefs and values that ideology has chosen to defend and
propagate seem most dubious assumptions. An attitude at once critical
and apologetic toward the same situation is no intrinsic contradiction in
terms (however often it may in fact turn out to be an empirical one) but a
sign of a certain level of intellectual sophistication. One remembers the
story, probably *ben trovato*, to the effect that when Churchill had finished
his famous rally of isolated England, 'We shall fight on the beaches, we
shall fight on the landing grounds, we shall fight in the fields and in the
streets, we shall fight in the hills . . . ', he turned to an aide and whispered,
'and we shall hit them over the head with soda-water bottles, because we
haven't any guns'.

The quality of social rhetoric in ideology is thus not proof that the
vision of sociopsychological reality upon which it is based is false and that
it draws its persuasive power from any discrepancy between what is
believed and what can, now or someday, be established as scientifically
correct. That it may indeed lose touch with reality in an orgy of autistic
fantasy – even that, in situations where it is left uncriticized by either a
free science or competing ideologies well-rooted in the general social
structure, it has a very strong tendency to do so – is all too apparent. But
however interesting pathologies are for clarifying normal functioning
(and however common they may be empirically), they are misleading as
prototypes of it. Although fortunately it never had to be tested, it seems
most likely that the British would have indeed fought on the beaches,
landing grounds, streets, and hills – with soda-water bottles too, if it came
to that – for Churchill formulated accurately the mood of his countrymen
and, formulating it, mobilized it by making it a public possession, a social
fact, rather than a set of disconnected, unrealized private emotions. Even
morally loathsome ideological expressions may still catch most acutely

the mood of a people or a group. Hitler was not distorting the German conscience when he rendered his countrymen's demonic self-hatred in the tropological figure of the magically corrupting Jew; he was merely objectifying it – transforming a prevalent personal neurosis into a powerful social force.

But though science and ideology are different enterprises, they are not unrelated ones. Ideologies do make empirical claims about the condition and direction of society, which it is the business of science (and, where scientific knowledge is lacking, common sense) to assess. The social function of science *vis-à-vis* ideologies is first to understand them – what they are, how they work, what gives rise to them – and second to criticize them, to force them to come to terms with (but not necessarily to surrender to) reality. The existence of a vital tradition of scientific analysis of social issues is one of the most effective guarantees against ideological extremism, for it provides an incomparably reliable source of positive knowledge for the political imagination to work with and to honor. It is not the only such check. The existence, as mentioned, of competing ideologies carried by other powerful groups in the society is at least as important; as is a liberal political system in which dreams of total power are obvious fantasies; as are stable social conditions in which conventional expectations are not continually frustrated and conventional ideas not radically incompetent. But, committed with a quiet intransigence to a vision of its own, it is perhaps the most indomitable.

Notes

1. K. Burke, *The Philosophy of Literary Form, Studies in Symbolic Action* (Baton Rouge, 1941). In the following discussion, I use 'symbol' broadly in the sense of any physical, social, or cultural act or object that serves as the vehicle for a conception. For an explication of this view, under which 'five' and 'the Cross' are equally symbols, see S. Langer, *Philosophy in a New Key*, 4th edn (Cambridge, Mass., 1960), pp. 60–6.
2. Useful general summaries of the tradition of literary criticism can be found in S.E. Hyman, *The Armed Vision* (New York, 1948) and in R. Welleck and A. Warren, *Theory of Literature*, 2nd edn (New York, 1958). A similar summary of the somewhat more diverse philosophical development is apparently not available, but the seminal works are C.S. Peirce, *Collected Papers*, ed. C. Hartshorne and P. Weiss, 8 vols (Cambridge, Mass., 1931–58); E. Cassirer, *Die Philosophie der symbolischen Foremen*, 3 vols (Berlin, 1923–29); C.W. Morris, *Signs, Language and Behavior* (Englewood Cliffs, N.J., 1944); and L. Wittgenstein, *Philosophical Investigations* (Oxford, 1953).
3. W. Percy, 'The Symbolic Structure of Interpersonal Process,' *Psychiatry*, 24 (1961): 39–52. Italics in original. The reference is to Sapir's 'The Status of Linguistics as a Science', originally published in 1929 and reprinted in D. Mandlebaum (ed.),

Selected Writings of Edward Sapir (Berkeley and Los Angeles, 1949), pp. 160–6.

4. A partial exception to this stricture, although marred by his obsession with power as the sum and substance of politics, is LASSWELL's 'Style in the Language of Politics', in LASSWELL et al., *Language of Politics*, pp. 20–39. It also should be remarked that the emphasis on verbal symbolism in the following discussion is merely for the sake of simplicity and is not intended to deny the importance of plastic, theatrical, or other nonlinguistic devices – the rhetoric of uniforms, floodlit stages, and marching bands – in ideological thought.

5. SUTTON et al., *American Business Creed*, pp. 4–5.

6. An excellent recent review is to be found in P. Henle (ed.), *Language, Thought and Culture* (Ann Arbor, 1958), pp. 173–95. The quotation is from LANGER, *Philosophy*, p. 117.

7. W. PERCY, 'Metaphor as Mistake', *The Sewanee Review*, 66 (1958): 79–99.

8. Quoted in J. CROWLEY, 'Japanese Army Factionalism in the Early 1930s', *The Journal of Asian Studies*, 21 (1958): 309–26.

9. HENLE, *Language, Thought and Culture*, pp. 4–5.

10. K. BURKE, *Counterstatement* (Chicago, 1957), p. 149.

11. SAPIR, 'Status of Linguistics', p. 568.

12. Metaphor is, of course, not the only stylistic resource upon which ideology draws. Metonymy ('All I have to offer is blood, sweat and tears'), hyperbole ('The thousand-year Reich'), meiosis ('I shall return'), synechdoche ('Wall Street'), oxymoron ('Iron Curtain'), personification ('The hand that held the dagger has plunged it into the back of its neighbor'), and all the other figures the classical rhetoricians so painstakingly collected and so carefully classified are utilized over and over again, as are such syntactical devices as antithesis, inversion, and repetition; such prosodic ones as rhyme, rhythm, and alliteration; such literary ones as irony, eulogy and sarcasm. Nor is all ideological expression figurative. The bulk of it consists of quite literal, not to say flat-footed, assertions, which, a certain tendency toward *prima facie* implausibility aside, are difficult to distinguish from properly scientific statements: 'The history of all hitherto existing society is the history of class struggles'; 'The whole of the morality of Europe is based upon the values which are useful to the herd'; and so forth. As a cultural system, an ideology that has developed beyond the stage of mere sloganeering consists of an intricate structure of interrelated meanings – interrelated in terms of the semantic mechanisms that formulate them – of which the two-level organization of an isolated metaphor is but a feeble representation.

13. PERCY, 'Symbolic Structure'.

14. G. RYLE, *The Concept of Mind* (New York, 1949).

15. E. GALANTER and M. GERSTENHABER, 'On Thought: The Extrinsic Theory', *Psychology Review*, 63 (1956): 218–27.

16. Ibid. I have quoted this incisive passage above (pp. 77–8), in attempting to set the extrinsic theory of thought in the context of recent evolutionary, neurological, and cultural anthropological findings.

17. W. PERCY, 'Symbol, Consciousness and Intersubjectivity', *Journal of Philosophy*, 55 (1958): 631–41. Italics in original. Quoted by permission.

18. Ibid. Quoted by permission.

19. S. LANGER, *Feeling and Form* (New York, 1953).

20. The quotations are from RYLE, *Concept of Mind*, p. 51.

21. T. PARSONS, 'An Approach to Psychological Theory in Terms of the Theory of

Action', in *Psychology: A Study of a Science*, ed. S. Koch (New York, 1959), vol. 3. Italics in original. Compare:

> In order to account for this selectivity, it is necessary to assume that the structure of the enzyme is related in some way to the structure of the gene. By a logical extension of this idea we arrive at the concept that the gene is a representation – blueprint so to speak – of the enzyme molecule, and that the function of the gene is to serve as a source of information regarding the structure of the enzyme. It seems evident that the synthesis of an enzyme – a giant protein molecule consisting of hundreds of amino acid units arranged end-to-end in a specific and unique order – requires a model or set of instructions of some kind. These instructions must be characteristic of the species; they must be automatically transmitted from generation to generation, and they must be constant yet capable of evolutionary change. The only known entity that could perform such a function is the gene. There are many reasons for believing that it transmits information, by acting as a model or template.
>
> (N.H. HOROWITZ, 'The Gene', *Scientific American*, February 1956, p. 5)

22. This point is perhaps somewhat too baldly put in light of recent analyses of animal learning; but the essential thesis – that there is a general trend toward a more diffuse, less determinate control of behavior by intrinsic (innate) parameters as one moves from lower to higher animals – seems well established.

23. Of course, there are moral, economic, and even aesthetic ideologies, as well as specifically political ones, but as very few ideologies of any social prominence lack political implications, it is perhaps permissible to view the problem here in this somewhat narrowed focus. In any case, the arguments developed for political ideologies apply with equal force to nonpolitical ones. For an analysis of a moral ideology cast in terms very similar to those developed in this paper, see A.L. GREEN, 'The Ideology of Anti-Fluoridation Leaders', *The Journal of Social Issues*, 17 (1961): 13–25.

24. That such ideologies may call, as did Burke's or De Maistre's, for the reinvigoration of custom or the reimposition of religious hegemony is, of course, no contradiction. One constructs arguments for tradition only when its credentials have been questioned. To the degree that such appeals are successful they bring, not a return to naive traditionalism, but ideological retraditionalization – an altogether different matter. See MANNHEIM, 'Conservative Thought', in his *Essays on Sociology and Social Psychology* (New York, 1953), especially pp. 94–8.

25. It is important to remember, too, that the principle was destroyed long before the king; it was to the successor principle that he was, in fact, a ritual sacrifice: 'When [Saint-Just] exclaims: "To determine the principle in virtue of which the accused [Louis XVI] is perhaps to die, is to determine the principle by which the society that judges him lives", he demonstrates that it is the philosophers who are going to kill the King: the King must die in the name of the social contract.'

> (A. CAMUS, *The Rebel* (New York, 1958), p. 114)

26. This point is, however, not quite the same as saying that the two sorts of activity may not in practice be carried on together, any more than a man cannot, for example, paint a portrait of a bird that is both ornithologically accurate and aesthetically effective. Marx is, of course, the outstanding case, but for a more recent successful synchronization of scientific analysis and ideological argument,

see E. SHILS, *The Torment of Secrecy* (New York, 1956). Most such attempts to mix genres are, however, distinctly less happy.

27. FALLERS, 'Ideology and Culture.' The patterns of belief and value defended may be, of course, those of a socially subordinate group, as well as those of a socially dominant one, and the 'apology' therefore for reform or revolution.

17 Marxism and Literary History

JOHN FROW

John Frow teaches in the department of Communications of Griffith University in Australia, and is one of Australia's foremost cultural theorists. His *Marxism and Literary History*, from which this passage is extracted, ranges from classical Marxism to Russian Formalism, semiotics and discourse theory, drawing upon these diverse sources for – among other things – a semiotic or discursive theory of ideology. Such a theory refuses the classical Marxist notions of ideology as a 'world view' determined by the economic 'base', or as the 'collective consciousness' of a 'class subject', for a more conjunctural sense of ideology as a mobile, disunified field in which discourse and power configurate in different ways. The passage is exemplary of a 'post-Marxist' theory of ideology, heavily indebted to the work of Michel Foucault but – unlike Foucault himself – retaining some vestigial Marxist categories.

I take the following to be the general requirements of a working theory of ideology. First, that it not assert a relationship of truth to falsity (and so its own mastery over error) but concern rather the production and the conditions of production of categories and entities within the field of discourse. Second, that it not deduce the ideological from the structure of economic forces or, directly, from the class positions of real subjects of utterance; that it theorize the category of subject not as the origin of utterance but as its effect. Third, that it not be an ontology of discourse, deriving effects of meaning from formal structure, but rather theorize the multiple and variable limits within which relations of power and knowledge are produced.

These requirements are largely negative, and there is perhaps a strong argument to be made against the normativeness of any conception of ideology – an argument that one should more properly attempt a

*Reprinted from JOHN FROW, *Marxism and Literary History* (Oxford: Basil Blackwell, 1986), pp. 61–7.

description of the determinations according to which discourses have historically been distributed between the true and the false.[1] But that would still leave unproblematized the position from which this description would be made. Marxist theory is inescapably involved in making political judgments about discourse, on the basis of categories which are necessarily provisional and are themselves positionally constituted. This political force of the concept of ideology must be retained. But if the ideological is not to be ontologized, it should be regarded as a *state* of discourse or of semiotic systems in relation to the class struggle. Rather than being thought through an opposition to theory (a space external to the determinations of ideological production), it would be thought as a differential relation to power. Given that all discourse is informed by power, is constituted *as discourse* in relation to unequal patterns of power, then political judgments can be made in terms of particular historically specific appropriations of discourse by dominant social forces.[2] Note that this involves two distinct theses: first, that of the productivity of power; second, that of the inequality of powers. This means that power is not simply on one 'side', and hence that the 'sides' in any situation may be mobile and tactically constituted; they are not necessarily pregiven (except in the limit case of simple social contradiction) and cannot necessarily be specified in advance, since ideology is both constituted by and involved in the constitution of social contradictions. But it also means that power is never monolithic, stable, or uniform in its effects. Every use of discourse is at once a judgment about its relation to dominant forms of power and either an assent or a resistance to this relation.

In so far as power invests all discourse, the category of ideology is a way of referring to systems of value in which all speakers are enclosed and which is the productive basis of all speech. In so far as power is always asymmetrically split, the category refers to a particular political functionalization of speech. It is both a 'universal' category and a category that refers to the tactical appropriation of particular positions by a dominant social class (in Engels's text, the 'universalizing' capture of the thoroughfares on behalf of the bourgeoisie). But it does not refer to specific 'class ideologies' or class cultures. Here I follow Nicos Poulantzas's argument against a 'number-plate' theory of ideology, according to which each class would possess its own distinct and characteristic view of the world, and his contention that 'the dominant ideology does not simply reflect the conditions of existence of the dominant class, the pure and simple subject, but rather the concrete political relation between the dominant and the dominated classes in a social formation'.[3] The hegemonic practice of the ruling class attempts to ensure that subordinate classes operate within limits defined by the dominant ideology. 'Subaltern groups are always subject to the activity of ruling groups, even when they rebel and rise up; only "permanent" victory breaks their subordination, and that not immediately.'[4]

This is not an argument that subordinate classes accept the tenets of a distinctly defined and externally imposed 'dominant ideology', nor is it an argument for the necessary effectivity of such an ideology in integrating a social formation and securing the reproduction of the relations of production. Nicholas Abercrombie, Stephen Hill and Bryan S. Turner have mounted what I think is a correct critique of functionalist conceptions of ideology (including a large part of recent Marxist theory) which assume that there *is* social coherence and that ideology is instrumental in securing it. But my argument concerns not 'an' ideology which would be separately specifiable, but rather the differential, and differentially effective, investment of discourse by power, and in particular ruling-class power. What is at stake in this process is the consolidation of class power (through the integration, in the first instance, of the disparate fractions of the ruling class and then, in so far as possible, of other classes) and the reproduction of the conditions for the extraction of surplus value (conditions which are always a combination of economic structures, the juridical and political relations buttressing them, judicial and military force or its potential, and the 'consent' of the working classes). But to describe what is at stake is not to describe an actual and necessary effectivity. Hegemonic strategies establish a shifting and tense balance between contradictory powers and concede greater or lesser degrees of autonomy to discursive positions occupied by subordinate classes (although even in yielding ground, such hegemonic strategies tend to define the terrain of struggle: to set the agenda of the thinkable and to close off alternative discursive possibilities). Hegemony is a fragile and difficult process of containment. Further, there are historically quite distinct degrees of coherence of the 'dominant ideology'. It may be the case either that one discursive domain (for example, religion in the feudal period) is so heavily invested as to constitute in itself the 'dominant ideology', or that the investment of power may range across a number of domains, no single one of which is dominant. It may be the total structure of a discursive domain which is appropriated because of its high correlation with a social function, or it may be one particular set of categories within a domain or across several discursive domains (the concepts of nation or individual, for example, which draw upon and pull together quite different discourses and practices); and it may be the case that the resulting stresses are neither coherent nor noncontradictory. It is quite true to say, then, that 'the functional relation of ideology and economy is . . . a contingent one, specifiable only at the level of concrete societies. There cannot be a general theory of ideology.'[5] Here, however, I attempt no a priori specification of which discursive domains were most heavily invested or appropriated in particular periods, since this is precisely a matter for reconstruction from textual analysis.

If the function of ideological investment (in Freud's sense of *Besetzung*) is to bring about an acceptance or a tolerance of the hegemonic position of a dominant class, resistance is nevertheless written into the structure of all discourse. If power is no longer thought of simply as a negative and repressive force but as the condition of production of all speech, and if power is conceived of as polar rather than monolithic, as an asymmetrical dispersion, then all utterances are potentially splintered, formally open to contradictory uses. Utterance is in principle dialogic. Both ideology and resistance are *uses* of discourse, and both are 'within' power. Ideological utterance is marked by redundancy, by an automatization which appears as a kind of semantic crust proclaiming its authority and its status as second nature.[6] Resistance is the possibility of fracturing the ideological from within or of turning it against itself (as in children's language games) or of reappropriating it for counterhegemonic purposes. This turning is an application of force. In both cases the conditions of possibility are given in the structure of discourse (although they are not necessarily grammatically marked), but they are not intrinsic qualities of the language; they take the form of enunciative acts, and of judgments about the status of those acts.

The concept of ideology is still predominantly reserved for systematic and immediately political or propositional conceptualization – for 'opinion' or 'world view'. But by ascribing political value only to what openly claims the status of political or philosophical discourse, this restriction of the ideological sphere impoverishes our understanding of the area in which class conflicts are fought out. In class societies, where the production and circulation of meaning function as a determined and determinant level within antagonistic social relations of production, all meaning is, in the fullest sense of the word, political. The concept of ideological system therefore needs to comprise not only explicitly conceptual systems but the totality of codes and values through which speakers make investments in the construction of realities. A theory of ideology is a theory of semiotic value, because within the symbolic order the position and intensity of values are the index of a mediated tactical assertion, the site of a struggle for symbolic power, and are charged with the traces of that struggle. The ideological structure is coextensive with the semiotic field – with the totality of signifying systems. Bakhtin/Vološinov makes this point when he writes that 'the domain of ideology coincides with the domain of signs. They equate with one another. Wherever a sign is present, ideology is present too. *Everything ideological possesses semiotic value*,' and 'without signs there is no ideology'.[7] This is not to claim the falsity of all signifying systems but to stress the arbitrariness of the sign – the fact that it signifies only by virtue of a social consensus, and that where this consensus is founded on social relations which are contradictory, the symbolic order is necessarily involved in this contradiction.

Bakhtin/Vološinov's conception of the sign as an entity which 'reflects and refracts another reality outside itself, i.e. possesses meaning, represents something other than itself',[8] however, ignores the extent to which meaning is produced by structural interrelationships within the signifying system, and instead locates the process of semiosis in the isolated act of representation, the relation between the sign and its referent. But ideological value does not reside in the falseness of a particular act of representation. It is only at the level of the articulation of the sign in a particular structure of signification that we can speak of a production of meaning, and here 'meaning' must be conceived strictly as a function of the diacritical coherence of the structure. Signification depends not on the correlation of signs with bits of reality but on the order of signs among themselves. A meaning is not the sign of something irreducible to which it points as its essence but a sign of its own position in a differential system.

Within the semiotic order language holds a privileged position insofar as the values generated in all other signifying systems can be translated into linguistic form: 'The field of linguistic value corresponds entirely to the field of meaning.'[9] At the lowest level of semantic structure the semiotic order could thus be defined as a collection of abstract positional units formed within a number of distinct systems of differential relations but corresponding to the signifieds of the language system.

At this level of definition the axioms of structural linguistics are crucial. Saussure's conception of the purely relational character both of the signifier and of the signified destroys the traditional empiricist notion of signification as a relation between a material signifier, an abstract concept, and a 'thing' for which the word 'stands'.[10] Language is no longer a secondary formation, an accretion superimposed on a naturally articulated reality, but rather it actively articulates our representations of reality.[11] The assumption that the sign simply associates a word with the thing it names presupposes 'that ready-made ideas exist before words';[12] whereas Saussure's conception of the closedness of the sign stresses just this gap which founds the *systematic* structure of language and the dependent independence of thought. It establishes that relative arbitrariness which enables us to grasp systems of representation as particular kinds of games rather than as a reflection of the real; and it demolishes the privileged position that substantives enjoy in any empiricist typology, making it possible to think of relations, processes, and qualities, as well as entities, as objects of signification.

Language thus, in Eco's words, establishes 'a "cultural" world which is neither actual nor possible in the ontological sense; its existence is limited to a cultural order, which is the way in which a society thinks, speaks and, while speaking, explains the "purport" of its thought through other thoughts.'[13] The referent cannot therefore be understood as a transcendental signified external to the order of language, since 'the so-called "thing itself" is always already a *representamen* shielded from the simplicity of intuitive evidence. The *representamen* functions only by giving rise to an *interpretant* that itself becomes a sign and so on to infinity. The self-identity of the signified conceals itself unceasingly and is always on the move.'[14] Meaning is an endless chain of semiosis,[15] a movement between units which are virtual, positional, and therefore irreducible.

The articulation of the semantic realm into pure differential values depends, however, on an implicit hypostatization of the signified (or more correctly of the empty content-form) as a position defined outside of particular systems of signification. It deals in atomized units and rests on something like the lexicographer's convenient fiction of the existence of stable lexemes. In fact, the *double* relationality of the levels of form and content means that the correlation of signifier to signified, and so the production of meaning, takes place only within specific relations of signification. The system of these relations I shall refer to as discourse (I include in this term nonverbal semiotic systems). If we follow Foucault's terminology, the mode of existence of language in discourse is the statement (*énoncé*), whereas the sentence is the relevant unit of analysis at the level of grammar or language system (*langue*). What distinguishes the statement from the sentence, the speech act, or the proposition is not an *addition* of meaning (since isolated sentences and propositions can be meaningful) but the mobilization of the complex of rules and conventions of the language games that constitute meaning in use. The statement is not a *unit* of discourse but rather a function cutting across the other domains of structure such as grammar and acting as the condition of possibility of linguistic manifestation in these domains. Statements are by definition contextual, but they are not the direct projection of an actual situation. Rather, the statement is always a component of 'an enunciative field in which it has a place and a status'. It belongs to textual and intertextual systems, so that 'if one can speak of a statement, it is because a sentence (a proposition) figures at a definite point, with a specific position, in an enunciative network that extends beyond it.'[16]

On this definition, discourse cannot be equivalent to speech in the linguistic sense of *parole* (it is closer to the extended sense that Derrida gives to *écriture*). Here again it is Bakhtin who has done the pioneering theoretical work. Michael Holquist summarizes it this way:

> Utterance, as Bakhtin uses it, is *not* . . . unfettered speech, the individual ability to combine *langue* elements with freely chosen combinations. As he says, 'Saussure ignores the fact that besides the forms of language there exist as well forms of combination of these forms.' If we take into account the determining role of the other in actual speech communication, it becomes clear that there is not only system in language independent of any particular articulation of it, but there is as well a determining system that governs any actual utterance. We might

say the world of *parole*, like the sphere of *langue*, is controlled by laws; but to say so would be to change completely the definition of *parole* as used by Saussure.[17]

Recent linguistic analysis, however, has largely failed to move beyond the *langue/parole* opposition. It has been dominated on the one hand by a formalism which treats the text as an extension of the syntactic and logical structuring of the sentence, and on the other hand by an embarrassed empiricism which, in attempting to take into account the role of context and enunciation in the shaping of text, finds itself unable to formalize the infinity of possible speech situations.[18] In both cases the result is a renewal of the traditional dichotomy between text and context or between *énoncé* and *énonciation*, in which only the former is seen as properly linguistic,[19] and the situation of utterance is conceived as contingent, circumstantial, 'subjective', nonsystematic.

Notes

1. MICHEL FOUCAULT, *Power/Knowledge*, ed. and trans. Colin Gordon (New York: Pantheon, 1980), p. 118.
2. Anthony Giddens argues that the concept of ideology 'is *empty of content* because what makes belief systems ideological is their incorporation within systems of domination', and that 'to understand this incorporation we must analyze the mode in which patterns of signification are incorporated within the medium of *day-to-day practices*'; 'Four Theses on Ideology', *Canadian Journal of Political and Social Theory*, 7, nos 1 and 2 (1983): 18.
3. NICOS POULANTZAS, *Political Power and Social Classes*, trans. Timothy O'Hagan (London: New Left Books and Sheed and Ward, 1973), p. 203.
4. ANTONIO GRAMSCI, *Selections from the Prison Notebooks*, ed. and trans. Quinton Hoare and Geoffrey Nowell Smith (New York: International Publishers, 1971), p. 55.
5. NICHOLAS ABERCROMBIE, STEPHEN HILL and BRYAN S. TURNER, *The Dominant Ideology Thesis*, 2nd edn (1980; reprint, London: George Allen and Unwin, 1984), p. 185.
6. Cf. GEORG LUKÁCS, *History and Class Consciousness*, trans. Rodney Livingstone (Cambridge, Mass.: MIT Press, 1971), p. 86.
7. MIKHAIL BAKHTIN and V.N. VOLOŠINOV, *Marxism and the Philosophy of Language*, trans. L. Matejka and I.R. Titunik (New York: Seminar Press, 1973), p. 10.
8. Ibid., p. 9.
9. ROSSI-LANDI, *Linguistics and Economics*, Janua Linguarum, Series Major 81 (The Hague: Mouton, 1975), p. 139.
10. Cf. CHARLES K. OGDEN and IVOR A. RICHARDS, *The Meaning of Meaning*, 8th edn (1923; reprint, New York: Harcourt, Brace, 1956), p. 11.
11. FERDINAND DE SAUSSURE, *Course in General Linguistics*, trans. Wade Baskin (New York: McGraw-Hill, 1966), p. 112.

12. Ibid., p. 65.
13. UMBERTO ECO, *A Theory of Semiotics* (Bloomington: Indiana University Press, 1976), p. 61.
14. JACQUES DERRIDA, *Of Grammatology*, trans. Gayatri Chakravorty Spivak (Baltimore: Johns Hopkins University Press, 1976), p. 49.
15. ECO, *A Theory of Semiotics*, p. 68.
16. MICHEL FOUCAULT, *The Archaeology of Knowledge*, trans. A.M. Sheridan Smith (London: Tavistock, 1972), pp. 87–8, 99; hereafter cited in the text. On Bakhtin's parallel distinction between sentence and utterance in his *Estetika* (1979) ('A sentence . . . lacks the capability of determining a response; it acquires this capability . . . only in the entirety comprised by an utterance'), cf. MICHAEL HOLQUIST, 'Answering as Authoring: Mikhail Bakhtin's Trans-Linguistics', *Critical Inquiry*, 10, no. 2 (1983): 313.
17. HOLQUIST, 'Answering as Authoring', p. 311.
18. For the second position, cf. TUEN VAN DIJK, *Text and Context: Explorations in the Semantics and Pragmatics of Discourse* (London: Longman, 1977), p. 91.
19. HERMANN PARRET, *Language and Discourse*, Janua Linguarum, Series Minor 119 (The Hague: Mouton, 1971), pp. 275–6.

Further Reading

(1) General introductions

JORGE LARRAIN, *The Concept of Ideology* (London: Hutchinson, 1979). An excellent, wide-ranging introduction to the field from Francis Bacon to the Frankfurt School.

TERRY EAGLETON, *Ideology: An Introduction* (London: Verso, 1991). Contains chapters on the definition of ideology, the Marxist and 'irrationalist' traditions, and discourse and ideology.

JOHN B. THOMPSON, *Studies in the Theory of Ideology* (Cambridge: Polity Press, 1984). Contains suggestive chapters on Habermas, Bourdieu, Anthony Giddens and several other major thinkers, along with some interesting general reflections on ideology and domination.

NORMAN BIRNBAUM, 'The Sociological Study of Ideology, 1940–1960', *Current Sociology*, vol. 9 (1960). A survey of theories of ideology from Marx to the modern day, along with an excellent bibliography.

A. NAESS et al., *Democracy, Ideology and Objectivity* (Oslo, 1956). For a useful summary of the various meanings of ideology.

GEORGE LICHTHEIM, 'The Concept of Ideology', in *The Concept of Ideology and Other Essays* (New York: Random House, 1967).

EDWARD SHILS, 'The concept and function of ideology', *International Social Sciences Encyclopaedia*, vol. 7 (1958). A classic statement of the 'end of ideology' case.

RAYMOND WILLIAMS, 'Ideology', in *Marxism and Literature* (Oxford: Oxford University Press, 1977).

D.J. MANNING (ed.), *The Form of Ideology* (London: George Allen and Unwin, 1980).

RAYMOND BOURDON, *The Analysis of Ideology* (Oxford: Basil Blackwell, 1989).

(2) The classical tradition

EMMET KENNEDY, *A Philosopher in the Age of Revolution: Destutt de Tracy and the Origins of 'Ideology'* (Philadelphia: University of Philadelphia Press, 1978). A meticulous exposition of the thoughts of the French ideologues, admirably detailed and erudite.

KARL MARX and FRIEDRICH ENGELS, *The German Ideology* (New York: International Publishers, 1986). Contains the first formulation of the Marxist doctrine of ideology.

KARL MARX, *Preface* to *A Contribution to the Critique of Political Economy*, in Marx and Engels: *Selected Works* (London: Lawrence and Wishart, 1968). The classic formulation of the doctrine of 'base and superstructure'.

KARL MARX, 'On the Fetishism of Commodities', *Capital*, vol. 1 (London: George Allen and Unwin, 1971). Marx's 'mature' sense of ideology as implicit in the material workings of capitalism.

GEORG LUKÁCS, *History and Class Consciousness* (Cambridge, Mass.: MIT Press, 1971). The key text of so-called Western Marxism; its chapter on 'Reification and the Consciousness of the Proletariat' makes a dramatically original contribution to the theory of ideology.

KARL MANNHEIM, *Ideology and Utopia* (London: Routledge and Kegan Paul, 1936). A central work in the 'sociology of knowledge', influenced by Marxism but critical of its major theses.

LUCIEN GOLDMANN, *The Hidden God* (London: Routledge, 1964). An important work in the Lukácsian tradition, and the founding text of so-called genetic structuralism.

THEODOR ADORNO, *Negative Dialectics* (London: Routledge, 1973). Perhaps the major philosophical work of the Frankfurt School, strongly influenced by Hegel and, in its conception of ideology as 'identity thinking', strikingly prefigurative of modern-day post-structuralism.

(3) Studies of the classical tradition

PERRY ANDERSON, 'The Antinomies of Antonio Gramsci', *New Left Review*, no. 100 (November 1976/January 1977). The best available account of Gramsci's concept of hegemony.

PERRY ANDERSON, *Considerations on Western Marxism* (London: New Left Books, 1976). A succinct and brilliant survey of the Western Marxist tradition, with particular attention to its focus on culture and ideology.

G.A. Cohen, *Karl Marx's Theory of History: A Defence* (Oxford: Oxford University Press, 1978). One of the seminal studies of Marxism of our day, not centrally concerned with ideology but with some suggestive comments on it.

N. Geras, 'Marxism and the Critique of Political Economy', in R. Blackburn (ed.), *Ideology in the Social Sciences* (Harmondsworth: Penguin, 1972).

Raymond Geuss, *The Idea of a Critical Theory* (Cambridge: Cambridge University Press, 1981). An excellent little study of the Frankfurt School in the light of a theory of ideology in general.

Gareth Stedman Jones, 'The Marxism of the early Lukács: An Evaluation', *New Left Review*, 70 (November/December 1971). A powerful critique of Lukács's brand of Hegelian Marxism from an Althusserian standpoint.

Joe McCarney, *The Real World of Ideology* (Brighton: Harvester, 1980).

John Mepham, 'The Theory of Ideology in *Capital*', in J. Mepham and D.-H. Rubin (eds), *Issues in Marxist Philosophy*, vol. 3 (Hemel Hempstead: Harvester Press, 1979).

Bhikhu Parekh, *Marx's Theory of Ideology* (London: Croom Helm, 1982).

Martin Seliger, *The Marxist Conception of Ideology* (Cambridge: Cambridge University Press, 1977).

Denys Turner, *Marxism and Christianity* (Oxford: Basil Blackwell, 1983). Contains a couple of illuminating chapters on the notions of ideology and science.

(4) The Althusserian legacy

Louis Althusser, *For Marx* (London: New Left Books, 1965). Sketches the main outlines of Althusser's psychoanalytic theory of ideology.

Louis Althusser, 'On Ideology and Ideological State Apparatuses', in *Lenin and Philosophy* (London: New Left Books, 1971). The single most influential account of ideology in recent times.

Ernesto Laclau, *Politics and Ideology in Marxist Theory* (London: New Left Books, 1977). A major work of Althusserian theory.

Gregory Elliott, *Althusser: The Detour of Theory* (London: Verso, 1987). Perhaps the single most perceptive and exhaustive study of Althusser's work.

Alex Callinicos, *Althusser's Marxism* (London: Pluto Press, 1976). An impressively compact and judicious assessment of Althusser's major tenets.

Ted Benton, *The Rise and Fall of Structural Marxism* (London: Macmillan, 1984). Another admirably judicious study of Althusser's career.

Jacques Rancière, 'On the Theory of Ideology – Althusser's Politics', in R. Edgley and P. Osborne (eds), *Radical Philosophy Reader* (London: Verso, 1985). A voice of dissent from within the Althusserian camp.

Paul Hirst, *Law and Ideology* (London: Macmillan, 1979). An exemplary text of British Althusserianism, with two important essays on Althusser's theory of ideology.

Etienne Balibar, 'The Vacillation of Ideology', in C. Nelson and L. Grossberg (eds), *Marxism and the Interpretation of Culture* (Urbana: University of Illinois Press, 1988). One of Althusser's most distinguished students reflects on the idea of ideology.

Pierre Macherey and Etienne Balibar, 'Literature as Ideological Form', in Robert Young (ed.), *Untying the Text* (London: Routledge, 1981). A strikingly original essay on ideology and literature by two of Althusser's colleagues.

Pierre Macherey, *A Theory of Literary Production* (London: Routledge, 1978). The single most interesting attempt to apply Althusserian theory to the field of literature.

Terry Eagleton, *Criticism and Ideology* (London: New Left Books, 1976). Another such attempt in a similar vein.

Edward Thompson, 'The Poverty of Theory: Or An Orrery of Errors', in *The Poverty of Theory* (London: Merlin, 1978). A devastating anti-Althusserian polemic from Britain's leading twentieth-century labour historian.

(5) Further studies

N. Abercrombie et al., *The Dominant Ideology Thesis* (London: George Allen and Unwin, 1980).

Roland Barthes, *Mythologies* (London: Paladin, 1973).

Daniel Bell, *The End of Ideology* (Glencoe: University of Illinois Press, 1960).

Terry Eagleton, 'Base and Superstructure in Raymond Williams', in T. Eagleton (ed.), *Raymond Williams: Critical Perspectives* (Cambridge: Polity Press, 1989).

Jon Elster, 'Belief, Bias and Ideology', in M. Hollis and S. Lukes (eds), *Rationality and Relativism* (Oxford: Basil Blackwell, 1982).

Clifford Geertz, 'Ideology as a Cultural System', in *The Interpretation of Cultures* (London: Hutchinson, 1973).

Alvin Gouldner, *The Dialectic of Ideology and Technology* (London: Macmillan, 1976).

JÜRGEN HABERMAS, *The Theory of Communicative Action*, vol. 1 (Boston: Beacon Press, 1984).

FREDRIC JAMESON, *The Political Unconscious* (London: Methuen, 1981).

GUNTER KRESS and RODGER HODGE, *Language as Ideology* (London: Routledge, 1979).

KENNETH MINOGHUE, *Alien Powers* (London: Weidenfeld and Nicolson, 1985).

W.J.T. MITCHELL, *Iconology* (Chicago: University of Chicago Press, 1986).

M. SELIGER, *Ideology and Politics* (London: George Allen and Unwin, 1976).

PETER SLOTERDIJK, *Critique of Cynical Reason* (London: Verso, 1988).

SLAVOJ ŽIŽEK, *The Sublime Object of Ideology* (London: Verso, 1989).

INDEX

Capital (Marx) 113, 115, 127, 213,
    214, 229
  on fetishism of commodities
    25-9
  on human labour 179
  on labour fund 225
  on phenomenal forms and real
    relations 218
  on theories of wage-form 224,
    236 n20
  theory of ideology 11, 99, 211-34
capitalism 12, 18, 23, 39, 41-4
  contradictions in 34, 41-3
  liberal 191, 198, 200
  state-regulated 192, 197
capitalist mode of production 127,
    150, 190-1, 217
  basis of class struggle 196
Carlyle, Thomas 45
Caudwell, Christopher 122
Chartism 232
children 202
China 239, 242, 251-2
Christianity 252
churches 90, 91, 94-8, 262-4
Churchill, Winston 7, 289, 290
class, definition 81
class conflict 41
class consciousness 31-49, 59, 132
class struggle 32, 44, 99, 101, 138
  concealment of 153-4
  forms of 158 n7, 159 n19
  ideological forms 109, 110-11, 143,
    146
  national in form 219
  under advanced capitalism 196,
    198
  in universities 142
cognitive dissonance 240
Cohen, G.A. 253, 254, 259 n59
cold errors 241-3
Cold War 18, 282
commodities 25-9, 227-8
commodity-form of production
    225-6
communications apparatus 94, 96
communism 88, 118
  see also Marxism

Communist Manifesto 42, 45, 98, 101,
    219
comprehension 80-1
Comte, Auguste 206
concrete analysis 35
concrete totality 35, 36
Condillac, Etienne Bonnot de 176,
    177
consciousness 1, 6, 13, 17, 24, 25,
    35-40
  actual 187
  collective 70, 74, 79
  definition 284
  effective 78
  epistemic properties 267-8
  forms of 267-74, 276 n26
  and ideology 88-9, 178, 179,
    184-5
  imputed 187
  philosophy of 57
  possible 77-80
  potential 187
  practical 187, 188
  products of 181
  real 77-80
  static conception 59
  theological forms 268
  see also class consciousness, false
    consciousness
contradictory beliefs 9
Council of Trent 262
Cultural Revolution 159-60 n19

Davidson, Donald 240, 256 n5,
    258 n39
debunking 56
deformation 170
depoliticization of the masses 193
deritualization of public
    communication 206
Derrida, Jacques 300
Descartes, René 155, 161
despots 102, 103
Destutt de Tracy, Antoine 2, 5, 99,
    176, 188
determinism 82-4
detraditionalization of society 203
Dewey, John 4